Building Appl
Spring 5 and Vue.js 2

Build a modern, full-stack web application using Spring Boot
and Vuex

James J. Ye

BIRMINGHAM - MUMBAI

Building Applications with Spring 5 and Vue.js 2

Commissioning Editor: Richa Tripathi
Acquisition Editor: Sandeep Mishra
Content Development Editor: Zeeyan Pinheiro
Technical Editor: Gaurav Gala
Copy Editor: Safis Editing
Project Coordinator: Vaidehi Sawant
Proofreader: Safis Editing
Indexer: Mariammal Chettiyar
Graphics: Alishon Mendonsa
Production Coordinator: Nilesh Mohite

First published: October 2018

Production reference: 2091118

Published by Packt Publishing Ltd.
Livery Place
35 Livery Street
Birmingham
B3 2PB, UK.

ISBN 978-1-78883-696-8

www.packtpub.com

To my beautiful wife, Sunny, and our lovely daughter, Selina

– James J. Ye

`mapt.io`

Mapt is an online digital library that gives you full access to over 5,000 books and videos, as well as industry leading tools to help you plan your personal development and advance your career. For more information, please visit our website.

Why subscribe?

- Spend less time learning and more time coding with practical eBooks and videos from over 4,000 industry professionals

- Improve your learning with Skill Plans built especially for you

- Get a free eBook or video every month

- Mapt is fully searchable

- Copy and paste, print, and bookmark content

Packt.com

Did you know that Packt offers eBook versions of every book published, with PDF and ePub files available? You can upgrade to the eBook version at `www.packt.com` and as a print book customer, you are entitled to a discount on the eBook copy. Get in touch with us at `customercare@packtpub.com` for more details.

At `www.packt.com`, you can also read a collection of free technical articles, sign up for a range of free newsletters, and receive exclusive discounts and offers on Packt books and eBooks.

Contributors

About the author

James J. Ye is an experienced software engineer and architect with a particular interest in full-stack engineering. James works at 6Connex Inc. as VP of Engineering. He manages the offshore engineering team in Suzhou, China. The team is responsible for all the engineering of the Virtual Experience SaaS platform. He has been using Spring since version 2.5.x and Vue.js since version 1.0. He also likes Angular, React, TypeScript, and Python.

About the reviewer

Vladimir Stanković is an independent software engineer, focused on designing lightweight solutions. He has helped various start-ups and enterprises to develop, scale, and perfect their products utilizing the agile methodology. While working in the healthcare industry, he has obtained hands-on experience with standards such as HIPAA, HL7, and FHIR. Kotlin is his weapon of choice when creating clean and expressive code that's easy to understand and maintain. In his spare time, he runs a blog (svlada) and maintains a community newsletter on microservices (microservicesweekly) for others to use and learn from.

Packt is searching for authors like you

If you're interested in becoming an author for Packt, please visit authors.packtpub.com and apply today. We have worked with thousands of developers and tech professionals, just like you, to help them share their insight with the global tech community. You can make a general application, apply for a specific hot topic that we are recruiting an author for, or submit your own idea.

Table of Contents

Preface

This book covers the full set of technologies that you need to know about to become a full-stack web developer with Spring and Vue.js. Spring is the most widely used framework for Java programming, and with its latest update to version 5, the framework has undergone some massive changes. Spring supports MVC architectural styles and is the most popular framework of its kind. Along with Spring in this stack, we will use Vue.js. Vue.js is a lightweight JavaScript framework. Since its release, it has managed to establish itself as one of the most popular frameworks for building user interfaces and is seeing a rapid adoption rate. In this book, you'll become familiar with these technologies while learning to develop a practical web application. You'll discover each technology in the full stack as you build an application up, one layer at a time, just as you'd do in a real project. From initial structuring to full deployment, this book provides step-by-step guidance for developing a web application from scratch with Vue.js and Spring. This book takes a very practical approach to becoming a full-stack web developer. You will create the different components of your application as you progress through each chapter. You will walk through the different tools in each of these frameworks to expedite your development cycle. Finally, this book will also demonstrate the key design patterns and best practices that underpin professional full-stack web development.

Who this book is for

This book is for developers who want to learn full-stack web application development with Spring Framework 5 and Vue.js 2. It introduces you to the full set of technologies and tools that you need for developing a practical web application. It doesn't assume that you have any prior knowledge of Vue.js or Spring Framework. However, you will be better prepared if you have some basic experience with HTML, CSS, and JavaScript on the frontend side, and the Java language, servlets, and JDBC on the server side.

What this book covers

Chapter 1, *Modern Web Application Development - This Is a New Era*, introduces JavaScript from a Java developer's perspective by highlighting the parts that confuse Java developers the most. It also introduces the basics of ES6.

Chapter 2, *Vue.js 2 - It Works in the Way You Expected*, introduces all aspects of Vue.js 2, from its fundamental concepts to its internal reactivity system.

Chapter 3, *Spring 5 - The Right Stack for the Job at Hand*, introduces the major features of Spring Framework 5, including **Inversion of Control (IoC)** and dependency injection, Spring MVC, Spring JDBC, JPA, Spring AOP, transaction management, and Spring Boot.

Chapter 4, *TaskAgile - A Trello-like Task Management Tool*, introduces requirement management in an Agile project, user story writing, and wireframe creation. It also discusses the Agile methodology and the skill sets a full-stack developer should have.

Chapter 5, *Data Modeling - Designing the Foundation of the Application*, introduces data modeling, the goal of data modeling, and the three stages of data modeling: from conceptual data modeling to logical data modeling, and then to physical data modeling.

Chapter 6, *Code Design - Designing for Stability and Extensibility*, introduces Agile code design, design principles, and design patterns. It also discusses the code design of TaskAgile applications.

Chapter 7, *RESTful API Design - Building Language Between Frontend and Backend*, introduces RESTful API characteristics, RESTful API design procedure, the implementation of Spring MVC, API consumption, and API testing.

Chapter 8, *Creating the Application Scaffold - Taking off Like a Rocket*, introduces how to create an application scaffold with Spring Initializr and `vue-cli`, as well as how to put these two ends together.

Chapter 9, *Forms and Validation - Starting with the Register Page*, is a step-by-step tutorial on how to create the register page of a TaskAgile application, from the frontend to the backend, including unit tests at both ends.

Chapter 10, *Spring Security - Making Our Application Secure*, is a step-by-step tutorial on how to create the login page of a TaskAgile application, from the frontend to the backend, including end-to-end testing of the register page and the login page.

Chapter 11, *State Management and i18n - Building a Home Page*, is a step-by-step tutorial on how to create the home page of a TaskAgile application, covering the use of Vuex and the implementation of i18n.

Chapter 12, *Flexbox Layout and Real-Time Updates with WebSocket - Creating Boards*, is a step-by-step tutorial on how to create a boards-based UI by using Flexbox, as well as how to implement real-time updates with WebSocket.

Chapter 13, *File Processing and Scalability - Playing with Cards*, is a tutorial on the implementation of cards on the boards page. It focuses on file processing and the use of the message queue.

Chapter 14, *Health Checking, System Monitoring - Getting Ready for Production*, focuses on the use of Spring Profile and Spring Boot Actuator to prepare for application release.

Chapter 15, *Deploying to the Cloud with Jenkins - Ship It Continuously*, introduces continuous delivery, the creation of API integration tests, and the use of Jenkins and Docker to ship an application.

Download the example code files

You can download the example code files for this book from your account at www.packt.com. If you purchased this book elsewhere, you can visit www.packt.com/support and register to have the files emailed directly to you.

You can download the code files by following these steps:

1. Log in or register at www.packt.com.
2. Select the **SUPPORT** tab.
3. Click on **Code Downloads & Errata**.
4. Enter the name of the book in the **Search** box and follow the onscreen instructions.

Once the file is downloaded, please make sure that you unzip or extract the folder using the latest version of:

- WinRAR/7-Zip for Windows
- Zipeg/iZip/UnRarX for Mac
- 7-Zip/PeaZip for Linux

The code bundle for the book is also hosted on GitHub at https://github.com/PacktPublishing/Building-Applications-with-Spring-5-and-Vue.js-2. In case there's an update to the code, it will be updated on the existing GitHub repository.

We also have other code bundles from our rich catalog of books and videos available at https://github.com/PacktPublishing/. Check them out!

Download the color images

We also provide a PDF file that has color images of the screenshots/diagrams used in this book. You can download it here: https://www.packtpub.com/sites/default/files/downloads/9781788836968_ColorImages.pdf.

Conventions used

There are a number of text conventions used throughout this book.

`CodeInText`: Indicates code words in text, database table names, folder names, filenames, file extensions, pathnames, dummy URLs, user input, and Twitter handles. Here is an example: "We will need to refactor `BoardPage` to make both routes work."

A block of code is set as follows:

```
// Close a card
    if (to.name === 'board' && from.name === 'card') {
        this.closeCardWindow()
        this.openedCard = {}
```

When we wish to draw your attention to a particular part of a code block, the relevant lines or items are set in bold:

```
watch: {
    '$route' (to, from) {
        // Switch from one board to another
        if (to.name === from.name && to.name === 'board')
```

Any command-line input or output is written as follows:

```
$ mvn install
```

Bold: Indicates a new term, an important word, or words that you see onscreen. For example, words in menus or dialog boxes appear in the text like this. Here is an example: "You can click the **Attachment** button to upload files."

 Warnings or important notes appear like this.

 Tips and tricks appear like this.

Get in touch

Feedback from our readers is always welcome.

General feedback: If you have questions about any aspect of this book, mention the book title in the subject of your message and email us at customercare@packtpub.com.

Errata: Although we have taken every care to ensure the accuracy of our content, mistakes do happen. If you have found a mistake in this book, we would be grateful if you would report this to us. Please visit www.packt.com/submit-errata, selecting your book, clicking on the Errata Submission Form link, and entering the details.

Piracy: If you come across any illegal copies of our works in any form on the Internet, we would be grateful if you would provide us with the location address or website name. Please contact us at copyright@packt.com with a link to the material.

If you are interested in becoming an author: If there is a topic that you have expertise in and you are interested in either writing or contributing to a book, please visit authors.packtpub.com.

Reviews

Please leave a review. Once you have read and used this book, why not leave a review on the site that you purchased it from? Potential readers can then see and use your unbiased opinion to make purchase decisions, we at Packt can understand what you think about our products, and our authors can see your feedback on their book. Thank you!

For more information about Packt, please visit packt.com.

Modern Web Application Development - This Is a New Era

The diversity of the modern web application development ecosystem is increasing at an astonishing rate. You can see new frameworks and libraries coming out almost every day. People seem to be happy with constantly reinventing the wheel. This could be daunting to new learners as the time it takes to master a new skill makes it sometimes difficult to keep pace with the rate with which technologies are evolving. And this has caused frequent complaints of making web development unnecessarily complicated, as there are many new libraries and frameworks to learn and a large number of new tools to familiarize yourself with.

The anxiety associated with the feeling that you might not be able to keep up with the mainstream can be released once you have learned how to create a full-stack modern web application and master the skill sets that are required to build such an application. And, with this book, you will learn these skill sets and realize that being a full-stack developer is not only about knowing how to write frontend and backend code. In this book, we will create a real-world, full-stack web application and cover most of the skills that a full-stack developer would require. And once you have finished reading it, you will understand that languages and frameworks are just tools in your toolbox. You can replace them with other languages and frameworks and also build great full-stack applications.

To start our journey, we will begin with the basics. Once you have those basics imprinted in your mind, you can learn the frameworks more efficiently. In this chapter, we will cover the following topics:

- An introduction to the full-stack web application we will build in this book
- Learning JavaScript from a Java developer's viewpoint
- Learning the features of ECMAScript 2015 that we will use in this book

Introduction

If you're creating a résumé page for your personal website, it will most likely be sufficient to write it in vanilla JavaScript, HTML 5, and some creative CSS style sheets that make it look special and unique. And if you're creating the jobs page of your company's official website, doing it barehanded might work. But if you use a number of frameworks to style the page and to process logic and animations, you will find yourself in a much better position that you can still go home from work earlier than usual and enjoy a cup of coffee with friends at the weekend. And if you're building something like Monster (`https://www.monster.com/`) I hope that you are not just carrying those favorite frameworks with you to the battlefield, and if you go barehanded, you wouldn't even make it there. With the level of complexity of such an application and the fact that you will need to keep improving or changing features because of the neverending stop-change requirements, you need to bring the tools for modern web application development with you.

 Sometimes, people use the term vanilla JavaScript to refer to using plain JavaScript without any additional libraries, such as jQuery, Lodash, and many more. That means that you write your code with only the APIs that the JavaScript language itself provides.

In this book, we will create a modern web application called `TaskAgile`, which is a Trello-like application for task management. Let's first get an overview of the technologies that we will use to build it.

For the frontend, we will use **Vue.js 2** as our frontend application framework, Bootstrap 4 as the UI framework, and we will write our frontend in ES6, also known as ECMAScript 2015, or ES 2015, and then use **Babel** to compile it into ES5 code. We will use ESLint to check our JS code to make sure it follows all the rules we defined and use Flow (`https://flow.org`) for static type checking. We will use **Jest** to write our frontend unit testing's and use **Nightwatch.js** to run our end-to-end test cases. We will use webpack 4 to bundle all the dependencies and use `npm` to take care of the package management.

For the backend, we will use Spring Boot 2 to create a Spring 5 application. And we will use Hibernate 5 as our **object-relational mapping (ORM)** framework, and MySQL as our database. We will use Spring Security for authentication and authorization, and we will implement a real-time-update feature with **Spring WebSocket**. We will use **Spring AMPQ** for asynchronously processing background tasks and **Spring Session** for server-side session management.

Now, before we introduce Vue.js 2 and Spring 5, for readers who are not familiar with JavaScript, let's learn the basics of it, starting with the part that Java developers would easily get confused with.

JavaScript from a Java developer's viewpoint

For readers who are new to JavaScript but who are familiar with the Java language, here are some differences between the two languages that may confuse you. And even though this section is written from a Java developer's perspective, if you're new to JavaScript, you will also find it informative.

Functions and methods

A function in JavaScript is quite different from a method in Java because it is actually an object created by the `Function` constructor, which is a built-in object of the language. Yes, that's right. `Function` itself is an object too. What is a method in JavaScript, then? When a function is a property of an object, it is a method. So, in JavaScript, a method is a function, but not all functions are methods.

Since a function is an object, it can also have properties and methods. To establish whether an object is a function or not, you can use `instanceof`, as follows:

```
var workout = function () {};
console.log(workout instanceof Function); // true
```

What is the difference between a function and other objects in JavaScript, apart from the fact that it is created by the `Function` constructor? First of all, a function is callable, while other objects are not. Another difference is that a function has a `prototype` property while other objects don't. We will talk about `prototype` later.

In JavaScript, you can use a function to create objects with `new`. In a case such as this, that function serves as a constructor. As a convention, when a function serves as a constructor, it should be capitalized. The following is a simple example of using a function as a `User` constructor. We will build the `User` constructor containing more details later:

```
function User () {
}
var user = new User();
```

Before we move on, let's see the different ways to create a function in JavaScript. Function declarations and function expressions are the most common ways to create functions. Other than that, you can use `new Function()` to create a function. However, this is not recommended due to its poor performance as well as its readability. The `User` function in the preceding code snippet is a function declaration. And `workout` is a function expression. The way that a function is created and invoked will affect the execution context that its function body will point to. We will talk about it later.

Objects and classes

In Java, you create a class to represent a concept, for example, a `User` class. The `User` class has a constructor, some fields, and methods. And you use its constructor to instantiate a `User` object. And every object in Java is an instance of the associated class that provides code sharing among its instances. You can extend the `User` class to create, for example, a `TeamMember` class.

In JavaScript, there are several ways to create an object:

- The `Object()` constructor method
- The object literal method
- The constructor function method
- The `Object.create()` method
- The creator function method
- The ES6 class method

Let's look at each method one at a time.

The `Object` constructor method looks like this:

```
// Call the Object constructor with new
var user = new Object();
user.name = 'Sunny';
user.interests = ['Traveling', 'Swimming'];
user.greeting = function () {
  console.log('Hi, I\'m ' + this.name + '.');
};
user.greeting(); // Hi, I'm Sunny.
```

The `Object` constructor creates an object wrapper. This is not a recommended approach, even though it is valid in JavaScript. In practice, it is better to use an object literal instead, which makes the code compact.

The object literal method looks like this:

```
// Create a user with object literal
var user = {
  name: 'Sunny',
  interests: ['Traveling', 'Swimming'],
  greeting: function () {
    console.log('Hi, I\'m ' + this.name + '.');
  }
}
user.greeting();   // Hi, I'm Sunny.
```

The object literal is a compact syntax to create an object in JavaScript and it is the recommended way of creating an object over `new Object()`. Starting from ES5, object literals also support getter and setter accessors, as can be seen here:

```
var user = {
  get role() {
    return 'Engineer';
  }
}
user.role;   // Engineer
```

And if you try to assign a value to `role`, it will stay unchanged because there is no setter accessor defined for the `role` property.

The constructor function method looks like this:

```
// Create a constructor function
function User (name, interests) {
  this.name = name;
  this.interests = interests;
  this.greeting = function () {
    console.log('Hi, I\'m ' + this.name + '.');
  }
}
// Call the constructor with new to create a user object
var user = new User('Sunny', ['Traveling', 'Swimming']);
user.greeting(); // Hi, I'm Sunny.
```

This syntax is very close to the one in Java. JavaScript is very tolerant, and you can omit the parenthesis when calling the constructor. However, this will not pass any arguments to the constructor, as can be seen here:

```
var user = new User;
console.log(user.name); // undefined
```

And again, even though this is valid in JavaScript, it is not recommended to omit the parenthesis.

The `Object.create()` method looks like this:

```
// Use Object.create() method with the prototype of
// User constructor function created above
var user = Object.create(User.prototype, {
  name: { value: 'Sunny' },
  interests: { value: ['Traveling', 'Swimming']}
});
user.greeting(); // Uncaught TypeError: user.greeting() is not a //function
```

The reason `greeting()` is not a function of the `user` object here is that the `Object.create()` method creates a new object with the constructor's prototype object. And the `greeting` function is not defined in `User.prototype`, or passed in the second argument of `Object.create()`. To make the user be able to greet, we can either pass the `greeting` function in the second argument, or we can add it to the `User` constructor's prototype object. The difference is that the first approach only adds the `greeting` function to the current `user` object. If you created another user without passing in the `greeting` function, that user won't have `greeting` function. On the other hand, adding the function to the prototype object will add the `greeting` function to all the objects created by that constructor. Let's add it to the `User` prototype object:

```
// Add greeting to prototype object
User.prototype.greeting = function () {
  console.log('Hi, I\'m ' + this.name + '.');
}
user.greeting(); // Hi, I'm Sunny.
```

Actually, using a prototype is how a superclass provides methods for subclasses to inherit in JavaScript. We will talk about that in detail later.

The creator function method looks like this:

```
// Use a creator function with an object as its return value
function createUser (name, interests) {
  var user = {};
  user.name = name;
```

```
    user.interests = interests;
    user.greeting = function () {
      console.log('Hi, I\'m ' + this.name + '.');
    };
    return user;
}
// Call the creator function with parameters
var user = createUser('Sunny', ['Traveling', 'Swimming']);
user.greeting(); // Hi, I'm Sunny.
```

The creator function here is a factory method, similar to the static factory method that used to instantiate an object in Java. And it is merely a pattern because underneath it wraps the object creation details inside of the creator function.

The ES6 class method looks like this:

```
// Create User class
class User {
  // Equivalent to User constructor function
  constructor (name, interests) {
    this.name = name;
    this.interests = interests;
  }
  // Equivalent to User.prototype.greeting
  greeting () {
    console.log('Hi, I\'m ' + this.name + '.')
  }
}
let user = new User('Sunny', ['Traveling', 'Swimming']);
user.greeting(); // Hi, I'm Sunny.
```

This is very close to the syntax in Java. Instead of using the class declaration, you can also use the class expression to create the class, as follows:

```
// Use class expression
let User = class {
  constructor (name, interests) {
    this.name = name;
    this.interests = interests;
  }
  greeting () {
    console.log('Hi, I\'m ' + this.name + '.')
  }
}
```

Even though it uses the same keyword, `class`, `class` in JavaScript is quite different from the `class` in Java. For example, there is no static class and no private class in JavaScript. We will talk more about `class` in the ES6 section.

Objects, properties, and property attributes

In Java, once an object is created, there is (almost) no way to modify its methods during runtime. Java is not a dynamic language. In JavaScript, things are quite different. You can create an object and modify it easily during runtime, such as adding new properties and replacing a method. That's what a dynamic language can do. Actually, that is not the special part. The special part is that `Object` is a language type in JavaScript, like other language types that JavaScript has, which includes `Undefined`, `Null`, `Boolean`, `String`, `Symbol`, and `Number`. Any value in JavaScript is a value of those types.

 The undefined type has a single value, `undefined`. The null type has a single value, `null`. A Boolean has two values: `true` and `false`.

In Java, an object has fields and methods. In JavaScript, an object is logically a collection of properties. A property has a name of the String type and a list of attributes. Attributes, in JavaScript, are used to define and explain the state of a property. There are two types of properties—data properties and access properties.

A data property has four attributes:

- `value`, which can be of any JavaScript language type
- `writable`, which defines whether a data property can be changed or not
- `enumerable`, which defines whether a property can be enumerated by using a `for-in` statement
- `configurable`, which defines whether a property can be deleted, changed to be an access property, changed to be not writable, or whether its `enumerable` attribute can be modified

An access property also has four attributes:

- `get accessor`, which can be a `Function` object or undefined
- `set accessor`, which can be a `Function` object or undefined
- `enumerable`, which defines whether a property can be enumerated by using a `for-in` statement

- `configurable`, which defines whether a property can be deleted, be changed to be a data property, or whether its other attributes can be modified.

To access a property of an object, you can use dot notation or bracket notation. The dot notation acts the same as how it does in Java. The bracket notation, on the other hand, is quite interesting. In JavaScript, property names must be strings. If you try to use a non-string object as a property name with bracket notation, the object will be casted into a string via its `toString()` method, as we can see here:

```
var obj = {};
obj['100'] = 'one hundred';
// Number 100 will be casted to '100'
console.log(obj[100]);  // 'one hundred'
// Both foo and bar will be casted to string '[object Object]'
var foo = {prop: 'f'}, bar = {prop: 'b'};
obj[foo] = 'Foo'
console.log(obj[bar])  // 'Foo'
```

In a nutshell, here is how an **object** appears, logically:

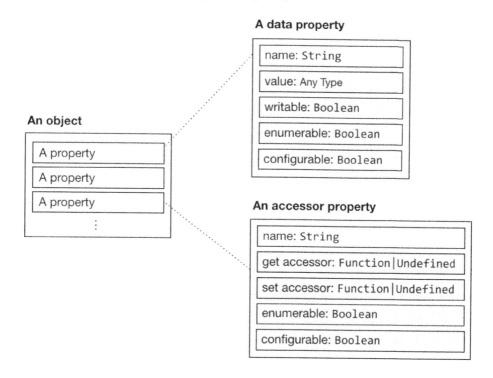

Figure 1.1: Object, properties, and property attributes

In JavaScript, you can use `Object.defineProperty` or `Object.defineProperties` to modify the properties of an object. Here is how it works:

```
1.  function User (name, department) {
2.    var _department = department;
3.    var _name = name;
4.    Object.defineProperty(this, 'name', {
5.      value: _name,
6.      writable: true,
7.      enumerable: true,
8.      configurable: false
9.    });
10.   Object.defineProperty(this, 'department', {
11.     get: function () {
12.       console.log('Retrieving department');
13.       return _department;
14.     },
15.     set: function (newValue) {
16.       console.log('Updating department value to "' + newValue + '"');
17.       _department = newValue;
18.     },
19.     enumerable: true,
20.     configurable: true
21.   });
24.   Object.defineProperty(this, 'greeting', {
25.     value: function () {
26.       console.log('Hi, I\'m ' + _name + '.');
27.     },
28.     enumerable: false,
29.     configurable: false
30.   });
31. }
```

As you can see from lines 4 to 9, we use `Object.defineProperty` to define `name` as a data property, and its actual data is stored in the internal property _name. In lines 10 to 21, we define `department` as an access property that has a `get accessor` and `set accessor`, and the actual value is kept in _department. In lines 24 to 30, we define `greeting` property as a data property and its value is a `Function` object:

```
32. var user = new User('Sunny', 'Engineering');
33. console.log(user.department);
34. user.department = 'Marketing';
35. user.greeting();
36. Object.defineProperty(user, 'name', {
37.   enumerable: false
38. });
39. delete user.name;
```

```
40. delete user.department;
41. for (var prop in user) {
42.    console.log(prop);
43. }
```

In line 32, we create a user object using the User constructor function. In line 33, we access the department property. Since it is a get accessor, the getter function will be invoked and the message Retrieving department will show up in the console before the actual department value. In line 34, we assign a new value to the department property. Since we have defined the set accessor, the setter function will be invoked. In line 35, since the greeting property of user object is defined as a function, we will need to invoke it. In lines 36 to 38, we try to redefine the name property. However, since it is not configurable, JavaScript will throw an error with this. The same is true with regard to line 39, where we try to delete this property. The deletion of department property in line 40 will work since it is configurable. In lines 41 to 43, the only property that will show up in the console is the name property, because the department has been deleted and the greeting property is not enumerable.

Prototype and inheritance

As has been briefly mentioned previously, inheritance in JavaScript is archived by using prototypes of constructor functions. In JavaScript, a prototype is an object that provides shared properties for other objects. And only a function object has a prototype because only a function object is callable and can create other objects. In ES6, arrow functions don't have prototypes. We will discuss that later.

You can think of a function as a factory and its prototype is the specification of the products that the factory manufactures. Every time you call a function with the new keyword, you place an order for its product. And the factory will produce it according to how it is specified in the prototype.

Now, let's see how inheritance works in code. We will create another constructor function, called `TeamMember`, and it will inherit properties from `User` and also override the `greeting()` method and provide a new method called `work()`. Later, we will add `eat()` method to `User` and `move()` to `Object`.

Here is how it is implemented in ES5:

```
1. function User (name, interests) {
2.    this.name = name;
3.    this.interests = interests;
4. }
5. User.prototype.greeting = function () {
6.     console.log('Hi, I\'m ' + this.name + '.');
7. }
```

In lines 1 to 4, we create a `User` constructor function. And what it really does is create a `function` object using the `Function` constructor. In JavaScript, you can check who created an object by using its `constructor` property, which references back to its creator, as follows:

```
console.log(User.constructor === Function);   // true
```

And once the `User` constructor function is created, it has a prototype object. And a `User` prototype object itself is created by the `User` constructor function, as you can see in the following:

```
console.log(User.prototype.constructor === User); // true
```

And in JavaScript, after you create a `user` object using the `User` constructor function, that object will have a `__proto__` property that references the `User` prototype object. You can see the link like this:

```
var user = new User();
console.log(user.__proto__ === User.prototype); // true
```

This `__proto__` reference serves as a link in the prototype chain. You will see what that means visually later.

Now back to the code. In lines 5 to 7, we create a greeting property on the User prototype. This will create a method that can be **inherited** by User subclasses. And, as we mentioned earlier, if you define the greeting method inside the User constructor function, subclasses won't see this greeting method. We will see the reason for this shortly:

```
8.   function TeamMember (name, interests, tasks) {
9.     User.call(this, name, interests);
10.     this.tasks = tasks;
11.  }
12.  TeamMember.prototype = Object.create(User.prototype);
13.  TeamMember.prototype.greeting = function () {
14.    console.log('I\'m ' + this.name + '. Welcome to the team!');
15.  };
16.  TeamMember.prototype.work = function () {
17.    console.log('I\'m working on ' + this.tasks.length + ' tasks');
18.  };
```

In lines 8 to 13, we create a TeamMember constructor function, and inside it, we invoke the User constructor function's call() method, which is inherited from the Function object to chain constructors, which is similar to invoking super() in a constructor of a Java class. One difference is that the call() method's first argument must be an object, which serves as the execution context. In our example, we use this as the execution context. Inside the call() method, the name and interests properties are initialized. And then, we add an additional property, tasks, to TeamMember.

In line 12, we use Object.create() to create a TeamMember prototype object using the User prototype object. In this way, objects created by the TeamMember constructor function will have the properties of the User prototype object and each team member object will have a __proto__ property that links to this TeamMember prototype.

In lines 13 to 15, we override the original greeting() method of the User prototype so that objects created by the TeamMember constructor function will have different behavior. This will not affect the User prototype object since they are essentially two different objects, even though these two prototype objects have the same constructor, as you can see in the following:

```
console.log(User.prototype === TeamMember.prototype);  // false
console.log(User.prototype.constructor ===
TeamMember.prototype.constructor); // true
```

In lines 16 to 18, we add a new method, `work()`, to the `TeamMember` prototype object. In this way, objects created by the `TeamMember` constructor function will have this additional behavior:

```
19. var member = new TeamMember('Sunny', ['Traveling'],
20.                            ['Buy three tickets','Book a hotel']);
21. member.greeting();   // I'm Sunny. Welcome to the team!
22. member.work();       // I'm working on 2 tasks
23
24. console.log(member instanceof TeamMember); // true
25. console.log(member instanceof User);       // true
26. console.log(member instanceof Object);     // true
27
28. User.prototype.eat = function () {
29.   console.log('What will I have for lunch?');
30. };
31. member.eat();      // What will I have for lunch?
32
33. // Add a method to the top
34. Object.prototype.move = function () {
35.   console.log('Every object can move now');
36. };
37. member.move();    // Every object can move now
38. var alien = {};
39. alien.move();     // Every object can move now
40. User.move();      // Even the constructor function
```

In line 19, we create a `member` object using the `TeamMember` constructor function. Line 21 shows that the `member` object can greet in a different way to objects created by the `User` constructor function. And line 22 shows that the `member` object can work.

Lines 24 to 26 show that the `member` object is an instance of all its superclasses.

In lines 28 to 30, we add the `eat()` method to the `User` prototype, and even though the `member` object is created before this, as you can see from line 31, it also inherits that method.

In line 34, we add the `move()` method to the `Object` prototype, which might turn out to be a really bad idea since, as you can see in lines 37 to 40, every object can move now, even those constructor function objects.

We just create an inheritance chain starting from `Object` | `User` | `TeamMember`. The prototype link is the key to this chain. Here is how it appears:

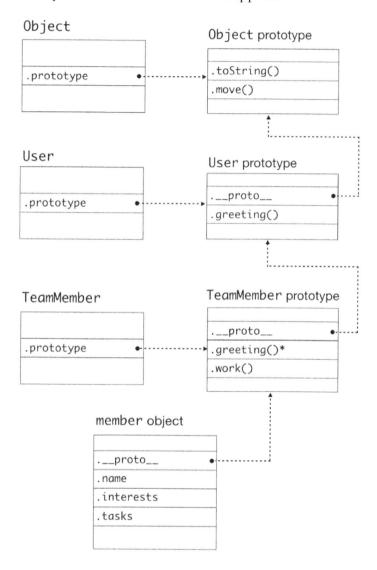

Figure 1.2: Prototype-based inheritance

On the left-hand side are the constructor functions, and on the right-hand side are their corresponding prototypes. The bottom is the member object. As you can see, the member object's __proto__ property references the prototype object of TeamMember. And the __proto__ property of the TeamMember prototype object itself references the prototype object of User. And the __proto__ property of the User prototype object references the top level, which is the prototype object of Object. To verify the link, you can do something like this:

```
console.log(member.__proto__ === TeamMember.prototype);       // true
console.log(TeamMember.prototype.__proto__ === User.prototype); // true
console.log(User.prototype.__proto__ === Object.prototype);    // true
```

So, be really careful with the __proto__ property. If you, let's say, accidentally change this property to something else, the inheritance will break:

```
User.prototype.__proto__ = null;
member.move(); // Uncaught TypeError: member.move is not a function
console.log(member instanceof Object); // false (Oops!)
```

It is recommended to use Object.prototype.isPrototypeof() to check the prototype chain:

```
TeamMember.prototype.isPrototypeOf(member);   // true
```

With the inheritance relationship map showing in the preceding diagram, you can easily see how JavaScript resolves a property through the prototype chain. For example, when you access a member object's name property, JavaScript finds that it is on the object itself and will not go up the chain. And when you access the move() method, JavaScript will go up the chain and check whether the TeamMember prototype has it and, since it doesn't, JavaScript will keep going up until it finds the method in the Object prototype. You can use an object's hasOwnProperty() method to check whether that object has a property as its own instead of inherited through the prototype chain:

```
member.hasOwnProperty('name');   // true
member.hasOwnProperty('move');   // false
```

Scope and closure

Scope is about the accessibility of variables. In Java, basically, a set of curly brackets { } defines a scope, including class-level scope, method-level scope, and block-level scope.

Let's take a look at the following example in Java:

```
1.   public class User {
2.       private String name;
3.       private List<String> interests;
4.
5.       public User (String name, List<String> interests) {
6.           this.name = name;
7.           this.interests = interests;
8.       }
9.
10.      // Check if a user is interested in something
11.      public boolean isInterestedIn(String something) {
12.          boolean interested = false;
13.          for (int i = 0; i < interests.size(); i++) {
14.              if (interests.get(i).equals(something)) {
15.                  interested = true;
16.                  break;
17.              }
18.          }
19.          return interested;
20.      }
21.  }
```

The name and interests properties are in the class-level scope and they are accessible anywhere within the class. The interested variable, defined in line 12, is in method-level scope, and it is only accessible within that method. The i variable, in line 13, is defined within the for loop and it is block-level scope only accessible within the for loop block. In Java, the scope of the variables is static and can be determined by the compiler.

In JavaScript, the scope of the variables is much more flexible. There is global scope and function scope, and block scope with the let and const keywords, which were introduced in ES6, which we will talk about later.

Let's look at the following JavaScript example:

```
1.   function bookHotel (city) {
2.     var availableHotel = 'None';
3.     for (var i=0; i<hotels.length; i++) {
4.       var hotel = hotels[i];
5.       if (hotel.city === city && hotel.hasRoom) {
6.         availableHotel = hotel.name;
7.         break;
8.       }
9.     }
10.    // i and hotel still accessible here
11.    console.log('Checked ' + (i+1) + ' hotels');// Checked 2 hotels
```

```
12.     console.log('Last checked ' + hotel.name);   // Last checked Hotel B
13.     {
14.       function placeOrder() {
15.         var totalAmount = 200;
16.         console.log('Order placed to ' + availableHotel);
17.       }
18.     }
19.     placeOrder();
20.     // Not accessible
21.     // console.log(totalAmount);
22.     return availableHotel;
23.   }
24.   var hotels = [{name: 'Hotel A', hasRoom: false, city: 'Sanya'},
                   {name: 'Hotel B', hasRoom: true, city: 'Sanya'}];
25.   console.log(bookHotel('Sanya')); // Hotel B
26.   // Not accessible
27.   // console.log(availableHotel);
```

The `hotels` variable declared in line 24, is in global scope and is accessible anywhere, such as inside the `bookHotel()` function, even though the variable is defined after the function.

The `availableHotel` variable declared in line 2 is in the scope of the `bookHotel()` function. It is a local variable and is not accessible outside of the function, as you can see from line 27. Inside its enclosing function, the `availableHotel` variable is accessible anywhere, even the nested `placeOrder()` function, as you can see in line 16. This is called **closure**. A closure is formed when a function is nested inside another function. And no matter how deeply you have nested a function, it will still have access to its parent function's scope, and all the way to the top scope, which is global scope. The `totalAmount` variable, defined in line 15, is a local variable of the `placeOrder()` function.

And in lines 3 and 4, we defined the `i` and `hotel` variables with the `var` keyword. Even though it is in a `for` loop block, it is still accessible outside the block, as shown in lines 11 and 12. In ES6, you can use the `let` keyword to define `i` and `hotel`, which will put these two variables in `for` loop block scope. We will talk more about this later.

The this keyword

In Java, `this` always refers to the current object. It is solid. In JavaScript, `this` behaves differently. In short, `this` refers to the current execution context, which is an object. And the way that JavaScript runtime determines the current execution context is much more complex than in Java.

In JavaScript, there is an execution context stack, logically formed from active execution contexts. When control is transferred from one executable code to another, control enters the new executable code's execution context, which becomes the current execution context, or what is referred to as the running execution context. At the bottom of the stack is the global context, where everything begins, just like the `main` method in Java. The current execution context is always at the top of the stack.

What is the executable code? There are three types in JavaScript:

- **Global code**, which is the code that runs from the place where a JavaScript program starts. In a browser, it is where `window` lives. And when you open a browser console and type in `var user = new User()`, you are writing global code.
- **Eval code**, which is a string value passed in as the argument of the built-in `eval()` function (do not use the `eval()` function unless you really know what you're doing).
- **Function code**, which is the code parsed as the body of a function. However, it doesn't mean all the code written inside a function is function code.

Now, to understand this better, let's look at the following example:

```
1.  function User (name) {
2.    console.log('I\'m in "' + this.constructor.name + '" context.');
3.    this.name = name;
4.    this.speak = function () {
5.      console.log(this.name + ' is speaking from "' +
6.        this.constructor.name + '" context.');
7.      var drink = function () {
8.        console.log('Drinking in "' + this.constructor.name + '"');
9.      }
10.     drink();
11.   };
12.   function ask() {
13.     console.log('Asking from "' +
14.       this.constructor.name + '"    context.');
15.     console.log('Who am I? "'  + this.name + '"');
16.   }
17.   ask();
18. }
19. var name = 'Unknown';
20. var user = new User('Ted');
21. user.speak();
```

Since an execution context is, in fact, an object, here we use its `.constructor.name` to see what the context is. And if you run the preceding code in the node command line, it will be `Object` instead of `Window`.

If you run the code from Chrome console, the output will be the following:

```
// I'm in "User" context.
// Asking from "Window" context.
// Who am I? "Unknown"
// Ted is speaking from "User" context.
// Drinking in "Window"
```

First, let's see which part is global code and which part is function code. The `User` function declaration, and lines 19 to 21, are global code. Lines 2 to 17 are the function code of the `User` function. Well, not exactly. Lines 5 to 10, except line 8, are the function code of the `speak()` method. Line 8 is the function code of the `drink()` function. Lines 13 and 14 are the function code of the `ask()` function.

Before we review the output, let's revisit the two commonly used ways of creating a function—function declarations and function expressions. When the JavaScript engine sees a function declaration, it will create a `function` object that is visible in the scope in which the function is declared. For example, line 1 declares the `User` function, which is visible in global scope. Line 12 declares the `ask()` function, which is visible inside the scope of the `User` function. And line 4 is a function expression that creates the `speak()` method. On the other hand, in line 7, we use a function expression to create a `drink` variable. It is different from the `speak()` method created in line 4. Even though it is also a function expression, the `drink` variable is not a property of an object. It is simply visible inside the `speak()` method.

In JavaScript, scope and execution context are two different concepts. Scope is about accessibility, while the execution context is about the **ownership** of running an executable code. The `speak()` method and the `ask()` function are in the same scope, but they have different execution contexts. When the `ask()` function is executed, as you can see from the output, it has global context and the `name` property resolves to the value `Unknown`, which is declared in global scope. And when the `speak()` method is executed, it has the `user` context. As you can see from the output, its access to the `name` property resolves to `Ted`. This can be quite confusing to Java developers. So what happened behind the scenes?

Let's review the preceding example from the JavaScript engine's view. When the JavaScript engine executes line 20, it creates a `user` object by calling the `User` constructor function. And it will go into the function body to instantiate the object. When the control flows from the global code to the function code, the execution context is changed to the `user` object. And that's why you see `I'm in "User" context.` in the output. And during the instantiation, JavaScript engine will not execute the code inside the `speak()` method because there is no invoking yet. It executes the `ask()` function when it reaches line 17. At that time, the control flows from the function code of the `User` constructor function to the `ask()` function. Because the `ask()` function isn't a property of an object, nor it is invoked by the `Function.call()` method, which we will talk about later, the global context becomes the execution context. And that's why you see `Asking from "Window"` `context.` and `Where am I? "Unknown"` in the output. After the instantiation of the `user` object, the JavaScript engine goes back to execute line 21 and invokes the `speak()` method on the `user` object. Now, the control flows into the `speak()` method and the `user` object becomes the execution context. And that's why you see `Ted is speaking from "User"` `context.` in the output. When the engine executes the `drink()` function, it resolves back to the global context as the execution context. And that is why you see `Drinking in` `"Window" context.` in the output.

As mentioned earlier, the execution context is affected by the way a function is created as well as by how it is invoked. What does that mean? Let's change line 16 from `ask()` to `ask.call(this)`. And if you run the preceding example again from Chrome's console, you can see the following output:

```
...
Asking from "User" context.
Who am I? "Ted"
...
```

And if you type in `user.speak.apply({name: 'Jack'})` into the console, you will see something interesting, like this:

```
Jack is speaking from "Object" context.
Drinking in "Window" context.
```

Or, if you change line 17 to `ask.bind(this)()`, you can see the answer to the question "Who am I?" is also "Ted" now.

So, what are these `call()`, `apply()`, and `bind()` methods? It seems that there are no definitions of them in the preceding example. As you might remember, every function is an object created by the `Function` object. After typing in the following code into the console, you can see that the `speak()` function inherits the properties from `Function` prototype, including the `call()`, `apply()`, and `bind()` methods:

```
console.log(Function.prototype.isPrototypeOf(user.speak));  // true
user.speak.hasOwnProperty('apply');                          // false
user.speak.__proto__.hasOwnProperty('apply');                // true
```

The `call()` method and the `apply()` method are similar. The difference between these two methods is that the `call()` method accepts a list of arguments, while the `apply()` method accepts an array of arguments. Both methods take the first argument as the execution context of the function code. For example, in `user.speak.apply({name: 'Jack'})`, the `{name: 'Jack'}` object will be the execution context of the `speak()` method of `user`. You can think of the `call()` and `apply()` methods as a way of switching execution context.

And the `bind()` method acts differently from the other two. What the `bind()` method does is create a new function that will be bound to the first argument that is passed in as the new function's execution context. The new function will never change its execution context even if you use `call()` or `apply()` to switch execution context. So, what `ask.bind(this)()` does is create a function and then execute it immediately. Besides executing it immediately, you can assign the new function to a variable or as a method of an object.

To wrap up, there are four ways to invoke a function:

- Constructor function invoking: `new User()`
- Direct function invoking: `ask()`
- Method invoking: `user.speak()`
- Switching context invoking: `ask.call(this)` or `ask.apply(this)`

When we are talking about constructor function invoking, the presence of `this` inside the function body, except those instances that are wrapped by functions of the other three types of invoking, refers to the object that the constructor creates.

When we are talking about direct function invoking, the presence of `this` inside the function body, except those instances that are wrapped by functions of the other three types of invoking, refers to the global context.

When we are talking about method invoking, the presence of `this` inside the function body, except those instances that are wrapped by functions of the other three types of invoking, refers to the object that the method belongs to.

When we are talking about switching context invoking, the presence of `this` inside the function body, except those instances that are wrapped by functions of the other three types of invoking, refers to the object that passed in as the first argument of the `call()` method.

Hoisting

This is another thing that Java developers usually easily get confused. Hoisting is a metaphor for the way that JavaScript interpreters will **lift** function declarations and variable declarations to the top of their containing scope. So, In JavaScript, you can see something that is obviously wrong and will definitely break the compilation if you write that in Java, but it is totally valid in JavaScript.

Let's see an example:

```
1. travel = 'No plan';
2. var travel;
3. console.log(travel); // Is the output: undefined?
4.
5. function travel() {
6.     console.log('Traveling');
7. }
8. travel(); // Is the output: Traveling?
```

What will the output be when the JavaScript engine executes line 3 and 8? It is not undefined, and not Traveling. Line 3 is "No plan" and line 8 is "Uncaught TypeError".

Here is what the JavaScript interpreter sees when it processes the preceding code:

```
1.  // Function declaration moved to the top of the scope
2.  function travel() {
3.    console.log('Traveling');
4.  }
5.  // Variable declaration moved under function declaration
6.  var travel;
7.  travel = 'No plan';
8.
9.  console.log(travel);  // No plan
10. travel();  // Uncaught TypeError: travel is not a function
```

JavaScript interpreter moves the function declarations up to the top, followed by variables declarations. Function expressions, for example, `var travel = function(){}`, are not lifted to the top as function declarations because they are also variable declarations.

Let's see another example:

```
1.   function workout() {
2.     goToGym();     // What will the output be?
3.     var goToGym = function () {
4.       console.log('Workout in Gym A');
5.     }
6.     return;
7.     function goToGym() {
8.       console.log('Workout in Gym B');
9.     }
10. }
11. workout();
```

What will the output be when line 2 is executed? It is "`Workout in Gym B.`". And here is what the interpreter sees when it processes the code:

```
1.   function workout() {
2.     function goToGym() {
3.       console.log('Workout in Gym B');
4.     }
5.     var goToGym;
6.     goToGym();
7.     goToGym = function () {
8.       console.log('Workout in Gym A');
9.     }
10.    return;
11. }
12. workout();
```

The interpreter moves the function declaration to the top of the scope and then the variable declaration, but not the assignment. So when `goToGym()` is executed, the assignment expression to the new function hasn't happened yet.

To wrap up, before executing, JavaScript interpreters will move the function declarations, and then variable declarations, without assignment expressions, up to the top of the containing scope. And it is valid to put function declarations after the `return` statement.

ES6 basics

ES6 (short for **ECMAScript 2015**), is the sixth version of ECMAScript, which is a general-purpose, cross-platform, and vendor-neutral programming language. ECMAScript is defined in ECMA Standard (ECMA-262) by Ecma International. Most of the time, ECMAScript is more commonly known by the name JavaScript.

Understanding ES6 is the key to writing web applications using modern JavaScript. Owing to the scope of this book, we will only cover the basics of new features introduced in ES6 here as you will see them in the rest of the book.

Block scoping, let, and const

As mentioned earlier, in ES6, you can use `let` to define variables or use `const` to define constants, and they will have block-level scope. And in the same scope, you can not redefine a variable using `let`. Also, you cannot access a variable or a constant that is defined with `let` or `const` before its declaration, since there is no variable hoisting with `let` or `const`.

Let's see the following `workout` example:

```
1.  function workout() {
2.    let gym = 'Gym A';
3.
4.    const gymStatuses = {'Gym A': 'open', 'Gym B': 'closed'};
5.    for (let gym in gymStatuses) {
6.      console.log(gym + ' is ' + gymStatuses[gym]);
7.    }
8.
9.    {
10.     const gym = 'Gym B';
11.     console.log('Workout in ' + gym);
12.     // The following will throw TypeError
13.     // gym = 'Gym C';
14.   }
15.
16.   console.log('Workout in ' + gym);
17.
18.   {
19.     function gym () {
20.       console.log('Workout in a separate gym');
21.     }
22.     gym();
23.   }
```

```
24.
25.    if (gymStatuses[gym] == 'open') {
26.      let exercises = ['Treadmill', 'Pushup', 'Spinning'];
27.    }
28.    // exercises are no longer accessible here
29.    // console.log(exercises);
30.
31.    try {
32.      let gym = 'Gym C';
33.      console.log('Workout in ' + gym);
34.      throw new Error('Gym is closed');
35.    } catch (err) {
36.      console.log(err);
37.      let gym = 'Gym D';
38.      console.log('Workout in ' + gym);
39.    }
40.  }
41. workout();
```

In line 2, we declare the gym variable, and it is visible in the workout() function body. In line 5, we declare the gym variable within the for loop block. It shadows the gym variable declared in line 2 and is only accessible within that for loop block.

In lines 9 to 14, we declare a new scope using a block statement. The gym constant declared in line 10 is only accessible within that scope. And as you can see in line 13, assigning a value to a constant will cause TypeError.

In line 16, the gym variable is back to the one declared in line 2. In lines 18 to 23, we declare the gym function and it is only accessible within that block.

In line 26, we define the exercises variable within the if block. And as you can see from line 29, it is no longer accessible outside the if block.

In lines 31 to 39, we declare a try-catch block. As you can see in lines 32 and 37, the try block and catch block are in different scopes.

To wrap up, using let and const, we can archive block-level scope with for loop blocks, if blocks, try-catch blocks, and block statements, as well as switch blocks.

Classes

ES2015 introduces classes, which is primarily a syntactical sugar over prototype-based inheritance. With the class syntax, you can create constructors, extends from a superclass, and create static methods, as well as getters and setters.

Let's see the following example that uses the class syntax to implement User, and TeamMember:

```
1.  class User {
2.    constructor(name, interests) {
3.      this.name = name;
4.      this.interests = interests;
5.    }
6.    greeting () {
7.      console.log('Hi, I\'m ' + this.name + '.');
8.    }
9.    get interestsCount () {
10.     return this.interests ? this.interests.length : 0;
11.   }
12. }
```

In lines 1 to 12, we define class User, which accepts two arguments via its constructor. It has a greeting() method and an interestsCount getter:

```
13. class TeamMember extends User {
14.   constructor(name, interests) {
15.     super(name, interests);
16.     this._tasks = [];
17.     this._welcomeText = 'Welcome to the team!';
18.   }
19.   greeting () {
20.     console.log('I\' m ' + this.name + '. ' + this._welcomeText);
21.   }
22.   work () {
23.     console.log('I\' m working on ' + this._tasks.length + '
        tasks.')
24.   }
25.   set tasks (tasks) {
26.     let acceptedTasks = [];
27.     if (tasks.length > TeamMember.maxTasksCapacity()) {
28.       acceptedTasks = tasks.slice(0,
          TeamMember.maxTasksCapacity());
29.       console.log('It\'s over max capacity. Can only take two.');
30.     } else {
31.       acceptedTasks = tasks;
32.     }
```

```
33.     this._tasks = this._tasks.concat(acceptedTasks);
34.   }
35.   static maxTasksCapacity () {
36.     return 2;
37.   }
38. }
```

In lines 13 to 38, we create a `TeamMember` class to extend from `User`. In its constructor, it calls the constructor of the `User` with `super` to instantiate the properties of `name` and `interests`. We also define two additional properties, `_tasks` and `_welcomeText`. The preceding underscore suggests that they are regarded as private properties and should not be changed directly from outside. However, nothing is private in JavaScript. You can still access these properties, for example, `member._tasks`, and `member._welcomeText`.

We override the `greeting()` method of `user` in line 20 and add a new `work()` method in line 22. In lines 25 to 34, we define a setter `tasks`, inside which we access the `maxTasksCapacity()` static method of `TeamMember`:

```
39. let member = new TeamMember('Sunny', ['Traveling']);
40. member.greeting();    // I' m Sunny. Welcome to the team!
41. member.tasks = ['Buy three tickets', 'Book a hotel', 'Rent a car'];
       // It's over max capacity. Can only take two.
42. member.work();        // I' m working on 2 tasks.
43. console.log(member.interestsCount); // 1
44. member.interestsCount = 2;          // This won't save the change
45. console.log(member.interestsCount); // 1
46. console.log(member.tasks);          // undefined
```

As you can see, in lines 39 to 43, the `member` object has all the features of the `User` class and `TeamMember`, working as expected. In lines 44 to 45, we try to make changes to `member.interestsCount`, but it won't work because there is no setter defined. And line 46 shows that accessing `member.tasks` results in `undefined` because we didn't define a getter for it.

You cannot use `member.constructor` to access the constructor of the `TeamMember` defined in line 14. It is for accessing the `member` object's constructor function, in this case, `TeamMember`.

And now let's see how to add a new method, `eat()`, to the `User` class:

```
User.prototype.eat = function () {
  console.log('What will I have for lunch?');
};
member.eat();   // What will I have for lunch?
```

You still need to add it to the prototype object of `User`. If you add it directly to `User` as follows, you will get `TypeError`:

```
User.sleep = function () {
  console.log('Go to sleep');
};
member.sleep();   // Uncaught TypeError: member.sleep is not a function
User.sleep();     // Go to sleep
```

It is because as a result of writing in this way that you add `sleep` as a property of the `User` class itself or, more precisely, the `User` constructor function itself. And you might have already noticed that `sleep` becomes a static method of the `User` class. When using the class syntax, when you define a method, behind the scene, JavaScript adds it to its prototype object, and when you define a static method, JavaScript adds it to the constructor function:

```
console.log(User.prototype.hasOwnProperty('eat'));   // true
console.log(User.hasOwnProperty('sleep'));           // true
```

Enhanced object literals

In ES6, object literals support setting prototypes, shorthand assignments, defining methods, making super calls, and computing properties with expressions.

Let's see the following example, which creates an `advisor` object with a `TeamMember` object as its prototype:

```
1.   const advice = 'Stay hungry. Stay foolish.';
2.
3.   let advisor = {
4.     __proto__: new TeamMember('Adam', ['Consulting']),
5.     advice,
6.     greeting () {
7.       super.greeting();
8.       console.log(this.advice);
9.     },
10.  [advice.split('.')[0]]: 'Always learn more'
11.  };
```

Line 4, assigning the object of `TeamMember` to the `advisor` object's __proto__ property makes `advisor` an instance of `TeamMember`:

```
console.log(TeamMember.prototype.isPrototypeOf(advisor));   // true
console.log(advisor instanceof TeamMember);                 // true
```

Line 5 is a shorthand assignment of `advice:advice`. Line 7 is creating the `greeting()` method of `TeamMember`, inside which it will invoke the `greeting` method of `TeamMember`:

```
advisor.greeting();    // I' m Adam. Welcome to the team!
                       // Stay hungry. Stay foolish.
```

In line 10, the `Stay hungry` property is calculated with bracket notation. And to access this property, in this case, because the property name contains a space, you need to use bracket notation, like this—`advisor['Stay hungry']`.

Arrow functions

ES6 introduces arrow functions as a function shorthand, using => syntax. Arrow functions support statement block bodies as well as expression bodies. When using an expression body, the expression's result is the value that the function returns.

An arrow syntax begins with function arguments, then the arrow =>, and then the function body. Let's look at the following different variations of arrow functions. The examples are written in both ES5 syntax and ES6 arrow function syntax:

```
const fruits = [{name: 'apple', price: 100}, {name: 'orange', price: 80},
{name: 'banana', price: 120}];

// Variation 1
// When no arguments, an empty set of parentheses is required
var countFruits = () => fruits.length;
// equivalent to ES5
var countFruits = function () {
  return fruits.length;
};

// Variation 2
// When there is one argument, parentheses can be omitted.
// The expression value is the return value of the function.
fruits.filter(fruit => fruit.price > 100);
// equivalent to ES5
fruits.filter(function(fruit) {
  return fruit.price > 100;
});
```

```
// Variation 3
// The function returns an object literal, it needs to be wrapped
// by parentheses.
var inventory = fruits.map(fruit => ({name: fruit.name, storage: 1})));
// equivalent to ES5
var inventory = fruits.map(function (fruit) {
  return {name: fruit.name, storage: 1};
});

// Variation 4
// When the function has statements body and it needs to return a
// result, the return statement is required
var inventory = fruits.map(fruit => {
  console.log('Checking ' + fruit.name + ' storage');
  return {name: fruit.name, storage: 1};
});
// equivalent to ES5
var inventory = fruits.map(function (fruit) {
  console.log('Checking ' + fruit.name + ' storage');
  return {name: fruit.name, storage: 1};
});
```

There is an additional note regarding variation 3. When an arrow function uses curly brackets, its function body needs to be a statement or statements:

```
var sum = (a, b) => { return a + b };
sum(1, 2);      // 3
```

The sum function won't work as expected when it is written like this:

```
var sum = (a, b) => { a + b };
sum(1, 2);      // undefined
// Using expression will work
var sum = (a, b) => a + b;
sum(1, 2);      // 3
```

Arrow functions have a shorter syntax and also many other important differences compared with ES5 function. Let's go through some of these differences one by one.

No lexical this

An arrow function does not have its own `this`. Unlike an ES5 function, that will create a separate execution context of its own, an arrow function uses surrounding execution context. Let's see the following shopping cart example:

```
1.  var shoppingCart = {
2.    items: ['Apple', 'Orange'],
3.    inventory: {Apple: 1, Orange: 0},
4.    checkout () {
5.      this.items.forEach(item => {
6.        if (!this.inventory[item]) {
7.          console.log('Item ' + item + ' has sold out.');
8.        }
9.      })
10.   }
11. }
12. shoppingCart.checkout();
13.
14. // equivalent to ES5
15. var shoppingCart = {
16.   items: ['Apple', 'Orange'],
17.   inventory: {Apple: 1, Orange: 0},
18.   checkout: function () {
19.     // Reassign context and use closure to make it
20.     // visible to the callback passed to forEach
21.     var that = this
22.     this.items.forEach(function(item){
23.       if (!that.inventory[item]) {
24.         console.log('Item ' + item + ' has sold out.');
25.       }
26.     })
27.   }
28. }
29. shoppingCart.checkout();
```

In line 6, `this` refers to the `shoppingCart` object itself, even it is inside the callback of the `Array.prototype.forEach()` method. As you can see in line 21, with the ES5 version, you need to use closure to keep the execution context available to the callback function.

And because an arrow function does not have a separate execution context, when it is invoked with `Function.prototype.call()`, `Function.prototype.apply()`, or `Function.prototype.bind()` method, the execution context that passed in as the first argument will be ignored. Let's take a look at an example:

```
1. var name = 'Unknown';
2. var greeting = () => {
```

```
3.    console.log('Hi, I\'m ' + this.name);
4.  };
5.  greeting.call({name: 'Sunny'});     // I'm Unknown
6.  greeting.apply({name: 'Tod'});      // I'm Unknown
7.  var newGreeting = greeting.bind({name: 'James'});
8.  newGreeting();                      // I'm Unknown
```

As you can see from line 3, in an arrow function, `this` always resolves to its surrounding execution context. The `call()`, `apply()`, or `bind()` method has no effect on its execution context.

 Unlike ES5 functions, arrow functions do not have their own `arguments` object. The `arguments` object is a reference to the surrounding function's `arguments` object.

Because arrow functions use its surrounding execution context, they are not suitable for defining methods of objects.

Let's see the following shopping cart example, which uses an arrow function for the checkout:

```
1.   var shoppingCart = {
2.     items: ['Apple', 'Orange'],
3.     inventory: {Apple: 1, Orange: 0},
4.     checkout: () => {
5.       this.items.forEach(item => {
6.         if (!this.inventory[item]) {
7.           console.log('Item ' + item + ' has sold out.');
8.         }
9.       })
10.   }
11. }
12. shoppingCart.checkout();
```

In line 4, we change `checkout` to an arrow function. And because an arrow function uses its surrounding execution context, `this` in line 5 no longer references the `shoppingCart` object and it will throw `Uncaught TypeError: Cannot read property 'forEach' of undefined`.

The preceding shopping cart example is written with object literals. Arrow functions do not work well when defining object methods using a prototype object either. Let's see the following example:

```
1.  class User {
2.    constructor(name) {
3.      this.name = name;
4.    }
5.  }
6.  User.prototype.swim = () => {
7.    console.log(this.name + ' is swimming');
8.  };
9.  var user = new User();
10. console.log(user.swim());    //  is swimming
```

As you can see from the output, in line 7, `this` does not reference the `user` object. In this example, it references the global context.

No prototype object

Arrow functions do not have prototype objects, hence, they are not constructor functions. And they cannot be invoked with a `new` operator. An error will be thrown if you try that. Here's an example:

```
const WorkoutPlan = () => {};
// Uncaught TypeError: WorkoutPlan is not a constructor
let workoutPlan = new WorkoutPlan();
console.log(WorkoutPlan.prototype);   // undefined
```

Default parameter value

In ES6, you can define the default values of a function's parameters. This is quite a useful improvement because the equivalent implementation in ES5 is not only tedious but also decreases the readability of the code.

Let's see an example here:

```
const shoppingCart = [];
function addToCart(item, size = 1) {
  shoppingCart.push({item: item, count: size});
}
addToCart('Apple');      // size is 1
addToCart('Orange', 2); // size is 2
```

In this example, we give the parameter `size` a default value, `1`. And let's see how we can archive the same thing in ES5. Here is an equivalent of the `addToCart` function in ES5:

```
function addToCart(item, size) {
  size = (typeof size !== 'undefined') ? size : 1;
  shoppingCart.push({item: item, count: size});
}
```

As you can see, using the ES6 default parameter can improve the readability of the code and make the code easier to maintain.

Rest parameters

In ES5, inside a function body, you can use the `arguments` object to iterate the parameters of the function. In ES6, you can use rest parameters syntax to define an indefinite number of arguments as an array.

Let's see the following example:

```
1.   // Using arguments in ES5
2.   function workout(exercise1) {
3.     var todos = Array.prototype.slice.call(arguments,
       workout.length);
4.     console.log('Start from ' + exercise1);
5.     console.log(todos.length + ' more to do');
6.   }
7.   // equivalent to rest parameters in ES6
8.   function workout(exercise1, ...todos) {
9.     console.log('Start from ' + exercise1);    // Start from
     //Treadmill
10.    console.log(todos.length + ' more to do'); // 2 more to do
11.    console.log('Args length: ' + workout.length); // Args length: 1
11.  }
12.  workout('Treadmill', 'Pushup', 'Spinning');
```

In line 8, we define a rest parameter `todos`. It is prefixed with three dots and is the last named parameter of the `workout()` function. To archive this in ES5, as you can see in line 3, we need to slice the `arguments` object. And in line 11, you can see that the rest parameter `todos` does not affect the length of the argument in the `workout ()` function.

Spread syntax

In ES6, when the three dot notation (. . .) is used in a function declaration, it defines a rest parameter; when it is used with an array, it spreads the array's elements. You can pass each element of the array to a function in this way. You can also use it in array literals.

Let's see the following example:

```
1. let urgentTasks = ['Buy three tickets'];
2. let normalTasks = ['Book a hotel', 'Rent a car'];
3. let allTasks = [...urgentTasks, ...normalTasks];
4.
5. ((first, second) => {
6.   console.log('Working on ' + first + ' and ' + second)
7. })(...allTasks);
```

In line 3, we use spread syntax to expand the urgentTasks array and the normalTasks array. And in line 7, we use spread syntax to expand the allTasks array and pass each element of it as arguments of the function. And the first argument has the value Buy three tickets, while the second argument has the value Book a hotel.

Destructuring assignment

In ES6, you can use the destructuring assignment to unpack elements in an array, characters in a string, or properties in an object and assign them to distinct variables using syntax similar to array literals and object literals. You can do this when declaring variables, assigning variables, or assigning function parameters.

Object destructuring

First of all, let's see an example of object destructuring:

```
1. let user = {name:'Sunny', interests:['Traveling', 'Swimming']};
2. let {name, interests, tasks} = user;
3. console.log(name);        // Sunny
4. console.log(interests);   // ["Traveling", "Swimming"]
5. console.log(tasks);       // undefined
```

As you can see, the `name` and `interests` variables defined in line 2 pick up the values of the properties with the same name in the `user` object. And the `tasks` variable doesn't have a matching property in the `user` object. Its value remains as `undefined`. You can avoid this by giving it a default value, like this:

```
let {name, interests, tasks=[]} = user;
console.log(tasks)  // []
```

Another thing you can do with object destructuring is that you can choose a different variable name. In the following example, we pick the value of the `name` property of the `user` object and assign it to the `firstName` variable:

```
let {name: firstName} = user;
console.log(firstName)  // Sunny
```

Array destructuring

Array destructuring is similar to object destructuring. Instead of using curly brackets, array destructuring uses brackets to do the destructuring. Here is an example of array destructuring:

```
let [first, second] = ['Traveling', 'Swimming', 'Shopping'];
console.log(first);   // Traveling
console.log(second);  // Swimming
```

You can also skip variables and only pick the one that you need, like the following:

```
let [,,third, fourth] = ['Traveling', 'Swimming', 'Shopping'];
console.log(third);   // Shopping
console.log(fourth);  // undefined
```

As you can see, we skip the first two variables and only require the third and the fourth. However, in our case, the `fourth` variable doesn't match any elements in the array and its value remains as `undefined`. Also, you can give it a default value, like this:

```
let [,,third, fourth = ''] = ['Traveling', 'Swimming', 'Shopping'];
console.log(fourth);  // an empty string
```

Nested destructuring

Similar to using object literals and array literals to create complex nested data structures with a terse syntax, you can use a destructuring assignment to pick up variables in a deeply nested data structure.

Let's see the following example, in which we only need the user's second interest:

```
1. let user = {name:'Sunny', interests:['Traveling', 'Swimming']};
2. let {interests:[,second]} = user;
3. console.log(second);     // Swimming
4. console.log(interests); // ReferenceError
```

In line 2, even though we put `interests` in the destructuring assignment, JavaScript doesn't really declare it. As you can see in line 4, accessing it will raise `ReferenceError`. What happens here is that JavaScript uses the part on left side of the colon (`:`), in this case, `interests`, to extract the value of the property of the same name, and uses the part on the right side to do further destructuring assignments. If you want to extract the `interests` property, as demonstrated previously, you need to write it in like this: `let {interests} = user;`.

Here is another example in which the `name` property of the second element in an array is destructured:

```
const fruits = [{name:'Apple', price:100},{name:'Orange', price:80}];
let [,{name:secondFruitName}] = fruits;
console.log(secondFruitName); // Orange
```

Rest elements

You can use the same syntax of the rest parameters in the destructuring assignment to put the remainder of the elements of an array into another array. Here is an example:

```
let [first, ...others] = ['Traveling', 'Swimming', 'Shopping'];
console.log(others);     // ["Swimming", "Shopping"]
```

As you can see, the second and third items of the array have been copied into the `others` variable. We can use this syntax to copy an array. However, this is only a shallow clone. When the elements of the array are objects, changes to an object's property of the copied array will be seen in the original array because essentially, the elements of both arrays reference the same object. Here is an example:

```
1. const fruits = [{name:'Apple', price:100},{name:'Orange', price:80}];
2. let [...myFruits] = fruits;
3. console.log(myFruits[0].name);          // Apple
4. myFruits.push({name:'Banana', price:90});
5. console.log(myFruits.length);           // 3
6. console.log(fruits.length);             // 2
7. myFruits[0].price = 110;
8. console.log(fruits[0].price);           // 110
```

As you can see in line 2, we use the destructuring assignment syntax to copy the `fruits` array into the `myFruits` array. And adding a new item to the copied array doesn't affect the original array, as you can see in lines 4 to 6. However, changing the value of the `price` property from the copied array will be also seen in the original array.

Function parameters destructuring

You can apply a destructuring assignment to function parameters as well. Let's see the following example:

```
1. function workout({gym}, times) {
2.   console.log('Workout in ' + gym + ' for ' + times + ' times');
3. }
4. let thisWeek = {gym: 'Gym A'};
5. workout(thisWeek, 2);   // Workout in Gym A for 2 times
```

As you can see, in line 1, we use object destructuring syntax to extract the `gym` variable from the first argument of the `workout()` function. In this way, the argument passed to the `workout()` function cannot be `null` or `undefined`. Otherwise, `TypeError` will be thrown. You can pass a number, a string, an array, or a function to the `workout()` function and JavaScript won't complain about it, although you will get `undefined` as a value for the `gym` variable.

Let's look at another example, in which we will perform a further destructuring of a destructured variable:

```
1. function workout({gym, todos}) {
2.   let [first] = todos;
3.   console.log('Start ' + first + ' in ' + gym);
4. }
5. let today = {gym: 'Gym A', todos: ['Treadmill']};
6. workout(today);         // Start Treadmill in Gym A
7. workout({gym: 'Gym B'}) // throw TypeError
```

In line 1, we do a parameter destructuring of the first argument, and in line 2 we do a further destructuring of the `todos` variable. In this way, the argument passed to the `workout()` function must have a `todos` property and its value is an array. Otherwise, `TypeError` will be thrown, as you can see in line 7. This is because, in line 2, JavaScript cannot do destructuring on `undefined` or `null`. We can improve this by giving `todos` a default value, as follows:

```
1. function workout({gym, todos=['Treadmill']}) {
2.   let [first] = todos;
3.   console.log('Start ' + first + ' in ' + gym);
```

```
4. }
5. workout({gym: 'Gym A'});  // Start Treadmill in Gym A
6. workout();                // throw TypeError
```

As you can see, in line 1, we only give `todos` a default value and we have to call the `workout()` function with a parameter. Calling it without any parameters, as in line 6, will still throw an error. It is because JavaScript still cannot do destructuring on `undefined` to get a value for the `gym` variable. And if you try to assign a default value to `gym` itself, such as `workout({gym='', ...})`, it won't work. You need to assign the entire parameter destructuring a default value, like this:

```
function workout({gym='', todos=['Treadmill']} = {}) {
    ...
}
```

Template literals

Template literals provide the ability to embed expressions in string literals and support multiple lines. The syntax is to use the back-tick (`` ` ``) character to enclose the string instead of single quotes or double quotes. Here is an example:

```
let user = {
  name: 'Ted',
  greeting () {
    console.log(`Hello, I'm ${this.name}.`);
  }
};
user.greeting();  // Hello, I'm Ted.
```

As you can see, inside the template literals, you can access the execution context via `this` by using the syntax `${...}`. Here is another example with multiple lines:

```
let greeting = `Hello, I'm ${user.name}.
Welcome to the team!`;
console.log(greeting);  // Hello, I'm Ted.
                        // Welcome to the team!
```

One caveat is that all the whitespaces inside the back-tick characters are part of the output. So, if you indent the second line as follows, the output wouldn't look good:

```
let greeting = `Hello, I'm ${user.name}.
                Welcome to the team!`;
console.log(greeting); // Hello, I'm Ted.
                       //                 Welcome to the team!
```

Modules

In ES6, JavaScript provides language-level support for modules. It uses `export` and `import` to organize modules and create a static module structure. That means you can determine imports and exports at compile time. Another important feature of ES6's module is that imports and exports must be at the top level. You cannot nest them inside blocks such as `if` and `try/catch`.

 Besides static declarations of imports and exports, there is a proposal to use the `import()` operator to programmatically load modules. The proposal is, at the time of writing, at stage 3 of the TC39 process. You can checkout the details at `https://github.com/tc39/proposal-dynamic-import`.

To create a module, all you need to do is to put your JavaScript code into a `.js` file. You can choose to use tools such as Babel (`http://babeljs.io`) to compile ES6 code into ES5, together with tools such as webpack (`https://webpack.js.org`) to bundle the code together. Or, another way to use the module files is to use `<script type="module">` to load them into browsers.

Export

Inside a module, you can choose to not export anything. Or, you can export primitive values, functions, classes, and objects. There are two types of exports—named exports and default exports. You can have multiple named exports in the same module but only a single default export in that module.

In the following examples, we will create a `user.js` module that exports the `User` class, a `tasks.js` module that tracks the count of total completed tasks, and a `roles.js` module that exports role constants.

Let's have a look at `user.js` file:

```
1. export default class User {
2.    constructor (name, role) {
3.       this.name = name;
4.       this.role = role;
5.    }
6. };
```

In this module, we export the `User` class inline as the default export by placing the keywords `export` and `default` in front of it. Instead of declaring an `export` inline, you can declare the `User` class first and then export it at the bottom, or anywhere that is at the top level in the module, even before the `User` class.

Let's have a look at `roles.js` file:

```
1. const DEFAULT_ROLE = 'User';
2. const ADMIN = 'Admin';
3. export {DEFAULT_ROLE as USER, ADMIN};
```

In this module, we create two constants and then `export` them using named exports in a list by wrapping them in curly brackets. Yes, in curly brackets. Don't think of them as exporting an object. And as you can see in line 3, we can rename things during `export`. We can also do the rename with `import` too. We will cover that shortly.

Let's have a look at `tasks.js` file:

```
1. console.log('Inside tasks module');
2. export default function completeTask(user) {
2.    console.log(`${user.name} completed a task`);
3.    completedCount++;
4. }
5. // Keep track of the count of completed task
6. export let completedCount = 0;
```

In this module, in line 2, we have a default export of the `completeTask` function and a named export of a `completedCount` variable in line 6.

Import

Now, let's create a module `app.js` to import the modules we just created.

Let's have a look at `app.js` file:

```
1.   import User from './user.js';
2.   import * as Roles from './roles.js';
3.   import completeTask from './tasks.js';
4.   import {completedCount} from './tasks.js';
5.
6.   let user = new User('Ted', Roles.USER);
7.   completeTask(user);
8.   console.log(`Total completed ${completedCount}`);
9.   // completedCount++;
10.  // Only to show that you can change imported object.
```

```
11. // NOT a good practice to do it though.
12. User.prototype.walk = function () {
13.   console.log(`${this.name} walks`);
14. };
15. user.walk();
```

In line 1, we use `default import` to import the `User` class from the `user.js` module. You can use a different name other than `User` here, for example, `import AppUser from './user.js'`. `default import` doesn't have to match the name used in the default export.

In line 2, we use `namespace import` to import the `roles.js` module and named it `Roles`. And as you can see from line 6, we access the named exports of the `roles.js` module using the dot notation.

In line 3, we use `default import` to import the `completeTask` function from the `tasks.js` module. And in line 4, we use `named import` to import `completedCount` from the same module again. Because ES6 modules are singletons, even if we import it twice here, the code of the `tasks.js` module is only evaluated once. You will see only one `Inside tasks module` in the output when we run it. You can put `default import` and `named import` together. The following is equivalent to the preceding lines 3 and 4:

```
import completeTask, {completedCount} from './tasks.js';
```

You can rename a `named import` in case it collides with other local names in your module. For example, you can rename `completedCount` to `totalCompletedTasks` like this:

```
import {completedCount as totalCompletedTasks} from './tasks.js';
```

Just like function declarations, imports are hoisted. So, if we put line 1 after line 6 like this, it still works. However, it is not a recommended way to organize your imports. It is better to put all your imports at the top of the module so that you can see the dependencies at a glance:

```
let user = new User('Ted', Roles.USER);
import User from './user.js';
```

Continue with the `app.js` module. In line 7, we invoke the `completeTask()` function and it increases the `completedCount` inside the `tasks.js` module. Since it is exported, you can see the updated value of `completedCount` in another module, as shown in line 8.

Line 9 is commented out. We were trying to change the `completedCount` directly, which didn't work. And if you uncomment it, when we run the example later, you will see `TypeError`, saying that you cannot modify a constant. Wait. `completedCount` is defined with `let` inside the `tasks.js` module; it is not a constant. So what happened here?

Import declarations have two purposes. One, which is obvious, is to tell the JavaScript engine what modules need to be imported. The second is to tell JavaScript what names those exports of other modules should be. And JavaScript will create constants with those names, meaning you cannot reassign them.

However, it doesn't mean that you cannot change things that are imported. As you can see from lines 12 to 15, we add the `walk()` method to the `User` class prototype. And you can see from the output, which will be shown later, that the `user` object created in line 6 has the `walk()` method right away.

Now, let's load the `app.js` module in an HTML page and run it inside Chrome.

Here is the `index.html` file:

```
1. <!DOCTYPE html>
2. <html>
3. <body>
4.   <script type="module" src="./app.js"></script>
5.   <script>console.log('A embedded script');</script>
6. </body>
7. </html>
```

In line 4, we load `app.js` as a module into the browser with `<script type="module">`, which is specified in HTML and has the `defer` attribute by default, meaning the browser will execute the module after it finishes parsing the DOM. You will see in the output that line 5, which is script code, will be executed before the code inside `app.js`.

Here are all the files in this example:

```
/app.js
/index.html
/roles.js
/tasks.js
/user.js
```

You need to run it from an HTTP server such as NGINX. Opening `index.html` directly as a file in Chrome won't work because of the **CORS** (short for **Cross-Origin Resource Sharing**) policy, which we will talk about in another chapter.

If you need to spin up a simple HTTP server real quick, you can use `http-server`, which requires zero configuration and can be started with a single command. First of all, you need to have Node.js installed and then run `npm install http-server -g`. Once the installation completes, switch to the folder that contains the example code, run `http-server -p 3000`, and then open `http://localhost:3000` in Chrome.

You will need to go to Chrome's Developer Tools to see the output, which will be similar to the following:

```
A embedded script
Inside tasks module
Ted completed a task
Total completed 1
Ted walks
```

As you can see from the output, the browser defers the execution of the module's code, while the script code is executed immediately, and the `tasks.js` module is only evaluated once.

Starting from ES6, there are two types in JavaScript—scripts and modules. Unlike scripts code, where you need to put `'use strict';` at the top of a file to render the code in strict mode, modules code is automatically in strict mode. And top-level variables of a module are local to that module unless you use `export` to make them available to the outside. And, at the top level of a module, `this` refers to `undefined`. In browsers, you can still access a `window` object inside a module.

Promises

Promises are another option in addition to callbacks, events for asynchronous programming in JavaScript. Before ES6, libraries such as `bluebird` (`http://bluebirdjs.com`) provided promises compatible with the Promises/A+ spec.

A promise represents the eventual result of an asynchronous operation, as described in the Promises/A+ spec. The result would be a successful completion or a failure. And it provides methods such as `.then()`, and `.catch()` for chaining multiple asynchronous operations together that would make the code similar to synchronous code that is easy to follow.

The features of ES6 promises are a subset of those provided by libraries such as `bluebird`. In this book, the promises we use are those defined in the ES6 language spec unless otherwise specified.

Let's look at an example in which we will get a list of projects from the server and then get tasks of those projects from the server in a separate API call. And then we will render it. The implementation here is a simplified version for demonstrating the differences between using callbacks and promises. We use `setTimeout` to stimulate an asynchronous operation.

First of all, let's see the version that uses callbacks:

```
1.  function getProjects(callback) {
2.    // Use setTimeout to stimulate calling server API
3.    setTimeout(() => {
4.      callback([{id:1, name:'Project A'},{id:2, name:'Project B'}]);
5.    }, 100);
6.  }
7.  function getTasks(projects, callback) {
8.    // Use setTimeout to stimulate calling server API
9.    setTimeout(() => {
10.     // Return tasks of specified projects
11.     callback([{id: 1, projectId: 1, title: 'Task A'},
12.               {id: 2, projectId: 2, title: 'Task B'}]);
13.   }, 100);
14. }
15. function render({projects, tasks}) {
16.   console.log(`Render ${projects.length} projects and
      ${tasks.length} tasks`);
17. }
18. getProjects((projects) => {
19.   getTasks(projects, (tasks) => {
20.     render({projects, tasks});
21.   });
22. });
```

As you can see in lines 18 to 22, we use callbacks to organize asynchronous calls. And even though the code here is greatly simplified, you can still see that the `getProjects()`, `getTasks()`, and `render()` methods are nested, creating a pyramid of doom or callback hell.

Now, let's see the version that uses promises:

```
1.  function getProjects() {
2.    return new Promise((resolve, reject) => {
3.      setTimeout(() => {
4.        resolve([{id:1, name:'Project A'},{id:2, name:'Project B'}]);
5.      }, 100);
6.    });
7.  }
8.  function getTasks(projects) {
```

```
9.      return new Promise((resolve, reject) => {
10.       setTimeout(() => {
11.         resolve({projects,
12.                 tasks:['Buy three tickets', 'Book a hotel']});
13.       }, 100);
14.     });
15.   }
16.   function render({projects, tasks}) {
17.     console.log(`Render ${projects.length} projects and ${tasks.length}
tasks`);
18.   }
19.   getProjects()
20.   .then(getTasks)
21.   .then(render)
22.   .catch((error) => {
23.     // handle error
24.   });
```

In lines 1 to 15, in the getProjects() and getTasks() method, we wrap up asynchronous operations inside a Promise object that is returned immediately. The Promise constructor function takes a function as its parameter. This function is called an executor function, which is executed immediately with two arguments, a resolve function and a reject function. These two functions are provided by the Promise implementation. When the asynchronous operation completes, you call the resolve function with the result of the operation or no result at all. And when the operation fails, you can use the reject function to reject the promise. Inside the executor function, if any error is thrown, the promise will be rejected too.

A promise is in one of these three states:

- **Pending**: The initial state of a promise
- **Fulfilled**: The state when the operation has completed successfully
- **Rejected**: The state when the operation didn't complete successfully due to an error or any other reason

You cannot get the state of a promise programmatically. Instead, you can use the .then() method of the promise to take action when the state changes to fulfilled, and use the .catch() method to react when the state changed to rejected or an error are thrown during the operation.

The .then() method of a promise object takes two functions as its parameters. The first function in the argument is called when the promise is fulfilled. So it is usually referenced as onFulfilled, and the second one is called when the promise is rejected, and it is usually referenced as onRejected. The .then() method will also return a promise object. As you can see in lines 19 to 21, we can use .then() to chain all the operations. The .catch() method in line 22 is actually a syntax sugar of .then(undefined, onRejected). Here, we put it as the last one in the chain to catch all the rejects and errors. You can also add .then() after .catch() to perform further operations.

The ES6 Promise also provides the .all(iterable) method to aggregate the results of multiple promises and the .race(iterable) method to return a promise that fulfills or rejects as soon as one of the promises in the iterable fulfills or rejects.

Another two methods that ES6 Promise provides are the .resolve(value) method and the .reject(reason) method. The .resolve(value) method returns a Promise object. When the value is a promise, the returned promise will adopt its eventual state. That is when you call the .then() method of the returned promise; the onFulfilled handler will get the result of the value promise. When the value is not a promise, the returned promise is in a fulfilled state and its result is a value. The .reject(reason) method returns a promise that is in a rejected state with the reason passed in to indicate why it is rejected.

As you might have noticed, promises do not help you write less code, but they do help you to improve your code's readability by providing a better way of organizing code flow.

Summary

In this chapter, you learned the differences between the JavaScript language and the Java language. Keep these differences in mind. They can help you to avoid pitfalls when you write JavaScript code.

You also learned the basics of ES6. ES6 mastery is considered to be one of the basic skill sets that a web developer should have. You can write less code and also better code with ES6.

In the next chapter, you will learn the fundamental concepts of Vue.js 2, and you will be able to understand how Vue.js 2 works internally and become a master of Vue.js.

Vue.js 2 - It Works in the Way You Expected

2

Vue.js is simple and powerful, and it is easy to learn. Once you understand the basics of the framework, everything will work in just the way you expect. The framework will help you to keep focused on writing the logic of your application instead of remembering a bunch of APIs that are hard to use.

In this chapter, you will do the following:

- Learn fundamental concepts in Vue.js
- Learn how the Vue.js reactivity system works
- Learn about the internal implementation of Vue.js
- Learn about Vue.js logic and designs

Along the way, we will create a sample application. It will show you how Vue.js works and you can write the application step by step as you read. And, by the end of this chapter, you will have a **single-page application (SPA)** that demonstrates most of the features in Vue.js 2, and you will have a deep understanding of how Vue.js works internally.

Fundamental concepts

When you start a Vue application, what you need to keep in mind is your application's logic itself. You don't need to remember a set of APIs so that you can connect different pieces of your code. Vue.js, which is a progressive framework, provides you with an intuitive way of writing web applications, starting small and growing incrementally into a large-scale application. If you have used other frameworks before, you may wonder why they make things unnecessarily complicated. Now, let's go through fundamental concepts in Vue.js and create the sample application.

Vue instance

Creating a Vue instance is the start of every Vue.js application. Typically, a Vue application consists of two types of Vue instance—the root Vue instance and component instances. You create the root instance with the Vue function, as follows:

```
new Vue({/* options */});
```

The options object here is where you describe your application. Vue.js takes this object and initializes the Vue instance.

Let's create a simple application, called the Messages App and see how to use the options object. This SPA has the following features:

- Add a message
- View messages list
- Delete a message
- Automatically disable the add feature under certain conditions

We will start by creating the index.html file and, from there, we will build our application incrementally.

Let's have a look at the index.html file:

```
1.   <!DOCTYPE html>
2.   <html>
3.   <head><title>Messages App</title></head>
4.   <body>
5.     <div id="app"></div>
6.     <script src="https://unpkg.com/vue@2.5.13/dist/vue.js"></script>
7.     <script>
8.     let vm = new Vue({
9.       el: '#app'
10.    });
11.    </script>
12.  </body>
13.  </html>
```

In line 5, we create a <div> element with an app id in the DOM. And in line 9, we mount our application to this element by using the el property of the options object. el is short for **element**, and its value can be a CSS selector string, like the one we use here, '#app', or it can be the HTMLElement itself, document.getElementById('app'). In line 8, we assign the Vue instance to the vm variable, which is short for ViewModel.

Now, let's define our data model of the application. We need an array to hold those added messages and a string to bind to the form's input which will accept new messages. Here is how the `data` object appears:

```
...
let vm = new Vue({
  el: '#app',
  data: {
    messages: [],
    newMessage: ''
  }
});
...
```

We add the `data` object using object literals. As you can see, it is quite straightforward. We give them initial values so that you can easily tell that `messages` is an array and `newMessage` is a string. Providing initial values for the `data` object properties is a good practice. It not only helps you understand the data model better, but also makes those properties reactive by default. We will see what this means when we discuss the reactivity system in the next section.

Besides using a plain object as the value of the `data` property of the `options` object, you can also use a function that returns a plain object, as in the example:

```
...
data () {
  return {
    messages: [],
    newMessage: ''
  }
}
...
```

Using a function is required when you define the data structure for a component because, in that way, Vue.js will always create a fresh data model for the new component. If you use a plain object to define a component's data model, all of the instances of that component will share the same `data` object, which is not desired. For our root Vue instance here, we are safe to use a plain object.

For now, we have only defined the data model, and we haven't told Vue.js what to do with the `data` object. Let's add a template for displaying and adding messages. You can add a template in three ways. One is to add an inline template string using the `template` property of the `options` object. It is appropriate to adopt this approach when you create a component that doesn't have a lot of markups. The second way is to put the template directly inside the mounting point, `<div id="app"></div>`. Vue.js will parse the template inside `#app` and replace it with HTML generated by Vue.js. The third way is to put the template markup inside a `script` tag, for example, `<script type="x-template" id="tmplApp">`, and put `'#tmplApp'` as the value of the `template` property of the `options` object. We will adopt the second approach here just so we can have the template markup close to the final output.

Here is how the template appears:

```
. . .
 5.  <div id="app">
 6.    <ul>
 7.      <li v-for="message in messages">
 8.        {{ message.text }} - {{ message.createdAt }}
 9.      </li>
10.    </ul>
11.    <form v-on:submit.prevent="addMessage">
12.      <textarea v-model="newMessage" placeholder="Leave a message">
13.      </textarea>
14.      <div><button type="submit">Add</button></div>
15.    </form>
16.  </div>
. . .
```

In line 7, we use the Vue built-in `v-for` directive to render the messages list. The syntax of the `v-for` directive is `alias in source`. In our code, `message` is `alias` and `messages` is `source`. We don't need to write `vm.messages` in order to access the `messages` property. Just use the exact name that you put in the `data` object. And by adding the `v-for` directive to the `li` tag, we create a `v-for` block inside the `li` tag, and that's where the `alias message` will be available. You can think of the `v-for` block as being equivalent to the `for-loop` block in JavaScript.

In line 8, we use **Mustache** syntax to output the `text` property and `createdAt` property of a `message` object of the `messages` list. The `createdAt` property is a `Date` object that we add when saving a new message. When Vue.js parses the template and interpolates a Mustache tag, for example, `{{message.text}}`, it creates data binding between the output and the data. It will replace the tag with the actual value and update the output whenever the `text` property has been changed. The text interpolation also supports JavaScript expression. For example, you can make the `text` property always in lower case with `{{message.text.toLowerCase()}}`.

In line 11, we use another built-in directive, `v-on`, to attach an event listener to the form's `submit` event. `prevent` is a modifier, telling Vue.js to call `event.preventDefault()` so that the browser won't actually submit the form. `addMessage` is a method that will be invoked when the form's `submit` event is triggered. We will create this method shortly. You can use `v-on` to attach listeners to all of the normal DOM events, for example, `click` and `mouseover`. You can also use it to listen to custom events of Vue's custom components in the same way. We will see how that works shortly.

In line 12, we use the built-in `v-model` directive to create a two-way binding between the `textarea` element and `newMessage` property of the `data` object. In this way, whenever the value of the `textarea` element is changed, the `newMessage` will be updated automatically. And when `newMessage` is changed, `textarea` will be updated accordingly. This is such a nice feature that you can get the value of the `textarea` element without touching it yourself specifically. It works just as you would imagine it should.

In line 14, we add a button with `type="submit"` to trigger the `submit` event of the form. Now, let's create our `addMessage` method to listen to that event. We can do it by using the `methods` property of the `options` object.

Here is how the `options` object appears with the `addMessage` method:

```
...
let vm = new Vue({
  ...
  data: {
    ...
  },
  methods: {
    addMessage (event) {
      if (!this.newMessage) {return;}
      this.messages.push({
        text: this.newMessage, createdAt: new Date()});
      this.newMessage = '';
    }
```

```
    }
});
...
```

The `methods` property of the `options` object takes an object, where you put all of your methods. And inside these methods, you have access to the properties of the `data` object via `this`, as you can see that we use `this.newMessage` and `this.messages` inside the `addMessage` method to access them. The method syntax we use here is ES6, but you can also use function expression, as follows:

```
addMessage: function (event) {
    // Logic goes here
}
```

However, you should not use arrow functions syntax to create methods because you will lose access to the Vue instance via `this`.

Inside the `addMessage` method, we add the new message to the `messages` array using the `push()` method, and then we reset the `newMessage` property. Accordingly, Vue.js will clear `textarea` in the UI automatically. This is the magic of two-way binding, which will be revealed soon.

Now, let's add a way to delete a message from the UI. Here is what we change in the template:

```
...
<li v-for="message in messages">
    {{ message.text }} - {{ message.createdAt }}
    <button @click="deleteMessage(message)">X</button>
</li>
...
```

We add a button and use `@click`, the short-hand of `v-on:click`, to attach the listener `deleteMessage` method to the `click` event. Instead of putting the method's name here, we use an inline statement to pass the `message` object to the method. And here are the updated `methods` of the `options` object:

```
...
let vm = new Vue({
    ...
    methods: {
        ...
        deleteMessage (message) {
            this.messages.splice(this.messages.indexOf(message), 1)
        }
    }
```

```
});
...
```

We delete the selected message from the `messages` array using the
`Array.prototype.splice()` method. Vue.js will detect this change and update the DOM
automatically. You don't need to manipulate the DOM at all.

Now, let's add the ability to automatically disable the `add` feature. Let's say we want to
disable the `Add` button when there are `10` messages in the list. To do that, we can use the
built-in `v-bind` directive to bind the `Add` button's `disabled` attribute with the
`messages.length >= 10` expression. In this way, Vue.js will update the `disabled`
attribute automatically when the length of the `messages` array changes. Here is the
updated template:

```
...
<form @submit.prevent="addMessage">
  ...
  <div>
    <button v-bind:disabled="messages.length >= 10"
    type="submit">Add</button>
  </div>
</form>
...
```

What if we want to change the logic so that the `Add` button is disabled when the length of
the `textarea` input exceeds 50 characters? You will need to change the value of the `v-bind` directive to `newMessage.length > 50`. What if we want to disable the button when
there are already `10` messages, or the length of `newMessage` exceeds 50 characters? We can
change the directive value to `messages.length >= 10 || newMessage.length > 50`.
It still works. However, as you can see, the code starts to bloat and it would become hard to
maintain when you need to add more logic to decide when the `Add` button should be
disabled.

Here, we can use `computed` properties. As the name suggests, the value of such a property
is computed rather than defined as those in the `data` object. And Vue.js will track the
dependencies of a `computed` property and update the property's value when the
dependencies change. Let's add the `computed` property `addDisabled` to
the `options` object:

```
let vm = new Vue({
  data {
    ...
  },
  computed: {
```

```
        addDisabled () {
            return this.messages.length >= 10 || this.newMessage.length > 50;
        }
    },
    ...
});
```

As you can see, the `addDisabled` computed property is defined as a method of the `computed` object of the `options` object. Inside the method, you also have access to the Vue instance via `this`. For the `v-bind` directive, there is also a shorthand option, which is a colon (`:`). Let's update the `Add` button in the template to the following:

```
<button :disabled="addDisabled" type="submit">Add</button>
```

As you can see, our template becomes much easier to follow and maintain since you keep most of the logic in the JavaScript rather than in the HTML template.

For the `v-bind` directive, you can use it to bind the HTML element's built-in attributes, for example, `class` and `style`. You can also use it to bind a Vue's custom component property. We will see how that works shortly.

By now, we have implemented all of the features of the Messages App. Since we didn't use `<script type="module">`, you can open `index.html` directly using Chrome. If you try it now, you will see something strange. Immediately after opening the file, you can see the template markups that we put inside the mounting point, `<div id="app">`, which is awkward. The reason that it behaves in this way is that, before the browser loads Vue.js and executes it, it will display the HTML in the manner it is defined until Vue.js takes control of the DOM and removes the template markups from the mounting point and then replaces it with the new dynamically generated DOM. Let's fix this by adding the `v-cloak` directive to the mounting point and inserting a CSS rule to hide the template markups. Vue.js will remove the `v-clock` directive when the generated DOM is ready. The following are the updates to the `index.html` file:

```
<head>
    ...
    <style>
        [v-cloak] {display: none;}
        body > div {width: 500px; margin: 0 auto;}
        textarea {width: 100%;}
        ul {padding: 0 15px;}
    </style>
</head>
<body>
    <div id="app" v-cloak>
        ...
```

```
        </div>
    </body>
```

Besides the `[v-cloak]` CSS rule, we add a few other rules to style the UI a little bit, even though it is still very primitive with these rules. Now, if you open it again in the browser, there is no **flash** anymore.

By now, you've learned how to use the `data` object, the `computed` object, and the `methods` object of the `options` object of a Vue instance. And you can see that, even though the properties of these objects are defined separately, you can access them in the same way, which is via `this`.

Now, let's open the **Console** tab of Chrome's Developer tools. Instead of using the input field in the UI, let's add a new message from the console by interacting directly with the `vm` object, which is the root Vue instance that we created and made available in the global scope. As you can see from the following screenshot, it works as you would expect. This is its simplicity and powerfulness:

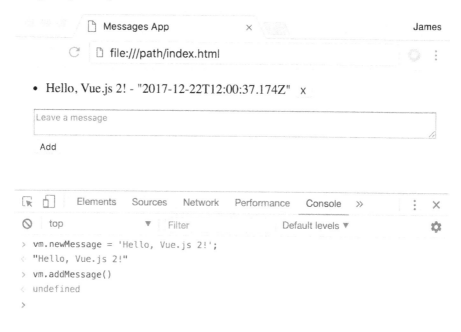

Figure 2.1: The Messages App in Chrome

Apart from the `data`, `computed`, and `methods` properties, the `options` object has many other properties that you can use to define a Vue instance. We will talk about them along the way. For now, let's move on to see another powerful feature of Vue.js.

Components

Components are the primary way of reusing code in a Vue application. With components, you can extend HTML elements and provide additional logic to make them reusable. You can define your elements and use them in the same way as native HTML elements. As we mentioned earlier, a Vue component is also a Vue instance. It accepts the same `options` object during creation.

You can register a component globally so that it is available across the entire application. To do that, you can use `Vue.component(id, [definition])`. The first argument is `component id`. It is also the tag name that you will use in the template. And the second argument is `definition` of the component, which can be an `options` object or a function that will return an `options` object. And you can also register a component locally to make it only available in the scope of another Vue instance. To do that, you add the component's `options` object to its parent's `components` property.

Let's update our Messages App to use a component to render the messages list. We call this component `MessageList`, and its tag name is `message-list`. It will extend the `<ul>` HTML element in our template, as well as everything inside of it. This component will also need to react to clicking on the **Delete** button.

In order to render the list, the `MessageList` component will need to access the `messages` property of the `data` object. In Vue.js, components have their own isolated scopes, meaning you cannot directly reference parent data in a child component. Vue.js provides a property called `props` in the `options` object. You can use it to define the data that can be passed to a component. The `props` property takes an array or an object as its value. Let's add property `items` to the `MessageList` component and use the v-bind directive to connect it to the `messages` data.

Now, we need to think about message delete actions. Since all of the messages are stored in the `messages` property, and we pass them to `MessageList` via the `items` property, it seems quite straightforward that we perform the delete operation directly within `MessageList`. This encapsulate logic inside the component itself. Is this a good approach? Let's step back and think about it. We put the rendering logic and the deleting logic into the `MessageList` component, but we have left the adding logic outside since `<form>` is not part of the `MessageList` component. Right, in that case, we can put that into `MessageList` too. Wait, does that sound like something `MessageList` should do? A component should only focus on one responsibility. We should make `MessageList` focus only on rendering the messages list. In that way, we can use it in other places that only require rendering but not adding or deleting. So, we will not move `<form>` into `MessageList`, nor will we delete the messages inside it.

Basically, we need a way to communicate back to the parent when a **Delete** button is clicked on a message inside the `MessageList` component. In Vue.js, we can do that with custom events. A Vue instance has a `$emit()` method that can trigger an event on the current instance. It takes the event name as the first argument and any additional data, if there is any, as the second argument. And the parent can use the `v-on` directive to attach listeners to that event. So, we can let `MessageList` trigger a `delete` event upon clicking on the **Delete** button and pass through the message that should be deleted.

Now, let's update the `index.html` file to use this component, even though we haven't defined it yet:

```
<div id="app" v-cloak>
  <message-list :items="messages" @delete="deleteMessage"></message-
  list>
  <ul>
    <li v-for="message in messages">
      {{ message.text }} - {{ message.createdAt }}
      <button @click="deleteMessage(message)">X</button>
    </li>
  </ul>
  ...
</div>
```

`:items="messages"` is the shorthand of `v-bind:items="messages"`, and `@delete="deleteMessage"` is the shorthand of `v-on:delete="deleteMessage"`. As you can see, we can do data binding and attach event listeners to the same with custom components and native HTML elements. It's another level of simplicity.

It's time to create the `MessageList` component. We can stay in `index.html` and put the code of `MessageList` above `let vm = new Vue({...})`, because Vue.js needs to register components first to use them in the parent. Another way, which is recommended, is to put everything that a component requires in a separate file so that we can use import to reuse it wherever needs it. Let's create a file called `MessageList.js` under the `components` folder.

Let's have a look at the `components/MessageList.js` file:

```
1.   export default {
2.     name: 'MessageList',
3.     template: `<ul>
4.       <li v-for="item in items" :item="item">
5.       {{ item.text }} - {{ item.createdAt }}
6.       <button @click="deleteMessage(item)">X</button></li></ul>`,
7.     props: {
8.       items: {
9.         type: Array,
```

```
10.      required: true
11.    }
12.  },
13.  methods: {
14.    deleteMessage (message) {
15.      this.$emit('delete', message);
16.    }
17.  }
18. };
```

This file is an ES6 module. It exports the component's definition, the `options` object, as the default export. In line 2, we add the `name` property, which is not mandatory, but it will help you during debugging and it is good practice to add it.

In line 3, we copy the `<ul>` object and everything inside of it from `index.html` here as an inline template. And we also add the `deleteMessage()` method in line 14 to listen to the `click` event on the **Delete** button. Inside this method, we use `$emit()` to trigger the `delete` event of `MessageList` so that its parent can listen to it via `@delete="..."`. You don't have to name the event `delete`; you can call it `onDelete` and trigger it like `this.$emit('onDelete', ...)` and use `@onDelete="..."` to listen to it.

In lines 7 to 12, we define the `items` property of `MessageList`. Here, we use an object instead of an array as its definition to give Vue.js details of the structure of the data that it needs to have. Here, we define it as an array and mandatory. If we mistakenly passed in a string or other value that is not an array, Vue.js will throw an error, so that we can capture this issue during development rather than troubleshoot it during production.

Now, let's register `MessageList` to the root Vue instance in `index.html`:

```
<script type="module">
import MessageList from './components/MessageList.js';
let vm = new Vue({
  ...
  components: {
    MessageList
  },
  ...
});
</script>
```

Since we create `MessageList.js` as an ES6 module, we need to add `type="module"` to the `<script>` tag and import `MessageList`. To register `MessageList` as a local component, we add it to the `options` object's `components` property by using the shorthand of `MessageList:MessageList`. Vue.js will convert the property name from Pascal case to kebab-case and use it as the `component` ID when registering it so that we can use it as `<message-list>` in the template.

Our Messages App is very simple and only has a few lines of code. An actual messaging application in the real world, for example, Disqus, supports features such as replies, markdown syntax, and embedding images. And if the Messages App was such an application, we do not want to only have a `MessageList` component. We want to have dedicated components to encapsulate specific features. A good start would be to move a single message rendering to a separate component, for example, `MessageListItem`. Let's do that.

Before we do that, let's talk about naming. `MessageList` is a long name and `MessageListItem` is even longer. So, why not just use `Messages` or `Msgs` for the list component and `Message` or `Msg` for the single message component? Most of the time, when you give something a name in the code, such as variable names and filenames, you need to consider whether or not that name is a good reflection of the domain that you're working on, and then whether or not it follows the naming convention or style guide. And then, you can turn to picking a shorter one. Vue.js has an official style guide. There is one guide about tightly coupled component names, which states: *Child components that are tightly coupled with their parent should include the parent component name as a prefix.* So, we're following that. And when you see the name `MessageListItem`, you know that its parent component is `MessageList`.

The `MessageListItem` component will extend the `<li>` tag and everything inside of it. And here is how it appears. Let's have a look at the `components/MessageListItem.js` file:

```
export default {
  name: 'MessageListItem',
  template: `<li>{{ item.text }} - {{ item.createdAt }}
    <button @click="deleteClicked">X</button></li>`,
  props: {
    item: {
      type: Object,
      required: true
    }
  },
  methods: {
    deleteClicked () {
```

```
        this.$emit('delete');
      }
    }
};
```

We define this component to accept data from the parent component using the property `item`, and it will trigger a `delete` event when clicking on the **Delete** button.

Here is the change to the `MessageList` component:

```
import MessageListItem from './MessageListItem.js';
export default {
  name: 'MessageList',
  template: `<ul><message-list-item v-for="item in items" :item="item"
    @delete="deleteMessage(item)"></message-list-item></ul>`,
  ...
  components: {
    MessageListItem
  }
  ...
};
```

As you can see, we import `MessageListItem` from the same directory and register it locally to `MessageList` and replace `<li>` with `<message-list-item>`. The v-for directive works the same way, and we pass data using `:item` and bind the listener using `@delete`.

When you run the application, you will see a tip from Vue.js in the console that says that component lists rendered with `v-for` should have explicit keys. In short, Vue.js is asking us to provide a key, which can be the unique id of the items in the list, so that it can track which element has been changed and only update that part of the DOM. It's related to the virtual DOM, which Vue.js 2 uses to keep track of changes it needs to make to the real DOM. We will talk about the virtual DOM in detail in a later section. For now, let's bind `key` for `<message-list-item>`.

Let's add the `id` property to `message` objects using the timestamp of creation, which is good enough in our case. Here are the changes to the `addMessage()` method:

```
addMessage (event) {
  ...
  let now = new Date();
  this.messages.push({
    id: now.getTime(), text:this.newMessage, createdAt:now});
  ...
}
```

And here is the change to the `MessageList` component:

```
export default {
  ...
  template: `<ul><message-list-item v-for="item in items"
    :item="item" :key="item.id" @delete="deleteMessage(item)">
    </message-list-item></ul>`,
  ...
};
```

By now, we have created a component-based Vue application. Here is its final structure:

```
/index.html
/components/MessageList.js
/components/MessageListItem.js
```

For building large-scale web applications, it is ideal to use single file components. With that, basically, you can put the template, the JavaScript code, and the CSS of a component in a single file that uses the `.vue` extension. We will see how that works when we build the TaskAgile app later.

Vue instance life cycle

Among these, life cycle hooks are special because they provide you with the ability to define logic for different stages during the instance's life cycle. Here are all life cycle hooks, listed from the first stage to the end:

- `beforeCreate`: Called after the instance's internal events and life cycle state have been initialized.
- `created`: Called after the instance's injections and reactivity system have been initialized. At this stage, the instance is functional, except the DOM hasn't been updated and users cannot see anything on the UI.
- `beforeMount`: Called after Vue.js finishes template compilation and is ready to render the generated DOM.
- `mounted`: Called after the DOM has been updated. At this point, users can interact with the UI, and the instance is fully functional.
- `beforeUpdate`: Called after the data changes and before the DOM is updated. In this hook, you can still perform changes to the data and they will not trigger additional DOM updates.
- `updated`: Called after the DOM has been updated based on the data changes.
- `activated`: Called when a kept-alive component is activated.

- `deactivated`: Called when a kept-alive component is deactivated.
- `beforeDestroy`: Called before the instance is destroyed. At this stage, the instance is still fully functional.
- `destroyed`: Called after the instance has been destroyed. At this stage, all of the directives of the instance have been unbound, all event listeners have been removed, and all of the children Vue instances have been destroyed.
- `errorCaptured`: Called whenever an error from any descendent component is captured.

Besides adding logic to life cycle, hooks, they are great ways of inspecting how Vue.js manage components' life cycles. It will help you understand how Vue.js works better. You can add hooks to the Messages App's components to try it out.

Directives

Directives play an important role in a Vue application. They reactively apply changes to the DOM when the value of its expression changes. For example, `v-for` renders the element or data block multiple times based on the source data, and `v-on` attaches listeners to a DOM element. Besides using the built-in directives, you can also create custom directives. To do that, you create directive definition objects and register them, either globally using `Vue.directive()` or locally to a component by using the `directives` property of that component.

In the definition object of a directive, you can add the following hook functions for Vue.js to notify the directive about what happens outside so that it can apply different logic accordingly:

- `bind`: Called only once when Vue.js first binds the directive to the element. This is where you perform the one-time setup.
- `inserted`: Called when Vue.js has inserted the bound element into its parent node. However, the parent node might not have been inserted into the DOM at this moment.
- `update`: Called when Vue.js has updated the containing component's VNode, but possibly before updating the VNodes of the component's children. We will talk about VNodes later.
- `componentUpdated`: Called after Vue.js has updated the containing component's VNode and the VNodes of its children.
- `unbind`: Called only once when Vue.js has unbound the directive from the element.

A good example of custom directives is to create one to automatically focus a forms input after a page has opened. Let's create a global directive, v-focus, and use it on the add message textarea of our Messages App.

Let's have a look at the directives/focus.directive.js file:

```
// The following example is borrowed from
// https://vuejs.org/v2/guide/custom-directive.html
// Register a global custom directive called `v-focus`
Vue.directive('focus', {
  // When the bound element is inserted into the DOM...
  inserted: function (el) {
    // Focus the element
    el.focus();
  }
});
```

Let's have a look at the index.html file:

```
...
<textarea v-focus ...></textarea>
...
<script type="module">
import MessageList from './components/MessageList.js';
import './directives/focus.directive.js';
...
</script>
```

We name our directive files in this format: ${directiveName}.directive.js. In this way, when you open it in your editor, you can know it is a directive from the suffix.

Filters

Filters in Vue.js are different from the filters in Java EE. In a Vue application, you use filters to format texts in Mustache interpolations or v-bind expressions. A filter is a JavaScript function that takes an expression's value as its first argument. Vue.js provides two types of filter registration—globally with Vue.filter(), and locally with the filters property of a component's options.

In our Messages App, the default date and time format that we used on the message's createdAt property aren't looking good. Let's create a global filter, datetime, to provide a better format.

As a convention, we will put the filter file under the `filters` directory and name it in this format: `${filterName}.filter.js`, similar to the names of the directives. We use `Intel.DateTimeFormat` to do the formatting. Alternatively, you might want to use libraries such as `date-fns` or `moment.js`, which provide much richer APIs.

Let's have a look at the `filters/datetime.filter.js` file:

```
const formatter = new Intl.DateTimeFormat('en-US', {
  year: 'numeric', month: 'long', week: 'long', day: 'numeric',
  hour: 'numeric', minute: 'numeric', second: 'numeric'
});
Vue.filter('datetime', function(value) {
  if (!value) return '';
  return formatter.format(value);
});
```

To enable this filter, we need to import it into `index.html` as well. Let's have a look at the `index.html` file:

```
...
<script type="module">
...
import './filters/datetime.filter.js';
...
</script>
```

To use this filter, we append it to the end of `item.createdAt`, separated with the pipe.

Let's have a look at the `components/MessageListItem.js` file:

```
export default {
  ...
  template: `<li>{{ item.text }} - {{ item.createdAt | datetime }}
    <button @click="deleteClicked">X</button></li>`,
  ...
};
```

You can chain multiple filters like this—`{{ expression | filterA | filterB }}`. The result of `expression` will be the first argument of `filterA`, and the result of `filterA` result will be passed to `filterB` as its first argument.

You can also provide additional arguments to a filter. For example, when using the `date-fns` library, we can support date and time formatting with different patterns with only a few lines of code. We can add a second parameter to the `filter` function for passing desired patterns, as follows:

```
Vue.filter('datetime', function(value, pattern) {
  ...
});
```

And here is how to specify a pattern when using the filter:

```
{{ item.createdAt | datetime('MM/DD/YYYY') }}
```

The `MM/DD/YYYY` string will be passed in as the second argument. You can also define the format pattern as a variable and pass it to the filter.

Mixins

Besides using components, mixins are another way to reuse code. A mixin is just a plain JavaScript object that can contain any component options. As suggested by the name mixin, Vue.js mixes a mixin into your Vue components' `options` objects. In this way, you can write cross-component functionalities.

When a mixin and a component both contain the same options, Vue.js will merge them with different strategies, depending on the value of the option. For example, if a mixin and a component both contain a `created()` life cycle hook, Vue.js will put both methods into an array and call the mixin's method first. And if they both contain an option that expects object values (for example, methods, components, directives, and filters) Vue.js will merge the options into the same object and the component's option will take priority.

You can apply a mixin locally or globally. This is unlike components, filters, and directives that, even if registered globally, still need to be declaratively used. Once you apply a mixin globally, it will affect every Vue instance created afterward automatically. So, use it with caution.

Let's create a mixin, `lifecycle-logger`, for inspecting Vue instances' life cycles by defining several hooks that we're interested in.

By convention, we will put the mixin under the `mixins` directory and name it in this format—`${mixinName}.mixin.js`.

Let's have a look at the `mixins/lifecycle-logger.mixin.js` file:

```
export default {
  created () {
    console.log(`${this.$options.name} created`);
  },
  beforeMount () {
    console.log(`${this.$options.name} about to mount`);
  },
  mounted () {
    console.log(`${this.$options.name} mounted`);
  },
  destroyed () {
    console.log(`${this.$options.name} destroyed`);
  }
};
```

In each hook function, we will simply log the instance's name and the stage. As you can see, inside the mixin, we can also access the instance via `this.$options`. The `$option` is a property of a Vue instance and it references the `options` object that we use to define a Vue component. So, we can access the component's name using `this.$options.name`. Let's add the `name` property to our root Vue instance as well.

Here are the changes to the `index.html` file:

```
<script type="module">
  ...
  import lifecyleLogger from './mixins/lifecycle-logger.mixin.js';
  ...
  let vm = new Vue({
    ...
    name: 'MessagesApp',
    mixins: [lifecyleLogger],
    ...
  });
</script>
```

Here are the changes to the `MessageList` component:

```
import lifecyleLogger from '../mixins/lifecycle-logger.mixin.js';
export default {
  name: 'MessageList',
  mixins: [lifecyleLogger],
  ...
};
```

Here are the changes to the `MessageListItem` component:

```
import lifecyleLogger from '../mixins/lifecycle-logger.mixin.js';
export default {
  name: 'MessageListItem',
  mixins: [lifecyleLogger],
  ...
};
```

If you run the app now, you can see different stages of all of the instances' life cycles. If you have experience with AOP in Java, you might feel that this life cycle mixin looks familiar.

Mixins provide a way of reusing code and, in fact, Vue.js uses mixins heavily to bootstrap the Vue constructor itself. However, it doesn't mean that this could be a good option for your application code since mixins might make your code less readable because mixin options are **merged** with those of a component, which creates some level of obscurity.

Plugins

Plugins are a great way to provide extensibility to the Vue.js framework. As a matter of fact, Vuex and Vue Router, the two most widely-used core libraries in the Vue.js ecosystem, are plugins. And the validation framework that we will use in the TaskAgile app, Vuelidate, is also a Vue.js plugin.

Creating a plugin in Vue.js is simple. You create a plain object with an `install()` method. This method will take two arguments. The first one is the `Vue` constructor, which is where all of the extended functionalities will be applied, and the second one is an `options` object, which allows a plugin to define options that can be used to configure the plugin itself.

Inside the `install()` method, you can add a static method or property to the Vue constructor. You can also create custom directives, filters, components, and mixins. And you can add instance methods to `Vue.prototype` as well.

You might have noticed that, in our previous section, in order to use the life cycle mixin, we need to import it first. And if we want to disable it in several components, we will need to change multiple files, which is not ideal. Let's use a plugin to track instances' life cycles instead. This plugin will provide switches so that you can turn off the hooks you're no longer interested in.

Let's call this plugin `lifecycle-logger`. And, by convention, we will add it to the `plugins` directory and name the file in this format: `${pluginName}.plugin.js`.

Let's have a look at the `plugins/lifecycle-logger.plugin.js` file:

```
const switchers = {
  created: true,
  beforeMount: true,
  mounted: true,
  destroyed: true
}
export default {
  install (Vue, options) {
    Object.assign(switchers, options)
    Vue.mixin({
      created () {
        if (switchers.created) {
          console.log(`${this.$options.name} created`)
        }
      },
      beforeMount () {
        if (switchers.beforeMount) {
          console.log(`${this.$options.name} about to mount`)
        }
      },
      mounted () {
        if (switchers.mounted) {
          console.log(`${this.$options.name} mounted`)
        }
      },
      destroyed () {
        if (switchers.destroyed) {
          console.log(`${this.$options.name} destroyed`)
        }
      }
    })
  }
}
```

We use the `Object.assign()` method to merge `switchers` in the `options` object into predefined `switchers`. And we apply the life cycle hook functions as a global mixin.

To use a plugin in a Vue application, all you need to do is to import it and call `Vue.use()`.

To use our `lifecycle-logger` plugin, we need to remove the `lifecycle-logger` mixin first. Once that is done, update `index.html` as follows:

```
<script type="module">
    ...
    import LifecycleLogger from './plugins/lifecycle-logger.plugin.js'
    import './directives/focus.directive.js'
    ...
    Vue.use(LifecycleLogger, {beforeMount: false})
    ...
</script>
```

As you can see, we disable the `beforeMount` hook tracking by using an `options` object.

Behind the scene

By now, we have covered most of the concepts in Vue.js. Those that we haven't talked about will be discussed when we build the TaskAgile application. For now, let's see what is behind the scene and how Vue.js makes the magic happen.

Reactivity system

The simplicity and powerfulness of Vue.js originate from its reactive data binding system. It is designed to be intuitive, and it doesn't require your attention to keep the data and the view in sync.

Essentially, to archive this ubiquitous reactivity, internally, Vue.js implements a variant of the observer design pattern to collect dependencies of the data and notify watchers when data is changed. During the initialization of a Vue instance, Vue.js makes every property of the `data` object reactive by using the `Object.defineProperty()` method to create a getter and a setter function for accessing that property and updating its value respectively. When the render function updates the DOM, it invokes the getter functions of the properties that are used in the template. And for every Vue component instance, Vue.js creates a Render **Watcher** to collect those properties as the render function's dependencies. And whenever the value of a property needs to be changed, Vue.js will notify the Render **Watcher** about that and the Render **Watcher** will trigger the render function to update the DOM. That is basically what reactive means. And the following diagram, which is cited from the official guide of Vue.js, provides a good visual explanation:

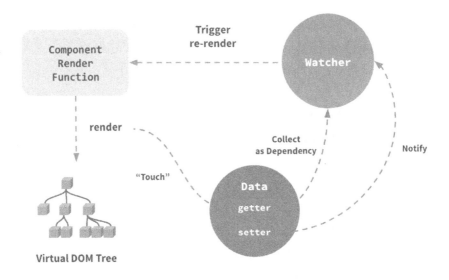

Figure 2.2: How Vue.js tracks changes
Source: https://vuejs.org/v2/guide/reactivity.html

Now that you have a basic understanding of its reactivity system, let's take a deep dive into the internal workings of Vue.js to see how it implements this reactivity system. And we will use the Messages App as an example to walk you through this.

Let's start from the root Vue instance, `vm`. In its `options` object, we define the following `data` object and `computed` object:

```
data: { messages:[], newMessage:'' },
computed: { addDisabled(){...} }
```

When Vue.js initializes this instance, it creates vm._data to store the actual data and creates proxies for accessing vm.messages and vm.newMessage by defining getters and setters with Object.defineProperty for these two properties. In this way, when you access vm.messages, you are proxied to vm._data.messages. So, the reactivity of the two properties actually happens in vm._data.

To make vm._data reactive, Vue.js observes it. In other words, Vue.js creates an observer object and assigns that object to vm._data.__ob__ to mark it as being observed. This observer object will walk through all of the properties of vm._data, in our case the messages and newMessage properties. For the newMessage property, Vue.js will simply define a reactive getter and a reactive setter for it because it is a primitive value. The reason they are called reactive getter and reactive setter is that inside the getter function, dependencies are collected, and inside the setter function, watchers are notified of the data change. In this way, the newMessage property becomes observable. On the other hand, for the messages property, besides defining a reactive getter and a reactive setter for it, Vue.js will observe it further because it is an array. Without performing a further observation, changes to the messages array won't be noticed because the reactive getter of the messages property will be invoked only when you access it via vm._data.messages, and its setter will be invoked only when you change it via vm._data.messages = [...] but not via vm._data.messages.push({...}). When Vue.js observes the messages array, it will create another Observer object and assign it to the array object's __ob__ property. And Vue.js also modifies Array.prototype by wrapping the original mutation method, including .push(), .pop(), .shift(), .unshift(), .splice(), .sort(), and .reverse(), inside another function in which watchers are notified of the data change. In this way, when you invoke messages.push({...}), the Render Watcher knows that and will trigger a re-render to update the DOM. Because we store objects inside the messages array, besides creating an Observer object for the messages array itself, Vue.js will also observe each message object in the array. It creates an Observer object for each message object in the array. This observer walks through all of the properties of that message object and it finds that the id property, the text property, and the createdAt property are neither an array nor a plain JavaScript object; it will simply define reactive getter and setter functions for them. By now, everyone in the data object of the options are reactive, aka, observable. No matter how complex the structure of the data object is, Vue.js will walk through the entire structure to make sure everything is reactive.

There are two types of changes that Vue.js cannot track. One type of change is inserting an item into an array using the index, for example, `vm.messages[itemIndex] = newItem`, or modifying the length of an array, such as `vm.messages.length = newLength`. JavaScript doesn't emit any event when you change an array in these two ways. To avoid losing reactivity of the array, use the mutation method instead, for example, `vm.messages.push(newItem)` and `vm.messages.splice(0)`. The other type of change is adding a new property to an object or deleting a property from an object. For example, adding a replies count to the `message` object, like this—`messageObject.repliesCount = 0`, or deleting the `createdAt` property, like this—`delete messageObject.createdAt`. Use `Vue.set(object, key, value)` and `Vue.delete(object, key)` instead, or the `vm.$set(object, key, value)` and `vm.$delete(object, key)` instance methods.

Now, let's see how Vue.js makes the `computed` property, `addDisabled`, reactive.

How Vue.js handles computed properties is different from how it handles `data` objects. For `addDisabled`, it creates a lazy watcher and puts it into `vm._computedWatchers`, which is a map implemented with a plain JavaScript object. The property's name `addDisabled` is the key and the watcher object is the value. This watcher is called a computed watcher. It is lazy because it evaluates the `addDisabled` property only when the render function touches it. Internally, Vue.js stores the value in the watcher's value property after evaluation. For public access, Vue.js creates a getter function for accessing `vm.addDisabled`. Inside this getter is where the computed watcher evaluates the `computed` property and collects dependencies.

In our Messages App, the `addDisabled` property depends on the `messages` array and the `newMessage` string. And it is bound to the `disabled` attribute of the **Submit** button. When Vue.js initializes the root Vue instance, both the `messages` array and the `newMessage` string are empty, and no changes have been made to these two during initialization. Even though Vue.js has created a getter for `vm.addDisabled`, access is not possible until Vue.js mounts the root instance to the mounting point.

When Vue.js mounts a component, it will invoke the component's render function. And the render function needs to know whether the **Submit** button should be disabled or not, so it invokes the `addDisabled` getter function. That's when the watcher starts the evaluation. Before the evaluation begins, the watcher will set itself as the only target of all of the dependencies collected during the evaluation. And during the evaluation, the following user-defined function is invoked:

```
addDisabled () {
  return this.messages.length >= 10 || this.newMessage.length > 50
}
```

As mentioned earlier, Vue.js defines reactive getters for `this.messages` and `this.newMessage`, making them observable. An `observable` property can let the target watcher know that it is a dependency and needs to be collected. So, after accessing `this.messages` and `this.newMessage`, the computed watcher of `addDisabled` will collect them as dependencies. And after the evaluation, the watcher will no longer be the target of the dependency collection.

Now, let's see how the **Submit** button gets disabled by Vue.js.

First of all, when Vue.js renders the DOM, it will figure out which parts of the DOM need to be updated. When the application is under initialization, the mounting point is empty, so it will just create all of the elements required for the initial rendering. In our template, we added a data binding to the `textarea` using the `v-model` directive, which supports two-way data binding. To archive that, Vue.js will add a listener to monitor the `input` event of `textarea`, so that when you type in `textarea`, the browser emits the `input` event, and the listener gets invoked with the latest value of `textarea`.

The listener passes the new value to the setter function of `vm.newMessage`. Inside that function, two watchers are notified. The first one is the Render Watcher. Internally, Vue.js puts the Render Watcher to `vm._watcher`. Instead of triggering the render function, the Render Watcher puts itself into the watcher's queue, which the Vue.js scheduler will schedule for a flush for the next DOM update cycle. The second watcher, which is the `addDisabled` watcher, gets notified. Instead of putting itself into the queue, it changes its flag, `dirty`, to `true` and then awaits evaluation. When the scheduler flushes the watchers' queue, the Render Watcher is invoked. It triggers the render function, and the render function, invokes the `addDisabled` getter function which triggers an evaluation of `addDisabled`.

Before the length of `vm.newMessage` exceeds 50, the result of the evaluation is always `false`. Vue.js finds that nothing needs to be updated in the DOM, so it won't manipulate the DOM. Once you type in the 51st character, the evaluation result is `true`, and Vue.js sees the difference and updates the **Submit** button's `disabled` property to `true`.

For each `computed` property, Vue.js will create a separate watcher. And it will tear down the Render Watcher, as well as all of the computed watchers of an instance when it destroys that Vue instance.

Now, let's see how Vue.js processes `props` of the `MessageList` component in our Messages App.

As a matter of fact, during the initializing of a Vue instance, Vue.js initializes `props` first, before the `data` object and `computed` properties. Internally, Vue.js creates an _props object to hold the data specified in `props` and puts it to `vm.$children[0]._props`. The vm here is the root Vue instance and `$children` is an internal property that contains the child component of the root instance. In our case, there is only one child component, which is the `MessageList` component. And when Vue.js creates the `MessageList` component instance, it knows that this component needs a `messages` array to be passed in as `items`, and it stores `items` to `vm.$children[0]._props.items` and creates a proxy for accessing `vm.$children[0].items`. Keep in mind that we look at this from the application level and the vm here references the root Vue instance. Inside the `MessageList` component, you access the `items` property using `items` in the template and `this.items` in the methods.

Because `messages` is an array, the value of `vm.$children[0]._props.items` is actually a reference that points to the place where the `messages` array's data is stored. If you type in the following expression into Chrome's console, you will see that the result is `true`:

```
// In the console, the vm is the root instance,
// and vm.$children[0] is one of MessageList.
vm.$children[0]._props["items"] === vm._data.messages
```

Vue.js doesn't create an `Observer` object for `vm._props`, because the props object should not be modified by the component. And the properties defined in `props` are considered as read-only. That is, inside the `MessageList` component, you should not try to modify the data of `props`. In fact, if you did, Vue.js will throw a warning in the console when the app is not running in production mode. Let's say, accidentally, inside the `MessageList` component, you change `items` by replacing it with a new array, like the following:

```
this.items = [{id: 1, text: 'Hello', createdAt: new Date()}]
```

If you want to change it in the browser's console, you will need to use the following statement:

```
vm.$children[0]._props.items = [{id: 1, text: 'Hello', createdAt: new
Date()}]
```

 Since we use `<script type="module">` in our Messages Apps, `let vm = new Vue({...})` means vm is not available in the global scope. In order to inspect vm, you need to change it to `window.vm = new Vue({...})`.

So, what will happen besides Vue.js throwing a warning after you make the change? First of all, the `MessageList` component's the Render Watcher will get notified and the UI will get updated. It looks like it works as expected. However, if you type anything into `textarea`, you will see that the UI restores to the one before the change was made. What happened? Well, Vue.js corrected the mistake. Let's take a look at the warning from Vue.js:

> *Avoid mutating a prop directly since the value will be overwritten whenever the parent component re-renders. Instead, use a data or computed property based on the prop's value, prop being mutated: "items."*

This doesn't make sense, does it? On the contrary, it totally makes sense. Here is why. When you assigned the new array to `vm.$children[0]._props.items`, you invoked the setter function of `_props.items`. Inside that function, Vue.js created a warning and told `_props.items`: *Here is the new location of the array. Hold it tight. Someone might ask you for it later*. Then, it observed `items` inside the new array before it notified the watchers that `items` has been changed. That's all of the things Vue.js did when you assigned that new array to `items`. The original `messages` array in the root Vue instance was untouched. So, when you typed in `textarea`, the render function of the root Vue instance was invoked and it found that the DOM of the `<message-list>` part was not in sync with the `messages` data, so it replaced it with a new one that was generated based on the `messages` data.

Now, let's say that you still want to modify `items` in the `MessageList` component. And instead of replacing the entire array, you want to use mutation methods that we mentioned earlier, for example, `this.items.splice(0)`. In this case, Vue.js won't complain about it. And the `messages` list will disappear in the UI. Also, the render function of the root Vue application won't update the UI with another version of the DOM because, with mutation methods, the change you make will be applied to the `messages` array itself. So, it seems that using mutation methods to change an array type property of the props of a component is a solid approach. Is that correct?

Not really. In our Messages App, just because it works in that way doesn't mean that it *should* work in that way. With the `items` property, the `MessageList` component expects the parent component to pass the data. From where and how the parent component gets the data, it doesn't know. And there is no need for it to know that. So, how could `MessageList` know how and where to change the data? All it has is a reference to the `messages` array. The parent component might change its implementation later to get `messages` from local storage or a server. Simply using the mutation methods to change the `messages` array won't preserve the change back to where it is stored. The parent component will refresh the array when it retrieves the data again next time.

Well, what if a few months later, you come back and find that it would make more sense to change the `messages` array inside the `MessageList` component? In that case, you should consider moving the code for retrieving the `messages` array from the parent component to the `MessageList` component and defining it in the `data` object instead of using a property.

A property of a component is for passing data down in a one-way direction, from the parent to the child. Also, there are some cases where you use a property for passing the initial value, and you definitely need to modify the data inside the child component. In such a case, you should define a local data property that uses that value passed down as its initial value. Or sometimes, when you only need to change the value when it has been updated, you can use a computed property to make the change so that whenever the source changes, the computed property's value will be updated automatically.

Summary

In this chapter, you learned about Vue instances and their life cycles. You created Vue components and created directives, filters, mixins, and plugins for the Messages App. You also took a deep dive into the internal implementation of Vue to understand its reactivity system.

We haven't covered slots, transitions, and animations in Vue.js. We will talk about them later when we build the TaskAgile application, along with two other core libraries—Vue Router and Vuex.

In the next chapter, we will move on to Spring 5, the backend technology that we will use to build the application. And we will also talk about the skillsets that a full-stack developer should have besides frontend and backend technologies.

Spring 5 - The Right Stack for the Job at Hand

3

The Spring Framework is a *de facto* standard for creating Java EE applications. It is lightweight, compared to its earlier competitor, **EJB** (short for **Enterprise JavaBeans**). In his book, *Expert One-on-One J2EE Development without EJB*, Rod Johnson, the creator of Spring Framework, wrote the following:

> *Lightweight Inversion of Control containers have huge benefits for implementing J2EE applications. I believe that Inversion of Control, along with AOP, provides the basis for next-generation J2EE architectures.*

And that was in 2004. He was right. In the past 16 years, since the initial release of the framework in 2002, Spring has become the first choice of frameworks that people use to build Java EE applications. And, with Spring Boot, building Spring applications has become much easier and more productive than ever before.

In this chapter, we will cover the fundamental concepts of Spring Framework 5. And you will do the following:

- Learn what **Inversion of Control (IoC)** and **dependency injection (DI)** are
- Learn Spring MVC
- Learn Spring JDBC and JAP for data accessing
- Learn aspect-oriented programming, Spring AOP, and its benefits
- Learn how Spring manages transactions
- Learn Spring Boot

Along the way, we will create the backend of the Messages App by using these technologies offered by Spring. Finally, we will integrate the frontend of the Messages App created in this chapter with this backend.

Spring IoC and dependency injection

By convention, in Spring, objects that are managed by Spring container are usually called **beans**. They form the backbone of our application. In Java, there are two ways to manage an object's dependencies. The first way is that the object itself either instantiates its dependencies, for example, inside its constructor, by invoking the constructors of its dependencies or locates its dependencies by using a look-up pattern. The following is an example of `RegistrationService`, which sends an email to users after a successful registration. For simplicity, we will focus on the dependencies part and skip the details of registration and sending emails.

The following code listing shows how `RegistrationService` instantiates `MailSender` in its constructor:

```
public class RegistrationService {
  private MailSender mailSender;
  public RegistrationService() {
    // Instantiate dependencies itself
    this.mailSender = new MailSender();
  }
  // ... other logics
}
```

As you can see, by instantiating `MailSender`, `RegistrationService` takes control of managing its dependencies. This is the first way of managing dependencies.

Let's take a look at the second way, which relies on a container, in our case, Spring, to inject its dependencies through its constructors or its setters. For example, we can change `RegistrationService` to the following:

```
public class RegistrationService {
  private MailSender mailSender;
  public RegistrationService(MailSender mailSender) {
    this.mailSender = mailSender;
  }
  // ... other logics
}
```

As you can see, we add a `MailSender` instance as an argument of the constructor of `RegistrationService`. In this way, `RegistrationService` has no control over its dependency. Spring takes responsibility for instantiating the `MailSender` instance now. The control of the dependency is inverted. And that's where the name, **Inversion of Control (IoC)**, comes from.

So, how does Spring know what dependencies a class needs? It uses the configuration metadata that we provide. In the configuration, we specify what objects need to be created and what their dependencies are. To set up a Spring container, the traditional way is to put the configuration metadata inside an XML file, usually named `applicationContext.xml`. Starting from Spring 2.5, we can use annotation-based configuration to spin up the container. And starting from Spring 3.0, we can use the Java-based configuration to define the configuration with zero XML configuration. Nowadays, the XML-based configuration is considered to be outdated and should be used in the legacy code. In our example, we will use the Java-based configuration.

Spin up the Spring container

In Spring, the `org.springframework.context.ApplicationContext` interface represents the Spring IoC container. In a standalone application, the typical way of setting up the container is to use `ClassPathXmlApplicationContext` or `AnnotationConfigApplicationContext`. Both are implementations of the `ApplicationContext` interface. And, as the name suggests, `ClassPathXmlApplicationContext` is used for XML-based configuration, while `AnnotationConfigApplicationContext` is used for Java-based configuration, and this is the one we will use.

Let's start building the backend of the Messages App. We will build it into a workable Spring Boot web application piece by piece as we introduce the features of Spring.

> All of the code in this book is written with Visual Studio Code (`https://code.visualstudio.com/`), and the following extensions are installed for the frontend code writing:
>
> - **ESLint** (`dbaeumer.vscode-eslint`)
> - **Vetur** (`octref.vetur`)

> The following extensions are installed for the backend code writing:
>
> - **Language support for Java ™** for Visual Studio Code (`redhat.java`)
> - **Java Extension Pack** (`vscjava.vscode-java-pack`)
> - **Debugger for Java** (`vscjava.vscode-java-debug`)
> - **Spring Boot Support** (`Pivotal.vscode-spring-boot`)
> - **Maven Project Explorer** (`vscjava.vscode-maven`)

We will create this application using Maven (https://maven.apache.org). For readers who are not familiar with Maven, you can think of it as npm in the Java world. A typical Maven project directory structure looks like this:

```
/src
/src/main/java
/src/main/resources
/src/main/webapp
/src/test/java
/src/test/resources
/pom.xml
```

The /src/main folder is the root of the application's source code. The /src/main/webapp is for web application to put views—static assets. However, because we are building a Spring Boot web application, we don't need this folder. The /src/test folder is the root of the application's test code. The pom.xml file is Maven's configuration file; you can think of it as package.json in Maven.

 Project Object Model (POM) is the unit of work in Maven. For more details, refer to https://maven.apache.org/guides/introduction/introduction-to-the -pom.html.

To start a Maven project, the first step is to create the pom.xml file. And our pom.xml file looks like this:

```
1.  <?xml version="1.0" encoding="UTF-8"?>
2.  <project xmlns="http://maven.apache.org/POM/4.0.0
3.          xmlns:xsi="http://www.w3.org/2001/XMLSchema-instance"
4.          xsi:schemaLocation="http://maven.apache.org/POM/4.0.0
            http://maven.apache.org/xsd/maven-4.0.0.xsd">
5.      <modelVersion>4.0.0</modelVersion>
6.
7.      <groupId>app.sample</groupId>
8.      <artifactId>messages</artifactId>
9.      <version>1.0-SNAPSHOT</version>
10.
11.     <properties>
12.        <spring.version>5.0.3.RELEASE</spring.version>
13.        <log4j.version>2.10.0</log4j.version>
14.     </properties>
15.
16.     <dependencies>
17.        <dependency>
18.           <groupId>org.springframework</groupId>
```

```
19.        <artifactId>spring-context</artifactId>
20.        <version>${spring.version}</version>
21.     </dependency>
22.     <dependency>
23.       <groupId>org.apache.logging.log4j</groupId>
24.       <artifactId>log4j-api</artifactId>
25.       <version>${log4j.version}</version>
26.     </dependency>
27.     <dependency>
28.       <groupId>org.apache.logging.log4j</groupId>
29.       <artifactId>log4j-core</artifactId>
30.       <version>${log4j.version}</version>
31.     </dependency>
32.   </dependencies>
33.
34. </project>
```

The root of `pom.xml` is the `<project>` element. In line 5, `modelVersion` is the version of the POM itself; usually, you don't need to change it. In lines 7 to 9, we define the details of the artifact of the application. If your application/library is published, the artifact is identified by a combination of `groupId`, `artifactId`, and `version`. In lines 11 to 14, we add properties of this POM to specify the versions of the dependencies that we use. And in lines 16 to 32, we add Spring Framework and Apache Log4j as the dependencies of this application.

Now, let's write source code that lives in the `app.messages` package. We will create the following four Java classes:

```
/src/main/java/app/messages/AppConfig.java
/src/main/java/app/messages/Application.java
/src/main/java/app/messages/Message.java
/src/main/java/app/messages/MessageRepository.java
/src/main/java/app/messages/MessageService.java
```

`AppConfig.java` is the configuration metadata Spring will use to instantiate the container. `Application.java` is the entry point of the application. It is where the `main()` method lives. `Message.java` defines the Message model, which has a very simple structure. `MessageRepository.java` is a demo of the repository that is responsible for saving messages. And `MessageService.java` is the application service that provides API's for its clients.

In our Messages App, we will define the repository and the service by using concrete classes instead of interfaces for reasons of simplicity. And, at this point, we don't have API available for HTTP-based access. Also, the code structure we're using for the Messages App is flat. Everything lives in the same package, which is not practical. You will see how the package grows by the end of this chapter.

Let's create `Message.java`. Here is what it looks like:

```
1. package app.messages;
2.
3. public class Message {
4.    private String text;
5.    public Message(String text){this.text = text;}
6.    public String getText(){return text;}
7. }
```

Line 1 defines the package in which the `Message` class lives. In line 4, we define a `private` field `text` of the `String` type. And in line 5, we define a `Message` class constructor. It accepts one parameter `text`, which is assigned to the private field `text`. In Java, a parameter's name can be the same as a class field. You can use the `this` keyword to distinguish them. In line 6, we define a getter method for others to access the `private` `text` field.

The code here has been reformatted so that it takes fewer lines. In practice, you should follow the convention of a Java-style guide, for example, `https://github.com/google/styleguide`.

`MessageRepository.java` looks like this:

```
1. package app.messages;
2.
3. import org.apache.commons.logging.Log;
4. import org.apache.commons.logging.LogFactory;
5.
6. public class MessageRepository {
7.
8.    private final static Log log =
      LogFactory.getLog(MessageRepository.class);
9.
10.   public void saveMessage(Message message) {
11.     // Save message to a database
12.     log.info("Saved message: " + message.getText());
13.   }
14.}
```

As you can see, in line 8, we create an instance of Log. And in lines 10 to 13, we create the saveMessage() method, which takes a Message object as its parameter. We leave the implementation of saving messages to databases for a later section. Here, we will simply print out a message to the log.

MessageService.java looks like this:

```
1. package app.messages;
2.
3. public class MessageService {
4.    private MessageRepository repository;
5.
6.    public MessageService(MessageRepository repository) {
7.       this.repository = repository;
8.    }
9.    public void save(String text) {
10.      this.repository.saveMessage(new Message(text));
11.   }
12.}
```

As you can see, in line 4, we define MessageRepository as the dependency of MessageService. And in lines 6 to 8, we create a constructor that takes an instance of MessageRepository as its parameter. And Spring will wire up the dependency for us through this constructor. In lines 9 to 11, we define a simple API save(String) method, which allows its client to pass a text of the String type and save it to the repository.

Now that the MessageService class and the MessageRepository class are ready, let's create the configuration AppConfig.java, which looks like the following:

```
1. package app.messages;
2.
3. import org.springframework.context.annotation.Bean;
4. import org.springframework.context.annotation.ComponentScan;
5. import org.springframework.context.annotation.Configuration;
6.
7. @Configuration
8. @ComponentScan("app.messages")
9. public class AppConfig {
10.
11.   @Bean
12.   public MessageRepository messageRepository() {
13.      return new MessageRepository();
14.   }
15.
16.   @Bean
17.   MessageService messageService() {
```

```
18.    return new MessageService(messageRepository());
19.  }
20.}
```

As you can see, in line 7, we apply the @Configuration annotation to tell Spring that this
AppConfig.java is for defining beans. The @ComponentScan annotation in line 8 is used
with @Configuration to tell Spring the base package for scanning for annotated
components. And we use the @Bean annotation to annotate the messageRepository()
method and the messageService() method. These methods are responsible for
generating beans. And the method name will be the bean's name; in other words, the
MessageRepository bean's name will be messageRepository. It is the same for
MessageService. And in line 18, we pass the MessageRepository instance to the
MessageService constructor.

Now, it is time to spin up the container in Application.java. It looks like the following:

```
1. package app.messages;
2.
3. import org.springframework.context.ApplicationContext;
4. import org.springframework.context.annotation.
   AnnotationConfigApplicationContext;
5.
6. public class Application {
7.   public static void main(String[] args) {
8.      ApplicationContext context = new
         AnnotationConfigApplicationContext(AppConfig.class);
9.      MessageService messageService =
         context.getBean(MessageService.class);
10.     messageService.save("Hello, Spring!");
11.  }
12.}
```

In line 7, we define the entry point of our application using the static-void-main method,
which takes an array of String objects as its parameter. In line 8, we create Spring
container by passing the AppConfig class to the constructor of the
AnnotationConfigApplicationContext class. In line 9, we retrieve the instance of the
MessageService bean by calling the getBean(Class<T>) method that was defined in the
org.springframework.beans.factory.BeanFactory interface, which is extended by
the ApplicationContext interface. At this point, the messageService bean we get from
the Spring container has been fully instantiated, notably, an instance of
MessageRepository has been injected to it. In line 10, we ask the service to save a
message.

Now, let's run the code. We will use Maven to generate a `.jar` file and run it from the command line. In order to do that, we will need to update the `pom.xml` file and add the following `<build>` section underneath the `<dependencies>` section.

Here is what it looks like:

```
    </dependencies>
    <build>
      <finalName>messages</finalName>
      <plugins>
        <plugin>
          <groupId>org.apache.maven.plugins</groupId>
          <artifactId>maven-assembly-plugin</artifactId>
          <executions>
            <execution>
              <phase>package</phase>
              <goals><goal>single</goal></goals>
              <configuration>
                <archiveBaseDirectory>${project.basedir}
                </archiveBaseDirectory>
                <archive>
                  <manifest>
                    <mainClass>app.messages.Application</mainClass>
                  </manifest>
                </archive>
                <descriptorRefs>
                  <descriptorRef>jar-with-dependencies</descriptorRef>
                </descriptorRefs>
              </configuration>
            </execution>
          </executions>
        </plugin>
      </plugins>
    </build>
    </project>
```

Basically, this adds the Maven plugin, `maven-assembly-plugin`, to the build process. And this plugin requires the information of the `main` class for the `.jar` file. We provide it in the `mainClass` tag. And in order to execute the `.jar` file from the command line, we will also need to include the application's dependencies, in our case, `spring-context-5.0.3.RELEASE.jar`, into the `.jar` file. That is the purpose of `<descriptorRef>`.

Before we build the application, we will need to add the Log4j configuration at `src/main/resources/log4j2.xml`, as follows:

```
<?xml version="1.0" encoding="UTF-8"?>
<Configuration status="WARN">
  <Appenders>
    <Console name="Console" target="SYSTEM_OUT">
      <PatternLayout pattern="%d{HH:mm:ss.SSS} [%t] %-5level
        %logger{36} - %msg%n"/>
    </Console>
  </Appenders>
  <Loggers>
    <Logger name="app.messages" level="INFO">
      <AppenderRef ref="Console"/>
    </Logger>
    <Root level="ERROR"/>
  </Loggers>
</Configuration>
```

As you can see, in this configuration, we define a console appender and a logger for our application. And the root level of the log is set to ERROR. If you're interested in the details of Log4j configuration, you can check its manual here: `https://logging.apache.org/log4j/2.x/manual/configuration.html`.

Now, open a Terminal in your macOS or a command line in Windows and switch to the root folder of the application where the `pom.xml` file lives and execute `mvn install`, which will download all of the required dependencies from the public Maven repository and then build the `.jar` file. The output will be placed under the `target` folder under the root folder of the application. Once the build finishes, execute the following command:

```
java -jar target/messages-jar-with-dependencies.jar
```

And you should see output similar to the following:

```
13:07:55.381 [main] INFO  app.messages.MessageRepository - Saved message:
Hello, Spring!
```

By now, you have successfully created a very simple Spring application.

Annotation-based configuration

In `AppConfig.java` we just created, we used the `messageRepository()` method and the `messageService()` method to instantiate `MessageRepository` and `MessageService` and incorporate them into the Spring container. This works well when you only have a handful of beans to initialize. However, it would require too much boilerplate code and too much attention to pass dependencies manually through constructors or setters when we have a lot of beans in the application.

Spring provides annotation-based configuration, which makes the dependencies management much easier. There are mainly two types of annotations that Spring provides. The first type is for declaring beans and the second type is for wiring up the dependencies.

Bean declaration

First of all, let's take a look at how to use Spring annotations to declare beans.

Spring provides a set of stereotype annotations for declaring beans, including `@Component`, `@Service`, `@Controller`, and `@Repository`. We can apply these annotations to the classes that need to be managed by Spring. And Spring will pick them up by scanning the packages, starting from the base package that we provide to the `@ComponentScan` annotation.

The `@Component` annotation is a generic stereotype. When a class is annotated with this annotation, Spring will instantiate an instance of that class. The `@Service` annotation is a specialization of `@Component`, and it indicates that the annotated class is a service, a term used in *Domain-Driven Design* (Evan, 2003), or a business service façade, a pattern in the Core J2EE. The `@Repository` annotation indicates that a component is a repository, also, a term used in *Domain-Driven Design*, or **Data Access Object (DAO)**, a traditional Java EE pattern. The `@Controller` annotation indicates that a component is a web controller that can accept HTTP requests. We will talk more about `@Service`, `@Repository`, and `@Controller` later. For now, let's simply use the `@Component` annotation. The following is the change made to `MessageService`:

```
...
import org.springframework.stereotype.Component;
@Component
public class MessageService {
...
```

As you can see, in order to have our beans managed by Spring, all we need to do is to apply the @Component annotation at the class-level. The following is the change made to MessageRepository:

```
...
import org.springframework.stereotype.Component;
@Component
public class MessageRepository {
...
```

And since we have already used @Component to declare beans of MessageService and MessageRepository, let's delete the messageRepository() and messageService() methods from AppConfig, since they are no longer required.

As a matter of fact, if we leave these two methods in AppConfig, Spring will still use them to create instances of MessageRepository and MessageService, and the @Component annotation applied to these two classes won't take effect. They are overridden by the @Bean annotation inside AppConfig.

Dependency injection

To wire up dependencies, we can use these two annotations provided by Spring—the @Required annotation and the @Autowired annotation. We can apply the @Required annotation to setter methods and the @Autowired annotation to constructor, methods, as well as fields.

To sum up, in Spring, there are three ways to inject dependencies:

- Constructor-based injection
- Setter-based/method-based injection
- Field-based injection.

Constructor-based injection

As its name suggests, this type of injection is done through the constructors. And, in our Messages App, a MessageRepository bean is injected into a MessageService bean through the constructor. We can apply the @Autowired annotation to the constructor, as follows:

```
@Autowired
public MessageService (MessageRepository repository) {
  this.repository = repository;
}
```

We can also omit the `@Autowired` annotation here and Spring still understands that it needs to inject a `MessageRepository` bean, thereby checking the `MessageService` constructor and finding out the types of the arguments.

Setter-based/method-based injection

The second way is to declare a method, usually a setter, and apply the `@Autowired` annotation or the `@Required` annotation to it. For example, we can remove the `MessageService` constructor and add a `setRepository(MessageRepository)` method, as follows:

```
public class MessageService {
   ...
   @Required
   public void setRepository(MessageRepository repository) {
      this.repository = repository;
   }
   ...
}
```

Or, you can name it something else, such as the following:

```
@Autowired
public void prepare (MessageRepository repository) {
   this.repository = repository;
}
```

Field-based injection

With the `@Autowired` annotation, you can apply it directly to a field. In this way, you don't need to declare a setter method for it, as in the following:

```
@Autowired
private MessageRepository repository;
```

Other annotations: Besides the built-in annotations, `@Required` and `@Autowired`, Spring also supports the `@javax.annotation.Resource` annotation specified in JSR-250 and the `@javax.inject.Inject` annotation from JSR-330.

 Java Specification Request (JSR): JSR 250 is for common annotations for the Java™ platform. JSR 330 is about dependency injection for Java. You can find more details at: `https://jcp.org/en/jsr/detail?id=250` and `https://jcp.org/en/jsr/detail?id=330`.

Best practices of dependency injection

For those mandatory dependencies, we should always inject them through constructors. In this way, after creation, the instance will be fully initialized and the dependencies will be read-only. No one can tempt you with dependencies anymore.

For those optional dependencies, we can inject them through setters/methods.

As for field-based injection, we should avoid using it. Spring makes the field injection by using Java Reflection, and it is considered to be harmful to use field injection. As a matter of fact, it should be avoided for the following reasons:

- It hides the information of the dependencies, such as how they are initialized and managed, and what these dependencies depend on.
- Field injection is very easy, as you only need to define a field and apply the `@Autowired` or `@Resource` annotation to it. Developers can get **addicted** to this and add too many dependencies and violate the **Single Responsibility Principle** (**SRP**), which we will talk about in `Chapter 6`, *Code Design - Designing for Stability and Extensibility*.

Spring MVC

Spring MVC provides the technologies for building web applications. It is based on the Java EE Servlet API. Before we dig into Spring MVC, let's take a look at how a Java EE web application works with servlet. This will help you to understand the role of Spring MVC easier.

Java EE Servlet

A Java EE Servlet, or servlet for short, lives inside a servlet container, which is usually an application server, for example, Tomcat (`https://tomcat.apache.org`). When an HTTP request arrives at a server, usually, it will go through a list of filters that perform filtering tasks, for example, authentication, logging, and auditing. And if the request doesn't get returned by any filter, the application server will hand it over to a servlet that is registered to process those requests that contain a URI that matches a certain pattern. Once the servlet finishes processing the request, an HTTP response will be sent back to the client after going through the same set of filters that processed the corresponding HTTP request.

Inside these filters, you can perform additional filtering tasks, such as adding certain HTTP headers to the response. The following diagram shows this flow:

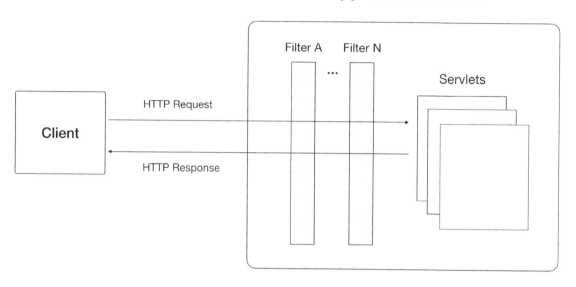

Figure 3.1: Java EE web application request/response flow

In Java EE, for every HTTP request, an instance of `HttpServletRequest` is created. And for every HTTP response, an instance of `HttpServletResponse` is created. To identify a user across multiple requests, the application server will create an instance of `HttpSession` upon receiving the first request. Each of the `HttpSession` instances has an ID, called a **session ID**. And the session id will be sent to the client in the HTTP response headers as a cookie. The client will store the cookie and send it back to the server in the next request. In this way, the server can recognize a user by looking up the `HttpSession` instance using the session ID found in the cookie.

In Java EE, you can create listeners to listen to events of `HttpSession` life cycle changes by implementing the `HttpSessionListener` interface or to listen to life cycle requests by implementing the `ServletRequestListener` interface.

To create a servlet, you can extend `javax.servlet.http.HttpServlet` and either annotate it with the `@WebServlet` annotation or register it in the traditional `web.xml` file, which is the configuration file for a Java EE web application. Either way, you need to map this servlet to one or more URI patterns so that the server can route requests of matching URIs to it.

Also, in a servlet, you can overwrite the following methods:

- `doGet`, for processing the HTTP GET requests
- `doPost`, for processing the HTTP POST requests
- `doPut`, for processing the HTTP PUT requests
- `doDelete`, for processing the HTTP DELETE requests

Inside these methods are the places where the logic of your application starts. And when using a servlet, if you need to access shared resources, such as in-memory data or performing I/O, what you need to keep in mind is the fact that your servlet typically handles concurrent requests, and changes made by one request might affect other requests.

DispatcherServlet

With Spring MVC, you don't have to create servlets. You can create a class and annotate it with the `@Controller` annotation and use the `@RequestMapping` annotation to map it to a certain URI pattern. By convention, the name of this class usually ends with `Controller`.

Spring uses a central servlet, the `DispatcherServlet`, to accept requests. This `DispatcherServlet` needs to be configured to process all requests and, based on the URI pattern specified in the `@RequestMapping` annotation, Spring will find a matching controller to handle a request.

The following diagram shows the request/response flow when using Spring MVC:

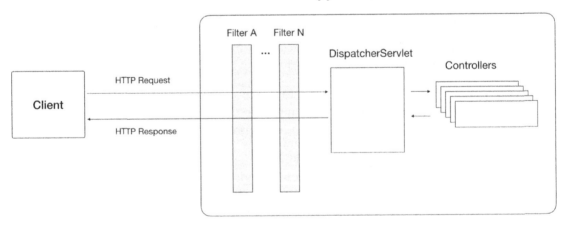

Figure 3.2: Spring DispatcherServlet and controllers

Now, let's turn the Messages App into a web application and add a controller to accept HTTP requests. To do that, let's add Spring Boot dependencies to the pom.xml file.

 In this book, all of the web applications that we build will be based on Spring Boot. And, by default, we use the Tomcat application server in embedded mode, which doesn't require the installation of Tomcat manually. Spring Boot will handle all of the heavy liftings.

Here is the change made to the pom.xml file:

```
...
<parent>
  <groupId>org.springframework.boot</groupId>
  <artifactId>spring-boot-starter-parent</artifactId>
  <version>2.0.0.RELEASE</version>
</parent>

<dependencies>
  <dependency>
      <groupId>org.springframework.boot</groupId>
      <artifactId>spring-boot-starter-web</artifactId>
  </dependency>
</dependencies>
...
```

The <parent> tag inherits the project artifacts from Spring Boot's parent starter. And the spring-boot-starter-web dependency includes the spring-context module we used previously. At the time of writing, Spring Boot 2.0 is still in release candidates, but we will need to specify the Spring's own Maven repository to download it.

Now, if you run mvn install, you can see that Maven will also download a bunch of dependencies that Spring Boot requires. And if you run the java -jar target/messages-jar-with-dependencies.jar command, you will see the debug information Spring printed out and, at the end of the output, is our message "Saved message: Hello, Spring!".

By now, our application is still not running as a web application. Let's change our Application.java to make it a Spring Boot web application.

Here is what it looks like:

```
1. package app.messages;
2. import org.springframework.boot.SpringApplication;
3. import org.springframework.boot.autoconfigure.SpringBootApplication;
4. @SpringBootApplication
5. public class Application {
```

```
6.    public static void main(String[] args) {
7.        SpringApplication.run(Application.class, args);
8.    }
9. }
```

In line 4, we apply the @SpringBootApplication annotation to the Application class so that Spring will do the **magic** autoconfiguration. And in line 7, we bootstrap our application using SpringApplication.run(), which will spin up the Spring container. We remove the MessageService saving message code because we will use controllers to handle HTTP requests.

Now, let's create a controller to accept HTTP requests. We will name it MessageController because we want to handle all message-related requests in this controller. For now, let's just add an API to display a hello message.

Here is how MessageController appears:

```
1. package app.messages;
2. import org.springframework.stereotype.Controller;
3. import org.springframework.web.bind.annotation.GetMapping;
4. import org.springframework.web.bind.annotation.RequestMapping;
5. import org.springframework.web.bind.annotation.ResponseBody;
6. @Controller
7. @RequestMapping("/messages")
8. public class MessageController {
9.     @GetMapping("/welcome")
10.    public String welcome() {
11.       return "Hello, Welcome to Spring Boot!";
12.    }
13. }
```

In line 6, we apply the @Controller annotation to make the MessageController class an actual Spring MVC controller. In line 7, we use the @RequestMapping annotation to map the controller to handle requests that match the URI pattern "/messages". In line 9, we use the @GetMapping annotation to map the welcome() handler method to handle requests that match the URI pattern; "/messages/welcome". The @GetMapping annotation is a shortcut variant of @RequestMapping to map an HTTP GET request. You can replace it with @RequestMapping(value = "/welcome", method = RequestMethod.GET). But @GetMapping is more succinct. In lines 10 to 12, the welcome() handler method returns a simple message that should be sent back in HttpServletResponse.

Now, if you run `mvn install` and then the `java -jar target/messages-jar-with-dependencies.jar` command, you can see that it won't work. You will see an error in the output saying `Application run failed`. This is because `maven-assembly-plugin` cannot run a Spring Boot application. Let's remove it from the `<build>` section and add `spring-boot-maven-plugin`, which is for running Spring Boot applications using Maven. Here is what the updated `<build>` section looks like:

```
<build>
  <finalName>messages</finalName>
  <plugins>
    <plugin>
        <groupId>org.springframework.boot</groupId>
        <artifactId>spring-boot-maven-plugin</artifactId>
    </plugin>
  </plugins>
</build>
```

Now, let's run the following command to start the application. With this command, you don't need to run `mvn install`:

```
mvn spring-boot:run
```

Once the application has started, you can see the following message in the output:

```
...
Mapped "{[/messages/welcome],methods=[GET]}" onto public java.lang.String
app.messages.MessageController.welcome()
...
Tomcat started on port(s): 8080 (http) with context path ''
...
```

It means that Spring has registered our `welcome()` handler with the `"/messages/welcome"` path for HTTP GET requests. And Tomcat server has started and is listening to HTTP requests that come in from port `8080`.

Let's open the `http://localhost:8080/messages/welcome` URL in Chrome browser to test it out. Wait, it is an error page, saying `HTTP 404 Not Found`, like the following:

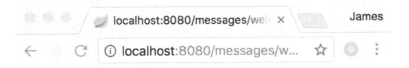

Whitelabel Error Page

This application has no explicit mapping for /error, so you are seeing this as a fallback.

Thu Feb 01 17:33:12 CST 2018
There was an unexpected error (type=Not Found, status=404).
No message available

Figure 3.3: Whitelabel HTTP 404 error page

That shouldn't be right. We have registered our `welcome()` handler correctly, as shown in the start-up output. Well, there is something else that we missed here. We haven't told Spring what to do with our return value, `"Hello, Welcome to Spring Boot!"`. And, by default, without any other configuration, Spring thinks of a `String` type return value as the path that the request should be forwarded internally. In our case, it tries to find a handler for the `"/Hello, Welcome to Spring Boot!"` path, which doesn't exist. And that's why the error message is `HTTP 404`.

To fix this, let's add the `@ResponseBody` annotation to the handler method, as follows:

```
@GetMapping("/welcome")
@ResponseBody
public String welcome() {
    return "Hello, Welcome to Spring Boot!";
}
```

With the `@ResponseBody` annotation, Spring will take the return value as the body of the HTTP response, and it will find a corresponding `HttpMessageConverter` to write the value to the response. You can also apply the annotation to the `MessageController` class that has the same effect of applying the annotation to all of the methods in this class.

Now, if you terminate the application and run `mvn spring-boot:run` again, you should see the hello message in the browser after refreshing it.

To build a RESTful API, you can also apply the `@RestController` annotation to controllers. The `@RestController` annotation is a combination of `@Controller` and `@ResponseBody`. We will talk about this more when we discuss RESTful APIs.

Views

In the `welcome()` handler, we returned a very simple `String` to the client side, which isn't what we want, since, for a web application, we usually need to send a chunk of HTML code to the browser to render a web page or send JSON data as a result of an API call. Indeed, HTML code and JSON data are all `String` objects passed in an HTTP response. And it is true that you can change the return value to something like the following, as an example, so that the browser will render a text in bold:

```
public String welcome() {
    return "<strong>Hello, Welcome to Spring Boot!</strong>";
}
```

However, putting HTML markups inside Java code isn't a practical way to create a web application. We need to follow the MVC pattern.

In the MVC pattern, **C** is our **controller**, **V** is the **view** where we put our HTML markups, and **M** is the **modal** that contains the data that the controller creates and that the view can use to render the final output that will be sent to the client in the HTTP response.

Let's change our application to use Thymeleaf (`http://www.thymeleaf.org/`), a template engine, to generate HTML code based on the HTML template we define. The first thing to do is to add the dependency. Here are the changes we make to the `pom.xml` file:

```
<dependencies>
  ...
  <dependency>
    <groupId>org.springframework.boot</groupId>
    <artifactId>spring-boot-starter-thymeleaf</artifactId>
  </dependency>
</dependencies>
```

As you can see, we didn't add the Thymeleaf library directly. Instead, we add the `spring-boot-starter-thymeleaf` starter module so that Spring Boot will configure this view technology for us automatically.

By default, the HTML template files that Thymeleaf will look for need to be placed under the `/src/main/resources/templates` directory. Let's add the `welcome.html` file to this folder.

Here is what the `welcome.html` looks like:

```
<strong th:text="${message}"></strong>
```

We keep this template very simple and only display a hello message showing in bold. `th:text` is a Thymeleaf syntax for rendering text and `${message}` is for getting the `message` value from the model that we will pass from `MessageController`.

Now, let's remove the `@ResponseBody` annotation from the handler method because it is not needed for the `welcome()` handler anymore. Spring will take the return value of the handler as the view's name and use Thymeleaf to generate the response.

Here is the change to the `welcome()` handler:

```
...
import org.springframework.ui.Model;
...
  @GetMapping("/welcome")
  public String welcome(Model model) {
    model.addAttribute("message", "Hello, Welcome to Spring Boot!");
    return "welcome";
  }
```

As you can see, we pass in the `Model` instance that Spring will create for us to the `welcome()` method and add the message as an attribute of `model`, with a key `"message"` that matches the one we use in the template, `${message}`. Now, if you restart the application, you will see a bold welcome message on the page. By now, we have added a view technology to our application.

Another way to utilize the model and view in Spring MVC is to return an instance of `org.springframework.web.servlet.ModelAndView` from the handler. Here is how the `welcome()` method appears when using `ModelAndView`:

```
  @GetMapping("/welcome")
  public ModelAndView welcome() {
    ModelAndView mv = new ModelAndView("welcome");
    mv.addObject("message", "Hello, Welcome to Spring Boot!");
    return mv;
  }
```

As you can see, we do not need to pass in a `Model` object to the handler method. Instead, we create a `ModelAndView` instance by passing the template file's name and add the data through the `addObject()` method. It works the same as the previous version, only in a different flavor. You can choose the one that you like.

Besides Thymeleaf, Spring also supports other view technologies, including Groovy Markup, FreeMarker, Mustache, and the traditional JSP. If you are fans of Velocity, currently, there is no out-of-the-box support for Velocity in the latest version of Spring Boot. But you can integrate Velocity with Spring MVC with a little extra work.

 There are a number of limitations with JSP when Spring Boot is running with an embedded application server. It is recommended that, when using Spring Boot, JPS should be avoided. In this book, we will use Thymeleaf.

Filters

Filters are another good technology of Java EE. It is an implementation of the **Chain of Responsibility** design pattern. It is useful when you want to perform filtering tasks to HTTP requests before they reach servlets.

Let's create an `AuditingFilter` to audit requests. For demonstration purposes, we will simply write the request information to log for now.

To create a filter, we need to implement the `javax.servlet.Filter` interface. Or, we can extend Spring's `org.springframework.web.filter.GenericFilterBean`, which provides a number of handy features. Let's go with `GenericFilterBean`.

Here is how `AuditingFilter` appears:

```
package app.messages;
...
public class AuditingFilter extends GenericFilterBean {
  @Override
  public void doFilter(ServletRequest req, ServletResponse res,
      FilterChain chain) throws IOException, ServletException {
    long start = new Date().getTime();
    chain.doFilter(req, res);
    long elapsed = new Date().getTime() - start;
    HttpServletRequest request = (HttpServletRequest) req;
    logger.debug("Request[uri=" + request.getRequestURI() + ", method="
      +
      request.getMethod() + "] completed in " + elapsed + " ms");
```

```
    }
  }
```

As you can see, we extend `GenericFilterBean` and overwrite the `doFilter()` method, which is the place that we perform the filtering tasks. At the beginning of this method, we mark the time before we invoke `chain.doFilter()`, which allows the chain to invoke further filters behind it if there are any. If you forgot to call `chain.doFilter()`, no response will be sent back to the client. And you can still perform some tasks after invoking the `chain.doFilter()` method. In our filter, we calculate the elapsed time and log it as debug information.

By now, we have created `AuditingFilter`. However, if you restarted the application and refreshed the page, nothing would be showing up in the output. This is because we haven't registered it yet.

There are two ways to register a filter in a Spring Boot application. You can register it by adding `<filter>` and `<filter-mapping>` to the `web.xml` file, or you can create `FilterRegistrationBean` to register it in the configuration class, `AppConfig`. The use of `web.xml` is for web applications as a `.war` file that is deployed to an application server. Since we are running Tomcat in embedded mode, and there is no `web.xml`, we will use `FilterRegistrationBean`.

Here is what the updated `AppConfig.java` looks like:

```
..
import org.springframework.boot.web.servlet.FilterRegistrationBean;
import org.springframework.context.annotation.Bean;
...
public class AppConfig {
  @Bean
  public FilterRegistrationBean<AuditingFilter>
    auditingFilterRegistrationBean() {
    FilterRegistrationBean<AuditingFilter> registration = new
      FilterRegistrationBean<>();
    AuditingFilter filter = new AuditingFilter();
    registration.setFilter(filter);
    registration.setOrder(Integer.MAX_VALUE);
    registration.setUrlPatterns(Arrays.asList("/messages/*"));
    return registration;
  }
}
```

We apply the `@Bean` annotation to the `auditingFilterRegistrationBean()` method to generate `FilterRegistrationBean` for `AuditingFilter`. As you can see from this method, to register `Filter`, we need to create a `Filter` instance and use the `setFilter()` method to set `Filter`. And we use the `setOrder()` method to position this `Filter` in the chain. The one with the smaller order value will be put to the front. In our case, `AuditingFilter` will be put at the end of the chain. The `setUrlPatterns()` method is for specifying the path that `Filter` will be registered against. In our case, `AuditingFilter` will only process requests whose paths begin with `/messages/`.

And in order to show the debug log in the output, we need to turn on the debug level log for `AuditingFilter`. To do that, let's create the `.properties` file, `application.properties`, under the `/src/main/resources/` directory. In this file, we will overwrite the default logging level of `AuditingFilter`. By now, we only have one custom property.

Here is what `application.properties` look like:

```
logging.level.app.messages.AuditingFilter=DEBUG
```

`logging.level.` is the property's prefix. And `app.messages.AuditingFilter` is the path of the class where we want to enable the debug level logging. You can use the path of a package that will enable the debug level logging for all of the classes inside that package.

Now, if you restart the application and refresh the page, you will see debug information similar to the following in the log:

```
Request[uri=/messages/welcome,method=GET] completed in 337 ms
```

Don't worry about the elapsed time showing in the preceding log. It took `337 ms` because it is the first request after the server has started and Spring needs to initialize `DispatcherServlet`. If you refresh the page again, you will see a much shorter duration. This is sometimes called **Server Warming Up**.

Spring Framework 5 introduces a new web stack, Spring WebFlux. It is a non-blocking web framework built to handle massive numbers of concurrent connections. In this book, we are going to use the traditional Spring MVC.

Spring JDBC and JPA

JDBC (short for **Java Database Connectivity**). The JDBC API defines how we can access the data stored in a relational database. A JDBC driver is the implementation of the JDBC API for a specific type of database. For example, `com.mysql.jdbc.Driver` is the driver class name for the MySQL database and `org.hsqldb.jdbcDriver` is the driver class name for HSQLDB, a relational database written in pure Java. Spring JDBC is an abstraction layer provided by Spring above the JDBC API to make it easier for us to interact with the database.

JPA (short for **Java Persistence API**). It defines a Java standard approach for Java objects persistence, using an **object-relational mapping (ORM)** mechanism to bridge the gap between an object-oriented model and the data stored a relational database. Hibernate ORM is the most popular implementation of JPA standard. Besides the standard APIs, Hibernate ORM also has its native APIs. In this book, we will use Hibernate ORM as our persistence solution, using the word **Hibernate** for Hibernate ORM.

JDBC and JPA are two sets of APIs for solving different issues. JDBC API solves interaction with the database, while JPA solves storing/retrieving of objects to/from databases in an object-oriented way. Underneath, JPA implementations rely on JDBC drivers to access databases.

In this section, we will implement the messages persistence feature of our Messages App adopting three different approaches—using JDBC driver directly, using Spring JDBC, and using Hibernate. In this way, you can see how the lower-level implementation works, as well as the benefits of using Spring JDBC and Hibernate. We will use MySQL Community Server as our database.

We will store messages in the `messages` table in the database. This table has three columns—id, `text`, and `created_date`. And we have a `Message` class in Java code, which has three fields—id, `text`, and `createdDate`. We will add an API to `MessageController` for saving new messages using the HTTP `POST` method. The new message will use JSON format.

The following shows the object/relational mapping between the objects live inside **Java Virtual Machine (JVM)** and the data records in the database:

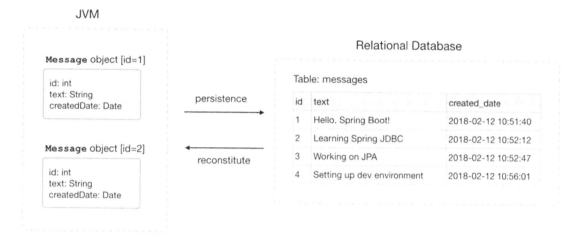

Figure 3.4: Object/relational database mapping

Before we start, if you don't have MySQL installed, you will need to download and install MySQL at `https://dev.mysql.com/downloads/mysql/`. At the time of writing, the latest version is 5.7. All of the code in this book will work with MySQL Version 5.6 and above. Once MySQL is ready, create a database named `app_messages`. After that, use the following SQL to generate the `messages` table:

```
DROP TABLE IF EXISTS `messages`;
CREATE TABLE `messages` (
  `id` int(11) NOT NULL AUTO_INCREMENT,
  `text` varchar(128) COLLATE utf8_bin NOT NULL DEFAULT '',
  `created_date` datetime NOT NULL DEFAULT CURRENT_TIMESTAMP,
  PRIMARY KEY (`id`)
) ENGINE=InnoDB DEFAULT CHARSET=utf8 COLLATE=utf8_bin;
```

JDBC driver

To use a JDBC driver to connect to a database directly in a Spring Boot application, we will need to add the following dependencies to the `pom.xml` file:

```
<dependencies>
  ...
  <dependency>
    <groupId>org.springframework.boot</groupId>
```

```
      <artifactId>spring-boot-starter-jdbc</artifactId>
    </dependency>
    <dependency>
      <groupId>mysql</groupId>
      <artifactId>mysql-connector-java</artifactId>
    </dependency>
  </dependencies>
```

With the `spring-boot-starter-jdbc` module, Spring Boot will spin up an instance of `javax.sql.DataSource` and make it available as a bean in the Spring container. It will also configure a database connection pool. The `mysql-connector-java` library is the JDBC driver for MySQL database and you can see why we didn't specify `<version>` for `mysql-connector-java`, which is normally required. Later in this chapter, we will discuss how Spring Boot works behind the scenes on this, as well as how it automatically configures the data source bean and connection pool.

The next thing we need to do is to configure the parameters that Spring needs to instantiate `DataSource`. Let's add the following properties to `application.properties`:

```
spring.datasource.url=jdbc:mysql://localhost:3306/app_messages?useSSL=false
spring.datasource.username=<username>
spring.datasource.password=<password>
spring.datasource.driver-class-name=com.mysql.jdbc.Driver
```

As you can see, the `url`, `username`, `password`, and `driver-class` objects are the minimal settings that we need to provide. If you need to ensure that the connection uses UTF-8 encoding , you can change the URL to `jdbc:mysql://localhost:3306/app_messages?useUnicode=true&amp;characterEncoding=UTF-8`. You will need to replace `<username>` and `<password>` with those of your own. The prefix of the property's `spring.datasource.` key is required by the `spring-boot-starter-jdbc` starter.

Now, let's make changes to the `MessageRepository` class. We need to ask Spring to inject a `DataSource` instance to `MessageRepository` so that we can get a database connection from it, as follows:

```
public class MessageRepository {
  private DataSource dataSource;
  public MessageRepository(DataSource dataSource) {
    this.dataSource = dataSource;
  }
  ...
}
```

The next thing is to implement the `saveMessage()` method. Here is what it looks like:

```
1.  public Message saveMessage(Message message) {
2.      Connection c = DataSourceUtils.getConnection(dataSource);
3.      try {
4.          String insertSql = "INSERT INTO message
            s (`id`, `text`,
            `created_date`) VALUE (null, ?, ?)";
5.          PreparedStatement ps = c.prepareStatement(insertSql,
            Statement.RETURN_GENERATED_KEYS);
6.          // Prepare the parameters for the SQL
7.          ps.setString(1, message.getText());
8.          ps.setTimestamp(2, new
            Timestamp(message.getCreatedDate().getTime()));
9.          int rowsAffected = ps.executeUpdate();
```

In line 1, we change our `saveMessage()` method to return the newly saved `message` object. In line 2, we use `DataSourceUtils`, a helper class of Spring, to get a database connection. And then, in line 4, we prepare our insert SQL. Since we use `AUTO_INCREMENT` for the `id` column of the `messages` table, we use the `null` value for it so that the database will generate a value for the ID. In line 5, we create `PreparedStatement` by passing the SQL and specify that we need the database to return the generated message `id`. In lines 7 to 8, we set the other two parameters. In line 9, we use the `executeUpdate()` method of `PreparedStatement` to execute the SQL against the database, and the return value of this method is the number of rows affected by the execution:

```
10.         if (rowsAffected > 0) {
11.             // Getting the newly saved message id
12.             ResultSet result = ps.getGeneratedKeys();
13.             if (result.next()) {
14.                 int id = result.getInt(1);
15.                 return new Message(id, message.getText(),
                    message.getCreatedDate());
16.             } else {
17.                 logger.error("Failed to retrieve id. No row in result
                    set");
18.                 return null;
19.             }
20.         } else {
21.             // Insert did not succeed
22.             return null;
23.         }
```

In lines 10 to 20, we check whether any row is affected. Since we're doing an insert, without any error, there should be one row affected, which is the newly inserted row. In line 12, we call the getGeneratedKeys() method of PreparedStatement to get the id of our message object from a ResultSet object. And you will need to call its next() method to move the cursor forward so that you can read the value in the ResultSet. Then, we create a new Message object with all three fields. Lines 16 to 22 are for dealing with failure. If there is no row affected or ResultSet is empty, we will return a null value, indicating that the message wasn't saved successfully. By now, we have completed a large part of this method. One last thing is that we must close the connection that we opened in line 2, otherwise, the connection won't be returned to the connection pool and reused by others:

```
24.    } catch (SQLException ex) {
25.      logger.error("Failed to save message", ex);
26.      try {
27.        c.close();
28.      } catch (SQLException e) {
29.        logger.error("Failed to close connection", e);
30.      }
31.    } finally {
32.      DataSourceUtils.releaseConnection(c, dataSource);
33.    }
34.    return null;
35. }
```

In lines 24 to 33, it is all about cleaning up connections. And in line 34, if the execution reaches here, it means that we didn't save the message object successfully.

As you can see, the JDBC API is a very low-level API and using it requires a lot of boilerplate code. You should avoid using it unless you don't have a choice.

Before we move on to implementation with Spring JDBC, let's change our MessageService and MessageController to provide an HTTP API for saving messages.

Here are the changes to the save() method of MessageService:

```
public Message save(String text) {
  return repository.saveMessage(new Message(text));
}
```

We make it return the result of the saved message. And we need to change our Message class as follows:

```
1. public class Message {
2.     private Integer id;
3.     private String text;
```

```
4.    private Date createdDate;
5.    public Message(String text) {
6.       this.text = text;
7.       this.createdDate = new Date();
8.    }
9.    public Message(int id, String text, Date createdDate) {
10.      this.id = id;
11.      this.text = text;
12.      this.createdDate = createdDate;
13.   }
14.   public Integer getId() {return id;}
15.   public String getText() {return text;}
16.   public Date getCreatedDate() {return createdDate;}
17.   // equals() and hashCode() omitted
18. }
```

In lines 2 and 4, we add a new `id` field and `createdDate`. The reason the `id` field is declared an `Integer` type is that, for a new `Message` object, it doesn't have an `id` generated, and its value will be `null`. Lines 5 to 8 include a constructor that takes a single parameter `text`. This is for creating a new message. And we will generate `createdDate` for it. Lines 9 to 13 include another constructor that is used for reconstituting a `message` object from the database. And in lines 14 to 16, the class only offers getters so you cannot change the value of any field. For now, this is good enough for our app.

Now, let's add a handler in `MessageController` so that clients can send an HTTP `POST` request like the following to save messages:

```
POST /messages
Content-Type: application/json
Request Body: {"text":"Add message here"}
```

Here is what our handle looks like:

```
@PostMapping("")
@ResponseBody
public ResponseEntity<Message> saveMessage(@RequestBody MessageData data){
  Message saved = messageService.save(data.getText());
  if (saved == null) {
    return ResponseEntity.status(500).build();
  }
  return ResponseEntity.ok(saved);
}
```

We use the `@PostMapping` annotation to map it to the `/messages` path. The return value of the handler is a Spring `ResponseEntity`, which allows us to set the response status, body, and headers. And this handler takes one parameter of the `MessageData` type, which we will create shortly. It is annotated with `@RequestBody`. In this way, Spring will convert the JSON format `String` passed in the HTTP request body to an instance of `MessageData`, so that we don't need to dig into the HTTP request to get the request body ourselves. Inside the handler, we simply pass the `text` field to `MessageService` and return the newly saved message using the `ResponseEntity.ok()` method, or, when it fails, we return the `500` status, an internal server error, to the client, telling them that there is something wrong on the server side.

Here is what the `MessageData` class looks like:

```
public class MessageData {
  private String text;
  public String getText() {return this.text;}
  public void setText(String text) {this.text = text;}
}
```

As you can see, it is a **Plain Old Java Object (POJO)** with only one `text` field. This `MessageData` is the definition of our API's request body. If you use another name for the `text` field, for example, `message`, the request body that the client sends over will then be changed to `{"message":"Add message here"}` accordingly.

Now, if you restart the application, we are ready to test it out. You can use an API test tool to send an HTTP `POST` request, for example, Postman (https://www.getpostman.com/), a free application with a friendly UI:

Figure 3.5: Postman headers tab

As shown in *Figure 3.5*, in Postman, after you create a new request and select `POST` for the method and the URL of the API, remember to add the `Content-Type` header with the `application/json` value. In this way, Spring knows that the request body is a JSON format string:

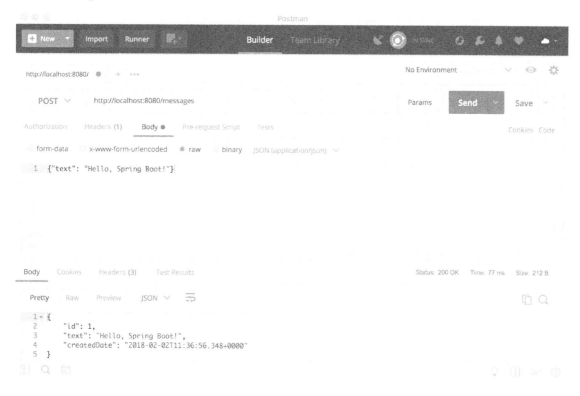

Figure 3.6: Postman body tab

As shown in *Figure 3.6*, in the **Body** tab, select **Raw** and **JSON** (`application/json`) and then put in the JSON string `{"text":"Hello, Spring Boot!"}`. After that, click the **Send** button. You should be able to see the result underneath without any difficulty, similar to the one in the screenshot.

> Before you try it out, make sure you have MySQL database installed, an `app_messages` database created, and a `messages` table created.

Spring JDBC

As mentioned earlier, Spring JDBC provides a layer of abstraction above the JDBC API. The `JdbcTemplate` class is the core of this layer. It helps you to manage connections and provides the workflow of interaction with the JDBC API. All you need to do is to prepare the statement and specify how you want to process the result set. The `NamedParameterJdbcTemplate` class wraps a `JdbcTemplate` object inside of it to provide the ability to use named parameters instead of a JDBC `"?"` placeholder.

Spring JDBC also provides `SimpleJdbcInsert` and `SimpleJdbcCall` to simplify JDBC operations by utilizing the metadata provided by the database. The metadata is retrieved by invoking the `connection.getMetaData()` method, which returns an instance of `DatabaseMetaData`. It includes information such as which tables are defined in the database and the columns that each table has. When using `SimpleJdbcInsert` and `SimpleJdbcCall`, you don't have to worry about the metadata. Spring takes care of that.

Spring JDBC also provides a way to model the JDBC operation as Java objects. You can create a `MappingSqlQuery` object to execute a database query, a `SqlUpdate` object to perform insert/update, and a `StoredProcedure` object to invoke a stored procedure on the database side. These objects are reusable and thread-safe.

We are going to use `NamedParameterJdbcTemplate` in `MessageRepository`. Here is what it looks like (the imports are omitted):

```
1.   public class MessageRepository {
2.      private static final Log logger =
         LogFactory.getLog(MessageRepository.class);
3.      private NamedParameterJdbcTemplate jdbcTemplate;
4.      @Autowired
5.      public void setDataSource(DataSource dataSource) {
6.         this.jdbcTemplate = new NamedParameterJdbcTemplate(dataSource);
7.      }
```

In line 3, we define the `jdbcTemplate` field of the `NamedParameterJdbcTemplate` type. And in lines 4 to 7, we use a setter method to ask Spring to inject `DataSource` so that we can instantiate the `NamedParameterJdbcTemplate` instance:

```
8.      public Message saveMessage(Message message) {
9.         GeneratedKeyHolder holder = new GeneratedKeyHolder();
10.        MapSqlParameterSource params = new MapSqlParameterSource();
11.        params.addValue("text", message.getText());
12.        params.addValue("createdDate",message.getCreatedDate());
13.        String insertSQL = "INSERT INTO messages (`id`, `text`,
           `created_date`) VALUE (null, :text, :createdDate)";
```

```
14.    try {
15.      this.jdbcTemplate.update(insertSQL, params, holder);
16.    } catch (DataAccessException e) {
17.      logger.error("Failed to save message", e);
18.      return null;
19.    }
20.    return new Message(holder.getKey().intValue(),
       message.getText(), message.getCreatedDate());
21.  }
22. }
```

Inside the `saveMessage()` method, in line 9, we declare `GeneratedKeyHolder`, which will hold the generated `id` of the new message. And in lines 10 to 12, we prepare the parameters for the inserted SQL declared in line 13. As you can see, we use the named parameter `text` and `createdDate` as placeholders for parameters. Their names need to match the ones we used during parameter preparation in lines 11 and 12. And in lines 14 to 19, we ask `jdbcTemplate` to execute the SQL inside a `try-catch` block, because the `update()` method could throw `DataAccessException` whenever there is a JDBC operation error. And in line 20, we return the newly saved message.

As you can see, the implementation of the `saveMessage()` method using Spring JDBC is much simpler compared with interaction using the JDBC API directly.

Hibernate

Now, let's see how to implement the `saveMessage()` method using Hibernate. First of all, let's update the `pom.xml` file to add the following two required dependencies:

```
<dependencies>
  ...
  <dependency>
    <groupId>org.springframework</groupId>
    <artifactId>spring-orm</artifactId>
  </dependency>
  <dependency>
    <groupId>org.hibernate</groupId>
    <artifactId>hibernate-core</artifactId>
  </dependency>
</dependencies>
```

The `spring-orm` library is Spring's ORM support, based on ORM technologies such as Hibernate. And the `hibernate-core` library is the Hibernate ORM framework.

Now, let's provide some metadata to Hibernate so that it knows how to map a `Message` object to the records in the `messages` table. Here, we will use the JPA annotation to add these metadata to the `Message` class.

Here is the change to the `Message` class:

```
@Entity
@Table(name = "messages")
public class Message {
  @Id
  @GeneratedValue(strategy = GenerationType.IDENTITY)
  @Column(name = "id", nullable = false)
  private Integer id;

  @Column(name = "text", nullable = false, length = 128)
  private String text;

  @Column(name = "created_date", nullable = false)
  @Temporal(TemporalType.TIMESTAMP)
  private Date createdDate;

  public Message() {}
  ...
}
```

The `@javax.persistence.Entity` annotation is to mark the `Message` class as an `Entity` class. And the `@javax.persistence.Table` annotation is used to specify the `messages` table that the `Message` class is mapped to.

And for the `id` field, we use the `@javax.persistence.Id` annotation to make it the primary key of this entity. And the `@javax.persistence.GeneratedValue` annotation is to specify how we want the value of `id` to be generated. In our case, we use the `GenerationType.IDENTITY` strategy, which means the database will generate the value for us. It is a perfect match for our `id` column's `AUTO_INCREMENT` setting. And the `@javax.persistence.Column` annotation is to map the `id` field to the `id` column of the `messages` table. And we specify it as not nullable.

For the `text` field, we map it to the `text` column and mark it as not nullable too, and set the column's length as `128`.

For the `createdDate` field, we map it to the `created_date` column, also marking it as not nullable. And the `@javax.persistence.Temporal` annotation is required for annotating a field of the `java.util.Date` or `java.util.Calendar` type. Its value, `TemporalType.TIMESTAMP`, is to map the `createdDate` field to a value of the `java.sql.Timestamp` type that the JDBC driver understands.

The default `public Message(){}` constructor is required by Hibernate. When Hibernate loads message records from the database and reconstitutes `Message` objects, it uses the default constructor to create those objects.

 Hibernate won't perform a data validation based on the nullable setting and the length attribute of the `@Column` annotation. It uses this metadata in its `hbm2ddl` feature, which generates **Data Definition Language (DDL)** from the Hibernate mapping (`hbm`). You can use the DDL scripts to create/update/drop data structures in a database. The SQL provided earlier for creating the messages table is a DDL script. On the other hand, for data validation, we can use Bean Validation 2.0 (JSR 380), which we will talk about later in this book.

In Hibernate, `org.hibernate.Session` is the main interface for storing/retrieving entities. And you can create sessions from a Hibernate `SessionFactory` instance. To create an instance of `SessionFactory` with Spring ORM, we can use Spring's `LocalSessionFactoryBean`, which is Spring `FactoryBean`, which will produce an instance of `SessionFactory`.

Let's change the `AppConfig` class to define `LocalSessionFactoryBean`.

Here are the changes made to `AppConfig`:

```
...
@Configuration
@ComponentScan("app.messages")
public class AppConfig {

  private DataSource dataSource;

  public AppConfig(DataSource dataSource) {
    this.dataSource = dataSource;
  }
  ...
  @Bean
  public LocalSessionFactoryBean sessionFactory() {
    LocalSessionFactoryBean sessionFactoryBean = new
```

```
        LocalSessionFactoryBean();
        sessionFactoryBean.setDataSource(dataSource);
        sessionFactoryBean.setPackagesToScan("app.messages");
        return sessionFactoryBean;
    }
}
```

The creation of `LocalSessionFactoryBean` requires an instance of
`javax.sql.DataSource`, which we ask Spring to inject into the configuration class. And
we also need to use the `setPackagesToScan()` method to specify the packages for
Hibernate to scan in order to find entity classes.

Now, everything is ready. Let's change the `MessageRepository` class to implement the
saving `message` objects with Hibernate. Here is what it looks like:

```
import org.hibernate.Session;
import org.hibernate.SessionFactory;
...
public class MessageRepository {
  private SessionFactory sessionFactory;
  public MessageRepository(SessionFactory sessionFactory) {
    this.sessionFactory = sessionFactory;
  }
  public Message saveMessage(Message message) {
    Session session = sessionFactory.openSession();
    session.save(message);
    return message;
  }
}
```

As you can see, we ask Spring to inject an instance of `SessionFactory` and then, inside the
`saveMessage()` method, we obtain an instance of `Session` by invoking the
`openSession()` method of the `sessionFactory` instance and use the `save()` method of
the `session` object to store the `message` object. With Hibernate, we don't have to worry
about getting the generated `id` of the `message` object. Hibernate takes care of that. All we
need to do now is simply return the `message` object after saving it.

As you can see, the Hibernate way of storing objects into a rational database is much
simpler. It saves a lot of boilerplate code and helps us to focus on implementing the logic of
the application itself.

Now, if you restart the application and run the test again, you can see that the messages are
saved successfully.

In this section, we only introduced the basics of Hibernate. We will talk about advanced Hibernate topics when we implement our TaskAgile application.

So, among these three approaches, using JDBC API directly, using Spring JDBC, and using Hibernate—which way is better? First of all, do not use the JDBC API directly unless you really don't have a choice. Between Spring JDBC and Hibernate, the answer is that it depends. Sometimes, you might find that using Hibernate is more straightforward and quicker to get things done. Sometimes, you might find the overhead brought by Hibernate causes performance issues, so you might want to use Spring JDBC or another framework, such as MyBatis (http://www.mybatis.org), a SQL mapper framework for Java. Or, sometimes, you might end up with using both for different scenarios.

 We won't cover the use of MyBatis in this book. If you're interested, you might want to check https://github.com/mybatis/spring-boot-starter, which is a Spring Boot starter module for MyBatis offered by the MyBatis team.

Spring AOP

Our Messages App is a simplified demo application. It doesn't have many features that a typical web application should have. For example, it lacks security checking. Currently, we allow anyone to post messages via the /messages (POST) API. A simple fix is to add security check logic inside the API handler, the MessageController.saveMessage() method, as follows:

```
public ResponseEntity<Message> saveMessage(@RequestBody MessageData data) {
   checkSecurity();
   ...
}

private void checkSecurity() throws NotAuthorizedException {
   // Do security checking
   ...
}
```

Inside the saveMessage() method, we invoke the checkSecurity() method immediately and, if the request is not authorized, NotAuthorizedException will be thrown.

Our Messages App doesn't have a user system. Hence, we cannot check whether a request is from an authenticated user. However, there are still several types of security checking we can perform here. For example, we can only allow requests coming from a specific IP address. Requests from all other IP addresses will be considered not authorized. Or, we can hardcode credentials into the code and the client-side needs to pass them in the request header to pass the security checking. Owing to the scope of this book, we will implement security checking in our TaskAgile application.

This would work fine in our app. However, it would cause code duplication in applications that have dozens of APIs that need to execute security checking as you will see this boilerplate code at the beginning of every API handler.

It is preferable to perform security checking in a central place and, when the code execution reaches the API handler, the security has already been checked. From there, it does pose any further concern.

We can create `SecurityFilter`, which will be responsible for security checking against requests. Inside the filter, we can use `request.getRequestURI()` and `request.getMethod()` to know which API the request is targeting and then check whether the request is authorized. This works perfectly when we only want security checking at the request-level.

In a complex application, you might want to check security at the method-level. For example, you might want to perform additional security checks on the `MessageService.save()` method. In such a case, performing security checking in `Filter` won't work. You will need to use AOP technology.

AOP is a different way of thinking about application structure compared with object-oriented programming. Let's introduce the basic concepts of AOP, before implementing security checking with AOP in our Messages App.

Concerns

In AOP, the security check is a security concern, or you can think of it as a goal that an application must meet. Usually, concerns span across multiple classes. Other types of concern include performance logging of application service APIs, transactional management, which we will discuss in the next section.

Aspects

An aspect is a modularization of such a concern. Instead of scattering code across many classes, we put the logic of handling the concern into an aspect. In Spring AOP, you can implement an aspect in a regular class and annotate it with the `@Aspect` annotation, which is an annotation from AspectJ (`https://www.eclipse.org/aspectj`).

Let's say we have `methodA()` in `ClassA`, `methodB()` in `ClassB`, and `methodC()` in `ClassC`, and we need to do security checking inside all of these methods. Before using AOP, we need to add code to handle security checks in all of these methods. And if we also need to execute a security check in other methods, we will need to add `checkSecurity()` to those methods too. After using AOP, we extract the security check logic into the `SecurityChecker` aspect, which is a regular Java class. And inside this class, the `checkSecurity()` method is annotated with the `@Around` annotation, which is an annotation from AspectJ. The value of the `@Around` annotation is an expression that is used to specify when the `checkSecurity()` method will be executed. In the example in *Figure 3.7*, the expression means whenever a method of any class inside the `app.message` package is executed:

Figure 3.7: AOP for security checking

With the `@Around` annotation, in runtime, the code execution will first reach the `SecurityChecker.checkSecurity()` method. Inside this method, you can decide whether the execution should proceed. If it should proceed, then you will invoke the target method and, once that method completes, the code execution will go back to the `checkSecurity()` method. At that point, normally you will return the code execution to the caller. On the other hand, if the execution should not proceed, you can throw an exception and the target method won't be executed.

As you can see from *Figure 3.7*, those methods requiring security checks no longer need the boilerplate code. All of the logic of the security checks has been centralized to the `SecurityChecker` aspect.

Join points

In AOP, `methodA()`, `methodB()`, and `methodC()` are join points—the points during the execution of a program. In Spring AOP, a join point always represents a method invocation. Other implementations of AOP, such as AspectJ, also support join points of field access and exception throwing.

Advices

In AOP, the `checkSecurity()` method inside `SecurityChecker` is an advice, which is an action to take care of a specific concern, in this case, a security concern. And there are different types of advice, including the following:

- **Before advice**: Advice to be executed before a join point, which cannot prevent the code execution reaching the join point unless it throws an exception. You can specify *before advice* with the `@Before` annotation.
- **After returning advice**: Advice to be executed after a join point completes normally without throwing an exception. You can specify *after returning advice* with the `@AfterReturning` annotation.
- **After throwing advice**: Advice to be executed when a method exits by throwing an exception. You can specify *after throwing advice* with the `@AfterThrowing` annotation.

- **After advice**: Advice to be executed regardless of the execution of a join point. It is like the final block in a `try...catch`. You can specify *after advice* with the `@After` annotation.
- **Around advice**: Advice surrounding a join point. This type of advice has full control of the code execution and hence is the most powerful. You can specify *around advice* with the `@Around` annotation, just as in the preceding example.

Pointcuts

In AOP, a pointcut is a predate that matches join points. The value of the `@Around` annotation, `"execution(* app.messages..*.*(..))"`, from the preceding example is a pointcut expression, which specifies when the `checkSecurity()` around advice should be fired. You can also use the `@Pointcut` annotation to declare a pointcut signature, as follows:

```
@Aspect
@Component
public class SecurityChecker {

    @Pointcut("execution(* app.messages..*.*(..))")
    public void everyMessageMethod() {}

    @Around("everyMessageMethod()")
    public Object checkSecurity (ProceedingJoinPoint joinPoint) {
        ...
    }
}
```

In the `SecurityChecker` aspect, we create an `everyMessageMethod()` public method and annotate it with the `@Pointcut` annotation. Since we only define a pointcut signature here, this method has no return value and is empty. In the `@Around` annotation of the `checkSecurity()` method, we use this method as a pointcut expression.

The execution in the previous pointcut expression is a **pointcut designator** (**PCD**), which tells Spring AOP what to match. Another useful PCD is `@annotation`. With this PCD, instead of using a regular expression to match join points, you can match only those methods annotated with a specific annotation.

AOP proxy

In our security check example in *@SecurityCheck* section, the objects of `ClassA`, `ClassB`, and `ClassC` are the target objects of the `SecurityChecker` aspect or are referred to as advised objects. In Spring AOP, the framework will create proxy objects for these objects in runtime to fulfill the `SecurityChecker` aspect contract. By default, Spring AOP uses standard JDK dynamic proxies to create AOP proxies. The JDK dynamic proxy can only proxy by an interface. If a target class doesn't implement an interface, Spring AOP will use CGLIB (`https://github.com/cglib/cglib`) to create a proxy by subclassing the target class. In our security check example, Spring AOP will create proxy objects using CGLIB.

Weaving

In AOP, weaving is the process of creating advised objects by linking aspects with other required objects. In Spring AOP, weaving happens at runtime, while AspectJ performs weaving at compile time or load time.

@SecurityCheck

Now, let's implement a simplified security check to our Messages App. We will create an *@SecurityCheck* annotation, which can be applied to any method to perform a security check.

Here is what the `@SecurityCheck` annotation looks like:

```
@Target(ElementType.METHOD)
@Retention(RetentionPolicy.RUNTIME)
public @interface SecurityCheck {
}
```

As you can see, this is a simple annotation that can be applied to methods.

And here is how the `SecurityChecker` aspect appears:

```
package app.messages;
...
import org.aspectj.lang.ProceedingJoinPoint;
import org.aspectj.lang.annotation.Around;
import org.aspectj.lang.annotation.Aspect;
import org.aspectj.lang.annotation.Pointcut;
...
@Aspect
```

```
@Component
public class SecurityChecker {
    ...

    @Pointcut("@annotation(SecurityCheck)")
    public void checkMethodSecurity() {}

    @Around("checkMethodSecurity()")
    public Object checkSecurity (ProceedingJoinPoint joinPoint) throws
    Throwable {
        logger.debug("Checking method security...");
        // TODO Implement security check logics here
        Object result = joinPoint.proceed();
        return result;
    }
}
```

As you can see, the `SecurityChecker` aspect is a regular Spring bean. What is special about it is that it has the `@Aspect` annotation. Spring supports XML-defined AOP configuration via the `<aop:config>` element, as well as the AspectJ annotations definition, which is the one we are using here.

Inside the `SecurityChecker` aspect, we create a pointcut signature, `checkMethodSecurity()`, with the `@Pointcut` annotation by using the `@annotation` PCD for the `@SecurityCheck` annotation.

In the `checkSecurity()` advice, we use the `@Around` annotation to specify that the advice is *around advice* with the pointcut expression, `"checkMethodSecurity()"`. Our advice is only implemented for demo purposes so that we only write a message to the log. In order to see the log message, you will need to add the following configuration to the `application.properties` file:

```
logging.level.app.messages.SecurityChecker=DEBUG
```

Now, the last step is to apply the `@SecurityCheck` annotation to the methods that we want to perform a security check. Let's apply it to the `MessageService.save()` method. Here is how the method appears:

```
@SecurityCheck
public Message save(String text) {
    return repository.saveMessage(new Message(text));
}
```

If you restart the Messages App and call the /messages (POST) API, you will see a debug message similar to the following in the log:

```
...
app.messages.SecurityChecker : Checking method security...
app.messages.AuditingFilter : Request[uri=/messages, method=POST] completed
in 273 ms
```

Spring Security uses Filter objects for request-level access control and AOP for method-level access control by using the @Secure annotation.

AOP execution flow

In our security checker example, without applying the @SecurityCheck annotation to the MessageService.save() method, the code execution flows directly from the MessageController.saveMessage() method to the MessageService.save() method. After applying the @SecurityCheck annotation, during runtime, the code execution flows from the MessageController.saveMessage() method to the AOP proxy object that Spring AOP creates. In our example, MessageService doesn't implement any interface, so the AOP proxy object is an instance of the MessageService subclass that Spring AOP creates with CGLIB. From the AOP proxy object, the execution flows to the checkSecurity() advisor. Inside the advisor, the MessageService.save() target method is invoked. And later, after MessageService.save() completes, the execution flows back to the MessageController.saveMessage() method. The following *Figure 3.8* demonstrates the execution flow with AOP:

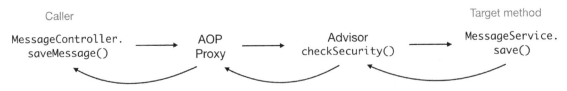

Figure 3.8: AOP execution flows

Spring transaction management

Spring's transaction support provides an abstraction over different transaction APIs, including the **Java Transaction API (JTA)** that works with global transactions, as well as the JDBC API, Hibernate transaction API, and JPA transaction API. The latter three APIs work with local transactions.

A global transaction can work with multiple transaction resources, typically relational database and message queues (JMS). And it is the application server that manages global transactions through JTA. On the other hand, a local transaction is resource-specific, for example, a transaction associated with a JDBC connection. Local transactions cannot work with multiple resources.

Spring transaction management supports both programmatic and declarative transaction management. You can use Spring's `TransactionTemplate` API to manage transactions programmatically or use the `PlatformTransactionManager` API directly. For declarative transaction management, you can apply the `@Transactional` annotation to the classes or methods where you want transaction management. The implementation of Spring's declarative transaction management is based on Spring's AOP framework, and it works in any environment for both global or local transactions.

Both programmatic and declarative transaction management support rollback rules, in other words, you can declare what exceptions can or cannot cause automatic rollback.

PlatformTransactionManager

Spring's transaction abstraction is based on a transaction strategy. That is, for different underlying transaction APIs, there is a specific implementation. And all of these implementations implement the `org.springframework.transaction.PlatformTransactionManager` interface, which is quite simple and looks like this:

```
public interface PlatformTransactionManager {
    TransactionStatus getTransaction(TransactionDefinition definition) throws
TransactionException;
    void commit(TransactionStatus status) throws TransactionException;
    void rollback(TransactionStatus status) throws TransactionException;
}
```

You can use the `getTransaction()` method with a `TransactionDefinition` object to get an object of `TransactionStatus`. And the returned `TransactionStatus` object could represent a new transaction or an existing one when there is a matching transaction that exists in the current call stack. With the `TransactionStatus` object, you can perform a commit or a rollback.

And for Hibernate, the implementation of `PlatformTransactionManager` is `HibernateTransactionManager`. For JDBC, the implementation is `DataSourceTransactionManager`. For JPA, the implementation is `JpaTransactionManager`. For, JTA, the implementation is `JtaTransactionManager`. And for JMS, the implementation is `JmsTransactionManager`. For different APIs, you need to create the corresponding implementation of `PlatformTransactionManager`.

Declarative transaction management

Now, let's see how we can implement Spring declarative transaction management.

Our Messages App is so simple that it works fine without transaction management. For demonstration purpose, let's add another requirement to the /messages (POST) API. Let's say we want to have a report to show the statistics of hourly posted messages. We can calculate the statistics using an SQL query. Or we can update the statistics after saving a message and save it into a table that will hold this information in the database. Let's go with the second approach so that we can use declarative transaction management.

 In practice, if our Message App had traffic like Disqus (`https://disqus.com`), you would probably want to take a different approach to update statistics, for example, send out an event to an MQ server and process the updating of statistics asynchronously.

To use declarative transaction management, we need to change `AppConfig`. Here are the changes:

```
...
@EnableTransactionManagement
public class AppConfig {
  ...
  @Bean
  public HibernateTransactionManager transactionManager() {
    HibernateTransactionManager transactionManager =
      new HibernateTransactionManager();
    transactionManager.setSessionFactory(sessionFactory().getObject());
    return transactionManager;
```

```
      }
   }
```

As you can see, we apply the `@EnableTransactionManagement` annotation to `AppConfig` and create a `HibernateTransactionManager` bean with the `transactionManager()` method. Inside this method, we set the same `SessionFactory` instance to this transaction manager.

By now, we've added transaction management to our app. Let's apply the `@Transactional` annotation to the `MessageService.save()` method. Here are the changes to the `MessageService` class:

```
public class MessageService {
   ...
   @SecurityCheck
   @Transactional
   public Message save(String text) {
      Message message = repository.saveMessage(new Message(text));
      log.debug("New message[id={}] saved", message.getId());
      updateStatistics();
      return message;
   }
   private void updateStatistics() {
      throw new UnsupportedOperationException("This method is not
      implemented yet");
   }
   }
}
```

As you can see, we apply the `@Transactional` annotation to the `save()` method. And we refactor the method to call the `updateStatistics()` method that is not implemented and will throw `UnsupportedOperationException`. This will cause the transaction's rollback. And we add a debug message to the log so that you can see the message has been saved and is then rolled back.

If you restart the application and call the `/messages` (`POST`) API, you will see the following exception:

```
java.lang.ClassCastException:
org.springframework.orm.jpa.EntityManagerHolder cannot be cast to
org.springframework.orm.hibernate5.SessionHolder
```

This is because, by default, Spring Boot creates `OpenEntityManagerInViewInterceptor`, which registers `EntityManager`, an interface from JPA, to the current thread. And we're using Hibernate's `SessionFactory` in the repository. And, in the transaction advice, Spring will try to cast `EntityManager` to `SessionFactory`. To solve this issue, we can change our repository to use `EntityManager` instead of `SessionFactory`. Or we can turn this feature off by changing `application.properties`.

Here are the changes to `application.properties`:

```
logging.level.app.messages.MessageService=DEBUG
...
spring.jpa.open-in-view=false
```

We turn on the debug level logging of `MessageService` so that we can see the log in the output. And we set `spring.jpa.open-in-view` to `false` to overwrite the default setting to turn off the creation of `OpenEntityManagerInViewInterceptor`.

 In Spring Boot 2, by default, a warning message shows up in the log when `spring.jpa.open-in-view` is not set to `false`. There are discussions regarding whether this should be turned on by default or not. If you're interested, you can check the discussion here: `https://github.com/spring-projects/spring-boot/issues/7107`.

Now, if you restart the application, you will see log information similar to the following in the console:

```
...
app.messages.SecurityChecker : Checking method security...
app.messages.MessageService : New message[id=6] saved
o.a.c.c.C.[.[.[/].[dispatcherServlet] : Servlet.service() for servlet
[dispatcherServlet] in context with path [] threw exception [Request
processing failed; nested exception is
java.lang.UnsupportedOperationException: This method is not implemented
yet] with root cause
...
```

As you can see, the `checkSecurity()` advice was invoked. After that, we created a message and the exception was thrown as expected. However, if you check the `messages` table, `message` of `id=6` is still there. It is not rolled back! What happened?

To find out what is wrong, first of all, let's review Spring's declarative transaction management, which is built on top of Spring AOP. As shown in *Figure 3.9*, Spring's transaction advisor creates transactions when the control flows in from the `checkSecurity()` advisor and either commits or rolls back the transaction after the control flows back to the transaction advisor. As mentioned earlier, a local transaction is associated with a JDBC connection. Therefore, when the transaction is created, a database connection is obtained from `DataSource`:

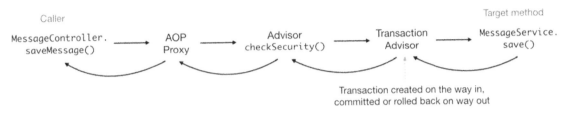

Figure 3.9: Transaction control flow

Let's take a look at the `MessageRepository.saveMessage()` method. Inside this method, we obtain a Hibernate session via `sessionFactory.openSession()`. The `openSession()` method will obtain a JDBC connection from `DataSource`. So, it seems that the connection obtained from this method is not the same one that the transaction advisor obtained.

This makes sense now. The `MessageRepository.saveMessage()` method uses a different JDBC connection to save the message and the transaction advisor cannot roll back a transaction of an unrelated connection.

Let's change the `MessageRepository.saveMessage()` method as follows:

```
public Message saveMessage(Message message) {
   Session session = sessionFactory.getCurrentSession();
   ...
}
```

`sessionFactory.getCurrentSession()` will obtain the current session that is in the current Hibernate context which is shared with the transaction advisor. In this way, the transaction advisor can roll back the saved message upon the thrown exception.

Now, if you restart the application and call the `/messages` (POST) API, you can see the saved message is rolled back because of the exception thrown by the `updateStatistics()` method.

As mentioned earlier, Spring transaction management supports rollback rules. We can declare those exceptions where we want the transaction advisor to roll back the transaction and those exceptions where we don't want the rollback.

With declarative transaction management, we can declare the rules with the `@Transactional` annotation. Now, let's change it to make it not roll back for `UnsupportedOperationException`.

Here is the updated `MessageService.save()` method:

```
@Transactional(noRollbackFor = { UnsupportedOperationException.class })
public Message save(String text) {
    ...
}
```

Now, if you restart the application and call the API again, you will see that the message is saved in the `messages` table as expected.

We will discuss more about Spring transaction management when we create the TaskAgile application.

Spring Boot

By now, you have been using Spring Boot to create the backend of Messages App along the way. As you can see, using Spring Boot to create a web application is quite straightforward. Now, let's take a closer look at it to see how it boosts developer's productivity.

Spring Boot takes an opinionated view of building production-ready applications. Its opinion is mostly expressed through its starters and its autoconfiguration mechanism. And, because of that, most Spring Boot applications need much less Spring configuration than traditional Spring applications.

A Spring Boot application typically inherits from the `spring-boot-starter-parent` project, which provides Maven defaults and a dependency management section so that you don't need to specify the version of those dependencies that Spring Boot supports. All you need to do is to specify Spring Boot version. On the other hand, you can still specify a version and override Spring Boot's recommendation.

If you're interested in the dependencies that Spring Boot supports by default, you can go to the `https://github.com/spring-projects/spring-boot` and check the `spring-boot-project/spring-boot-dependencies/pom.xml` file.

Also, Spring Boot supports a variety of technologies that can be used to build almost anything. To get started with a specific technology, all you need to do is simply add the starter that supports such a technology to your dependencies, and Spring Boot will take care of the initialization of the beans you need. For example, in our Messages App, we need to use JDBC, so we add the `spring-boot-starter-jdbc` starter and Spring Boot will create the `DataSource` bean by using the data source parameters we defined in `application.properties`.

Starters

Spring Boot starters are sets of convenient dependency descriptors, and they only contain a dependency descriptor file, which is the `pom.xml` file. By convention, all official starters follow the naming pattern—`spring-boot-starter-*`, where * is a particular technology, for example, `jdbc`, and `web`. Spring Boot also has a core starter, which is `spring-boot-starter`. All other starters depend on this starter, mostly for the autoconfiguration support it provides. The core starter is also a dependency descriptor, and its autoconfiguration ability comes from its `spring-boot-autoconfigure` dependency. We will discuss autoconfiguration soon.

Let's take a close look at the `spring-boot-starter-jdbc` starter. In this starter's `pom.xml` file, listed dependencies include `spring-boot-starter`, `HikariCP`, and `spring-jdbc`. And, by adding this starter to our app, we don't need to worry about `HikariCP`, `spring-jdbc`, or dependencies on which these two libraries depend. The build system you use, in our case, Maven, takes care of that.

Besides official starters, you can use custom starters provided by the community. For example, if you need to use MyBatis, you can use `mybatis-spring-boot-starter`. You can also create your own starters. All custom starters also need to depend on the core starter.

Due to the scope of this book, we're not going to discuss how to create a custom starter. If you're interested, you might want to take a look at the MyBatis starter (`https://github.com/mybatis/spring-boot-starter`).

Autoconfiguration

As mentioned earlier, the autoconfiguration ability of Spring Boot starters comes from `spring-boot-autoconfigure`. This project is the autoconfiguration implementation of Spring Boot's official starters.

The `@SpringBootApplication` annotation is the trigger for the autoconfiguration. This annotation is a combination of these three annotations:

- `@SpringBootConfiguration`
- `@EnableAutoConfiguration`
- `@ComponentScan`

The `@SpringBootConfiguration` annotation indicates that a class is a Spring Boot application configuration class. The `@EnableAutoConfiguration` annotation is the one that actually enables autoconfiguration, as its name suggests. The `@ComponentScan` annotation is to enable Spring's component scan feature.

With the `@EnableAutoConfiguration` annotation, `spring-boot-autoconfigure` will load metadata from the `META-INF/spring.factories` resource file using the application's class loader. And all of the `spring.factories` files of the application's dependencies will be loaded, including official starters as well as custom starters. Inside the `spring.factories` metadata file, the autoconfiguration is hooked through the `org.springframework.boot.autoconfigure.EnableAutoConfiguration` property.

Let's take a look at the `spring.factories` file of `spring-boot-autoconfigure`, which contains the autoconfiguration hooks of all the official starters.

The following is a snippet of the official `spring.factories` file:

```
# Auto Configure
org.springframework.boot.autoconfigure.EnableAutoConfiguration=\
...
org.springframework.boot.autoconfigure.aop.AopAutoConfiguration, \
...
org.springframework.boot.autoconfigure.jdbc.DataSourceAutoConfiguration, \
...
```

As you can see, this metadata file has the same format as a `.properties` file, which is a list of key-value pairs. The value of the `org.springframework.boot.autoconfigure.EnableAutoConfiguration` key is a list of names of the autoconfiguration classes, separated by commas. `AopAutoConfiguration` and `DataSourceAutoConfiguration` are the two that we have used in the Messages App. An autoconfiguration class is also a Java class annotated with Spring's `@Configuration` annotation.

Inside these autoconfiguration classes, Spring will create beans as configured. The only special part of these classes is that their configurations are conditional. For example, if you have already defined a `DataSource` bean in your application's configuration class, Spring Boot will not create another `DataSource` bean. In our Messages App, we let Spring Boot do autoconfiguration for us by leaving the definition of a `DataSource` bean empty. This is called conditional configuration. To archive conditional configuration, Spring provides annotations such as `@Conditional`, `@ConditionalOnClass`, `@ConditionalOnMissingBean`, and other conditional annotations that you can use to specify under what conditions autoconfiguration should be applied. Take the `DataSourceAutoConfiguration` class as an example; autoconfiguration will only happen when there are `DataSource` classes available in the classpath. The connection pool HiKari will be initialized when there is no user-defined bean of the `DataSource` type in the Spring container.

We're not going to go into any more detail on the usage of conditional autoconfiguration. If you are interested, you can check the source code for `DataSourceAutoConfiguration` here: `https://github.com/spring-projects/spring-boot/blob/master/spring-boot-project/spring-boot-autoconfigure/src/main/java/org/springframework/boot/autoconfigure/jdbc/DataSourceAutoConfiguration.java`.

Custom starters follow the same autoconfiguration mechanism as the official starters.

Put it together

Now, let's put the frontend and the backend of the Messages App together. We will populate the messages list in the UI by querying messages from the database and save new messages to the database after clicking the **Add** button in the UI.

The following are the things we need to do to make the integration work:

- Place the frontend and backend code in the same project
- Add APIs to the backend for getting messages and saving new messages
- Add the ability to communicate with the backend to the frontend

Place code together

In Chapter 2, *Vue.js 2 - It Works in the Way You Expected*, we created the frontend and used `http-server` to serve the `index.html` file and the static `.js` assets. When the integration is done, the embedded Tomcat server will serve these files. Now, let's move the frontend code to the backend.

 Besides putting the frontend and the backend together in a single project and deploying it as a whole, you can also keep them separated and deploy them separately so that the team can benefit from this decoupling when they need to work on each end independently. In this book, we will keep both ends together.

As mentioned earlier in the Spring MVC section, when requests come in, they go through `Filter` and `DispatcherServlet` objects and then arrive at `Controller` objects. In our Messages App, we have two types of request—one is for rendering the UI and the other is for API requests, such as retrieving JSON messages and saving new messages.

Now, let's add an `index()` handler method to `MessageController` to render the UI so that you can open the app via `http://localhost:8080/messages`:

```
@Controller
public class MessageController {
  ...
  @GetMapping("/messages")
  public String index() {
    return "index";
  }
  ...
}
```

As you can see, the `index()` handler method is quite simple. It simply returns the view's name. And we will need to put the `index.html` file from the frontend code to `resources/templates/index.html`. For those static `.js` assets, we will need to put them into the `resources/static` directory. In this way, when you request `http://localhost:8080/vue.js`, Spring Boot will serve `resources/static/vue.js`.

The `resources/static` directory looks like this after moving the static `.js` assets inside:

```
resources/static/components
resources/static/directives
resources/static/filters
resources/static/mixins
resources/static/plugins
resources/static/axios.v0.18.0.min.js
resources/static/vue.js
```

And the `resources/templates` directory looks like this:

```
resources/templates/index.html
resources/templates/welcome.html
```

Add APIs

Since we will serve the UI from `http://localhost:8080/messages`, it is better that we separate the path for APIs. Let's put API requests under `/api/`.

We will need to make the following changes to `MessageController`:

- Change the existing `/messages` (POST) to `/api/messages` (POST) for saving new messages
- Add `/api/messages` (GET) for retrieving messages
- Remove the `@RequestMapping` annotation from the `MessageController` class level

Here is the updated `MessageController`:

```
@Controller
public class MessageController {
  ...
  @GetMapping("/api/messages")
  @ResponseBody
  public ResponseEntity<List<Message>> getMessages() {
    List<Message> messages = messageService.getMessages();
    return ResponseEntity.ok(messages);
```

```
    }

    @PostMapping("/api/messages")
    @ResponseBody
    public ResponseEntity<Message> saveMessage(@RequestBody MessageData data)
  {

        ...

    }
  }
```

The `getMessages()` handler for the `/api/messages` (GET) API is the new one we add here. Inside this method, we invoke `MessageService.getMessages()` to get messages.

Here are the changes to `MessageService` to add the `getMessages()` method:

```
  public class MessageService {
    ...
    @Transactional(readOnly = true)
    public List<Message> getMessages() {
      return repository.getMessages();
    }

    @SecurityCheck
    @Transactional
    public Message save(String text) {
      return repository.saveMessage(new Message(text));
    }
  }
```

As you can see, we add the `@Transactional` annotation here to create a transaction because we are going to use `sessionFactory.getCurrentSession()` to get a Hibernate session in the repository. And, because it is just a `read` operation, we mark it as read-only. We also need to change the `save()` method of `MessageService` to remove the `updateStatistics()` method because we don't need it here.

Here is the change to `MessageRepository`:

```
  public class MessageRepository {
    ...
    public List<Message> getMessages() {
      Session session = sessionFactory.getCurrentSession();
      String hql = "from Message";
      Query<Message> query = session.createQuery(hql, Message.class);
      return query.list();
    }
  }
```

In the `getMessages()` method, after getting a Hibernate session, we create a **Hibernate Query Language (HQL)**, to retrieve all of the messages. Hibernate will translate this HQL into an SQL similar to the following and send it to the database:

```
select message0_.id as id1_0_, message0_.created_date as created_2_0_,
message0_.text as text3_0_ from messages message0_
```

 You can open the debug log of Hibernate SQL as follows to print out the SQL that Hibernate
generates: `logging.level.org.hibernate.SQL=DEBUG`

To execute the HQL, we need to create a Hibernate `org.hibernate.query.Query` object and call its `.list()` method to ask Hibernate to execute the query and return all of the records in the `messages` table. Hibernate will take care of the relational-to-object mapping and provide us with a list of `Message` objects.

HTTP client – axios

Now, let's work on the last step, which is to use an HTTP client to communicate with the backend. We will use axios (`https://github.com/axios/axios`) for its simple promise-based API. Let's download it from CDN (`https://unpkg.com/axios/dist/axios.min.js`) and put it under the `resources/static/` directory. The version we use here is v0.18.0.

Once the messages page (`https://localhost:8080/messages`) is opened, in order to show the existing messages as soon as possible, we will need to add the logic of retrieving messages to the `created()` life cycle hook of the Vue instance. And we will also need to modify the `addMessage()` method.

Here are the changes to the `index.html` file:

```
...
<body>
  ...
  <script src="../axios.v0.18.0.min.js"></script>
  <script type="module">
    window.vm = new Vue({
      ...
      created () {
        axios.get('api/messages?_=' + new Date().getTime())
        .then((response) => {
          this.messages = response.data
        })
```

```
      ...
    },
    methods: {
      addMessage (event) {
        if (!this.newMessage) return
        axios.post('api/messages', {text: this.newMessage})
        .then((response) => {
          this.messages.push(response.data)
          this.newMessage = ''
        })
        ...
      }
    }
  })
  </script>
</body>
...
```

As you can see, inside the created() hook, we use axios.get() to send the retrieve message GET request. The appended ?_ parameter in the URL is designed to make the browser not use a previously cached response. Once the request completes, the message JSON data is passed in the data property of the response parameter.

In the addMessage() method, we use axios.post() to send a new message to the backend. Once the request completes, we add the saved message to the messages list.

By now, we have completed the integration in terms of getting messages and saving new messages. The deleting message logic is left as an exercise for you.

If you restart the application and open http://localhost:8080/messages, you will see those messages you previously added showing up on the page.

Package app.messages

At the beginning of this chapter, we decided to put everything inside the app.messages package. Let's take a look at it. Here is everything inside:

```
AppConfig.java              // Root configuration class
Application.java            // Application bootstrap class
AuditingFilter.java        // Requests audit Filter
Message.java               // Message Entity class
MessageController.java     // Message Controller for HTTP API
MessageData.java           // Saving message request data structure
MessageRepository.java     // Repository class of Message
MessageService.java        // Service class of Message
```

```
SecurityCheck.java            // Security Check annotation
SecurityChecker.java          // Security Checker aspect
```

As you can see, it is a pile of mud. And if we were going to build more features into this app, it would turn into chaos unless we reorganize it.

Let's reorganize it. Since our Messages App is quite small, it would be sufficient to break the `app.messages` package into subpackages based on the roles of the classes.

Here is the refactored structure of the `app.messages` package:

```
app.messages
 /config
    /AppConfig.java
 /model
    /Message.java
 /repository
    /MessageRepository.java
 /service
    /MessageService.java
 /web
    /AuditingFilter.java
    /MessageController.java
    /MessageData.java
 /security
    /SecurityCheck.java
    /SecurityChecker.java
 /Application.java
```

As you can see, we put all of the configuration classes into an `app.messages.config` package, the message entity class into an `app.messages.model` package, and the service and repository classes into their own packages. And since `AuditingFilter`, `MessageController`, and `MessageData` all deal with HTTP requests, they live in the `app.messages.web` package, while the `app.messages.security` package is for security-related items. The `Application.java` bootstrap class stays in the `app.message` package.

This is a typical structure of a layered application, which usually contains three layers—a web layer, a service layer, and a DAO layer. This type of structure isn't a silver bullet for all applications. We will discuss more about code design later in this book.

Summary

In this chapter, you have learned about Spring IoC and DI, Spring MVC, Spring JDBC, JPA/Hibernate, Spring AOP, Spring transaction management, and Spring Boot. You've also integrated the frontend and the backend of the Messages App.

In the next chapter, we will introduce a TaskAgile application so that you will know what kind of application we're going to create.

TaskAgile - A Trello-like Task Management Tool

It's time to build the main application of this book, TaskAgile, a Trello-like task management application. For the rest of this book, we will focus on building this application, from requirements to design and implementation, and then to deployment. We will adopt Agile methodologies through the life cycle of this application and practice **Domain-Driven Design (DDD)** and **Test-Driven Development (TDD)**. You will see how to create a full-stack web application right from the beginning.

In this chapter, we will introduce the requirements of this application and you will learn the following:

- Managing requirements in an Agile way
- Writing effective user stories
- Creating wireframes
- Understanding Agile
- Full-stack developer skillsets

Managing requirements in an Agile way

In waterfall projects, business analysts write comprehensive requirement documents and then hand them over to developers and testers. Developers will create the application according to all of the details specified in the document, and testers use these documents to create test cases. Once the code is complete and integration is done, testers will do quality assurance and developers will fix bugs before the customer performs the acceptance test.

Since the required documents need to include all of the details, it usually takes months for requirement development. And if the schedule is tight, requirements might not be accurate, or worse, not documented. Or later during the implementation, customers might change their mind and some features may have to be discarded even though they have already been built.

There are many other kinds of risks and frustrations associated with a waterfall project because of the way of managing requirements.

Teams that adopt an Agile methodology manage requirements in a quite different way. Before we introduce that, let's see the levels of requirements. It will help us know how to manage them better.

Levels of requirements

In the book entitled *Software Requirements, 3ʳᵈ edition*, by Karl Wiegers and Joy Beatty, the authors classify software requirements into three levels—business requirements, user requirements, and functional requirements:

- **Business requirements**: These are the high-level business objectives of an organization, why the organization needs to build the system, and what the benefits are to the business. Suppose a software outsourcing company wants to provide better training to their employees. This is a business requirement. To achieve this goal, the executive team decides to build an internal training and learning system to include all of the technologies the company uses, together with sample applications of each technology.
- **User requirements**: These define the tasks that users can perform with the system. These requirements can be written as use cases or user stories. For example, in the training system, users can take exams and, once they pass these exams, they can gain certificates. This is a user requirement that specifies the tasks users can perform with the system.
- **Functional requirements**: These specify the behaviors of the system in terms of how users can fulfill the tasks defined in user requirements. They describe what engineers must build into the system so that users can accomplish their tasks. For example, in the training system, users should be able to retake an exam only if they have failed that exam less than three times.

As you can see, business requirements establish the goals and objectives of a system. User requirements focus on what users can do in the system to achieve that goal, while functional requirements provide the details of the behavior that the system should have under specific conditions.

Business requirements are usually written in the vision and scope document, while user requirements are stored in the **User Requirements Document** (URD), and functional requirements are written in the **Software Requirements Specification** (SRS). Large projects tend to write all of these documents upfront. Teams that use Agile methodologies adopt another approach.

Writing a requirement in an Agile project

Many people think that Agile project teams do not need to write documents, especially if they use extreme programming methodology. This is is a common misunderstanding.

Even though, in Agile teams, developers usually have closer interaction with customers, a business requirement document is still a must because it is the guidance on how the product should be built. It sets the direction of all development activities. Teams without a business requirement document or a well-defined one often face disasters during implementation. It can also be used to validate the changes requested by customers to keep everyone's focus on delivering a product that meets the objectives of the business.

At a lower level, user requirements are written as user stories in the product backlog in Agile teams. Because of the close collaboration with customers, developers usually need fewer details written in user stories than on a traditional team. Agile methodologies encourage creating minimal documentation that can accurately guide the team to implement the features, and any documentation beyond that could be a waste of time because a working software provides more value to customers than comprehensive documentation.

As for functional requirements, in Agile teams, you add them to your unit tests and automation tests and run them repeatedly to verify the system's behavior. In this way, you will have the confidence of delivering a working software that meets customers' expectations. Do not write functional requirements in a requirement document because you cannot use that document to perform repeated automatic tests. Also, soon enough, those documents will become obsolete because of the changes to requirements. Another benefit of keeping details of functional requirements in the test code is that whenever you implement a requirement change, you will have to update the test code and this will always keep them up to date.

For TaskAgile applications, the business requirement is to build an open source Trello-like task management application that can be extended and customized by the open source community. In the next section, we will write user stories for this application.

Writing effective user stories

In an Agile project team, the product owner is responsible for keeping a product backlog, but not necessarily for writing all user stories. Writing user stories should be a team effort. It is a collaboration between the product owner and developers. In this way, the creativity and knowledge of the whole team are involved in producing better user stories.

Tips on writing user stories

Before we write the user stories of the TaskAgile applications, let's go through some tips on how to write effective user stories:

- **Tip 1**: Write user stories in the following format if you can:

    As a <type of user>, I want to <do something>, so that I <get some benefit>.

    That is a user story that basically consists of who, what, and why. However, don't force your stories into this template if they do not fit. And you don't want to stick with *I want to*, you can choose other phrases, such as *I can* or *I'd like to*, as you see fit. For example, the following is a user story of TaskAgile about user login:

    As a registered user, I can use my username or email address with the password to log into the application.

    In this user story, you don't have to write the `so that` part because the reason you log into the application might be that you want to check tasks in progress or create a new team. It wouldn't make sense to put all of these into the `so that` part.

- **Tip 2**: Make sure that user stories can provide end-to-end functionalities to users. For example, if one user story is about filling out the registration form and another user story is about creating the user account with the details provided in the form when the first user story is finished, users won't be able to actually perform the registration action. It doesn't provide a functionality that can let users accomplish something.
- **Tip 3**: Keep user stories small and feasible. User stories need to be small enough so that they can fit into an iteration during the planning stage. When a user story is too large, it usually means that there are undiscovered details and developers usually cannot implement it directly. For example, in TaskAgile applications, there can be a user story like this:

    As a board member, I can manage cards.

This story is too large because there are many details regarding how to manage cards that are not specified. On the other hand, when a user story is too small, it won't be able to provide a useable functionality to users, like the example mentioned in tip 2.

Large user stories are epics, and they should be broken into smaller stories. For example, the preceding user story can be broken into the following stories:

- As a board member, I can create cards
- As a board member, I can archive cards
- As a board member, I can move cards between card lists
- As a board member, I can change card positions
- As a board member, I can delete archived cards

- **Tip 4**: Add acceptance criteria to user stories. Acceptance criteria, or conditions of satisfaction, provide additional details to user stories. They are the conditions that will be true when the story is complete. For example, the following is a TaskAgile user story about user registration:

    As a visitor, I want to register a user account with my email address, username, and password.

The acceptance criteria is as follows:

- The email address must not already exist in the system
- The username must not already exist in the system
- The password must be at least six characters
- The password must contain at least one number
- The password must contain at least one letter

If you use a paper card for writing user stories, put these conditions at the back of the card. Make them no more than five items so that they can fit in one card. And when you implement this user story, these conditions should be included in your automation test.

- **Tip 5**: Avoid including user interfaces in user stories. There is a tendency to add user interface-related details to user stories. For example, in a user management system, there can be a user story such as the following:

    *As an administrator, I want to click the **Open Filters** button to open filters so that I can use the keyword field and date selector to search users by name, email address, and registration date.*

In fact, a user interface is more like a specific solution to a requirement, rather than the requirement itself. It is better to change the preceding user story to the following:

> *As an administrator, I want to search users by name, email address, and registration date so that I can find a user quickly.*

- **Tip 6**: Use themes to group user stories. A theme is a collection of user stories that share a common attribute. For example, we can use a theme named **Cards** and group all the card-related user stories in this theme. Themes are a way to organize your user stories.

- **Tip 7**: Use short titles instead of numbers to reference user stories. When the team has discussions about user stories, it would be confusing to reference cards with numbers. For example, *Let's discuss story 39*. And then everybody else has to think about what *story 39* is about, and every time the name story 39 pops up, people need to do the translation. The discussion will be much easier when stories have short titles. For example, *story edit card title* is much better than *story 39*.

TaskAgile user stories

In this section, we will write all of the user stories for TaskAgile. And we keep all stories small and feasible.

The user stories will be grouped into the following themes:

- **Users**: This contains all user-related stories
- **Teams**: This contains all team-related stories
- **Boards**: This contains all board-related stories
- **Card lists**: This contains all card list-related stories
- **Cards**: This contains all card-related stories

And we will have the following user roles:

- **Visitor**: Anonymous visitors that the system does not recognize
- **Registered user**: A user that has registered in the system
- **Team creator**: A user who creates that team
- **Board creator**: A user who creates that board
- **Board member**: A user who is added to a board by the board creator

Users

The following are the user stories with the title of the Users theme:

- **Register**: As a visitor, I want to register a user account with my email address, username, and password.

  The acceptance criteria is as follows:

  - The email address must not already exist in the system
  - The username must not already exist in the system
  - The password must be at least six characters
  - The password must contain at least one number
  - The password must contain at least one letter

- **Log in**: As a registered user, I can use my username or email address with the password to log into the application.

Teams

The following are the user stories with the title of the Teams theme:

- **Create a team**: As a registered user, I want to create teams so that I can organize tasks of different teams.

- **Change team name**: As a team creator, I can change the name of the team that I created.

Boards

The following are the user stories with the title of the Boards theme:

- **Create a personal board**: As a registered user, I can create a personal board so that I can organize personal tasks.

- **Create a team board**: As a registered user, I can add a board to a team so that I can organize the tasks of that team.

- **Add board member**: As a board creator, I can add registered users to a board as board members so that they can access cards in the board.

- **View board activities**: As a board member, I can view all activities within that board so that I can understand what happened.

Card Lists

The following are the user stories with the title of the Card Lists theme:

- **Create a card list**: As a board member, I can add card lists in a board so that I can arrange cards in that list.

- **Rename card list**: As a board member, I can rename a card list.

- **Archive card list**: As a board member, I can archive a card list in that board.

- **Change card list position**: As a board member, I can change the position of a card list in that board.

- **View card list**: As a board member, I can view the cards added to a card list in that board.

Cards

The followings are the user stories with the title of the Cards theme:

- **Add card**: As a board member, I can add cards to card lists in that board.

- **View card**: As a board member, I can view the details of a card in that board.

- **Edit card title**: As a board member, I can edit the title of a card in that board.

- **Edit card description**: As a board member, I can edit the description of a card using plain text or markdown formatted text in that board.

- **Assign member to the card**: As a board member, I can add board members to a card.

- **Change the card position**: As a board member, I can rearrange cards by changing their positions in the same card list so that I can better prioritize them.

- **Move card**: As a board member, I can move cards between card lists in that board.

- **Archive card**: As a board member, I can archive a card in that board.

- **Delete card**: As a board member, I can delete an archived card in that board.

- **Add card attachment**: As a board member, I can attach an attachment to a card in that board.

- **Download card attachment**: As a board member, I can download the attachments of a card in that board.

- **Delete card attachment**: As a board member, I can delete card attachments of a card in that board.

- **Add card comment**: As a board member, I can add comments to a card in that board.

- **Edit card comment**: As a board member, I can edit my own card comments in that board.

- **Delete card comment**: As a board member, I can delete my own card comments in that board.

- **View card activities**: As a board member, I'd like to view all the activities of a card so that I can track the history of that card.

We will learn how to implement all of these user stories in this book, using Spring Framework and Vue.js. And you will be able to download the source code of the application. A live demo of the application is hosted in `https://taskagile.com`.

Creating wireframes

When you look at the user stories of the TaskAgile applications that we just wrote, they are clear and small. But they omit important details that developers need in order to start the implementation.

In fact, user stories are only starting points for discussions on requirements. For example, when you look at a story login, you would ask questions such as, do we need to add a placeholder for each input field? Do we need to add labels for these fields? If we do, should the labels be to the right of the fields or above the fields? Different people can have different ideas about how to implement a user story.

Creating wireframes for user stories can help everybody understand what needs to be built. And you can link wireframes back to user stories which will become the pointers of implementation details.

You can use paper and pencils to create the wireframe or write them on a whiteboard. These two ways are straightforward, but not maintainable and not easy to be shared within the team online. You can also use online wireframe tools to create wireframes.

Another way to create a wireframe, which is the way we will use, is to use PowerPoint or Keynote. Here are some tips for using these tools for creating wireframes:

- **Tip 1**: Set the **Slide Size** to the same size as your display's resolution. For example, if your display resolution is 1280 pixels x 800 pixels, in PowerPoint, go to the **Page Setup** and type in 1280 pixels and 800 pixels. By default, PowerPoint will convert these values from a pixel unit to an inch unit. The benefit of this is that, when you play the slide, it will be in fullscreen. And for all of the elements on the page, you can give them values using the same measurement. For example, you can set the input field to be 30 pixels high by 350 pixels wide. The following is a screenshot of how the log in page wireframe appears in PowerPoint:

Figure 4.1 Creating a wireframe using PowerPoint

- **Tip 2**: Use Master Slides to create page templates. When there are several pages that share the same elements, creating page templates using Master Slides can save you time when you need to change those shared elements on multiple pages.
- **Tip 3**: Use Font Awesome to create icons. Font Awesome 5 (`http://fontawesome.com`) provides almost 1,000 free icons. You can download its free version and install the fonts on your computer. If you're using Keynote, you can add text and type `home`, and then select **Font Awesome 5** as its font and Keynote will change the text to the home icon. If you're using PowerPoint, after installing the font, you will need to go to Font Awesome Cheatsheet (`https://fontawesome.com/cheatsheet`) and copy an icon itself, not the text, and then paste it in PowerPoint. If you copy a solid icon, remember to change the font to **Font Awesome 5 Free Solid** in PowerPoint.
- **Tip 4**: Use **Lock** to prevent elements from being selected. This tip only applies to Keynote. In Keynote, you can select a shape and then right-click on it and choose **Lock** from the menu to lock the shape so that it cannot be selected. This is quite useful when you don't want to freeze shapes on the slide.
- **Tip 5**: Practices make perfect. The more wireframes you create with PowerPoint or Keynote, the better your skills will be.

With PowerPoint or Keynote, you can also create simple UI designs in the same way you create wireframes. The only difference is that you need to pay more attention to details, such as the text colors, background colors, border sizes, and border colors. The following is a screenshot of TaskAgile's board page UI created with Keynote:

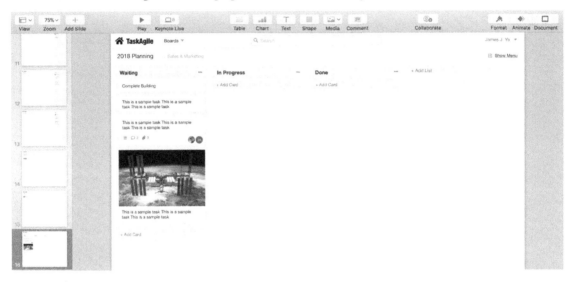

Figure 4.2 Create simple design works with Keynote

No matter what tool you use to create them, wireframes are always an efficient way to communicate your ideas to the rest of the team. You can use them to clarify requirements and explore UI alternatives by creating wireframes of different solutions for the same user story.

Understanding Agile

More and more teams are using Agile methodologies. Many of them have great success. Others might only get a better-than-not-doing-it result. In this book, we're going to use Agile to build the TaskAgile application. Since this is a full-stack development experience for one developer, we will only be able to practice some Agile methods. For example, there won't be a daily standup meeting for the obvious reason.

Before moving on, let's discuss what Agile software development is so that we can have a better understanding of the methods that we will use.

When talking about Agile development, Scrum, Extreme Programming, Lean, and Kanban are the buzzwords. We're not going to discuss these here. Instead, let's go back to the values in the Agile manifesto (`http://agilemanifesto.org`). Everything else is based on that.

The Agile manifesto

The four values in the manifesto are as follows:

- **Individuals and interactions** over processes and tools
- **Working software** over comprehensive documentation
- **Customer collaboration** over contract negotiation
- **Responding to change** over following a plan

As it is stated in the manifesto, while there is value in the items on the right, we value the items on the left more. Let's discuss these values respectively.

Individuals and interactions over processes and tools

Good processes and useful tools can improve the team's productivity. There is no doubt about that. And that's why there are many best practice, and people keep inventing new tools. However, if the members of a team follow processes or best practices blindly, or a tool that works so great in a previous project is not appropriate in the current project, these processes and tools would become counter-productive. It is always important to remember that it is the people on the team that move the project forward. Instead of relying on processes and tools, we should get to know each other's thoughts better, as a team, and utilize a team's collective intelligence. In Agile, practices such as daily standup meetings and retrospectives are the ones that align with this value.

Working software over comprehensive documentation

In an Agile team, people value a working software over comprehensive documentation. As mentioned previously, it doesn't mean there should be no documentation in an Agile team. In fact, you need vision and scope documentation to guide you through the project, user stories to bring up the conversations of requirement discussions, wireframes and UI design works for the implementation, documents of business rules and system requirements to specify the constraints of the system, and technical design documents to help the team understand the logic of the system. These documents don't need to be comprehensive. They should only contain sufficient detail to accurately guide the team. For example, in the technical design documents, you don't need to write every detail regarding the logic, just the important parts. These documents only serve as guidance. For the actual logic, you keep them in the code, and, even better, write automation tests to verify those logics, because a working software brings actual value to the customer, not those comprehensive documents.

Customer collaboration over contract negotiation

We need contracts and contract negotiations. One of the values of a contract is to have an agreement on the scope of the project. And contract negotiation is a process in which changes requested by customers can be denied. Besides that, to both sides, a contract is protection. However, when contracts are used as weapons and shields by either side, the trust, collaboration, and momentum are gone. And conversations start to begin with: According to the contract..., and there will be times when customers point out that a feature isn't functional, to which developers might reply—I built that strictly according to the requirements specified in the contract. Or, when developers try to discuss an alternative solution to a feature where the team has difficulty with the underlying technology, the customer might say: No, you have to build it in that way. It is written in the contract. These are the moments when a project stalls.

On the other hand, when developers and customers work as partners, everybody works toward the same goal, and there is a much bigger chance of achieving success.

Responding to change over following a plan

The only thing that is constant is change. Most of the time, changes mean evolving. Operating systems keep changing with new versions and upgrades, while frameworks and libraries keep changing with new releases. Applications keep changing with new versions. Those that do not change are the systems that either are not being actively used or are abandoned. Changes are inevitable.

Making plans is to keep things organized. And it takes an effort to build a plan. However, the following one doesn't mean you must not change it when a change is really needed. Sticking to a plan that is no longer heading in the right direction will either end in failure or will require much greater efforts to get it back on track later.

Due to the scope of this book, we're not going to discuss the twelve principles in the Agile manifesto. If you're interested to learn more about Agile, I recommend the book *Learning Agile*, by Andrew Stellman and Jennifer Greene. It's a must-read for Agile practitioners. Another interesting book is *Succeeding with Agile: Software Development Using Scrum*, by Mike Cohn, which is a guide to starting Agile with Scrum.

Full-stack developer skillsets

In `Chapter 2`, *Vue.js 2 - It Works in the Way You Expected*, you learned the basics of the frontend technology and the basics of Java backend technology, and you successfully integrated the frontend and the backend. This might seem to be sufficient for a full-stack developer. In fact, to become a full-stack developer, you need more than simply learning frontend and backend code skills.

The start point of being a full-stack developer is to change your mindset. You should not only focus on writing code. You need to look at the application development life cycle from a higher level and participate in all its phases. And there might be some phases that you don't think are necessary for a developer to work on. Now is the time to make a change.

The development of an application usually begins with the requirements, followed by design, implementation, testing, and deployment. In Agile development, the process is similar, but at a feature level or a group of features level.

Let's go through the skillsets of a full-stack developer one by one.

Requirement analyzing

To start with, you need to understand the value of the application, what the customer and business need, what the application will bring to its users, and how it can help its users to achieve their goals. This is the foundation of building an application. As a full-stack developer, you need to analyze the requirement and see features that are missing or incomplete. You should no longer be satisfied with simply accepting requirements. You will need to detect the flaws in the business logic or even propose new ideas, because if the requirements don't get sorted out, sooner or later, issues will pop up. And the effort required to fix those issues is usually not insignificant.

As a software developer, whenever you work on a feature or bug fixing, you will need to understand its requirements and the business logic behind it. If you don't feel that you are good at requirement analyzing, most of the time, it is because you need more analytical thinking. Next time, ask more questions, such as the following:

- Why do we need this feature?
- What is the business value of this feature?
- Does this feature fit into the whole application?
- Are there any improvements we can do to make it better?

Communication

Communication is a fundamental skill of a full-stack developer, as there are a lot of people that you need to communicate with—business owners, application users, product managers, UI designers, QA, and DevOps. It's time to open up communication and avoid limiting yourself to just writing code. You need to communicate issues, ideas, development status, and feedback to these people. More or less, you're taking part in a project manager's role.

Wireframes creating

Wireframes can eliminate people's misinterpretation of requirements that are not clearly stated. And the effort to draw wireframes are much lower than creating sophisticated UI design works. You can create them easily by using paper and pencil, a whiteboard with a marker, or PowerPoint/Keynote. As a full-stack developer, you will find that creating wireframes to communicate requirements with others in the team is an efficient way of keeping everybody on the same page. And it requires your patience and attention to detail.

Data modeling

Data modeling is so critical that you will want to spend a good chunk of your time on that. Most of the features in your application are built on top of the data models that you created. If your data model design has flaws, you will need to introduce weird logic to cover corner cases that are not included in the data models. And, in the worst case, as the application evolves, the terms in the code no longer match their meanings in the data models.

A good data model design is a result of a deep understanding of the requirements, solid knowledge of the database, and the practicing of domain-driven design.

API designing

There are different levels of API design in an application development. When you create a class, its public methods are its API. When you create a package, those publicly available classes inside that package are the API of the package. When you create a web application, those HTTP endpoints that the backend provides are the APIs of the application. And you can design them in SOAP, make them RESTful, or use GraphQL. No matter what level of API you're designing, you need to make sure it is clear, consistent, and simple to use.

Frontend coding

You will need HTML, CSS, and JavaScript skills, as well as an understanding of the basics of these technologies. For example, in JavaScript, you need to understand the prototype chain and ES6 features; in CSS, you need to understand what `relative`, `absolute`, and `fixed` means for `position` property, and how float works and when you need to use clear. On top of that, you need to master several frameworks, for example, Bootstrap, Backbone.js, React, Angular, or Vue.js.

Besides that, you also need to understand the way browsers work and how the JavaScript engine works, because it will help you understand how your frontend code is executed.

Backend coding

As a Java developer, you need to understand Java EE Servlet and how an application server handles cookies, session management, HTTP requests, and responses. You will need to master at least one application framework, such as Spring Framework, and one data layer framework, such as Hibernate or MyBatis, and at least one database technology, such as a relational database or NoSQL database.

Unit tests and automation tests

The skill of writing unit tests and automation tests is important to a full-stack developer. It ensures code quality and improves productivity by avoiding repeating manual testing. Practicing test-driven development is a trait of experienced developers.

Continuous integration

Working with DevOps, a full-stack developer needs to know how to practice **Continuous Integration (CI)** or **Continuous Delivery (CD)** and keep the application in a workable state. Even though you might often work in a small team, sometimes solo on a project, as a full-stack developer, you should follow the disciples and best practices of CI.

Server monitoring and architecture awareness

A full-stack developer should know how to monitor servers in the production environment and work with DevOps to create a strategy to keep the system in a highly-available state and, from the architecture level, to make the system horizontally scalable. A full-stack developer should also keep a close eye on the application's performance and know how to troubleshoot performance issues and how to solve them.

In the rest of this book, we will address these skillsets while we create the TaskAgile application.

Summary

In this chapter, you have learned the levels of requirements and how to manage requirements in an Agile project. You have also learned tips to write effective user stories and tips to creating wireframes. We also reviewed the four values of the Agile manifesto and went through the skillsets of a full-stack developer.

In the next chapter, we will start the data model design of our TaskAgile applications.

Data Modeling - Designing the Foundation of the Application

5

Data models are the foundation of an application. Getting them right at the beginning is much easier than changing the foundation later because, at the design stage, all of the changes you need to make can be done with papers and pencils. On the other hand, making a change to data models during the implementation of the application usually involves modifying all of the code through each layer of the application, and as we mentioned before that changes are unavoidable, building good data models can help you make those changes much easier.

In this chapter, we will design the data models of the TaskAgile application, and you will learn the following:

- The basics of data modeling
- The goals of doing data modeling
- Conceptual data modeling with ER diagrams
- Logical data modeling
- Physical data modeling for RDBMS
- Physical data modeling for MongoDB

Introduction to data modeling

Data modeling is an essential step in the creation of an application like TaskAgile. Through data modeling, we discover the data requirements based on the requirements of our application, and then analyze and scope those data requirements and turn them into data models that define how the data of the application will be stored, retrieved, and updated. Additionally, the rest of the application will be built upon these data models.

In this section, we will talk about the basics of data modeling, including the stages and the deliverable of each stage, and terminologies used in data modeling. After that, we will start the data modeling of the TaskAgile application.

Data modeling stages and deliverables

Data modeling usually consists of three stages:

- Conceptual data modeling
- Logical data modeling
- Physical data modeling

In the following sections, we will learn about each of these stages in detail.

Conceptual data modeling

Conceptual data modeling is the stage where we discover the data requirements by going through the requirements of an application. We document these data requirements as conceptual data models using **Entity-Relationship** (**ER**) diagrams, which is an informal standard of documenting data models.

Let's look at an example. Based on the Register user story and the Log in user story in the TaskAgile application as created in Chapter 4, *TaskAgile - A Trello-like Task Management Tool*, under *Users* the section, we can discover that we need to store users' data upon registration and also provide the ability to query each user's data based on a username or an email address during login.

Let's use the Create a team user story created in Chapter 4, *TaskAgile - A Trello-like Task Management Tool*, under the *Teams* section as another example. As a registered user, I want to create teams so that I can organize the tasks of different teams. We can discover that we will need to store the teams, and also the relationship between users and teams, which is who created which teams, and with a closer look, you can discover that we will also need to store the task's data and probably the relationship between tasks and teams. There are no further details for this data requirement, but we will get a better understanding of it once we finish analyzing all of the other user stories.

Logical data modeling

Once we have conceptual data models, we go into the next stage, which is logical data modeling. In this stage, we do further analysis and scope of the data requirements. We will build out the details of the data models by asking questions or having discussions with business specialists. For example, you might have questions such as the following about the relationship between users and teams:

- How many teams can a user create?
- Does a user have to create a team?
- Besides creating a team, can a user join the teams created by other users?
- If so, how many teams can a user join?
- Can a user create a team with a name that is already being used by another team?
- How can we identify a team by its name?

With answers to questions like these, we start to gain a deeper understanding of the data requirements and the logic that haven't been revealed during the conceptual data modeling.

And, during logical data modeling, we will need to do normalization and usually denormalization. Normalization is a process for eliminating data redundancy and anomalies during data insertion, updating, and deletion and ensuring the data dependencies make sense. Denormalization is the opposite of normalization and is used mainly for performance improvement. We will also see an example of this later.

In both the conceptual data modeling stage and logical data modeling stage, usually, we will make generalizations with the use of subtypes and supertypes to adjust the data models. We will see an example of this later.

Physical data modeling

Once we have the logical data models, we are ready to create physical data models. This is the stage where you convert the logical data models into a database design for a specific **RDBMS** (short for **Rational Database Management System**), such as MySQL or PostgreSQL, or a NoSQL database, such as MongoDB. An important consideration during physical data modeling is performance. Most of the database systems support tools such as indexing, clustering, partitioning, and data compression to archive performance improvement without compromising the logical data model design. We will also discuss indexing in this book. But we will not discuss clustering, portioning, or data compression. They are beyond the scope of this book.

The output of this stage are the physical data models, and since we're using MySQL (5.7.21) as our database, we will use MySQL Workbench (`https://www.mysql.com/products/workbench`) for the physical data modeling. One of the nice features that MySQL Workbench supports is the ability to export physical data models as SQL that we can use to set up the database.

The following is an activity diagram that shows different data modeling stages and the deliverable of each stage. The round-cornered rectangles represent actions, such as creating **Conceptual Data Model**, while the square-cornered rectangles represent the object flows between actions, for example, the **Application Requirements** node is the input of creating **Conceptual Data Model**:

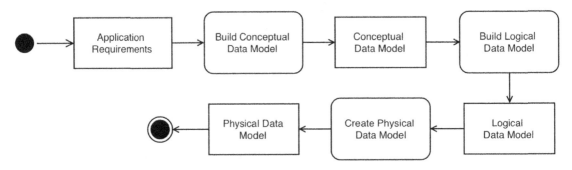

Figure 5.1 Data modeling stages and deliverables

Terminologies used in data modeling

Now, let's introduce the terminologies that we will use in data modeling.

Entities

In data modeling, we use the term **entities** to represent the things that we want to store in the database, and these things exist either physically or logically and can be uniquely identified. Entities are abstractions of the complexities of the things, a domain, that you're modeling. And, usually, they consist of only those characteristics that the application you're developing is interested in. For example, in the TaskAgile application, User entities represent the users of the application whose data needs to be stored in the database. During physical data modeling, if you're targeting an RDBMS, such as MySQL, these User entities will be stored inside a table, and each User entity will be a record of that table. Or, if you're targeting a NoSQL database, such as MongoDB, they will be stored inside a collection, and each User entity will be stored as a document inside that collection.

Attributes

We use the term **attributes** to represent the characteristics of an entity. For example, first name, last name, and email address are the attributes of User entities. And, for RDBMS, attributes will be converted into the columns of a table or, for NoSQL, such as MongoDB, they will be converted into the fields of documents. Among the attributes of an entity, there needs to be at least one that can be used to uniquely identify that entity. Take the User entities as an example; the email address of a user can be used to identify that user. Usually, there can be several such attributes.

Relationships

We use the term **relationships** to represent the relationships between two entities. Usually, a relationship has a name, for example, the relationship between creators and teams is a **create** relationship. And, relationships are usually mentioned with cardinality, for example, the create relationship is a **one-to-many** relationship. That is, one Team Creator can create zero or multiple teams and one team can be created by one Team Creator. The other cardinalities include one-to-one and many-to-many.

Primary keys

When we design entities, we choose an attribute or a combination of multiple attributes that can be used to uniquely identify an entity as the **primary key** of that type of entity.

By nature, primary keys are unique. For example, since two users cannot have the same email address, we could use it as the primary key of the User entities. However, that won't work in applications that allow users to change their email addresses. The attribute or a combination of the attributes that are used as the primary key must be stable. That is, the value of a primary key must not be changed throughout the life cycle of that entity, for the same reason that it is not a good idea to use an attribute username as the primary key for the User entities. Even though the email address and the username attribute cannot be used as a primary key, they can still be used to identify users, for instance, you can still use a user's email address or username to find that user. We call these types of attributes **candidate keys**.

In practice, it is common to use a system-generated unique value as the primary key of a type of entity. For example, we can let MySQL generate integer values for the `id` column of a table and use that column as the primary key. With MongoDB, the database will autogenerate a unique value for each document's `_id` attribute, which can be used as the primary key. Or, we can generate a **Universally Unique Identifier (UUID)**, such as `e7f71282-37c6-41fe-a413-8fc0d4d32eed`, in the application and use it as the value of a primary key. All of these system-generated primary keys are called surrogate keys.

Foreign keys

Foreign keys are the way to build relationships between different types of entities. For example, in the one-to-many relationship between team creators and teams, the Team entities will have an attribute Creator ID, which holds the value of the primary key of the team creator. We will talk about this in detail when we build the logical data model.

Goals of data modeling

As we mentioned at the beginning of this chapter, data modeling is an essential step in the creation of an application. It is the step that you don't want to skip. Even in a project where you don't want to create any other documents, data models should still be one that is worth the investment of your time and effort.

So, what do we want to archive with data modeling? Let's talk about this before starting data modeling for the TaskAgile application.

Completeness

The first goal of data modeling is to achieve completeness in covering the requirements of an application. However, this doesn't mean that we need all of the requirements of an application upfront when we start the data modeling, which adopts more of a waterfall way. The data models we design should be able to support the implementing of the features specified in the requirements that are currently available.

And, it also means that during data modeling, we should include those business rules that need to be applied to the database level so that we can be confident with the stored data.

Minimal redundancy

The second goal of data modeling is to achieve **minimal redundancy** in our database. When we store the same data multiple times or store a piece of data that can be derived from other data, we bring in redundancy to our database. Most of the time, redundancy is bad. The extra space that is required to store the redundant data is not the main reason for us to get rid of redundancy. It is the extra effort and the potential inconsistency in the data that require our effort to achieve minimal redundancy in data models.

For example, for our User entities, we will have a first name attribute and last name attribute. And, if we added another attribute, say, initials, which can be calculated based on the first name and last name, we introduced redundant data, and every time we changed the names, we would also have to update the initials and if somehow, which could happen, we forgot to do that, there would be inconsistency in our database. And it should be avoided when we design the data models.

On the other hand, sometimes we need to add redundant data, mainly for the performance improvement that it will provide. However, during conceptual data modeling, we should get rid of redundancy first, then, explicitly only add those that can improve performance during logical data modeling.

Extensibility

Another goal that we want to achieve during data modeling is extensibility. That is, the data models we build should be able to be extended to accommodate new requirements with minimal impact on the existing data structure, and the effort required to make those changes should be small. Being extensible doesn't mean that the data models should be able to adapt to all kinds of changes, which is impossible and usually leads to the model becoming over-designed. The extensibility that we should achieve is based on a deep understanding of the application requirements, and also through discussions with business specialists to foresee possible requirements in the near future. For example, in the TaskAgile application, we don't have the requirement to create organizations above teams or provide the ability to invite people to join a team (in the current user stories, we only allow adding people to boards). These are examples of features that we might need to implement in the next version. And, when we design the data models, we definitely need to keep these in mind and make sure we have extensibility in our data models.

Consistency

The **consistency** we talk about here is mainly about consistency in the naming of the entities and attributes of our data models, as well as consistency in the language that we use to discuss and communicate the requirements at the application level. For example, if the business specialists use team creator to refer to the user who created a team, in the data model, we should also use team creator instead of other terms, such as team owner. And we should have a naming convention to enforce the consistency. We will talk about naming convention for data modeling later.

Conceptual data modeling with ER diagrams

Now, let's start the conceptual data modeling for our TaskAgile application. First of all, let's go over the notation that we will use to create ER diagrams.

Crow's foot notation

The notation we use in this book is crow's foot notation. We use rectangles to represent entities. For example, the following represents **User** entities and **Team** Entities:

Figure 5.2: Entities

And, we use a line to connect rectangles to represent a relationship. For example, *Figure 5.3* represents the relationship between **User** entities and **Team** entities:

Figure 5.3: The relationship between User and Team

In this relationship, the symbol with double perpendicular lines on the left side means *one and only one,* and the symbol on the right side that is similar to a crow's foot means *zero or many.* It reads like this from left to right—*Each user may create zero or many teams.* And, it is like this when reading from right to left—*Each team must be created by one and only one user.*

Here are the relationship symbols in crow's foot notation:

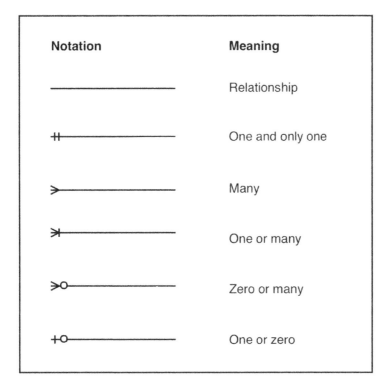

Figure 5.4: Relationship symbols in crow's foot notation

 The tool used to create the ER diagram is draw.io (`https://www.draw.io`). It is a great tool, and it is free and available as an online version as well as a desktop version. Also, you can use it to create many other types of diagrams besides ER diagrams.

The naming convention

In order to achieve consistency in the data models, we need to have a naming convention for the ER diagrams. The following is the one used in this book. You can choose the one that you see fit. The goal here is to be consistent:

- Entity names must be singular and non-collective. For example, **User** and **Team** but not Users, Teams, nor User Table. One exception is **Card List**, which is actually the name in the requirement.
- Entity names must be in title case. For example, **Board Member** rather than Board member, nor board member.
- Relationship names must be in infinitive form. For example, **create** rather than creates and **be created by** rather than is created by.
- Attribute names must be in title case.

TaskAgile conceptual data models

We start the conceptual data modeling by going through the user stories and finding the entities and the relationships between entities. We will leave the attributes to the logical data modeling stage, so we can focus on the high-level views of the data requirements and avoid being bogged down by details. Now, let's start going through user stories.

As mentioned before, the User entities and Team entities are in a one-to-many relationship, which covers the users and teams themes in the user stories.

And, based on the user story, Create personal board, that was created in Chapter 4, *TaskAgile - A Trello-like Task Management Tool*, we can see that there will be **Board** entities and the relationship between the **User** entities and **Board** entities is also a one-to-many relationship, as shown in *Figure 5.5*:

Figure 5.5: Relationship between User and Board

And, based on the user story, Create team board, that was created in Chapter 4, *TaskAgile - A Trello-like Task Management Tool*, we can discover that there is a relationship between **Board** entities and **Team** entities, which is a one-to-many relationship, as shown in *Figure 5.6*:

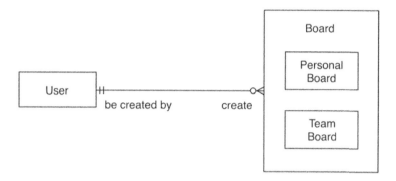

Figure 5.6: Relationship between Team and Board

In *Figure 5.6*, the relationship reads like this—*A Team may contain zero or many Boards, and a Board may belong to zero Teams when it is a personal board, or one team when it is a team board.* Wait, it seems that the relationship has hidden information about distinguishing between a personal board and team board. It would be better that we make this distinction explicit in the diagram by creating two subtypes of **Board** entities: **Personal Board** and **Team Board**, as shown in *Figure 5.7*:

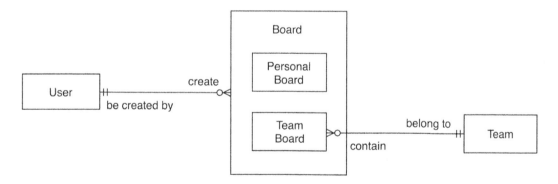

Figure 5.7: Relationship between User and Personal Board, and Team and Team Board

As you can see, we update the cardinality on Team's end from zero or one to one and only one, because a **Team Board** must belong to one and only one **Team**.

This is still not accurate because, based on this diagram, the relationship between **User** entities and **Team Board** entities is *Each User may create zero or many Team Boards*. That is, any registered user can add a board to any team, even those teams that are not created by that user. This is wrong. The correct logic should be that only a team creator can add boards to a team. And it is also wrong in the Create team board user story, which says *As a registered user*. It should be *As a team creator*. Let's correct the Create team board user story to the following:

- **Title—Create team board**: As a team creator, I can add a board to my team so that I can organize the tasks of that team, and we should also use **Team Creator** as a subtype of **User**. *Figure 5.8* is the revised diagram using subtypes of **User** and **Board**:

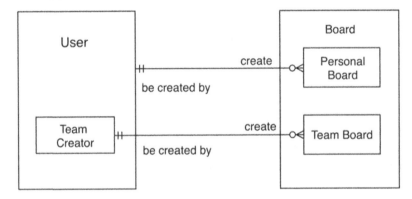

Figure 5.8: Subtypes of User and Board

Based on the diagram, one **Team Creator** can also create zero or many **Personal Boards**, which makes sense because a **Team Creator** is also a **User**. Or does it really make sense? We will come back to this later. For now, let's move on.

Based on the user story, Add board member that was created in Chapter 4, *TaskAgile - A Trello-like Task Management Tool*, we can see that there is another relationship between **User** and **Board**, which is a many-to-many relationship, as shown in *Figure 5.9*. In fact, when a user creates a board, that user should become the first member of that board. So, a **Board** must have one or many **Users** as its members:

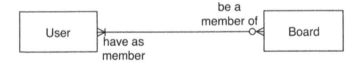

Figure 5.9: Another relationship between User and Board

Based on the user story, View board activities that was created in Chapter 4, *TaskAgile – A Trello-like Task Management Tool*, we can see there is a new type of entity, **Board Activity**. The relationship between **Board** and **Board Activity** is a one-to-many relationship, and the relationship between **Board Member** and **Board Activity** is a one-to-many relationship, as shown in *Figure 5.10*:

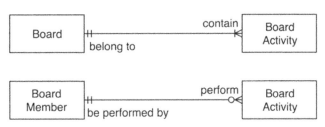

Figure 5.10: Board Member and Board Activity, Board and Board Activity

In the relationship between **Board** and **Board Activity**, the cardinality on the **Board Activity** end is a one or many cardinality because, when a board is created, there will be a **Board Creation Activity** generated. Hence, each **Board** must have at least one **Board Activity**

Based on the user story, Create card list, that was created in Chapter 4, *TaskAgile – A Trello-like Task Management Tool*, we can find the **Card List** entities and the relationship between **Board Member** and **Card List** is a one-to-many relationship. And, the relationship between **Board** and **Card List** is also a one-to-many relationship, as shown in *Figure 5.11*:

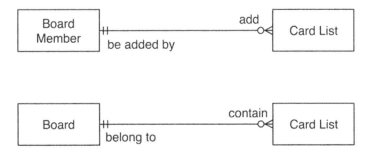

Figure 5.11: Card List

Here, **Board Member** is a subtype of **User**. We use **Board Member** instead of **User**, because not every user can add a card list in a board. Only those who are members of that board can do it. If we replaced **Board Member** with **User**, this business rule would be missing.

There are no new entities or relationships in the other user stories in the Card Lists theme. Let's move on to user stories in the Cards theme.

Based on the user story, Add card, that was created in `Chapter 4`, *TaskAgile – A Trello-like Task Management Tool*, we can find a new entity **Card**, and its relationship with **Board Member** is a one-to-many relationship, and its relationship with **Card List** is also a one-to-many relationship, as shown in *Figure 5.12*:

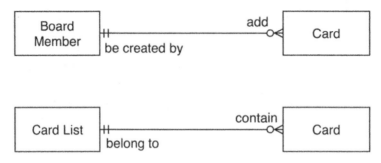

Figure 5.12: Card.

Based on the user story, Assign member to card, we can find another relationship between **Board Member** and **Card**, which is a many-to-many relationship, as shown in *Figure 5.13*:

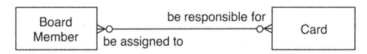

Figure 5.13: Board Member and Card

Based on the user story, Add card attachment, from `Chapter 4`, *TaskAgile – A Trello-like Task Management Tool*, we can see a new entity Attachment. The relationship between **Board Member** and **Attachment** is a one-to-many relationship. The relationship between **Card** and **Attachment** is a one-to-many relationship, as shown in *Figure 5.14*:

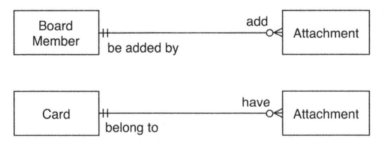

Figure 5.14: Board Member and Attachment, and Card and Attachment

Based on the user story, Add card comment created in Chapter 4, *TaskAgile – A Trello-like Task Management Tool* we can see that there is another type of entity, **Comment**. The relationship between **Board Member** and **Comment** is a one-to-many relationship. And the relationship between **Card** and **Comment** is also a one-to-many relationship, as shown in *Figure 5.15*:

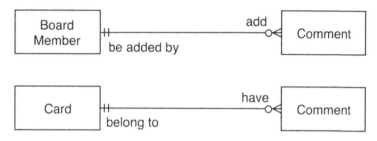

Figure 5.15: Board Member and Comment, and Card and Comment

Based on the user story, View card activities, that was created in Chapter 4, *TaskAgile – A Trello-like Task Management Tool*, we can find a new type of entity, **Card Activity**. And the relationship between **Board Member** and **Card Activity** is a one-to-many relationship, and the relationship between **Card** and **Card Activity** is also a one-to-many relationship, as shown in *Figure 5.16*:

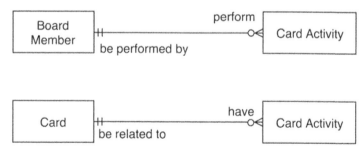

Figure 5.16: Board Member and Card Activity, and Card and Card Activity

Figure 5.17 is the ER diagram with all of the entities and relationships we have discovered:

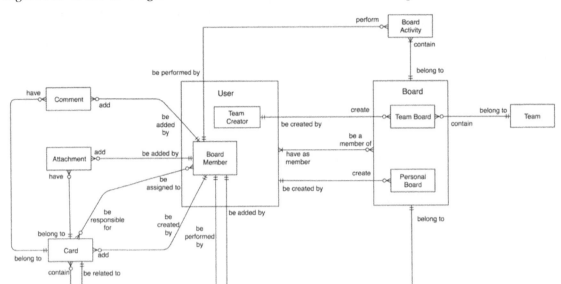

Figure 5.17: Conceptual data model of TaskAgile

If you take a closer look, you can see the relationship between **User** entities and **Board** entities is a membership relationship. But, we also have **Board Member** entities as a subtype of the **User** entities. As you can see, something smells here. It would become more obvious when we only have those relevant in the diagram, as shown in *Figure 5.18*:

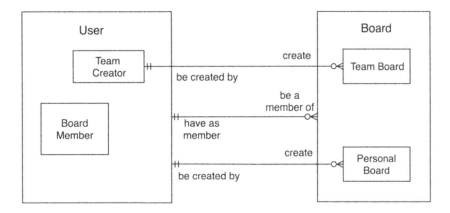

Figure 5.18: The part that smells

Let's do a test on the relationship between **Board Member** and **Board** based on this diagram. Since we make **Board Member** a subtype of **User**, it should inherit the relationship of its supertype. Therefore, the relationship reads like this from left to right: *A Board Member may be a member of zero of many Boards*. This can't be right because a **Board Member** must belong to one and only one **Board**. That's why it is called **Board Member**. To fix this, we will have to change the have as member/be of member of relationship. However, if we change it, the relationship between **User** and the **Board** will be wrong.

So, there is something wrong with this part. If it is not the relationship, it must be the entities. And, based on the test we just did, **Board Member** entities do not inherit that membership relationship of **User** entities. It means that they are not a subtype and supertype, even though it sounds true when you say **Board Member** is a subtype of **User**. Actually, it is true when they have the **Board Member** role and **User** role in the application.

Subtypes and supertypes

In data modeling, a subtype and its supertype share common attributes, and the relationships between the supertype and other entities can also be applied to the subtype. You can use this a rule to test two types of entities to see if they are subtype and supertype. If you try this with **Personal Board** and **Team Board**, you can see they are subtypes of **Board**. And if you test **Team Creator** with this rule, you can see it is not a subtype of **User**. *Figure 5.19* shows the corrected data model of TaskAgile:

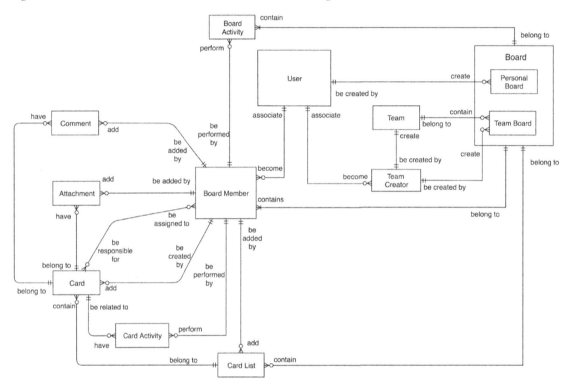

Figure 5.19: Revised conceptual data model of TaskAgile

Logical data modeling

Now, let's create the logical data models of TaskAgile. In this stage, we will add attributes to each type of entity in the conceptual data model by going through user stories by theme and implementing the relationships between entities, as well as the subtypes we used.

Based on Users theme and Teams theme, we create the following logical data models:

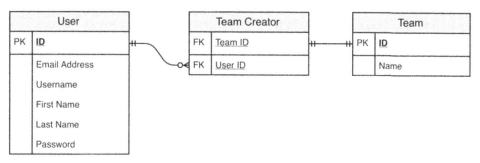

Figure 5.20: Logical data model of User and Team entities

As you can see in *Figure 5.20*, for **User** entities, we use surrogate key **ID** as its primary key because even though **Email Address** and **Username** can be used to identify a user, they can be changed. The system-generated **ID** will always stay the same. It is the same for **Team** entities. And the **User ID** attribute in the **Team Creator** entities is a foreign key. In the diagram, **PK** is short for **Primary Key**, and **FK** is short for **Foreign Key**. And, in **Team Creator** entities, the **Team ID** and **User ID** attributes form a composite key that can be used to uniquely identify a **Team Creator**.

Based on the user stories in the Boards theme, we update the logical data model, as shown in *Figure 5.21*:

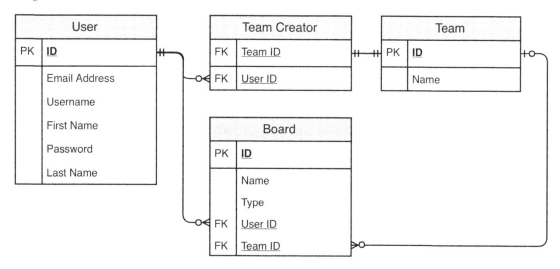

Figure 5.21: Logical data model with Board entities

In the conceptual data model, we have **Personal Board** and **Team Board** as subtypes of **Board**. Here, we only have **Board**. In the **Board** entities, we add an attribute, **Type**, to distinguish **Personal Board** and **Team Board**, and a foreign key, **User ID**, to build the create relationship between **User** entities and **Board** entities. And the foreign key, **Team ID**, is to build the one-to-many relationship between **Team** entities and **Board** entities.

As you can see, both **Board** entities and **Team Creator** entities have the foreign key **Team ID** and foreign key **User ID**, that can be used to identify the user who creates the team. However, based on this logical data model, the user who adds the board doesn't necessarily have to be a team creator. It can be anyone. If you want to enforce the constraint that only team creator can add a board on the database level, you can change the design, as shown in *Figure 5.22*:

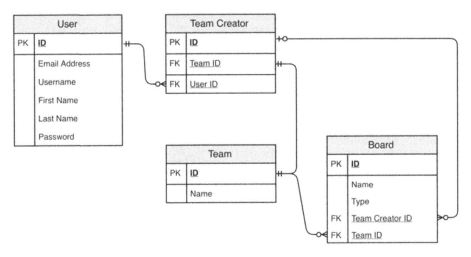

Figure 5.22: Enforce team creator constraint

As you can see, we add attribute **ID** to **Team Creator** entities and foreign key **Team Creator ID** to **Board** entities. This will make sure all of the boards are created by **Team Creator**. However, this could be the root of the rework when we need to allow other team members to create boards. The design in *Figure 5.21* provides extensibility, which makes it a better design from this perspective. As a tradeoff, we can enforce the constraint in the application's code. Another reason we should not use **Team Creator ID** in **Board** entities is that there will be an extra join of tables to query boards by **User ID**.

You might have noticed that in *Figure 5.21*, for Boards that are personal, the value of attribute **Team ID** will be null, and this is allowed. Foreign keys can have null values.

The following *Figure 5.23* is the logical data model with **Board**, **Board Member**, **Board Activity**, and **User** entities. For simplicity, we will keep **Team Creator** out of the diagram:

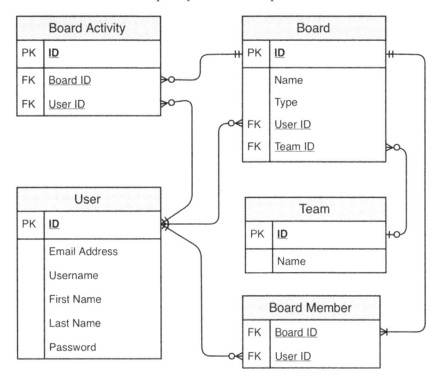

Figure 5.23: Logical data model with Board, Board Member, Board Activity, and Team

In **Board Member**, foreign key **Board ID** and foreign key **User ID** form a composite key that can be used to uniquely identify a board member. We use this composite key in **Board Activity** entities. And, between **Board Activity** entities and **User** entities, there is a one-to-many relationship. This is not the same as how it is in the conceptual data model, in which it is the **Board Activity** entities and **Board Member** entities that have the one-to-many relationship. The reason we make this adjustment is that we don't want to add a primary key **ID** to **Board Member** and use that primary key in **Board Activity** since **Board Activity** already has the **Board ID** attribute and **User ID** attribute, which is a composite key that can be used to identify a board member.

And, in the conceptual data model, **Board Member** has relationships with **Card List**, **Card**, **Comment**, **Attachment**, and **Card Activity**. For the same reason, we will use the composite key, `<Board ID and User ID>`, to build those relationships.

The following *Figure 5.24* is the logical data model with **Card**, **Card List**, and other related entities:

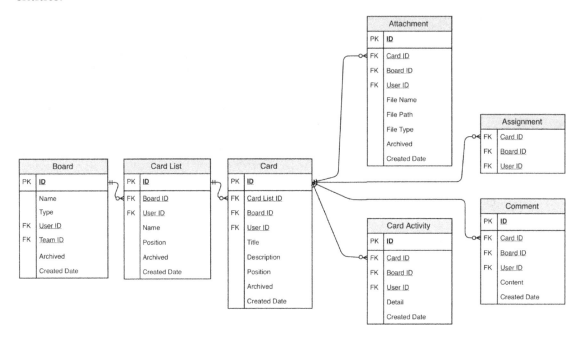

Figure 5.24: Logical data model with Card, Card List, and related entities

In this diagram, as you can see, we use the **Board Member** composite key (**Board ID**, and **User ID**) in **Card List**, **Card**, **Attachment**, **Card Activity**, **Assignment**, and **Comment** entities. But this has caused data redundancy, mainly with the **Board ID**. The reason **Board ID** is redundant is because it can be derived from other attributes. For example, the **Board ID** in the **Card** entities can be derived from **Card List** entities through the **Card List ID** in the **Card** entities. Another issue with this design is that when we need to implement a feature in the future, for example, moving cards between boards, we will have to update all of the **Board ID** in all those entities, which will cause not only the performance issue, but also data inconsistency. And the effort to solve these issues in the future would be significant.

So, let's remove **Board ID** from **Card**, **Attachment**, **Card Activity**, **Assignment**, and **Comment**. This will leave the **User ID** in these entities. And the relationships between **Board Member** and these entities will be moved to **User** entities. And because of this, we will need to enforce the constraint that only a board member can perform these related actions in the application code. With this adjustment, our data model will have no redundant **Board ID** and will also be extendable.

And, as you can see in *Figure 5.24*, we add the **Archived** attribute to entities that need to support being restored after removing. That is, when a card has been archived, the value of the **Archived** attribute will be `true` and the card will not show up in the UI. And a board member can restore it from the activities list of that board.

One more thing before we do the removal of **Board ID**. Let's take a second look at Board Activity, **Card Activity**, and the user story, View board activities, which goes as follows:

> *As a board member, I can view activities of everything in that board so that I can understand what happened within that board.*

This description is vague. What does everything include? It needs to be specified. Such is the moment when the data modeler needs to have an in-depth discussion with the business specialist.

For this version of TaskAgile, let's add the support of tracking the following activities:

• Create board	• Move card
• Add member to board	• Archive card
• Create card list	• Delete card
• Rename card list	• Add card attachment
• Archive card list	• Delete card attachment
• Add card	• Add card comment
• Edit card title	• Edit card comment
• Assign member to card	• Delete card comment

And, if we use Board Activity to refer to the first two activities, *Create board* and *Add member to board* in the preceding list, we will also need to have another new type of entity, Card List Activity, to refer those activities to card lists. And, in this way, we will have three types of entities: Board Activity, Card List Activity, and Card Activity.

This separation will cause issues when we need to pull data from three entities to render a list so that board members can view activities of everything in that board. For example, if by default a board member can view the latest 15 activities, we will need to pull 15 activities from each of these entities and combine them into a single sorted list, and then return only the latest 15 items as the result. This still seems manageable. But, how about getting activities from 16 to 30? The complexity of the implementation and performance issue is a sign of a bad data model design.

The following figure is the revised logical data model:

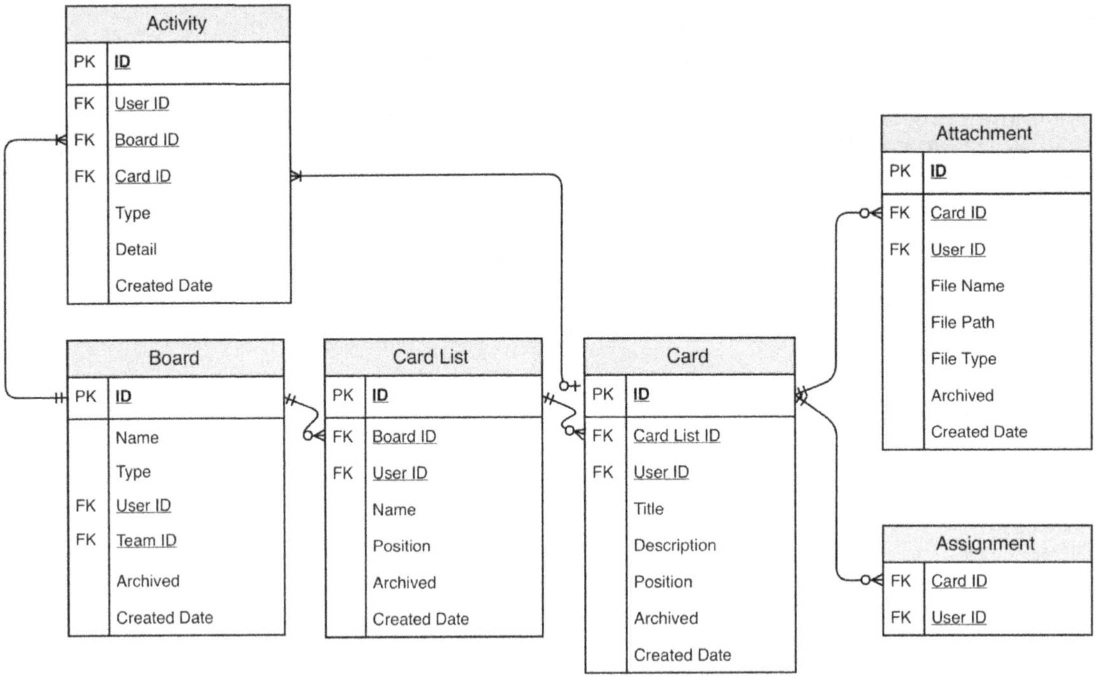

Figure 5.25: Revised logical data model with Card, Card List, and related entities

As you can see, we introduce **Activity** entities that will store activities of all the actions we listed, and also card comments. In this way, we can render card activities and card comments in the same timeline with much simpler queries. The **Type** attribute of **Activity** entities is for indicating if a record is an activity log, or if it is a card comment. And, the **Card ID** attribute is a foreign key, and the value of this attribute will be null if an activity is not related to a card. The **Detail** attribute will contain detailed data that is stored in JSON format. Since we use these generic **Activity** entities to store all the activities as well as card comments, we don't need **Comment** entities.

Let's put all the entities in one diagram, as shown in *Figure 5.26*. And, in this version, we add foreign key **User ID** to **Team** entities and remove **Team Creator** entities. The reason for that is because **Team** entities and **Team Creator** entities are a one-to-one relationship, and there is no other additional attribute beside **User ID**. One benefit we get from this change is that we can avoid a join of tables to query teams by **User ID**.

And, as you can see, there are many differences between the conceptual data model and the logical data model. Some of the constraints that we have in the conceptual data model have to be moved to the application's code so that we have better extensibility in the design as well as performance improvement with fewer joins of tables:

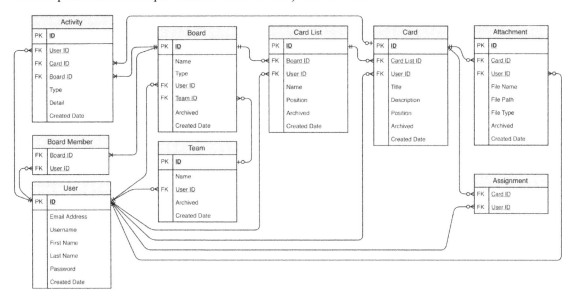

Figure 5.26: Complete logical data model

By now, we have finished conceptual data modeling and logical data modeling by taking a top-down approach, that is, we build the high-level conceptual data model first and then based on that build the logical data model. And now, let's create the physical data model based on the logical data model.

Physical data modeling for RDBMS

In this stage, we will convert the logical data model into the physical data model of the target RDBMS. As mentioned, we will use MySQL and will create the physical data model using MySQL Workbench.

Here is what we are going to do:

- Create a table for each entity.
- Create a column for each attribute. Besides the name, we will define columns type, length, nullability, and default value.
- Make primary keys auto increment.
- Create indexes.

The naming convention

The naming convention of the physical data model has some differences with the naming convention of the logical data model:

- We will use lowercase for tables, columns, and indexes, for example, the `user` table. And we will use underscore to connect multiple words, for example, the `card_list` table.
- For foreign key definition, the key's name starts with `fk_`. The naming convention of the foreign keys is `fk_<referencing table name>_<referenced table name>_<referencing field name>`. For example, the foreign key of the `user_id` field in the `activity` table is `fk_activity_user_user_id`.
- For index definition, the index name will end with `_idx`, or `_uidx` if it is a unique index.

The reason we use lowercase is that MySQL is case-sensitive in Linux/Unix and not case-sensitive in Windows. Making everything in lowercase can avoid issues caused by a mixture of difference cases.

The figure here is that of the physical data model of the TaskAgile application:

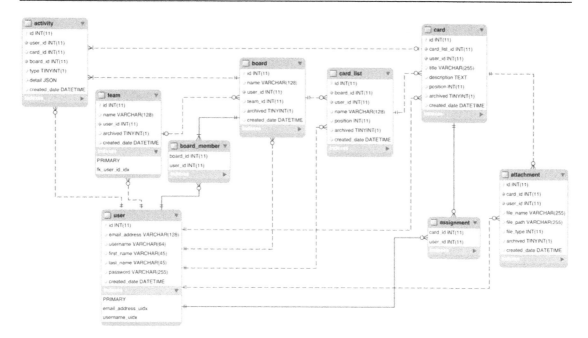

Figure 5.27: Physical data model of the TaskAgile application

The diagram created with MySQL Workbench is an **enhanced-entity-relationship** (**EER**) diagram. It uses solid lines to represent identifying relationships and dash lines to represent non-identifying relationships.

An identifying relationship means a child table cannot be uniquely identified without the parent table. For example, in the board_member table, the board_id column and the user_id column is the primary key. And, without a board ID or a user ID, a board member record cannot be uniquely identified. In other words, a relationship is an identifying relationship when the foreign key is part of the child table's primary key.

And, with MySQL Workbench, we can export our physical data model as a DDL script that can be used to set up our database.

 You can find the exported database setup SQL file, database-setup.sql, and the MySQL Workbench data model file, TaskAgilePhysicalDataModel.mwb, in the source code of this chapter.

Physical data modeling for MongoDB

Data stored in MongoDB has a very flexible schema. When we do the physical data modeling for MongoDB, instead of defining the structure of schemas, we write validators to enforce the rules on the fields that we have in our data model. In this way, we can make sure that each document in the collection will have those required fields we specified in the validator and they will be in the data type we require. And, as a naming convention of MongoDB, all of the collection's names will be plural, for example, User entities will be stored in collection users.

Let's look at an example; the following is a MongoDB script (for MongoDB Version 3.6 and later) that is used to create the `teams` collection. As you can see, most of this script is defining validation rules:

```
db.createCollection( "teams",{
    "storageEngine": {"wiredTiger": {}},
    "capped": false,
    "validator": {
        "$jsonSchema": {
            "bsonType": "object",
            "additionalProperties": false,
            "properties": {
                "_id": {"bsonType": "objectId"},
                "name": {"bsonType": "string"},
                "user_id": {"bsonType": "objectId"},
                "archived": {"bsonType": "bool"},
                "created_date": {"bsonType": "timestamp"}
            },
            "required": [
                "_id",
                "name",
                "user_id",
                "archived",
                "created_date"
            ]
        }
    },
    "validationLevel": "strict",
    "validationAction": "error"
});
```

Due to the scope of this book, we will not go through this script. You can find all of the MongoDB scripts for creating all of the entities defined in the logical data model in the source code of this chapter.

Summary

In this chapter, you have learned what data modeling is and the three stages of data modeling—conceptual data modeling, logical data modeling, and physical data modeling, as well as the deliverable of each stage.

You also learned the goals of performing data modeling, and how to do conceptual data modeling and logical data modeling using ER diagrams. You also learned how to create a physical data model for MySQL using MySQL Workbench, and you have seen the MongoDB script that is used to define scheme rules.

In the next chapter, we will discuss the code design of the application.

6
Code Design - Designing for Stability and Extensibility

Code design, or software design, is often thought of as a disjoint step in the development process of an application. A set of UML diagrams is the most common way to document designs. However, they will quickly become obsolete once the code has been written. There are differences between the implementation and the design, and those differences are not synced back to the design documents. The effort of keeping design documents up-to-date is considerable because there are always changes in the requirements. It feels like a battle that we keep losing.

So, should we do code design? Is it really necessary? Because we have the data models now, why don't we just start writing the code and get features implemented? We can refactor our code later, anyway. This sounds more Agile.

There is an old saying in China, *Grinding a chopper will not delay the work of cutting firewood.* Doing code design is like grinding a chopper where cutting firewood is like writing code.

So, let's talk more about code design, especially how to do it the correct way in an Agile project. In this chapter, you will learn about the following topics:

- Agile code design
- Design principles and design patterns
- TaskAgile code design

Agile code design

Most of the time, when we talk about doing code design, or software design, the first thing that pops up is drawing UML diagrams. UML diagrams are part of a design, but it is not the design. So, what is code design exactly?

What is code design?

Robert C. Martin said the following in his book, *Agile Software Development: Principles, Patterns, and Practices* (Martin, 2002):

> *The design of a software project is an abstract concept. It has to do with the overall shape and structure of the program as well as the detailed shape and structure of each module, class, and method. It can be represented by many different media, but its final embodiment is source code. In the end, the source code is the design.*

Wait for a second, how can the source code be the design? This doesn't make sense, does it? The source code is part of the final software product itself. If source code were the design, we wouldn't need to do design anymore because we just need to write code. This seems absurd, right?

This **fresh** point of view might strike you. And here, we will not try to prove that the source code is the design, as Jack W. Reeves wasn't proving it in his visionary essay *What is Software Design?*, which was first published in Fall, 1992 in the C++ journal, now available on developer.* (`http://www.developerdotstar.com/mag/articles/reeves_design_main.html`).

As a matter of fact, the idea that the source code is the design is not a formula that needs to be proved. It's just a different opinion about the relationship between software design and coding, looking from a different angle. And it is always a good idea to get a second opinion.

Traditional angle

Now, let's look at the relationship between the source code and coding from a traditional angle. The word **traditional** here doesn't imply that this angle is old. Actually, by 2018, the idea that the source code is the design is 26 years old, since Reeves published his essay.

Traditionally, when we talk about software design and coding, we often compare this relationship with the one between design blueprints and the process by which engineers build houses, or with the one between car design and car manufacturing. With this assumption, we require up-front software design to guide us during the implementation of the application.

However, how many times have we found that we cannot follow a design to write the code because something is missing in the design or the requirement has been changed? And the design documents become obsolete the moment the code is written. You might think that this is because the effort put into code design isn't enough or the design isn't comprehensive enough to cover all of the requirements. Based on that, you demand to allocate more time for designing before writing the code. In reality, this doesn't always work.

Here is what is common in software application development. At the beginning of a project, a clean and elegant code design is crafted. However, with new features being added or changes being implemented, things start to go wrong. The code isn't following the design anymore, and in order to catch up with a tight schedule that is already behind, developers are forced to make compromises between getting it done right and getting it done fast. And then, the code becomes messy and turns into a pile of **spaghetti code**. You could see a lot of hacks and comments such as *Refactor it later. This is a hack. Will come up with a better solution later* in the code. And then, a simple change to a feature would cascade to other parts of the code, even those that are not related, and the cost of maintenance rises exponentially. This means that the existing code has become so fragile that developers start to write new code around it, which makes things worse, and eventually, they tell their managers that, without a redesign or a rewrite, no more changes can be implemented, because they might break other features that are already working, and it would take weeks, even months, to fix those potential issues.

Will a redesign solve this problem? It seems optimistic because now we have a much better idea of the features of the application. A redesign can embody those changes not included in the initial design. However, as said by Robert C. Martin in his book *Agile Software Development: Principles, Patterns, and Practices*, such redesigns rarely succeed. This is because the old system will continue to evolve and change, and the new design must catch up. There will always be changes that the designer can't foresee unless there is a crystal ball. Even when the new design reaches its first release, it might be just the beginning of another round of the cycle.

A second angle

Writing code is a process of getting your understanding of the requirements, and the thoughts of how to implement those requirements, out of your head in the form of code that's written in the programming languages that you prefer. Creating design documents is a process of outlining solutions that you have in your mind in a form other than code, for example, UML diagrams. Essentially, code and design documents are the media that represent your thoughts.

Design documents are useful because they are the outlines of your solution. You can use them as guidance through code writing. And during writing code, usually, you can get inspiration for the solution. New ideas will come up or you will find flaws in the outlines. Eventually, the solution is written into the source code. From a product perspective, the only thing that is used to create the final product is also the source code, which is built into zeros and ones by computers. From this angle, you can think of computers as the workers in a factory, and the source code is the design they use to create products.

Differences between the two angles

What're the differences between this angle and the traditional one? The biggest difference is that, in the traditional view, the design process and the coding process are two disjointed steps. This separation cuts off the design activity from the coding activity. That is, you only do design in the design stage and you only write code in the implementation stage. This is, in fact, a failure to recognize that, when writing code inside our brain, what's happening is not a simple translation from the design to the source code, but an intense creative activity carried out by the brain.

On the other hand, when we say the source code is the design, it doesn't mean we are against using UML diagrams or any other tools and notations. In fact, we should use anything that helps to create the design. It's just that we must keep in mind that the source code is the final design and the other design documents are auxiliary documentation, which is as important for a software project as design blueprints are for building a house.

In this book, we consider that the source code is the design. And before we talk about how to do code design in Agile projects, let's look at different levels of code design.

Levels of code design

In Jack W. Reeves's essay, *What Is Software Design: 13 Years Later*, he mentioned three levels of design:

> *I would say we need good architectures (top level design), good abstractions (class design), and good implementations (low level design).*

Here, we will rephrase it into architecture level design, abstraction level design, and implementation level design.

Architecture level

In the design of this level, you can find answers to questions like the following:

- Is the system going to use the multilayer design?
- Is it a monolith or does it use microservices?
- What are subsystems, and how do they communicate using SOAP, REST, or AMQP?
- Is there any interaction with third-party systems? How do they communicate?

This level of design is fundamental and, most of the time, you do the architectural design up-front and, once it is done, you don't change it unless there is something fundamentally wrong or if the implementation of requirement changes would be impossible without a redesign at this level. You write the design of this level in design documents because figuring out the architecture level design by going through the source code is often a daunting experience and impossible when there is a significant amount of code built around that architecture.

Abstraction level

At this level, the design focuses on the packages and main components of a subsystem, and it should stay as a high-level design. You usually keep it in a design document or in the package—`info.java` class if it is relatively simple. The design of this level provides an abstract overview of a subsystem. You should only include only key classes and their relationship in the design. Any other details should be avoided as much as possible. When you look at the design of this level, you should be able to understand the structure and the main logic of that subsystem.

You do the abstraction level design when you start the implementation of a subsystem. Usually, the design at this level is, or is close to, stable. During the implementation, you might improve it as you gain more insight into the logic of the application. However, you should not need to change it often. Otherwise, this implies that there must be something wrong with the design itself.

Implementation level

At this level, the design focuses on the implementation of classes, mainly fields, and methods. It is full of details with concrete and low-level information. The source code is the main representation of the design at this level. You might create some UML diagrams for complicated logic, but you should keep them minimal because details change, and they change a lot. You certainly don't want to put too much effort into having to update those diagrams. Instead, you should invest more time in the source code itself. Keep it clean, simple, and expressive.

And at this level, because of these changes, there will be a lot of refactoring going on to keep the design as good as it can be.

Devil in the details

If you think of the design of the three levels that we just talked about is like a house, the architecture level is like the foundation and overall structure of that house; once you've built it, you don't change it. The abstraction level is like the walls inside that house. Sometimes, you might add another wall to divide a big room into two smaller ones, or you might tear down a wall to create more space. But you do not need to do that often. The implementation level is like the furniture, carpets, wallpaper, curtains, and so on, which are all those small and movable items in a house. You can change these frequently, for example, you can move the sofa closer to the TV, replace the dining table with a new one, or do another round of redecoration. You also need to keep cleaning the house on a regular basis. Otherwise, it will turn into a mess, no matter how beautiful it was in its initial design.

In a software application, all of the details are in the source code, and that is also the part that requires your constant effort to keep it clean, simple, and expressive. Otherwise, you will see the devil in the details.

Symptoms of bad design

When the devil in the details appears something is seriously wrong with the design. Usually, you will see symptoms of bad designs in the code.

The following are the design smells that Robert C. Martin mentioned in his book, *Agile Software Development: Principles, Patterns, and Practices*:

- **Rigidity**: The system is hard to change because every change forces many other changes to take place in other parts of the system
- **Fragility**: Changes cause the system to break in places that have no conceptual relationship to the part that was changed
- **Immobility**: It is hard to disentangle the system into components that can be reused in another system
- **Viscosity**: Doing things right is harder than doing things wrong
- **Needless complexity**: The design contains infrastructure that adds no direct benefit
- **Needless repetition**: The design contains repeating structures that could be unified under a single abstraction
- **Opacity**: It is hard to read and understand. It does not express its intent well

Among these design smells, rigidity, fragility, immobility, viscosity, and opacity are the symptoms of bad designs. Needless to say, complexity and needless repetition are two of the causes of those symptoms. Let's look at all of these symptoms closer.

Rigidity

When a software becomes rigid, changes are hard to make; not because a change itself is complicated, but because all of the subsequent changes caused by that change are usually more than you expected. And, even worse, you might not have a way to verify that, after the change, the system will still function correctly unless you do a manual test of all the features affected by that change, which can be quite daunting for applications that are not small in size. Because of this, a small change could take days, even weeks to get done and verified, which is much longer than the initial estimate.

Fragility

When a software becomes fragile, it breaks often and most of the time unexpectedly, even if the change you make is a simple one and remotely unrelated. Developers are afraid of making changes to the existing code because they might break the system unintentionally. However, as long as the software isn't abandoned, changes always come along. Making changes to a fragile system would probably make it even more fragile, and the complexity of the system would increase with hacks and corner case covering code.

Opacity

When a system suffers from opacity, reading the code is hard, and understanding it is even harder. Maintaining such a system requires much more effort than those that have a clear and expressive code. There could be many causes of opacity, for example, bad naming, needless complexity, and overdesign. It is easy to make simple things complicated, while it is much harder to make complicated things simple.

Immobility

Immobility is the opposite of reusability. It doesn't mean that a system is badly design when it doesn't have parts that can be reused by other systems. It means that the effort to make a part of the code reusable by another system is too high when such reusability is required. When a system has an immobility symptom, it also has rigidity and fragility symptoms.

Viscosity

When software becomes viscous, developers tend to choose a way that is easy to implement among the different solutions to implement a change. However, they don't preserve the design and abandon solutions that will preserve the design that is harder to implement. This could be that the design itself is too complicated, and the lack of clearness makes it impossible to get it done within a tight schedule.

Agile code design practices

Up until this point, we have talked about what code design is, three levels of code design, and also the symptoms of bad designs. In this section, we will talk about the practices of Agile code design at various levels.

Architecture level

When we start a new project, usually, we already have an idea of what kind of application we are going to build and, at the top level, how the system works. We should be able to create an architecture level design. Sometimes, there might be some new technologies introduced, and you will need to do some research or create prototypes to verify your design.

Abstraction level

At the beginning of implementing a subsystem, we should do the abstraction level design for that subsystem or module. As mentioned previously, this design should avoid details and only provide high-level information. It serves more like guidance so that developers can understand how that subsystem or module works internally when it is done.

Implementation level

The design of the implementation level requires the most effort so that you can keep the code as good as it can be. There are several practices you need to adopt, such as the following:

- **Test-driven development**: At the implementation level, we must practice test-driven development. This is critical for an Agile project because we rely on these unit tests to make sure that the code we write runs correctly after refactoring. We also use unit tests as the client of the source code to help us improve the code design, make it decoupled, and also increase code quality. And when we have test cases to verify our code, we can do frequent refactoring to clean up the mess in the code so that the system won't suffer from all those symptoms we talked about.

- **Acceptance tests**: Besides unit tests, we should also write acceptance tests to verify the details of user stories specified by the customer. These acceptance tests need to be able to run repeatedly. They provide a higher level of verification than the unit tests. Together, unit tests and acceptance tests act to verify the implementation level design and provide confidence during refactoring.

- **Refactoring**: Another practice, which we mentioned several times, is refactoring. It is like reorganizing the furniture of your house or doing housekeeping to prevent things from becoming messy. Refactoring is a technique to improve your design by changing the code in order to apply a design principle or use a design pattern whenever it is necessary. That is, when you write code, you start from simple and only write enough code to make it pass the test cases. No more, no less. In this way, you keep a simple design in the implementation level, and only when there is a change or a smell in the code do you refactor it.

- **Focus on current stories**: When doing code design at the implementation level, you should focus on the user stories of the current sprint and design the code to be as good as it can be. Don't worry too much about future user stories. You can keep them in mind, but do not write code for them. Here are the reasons why:
  - Future stories might be changed or discarded. In such cases, the code written for future stories would bring needless complexity into the design.
  - You can write them when the time comes. You are not at much of an advantage by writing them earlier. On the contrary, you're taking risks when doing that.

To sum this up, in practice, we create high-level architecture level designs and abstraction level designs. At the implementation level, we do the following:

- We adopt test-driven development practice and write acceptance tests to detect the problem of the code
- We apply design principles to find out code smells
- We apply appropriate design patterns to solve the problem through refactoring

So, Agile code design is more of a process than a set of design documents or an event. Robert C. Martin defined it as follows:

> *It's the continuous application of principles, patterns, and practices to improve the structure and readability of the software. It is the dedication of keeping the design of the system as simple, clean, and expressive as possible at all times.*

Design principles and design patterns

We mentioned design principles and design patterns earlier. In this section, we will talk about them further. We will start with SOLID, which is an acronym of the five design principles we will introduce. Due to the scope of this book, we will only talk about related design patterns along the way.

The SOLID design principles were introduced in Robert C. Martin's book, *Agile Software Development: Principles, Patterns, and Practices*, in which he gave a detailed explanation and examples of these principles. Here, we will introduce them as the principles that we will apply in our TaskAgile application.

SOLID design principles

Let's start with the first five design principles:

- SRP: **The Single Responsibility Principle**
- OCP: **The Open-Closed Principle**
- LSP: **The Liskov Substitution Principle**
- ISP: **The Interface Segregation Principle**
- DIP: **The Dependency Inversion Principle**

The Single Responsibility Principle (SRP)

A class should have only one reason to change.

This principle is one of the simplest of the principles, yet the easiest to get confused about, mostly because of its name.

As mentioned in the book, *Agile Software Development: Principles, Patterns, and Practices*, a responsibility, in the context of the SRP, is *a reason for a change*. That is when you change a class, and if you can think of another reason to change it separately, such as at a different time, then that class violates the SRP.

Another interpretation is that responsibility is *an axis of change*. Inside a class, all of the changes should occur around a central point or a continuum. You can think of a class as a discussion room. In one room, people are talking about hobbies, such as hiking, skiing, diving, and playing football how they like it. And then someone mentions watching movies, and suddenly several people start to have an intense discussion about what movies they like the best, who their favorite characters are, and the details of the scenes in those movies. And at that point, it would be better to divide the group into two different rooms; one continues talking about hobbies and the other discusses movies. In this way, the discussion of either group won't be affected by the other group. In this metaphor, the topic *hobbies* are the axis of change.

As Martin said: *An axis of change is an axis of change only if the changes actually occur.*

So, if there is no intense discussion of movies but only a brief mention of them, then there is no reason to move those people to another discussion room.

Because of the name of this principle, it is easy to think that each class should do one thing and one thing only. If we follow that interpretation when we design classes, we will add needless complexity into the design because we will destroy the cohesion of a class, which has its code bound together closely for a single responsibility, even though that class seems to be doing different things. It will also decrease the readability of the code because you will need to jump between different, smaller classes to link the fragments to understand the logic.

As a matter of fact, there is a principle saying that one method should do one, and only one, thing. However, that is for refactoring large methods into smaller ones, and it should be used at low-level design, which is the implementation level design.

The Open-Closed Principle (OCP)

A software artifact should be open for extension but closed for modification.

Bertrand Meyer coined the OCP in 1988, providing us with guidance on how to create a design that is stable in the face of changes.

Here, we're going to borrow the `DrawAllShapes` example from *Agile Software Development: Principles, Patterns, and Practices*, to explain this principle here. We will write the example in ES6; the unrelated details have been omitted:

```
class Circle extends Shape {
  constructor(radius, point) {
    this.type = 'circle'
    // ...
  }
}

class Square extends Shape {
  constructor(width, point) {
    this.type = 'square'
    // ...
  }
}

function drawCircle(circle) {
  // Draw circle logic here
}

function drawSquare(square) {
  // Draw square logic here
}
```

```
function drawAllShapes(shapes) {
  shapes.forEach((shape) => {
    if (shape.type === 'circle') {
      drawCircle(shape)
    } else if (shape.type === 'square') {
      drawSquare(shape)
    }
  })
}
```

As you can see, we have the `Circle` and `Square` classes, which extend `Shape`. Both of them have field types. `drawCircle()` and `drawSquare()` are two functions that are responsible for drawing circles and squares, respectively. Now, let's examine the `drawAllShapes()` function. It goes through an array of `shapes` and check each shape's type and call with the corresponding `draw` function to draw that shape. This `drawAllShapes()` function violates the OCP because it is not extendable without modification when we need to support new kinds of shapes. It is not closed against new changes.

We can refactor it to the following to make it conform to the OCP:

```
class Circle {
  //...
  draw() {
    // Draw circle logic here
  }
}

class Square {
  //...
  draw() {
    // Draw square logic here
  }
}

function drawAllShapes(shapes) {
  shapes.forEach((shape) => {
    shape.draw()
  })
}
```

As you can see, we move the draw function to each type of shape, and inside drawAllShapes() function, we simply call the draw() method of that shape. Now, the drawAllShapes() function supports Triangle, Rectangle, and any other type of shape, as long as it has a draw() function. This design now conforms to the OCP. It is changed by adding new code, such as Triangle and Rectangle, rather than changing existing code.

However, it is not really closed. It is closed to the requirement that needs to support a new type of shapes, but it is not closed against requirements, for example, if we need the application to draw all circles before drawing any square or we need to draw shapes in the order of their positions.

So, should we refactor our drawAllShapes() function to make it closed to the two requirements we just mentioned? No, not yet! We wait until the changes happen. That is, we only refactor the function when the change is needed. If it is still in the future, let's just wait for it. Because, as mentioned earlier, in an Agile project, changes happen frequently. Those requirements might be moved to the very end of the product backlog or might even no be longer needed. Refactoring it now will be an act of overdesign and the code will show the opacity symptom, not to mention the development time and effort to refactor it could be wasted.

The Liskov Substitution Principle (LSP)

In 1988, Barbara Liskov wrote this principle in the following way as a way to identify subtypes:

> *What is wanted here is something like the following substitution property: if for each object o1 of type S there is an object o2 of type T so that for all programs P defined in terms of T, the behavior of P is unchanged when o1 is substituted for o2, then S is a subtype of T.*

And it is paraphrased as the following by Robert C. Martin in his book, *Agile Software Development: Principles, Patterns, and Practices*:

> *Subtypes must be substitutable for their base types.*

Here, we're going to use the square/rectangle problem from *Agile Software Development: Principles, Patterns, and Practices*, as an example of a violation of LSP, since we know that, logically, a square is a rectangle. As shown in the following diagram, the Square class inherits from the Rectangle class. Usually, the inheritance is regarded as the **IS-A** relationship. The App class depends on the Rectangle class:

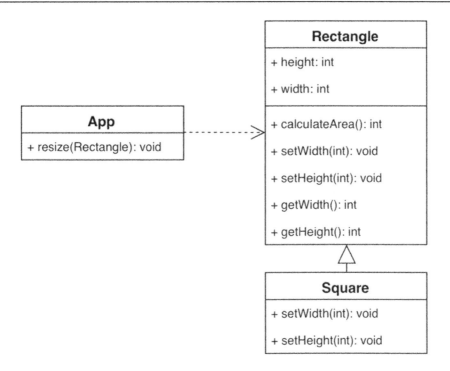

Figure 6.1: Rectangle and Square

As you can see, the `Rectangle` class has two fields and their setters and getters, as well as the `calculateArea()` method. In the `Square` class, the `setWidth()` and `setHeight()` methods override the setters in its base class.

The following is the code of the `Square` class and the `App` class. For the sake of brevity, the `Rectangle` class is not shown here:

```
public class Square extends Rectangle {
  public void setWidth(int width) {
    this.width = width;
    this.height = width;
  }
  public void setHeight(int height) {
    this.height = height;
    this.width = height;
  }
}

public class App {
  public void resize(Rectangle rectangle) {
```

```
        rectangle.setWidth(10);
        rectangle.setHeight(5);
        int area = rectangle.calculateArea();
        assert area == 50;
    }
}
```

As you can see in the `setWidth()` and `setHeight()` methods of the `Square` class, we keep the width and height the same value, which makes perfect sense.

So, what is the problem with this design? The problem is that inside the `resize()` method of the `App` class, when we call this method with an object of `Square`, the assertion will be `false`. After `rectangle.setHeight(5)`, inside that object, both the width and height will be at a value of 5. The value of `area` will be 25 instead of 50. However, the assertion will be `true` when the parameter we pass in is an object of `Rectangle`.

This is a violation of the LSP. The `Square` subtype cannot substitute its base type, `Rectangle`, in the `resize()` method. So, why this is a problem? Because, from the perspective of the `App` class, `Rectangle` and all its subtypes should behave the same.

The Interface Segregation Principle (ISP)

Clients should not be forced to depend on methods that they do not use.

This principle deals with **heavy** interfaces. The clients of these heavy interfaces are forced to carry extra burdens. That is, they are subject to changes that are requested by other clients. Let's see an example of this.

Future Drone is a company that produces drones. Their research and development department has recently designed a drone that can fly and drive. There are two separate remote control devices for this drone—one controls its flying and the other controls its driving. Here is the design of their `DroneController` API:

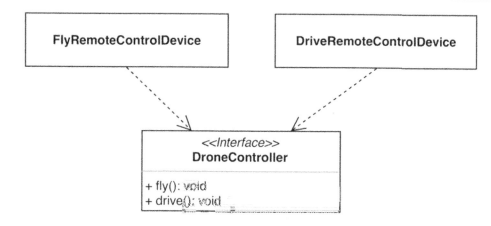

Figure 6.2: The DroneController API

As you can see, both remote control devices can access the methods that they don't need. This is seriously wrong. Why? Because the engineers from Future Drone's R&D department work very hard and they make drones that can also sail. Now, they need to add a `sail()` method to the `DroneController` API so that `SailRemoteControlDevice` can make a drone sail, as shown in the following diagram:

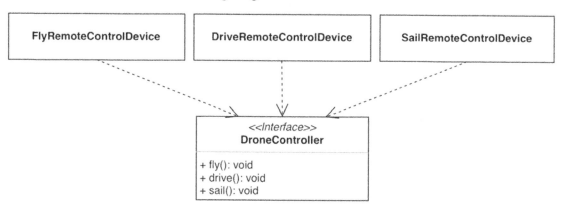

Figure 6.3: New version of the DroneController API

Now, the new version of `DroneController` forces `FlyRemoteControlDevice` and `DriveRemoteControlDevice` to be recompiled and redeployed to all of those remote control devices. This is why the design of `DroneController` is seriously wrong!

Let's refactor it according to the ISP, as shown in the following diagram:

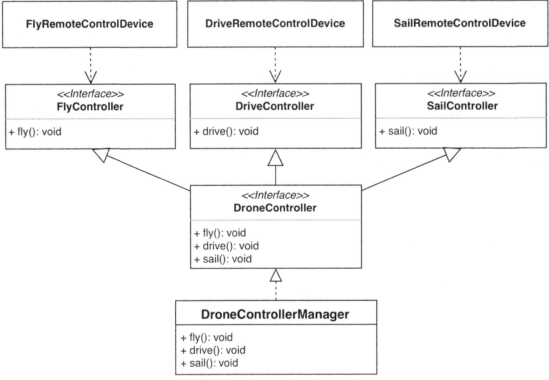

Figure 6.4: Segregated interface

As you can see, smaller interfaces are created for each device, respectively. This releases the unnecessary burdens that the `DroneController` API put on them. They are not affected by future changes on other interfaces.

However, this design still violates the SRP. `DroneControllerManager`, an implementation of `DroneController`, contains more than one reason of change. To make it conform with the SRP, `DroneController` should be faded out and deprecated. The `fly()`, `drive()`, and `sail()` implementations inside `DroneControllerManager` should also be moved into separate implementations of each smaller controller API, as shown in the following diagram:

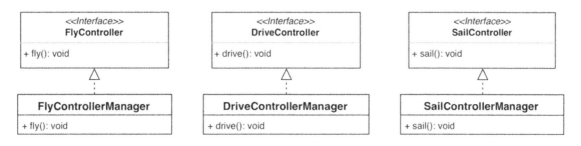

Figure 6.5: Implementation conforming to the SRP

Façade design pattern: This pattern is a part of the **Gang of Four (GoF)** design patterns, categorized under structural design patterns. This pattern is used to provide a unified interface to a set of interfaces in a subsystem. Façade defines a higher level interface that makes the subsystem easier to use.

In the following diagram, on the left-hand side, clients of a subsystem need to know the details of classes inside the subsystem. On the right-hand side, the **Façade** of the subsystem provides a unified interface to its clients and hides the implementation details of the subsystem. Changes inside the subsystem are not visible to the clients, as long as the APIs of the **Façade** stay the same:

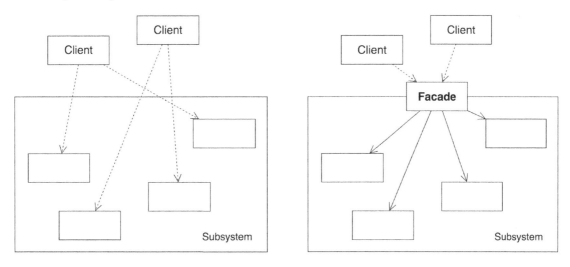

Figure 6.6: Facade design pattern

If you think about this **Façade** design pattern and the ISP, it seems that what the ISP suggests you do is the opposite of how **Façade** works. Clearly, the **Façade** design pattern is a violation of the ISP, right? It depends on which level you are going to apply the **Façade** design pattern on. What does this mean? Let's use Future Drone as an example:

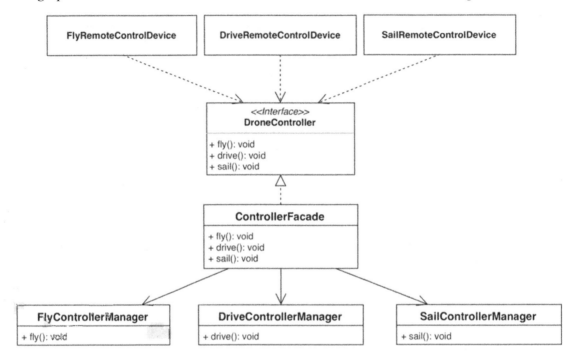

Figure 6.7: ControllerFacade

As you can see, `ControllerFacade` is an implementation of the `DroneController` API, and it delegates calls to other controller managers. This is a violation of the ISP.

However, if we apply the façade design pattern to the flight subsystem, which is responsible for controlling the flying ability of the drone, then this is not a violation of the ISP, as shown in the following diagram:

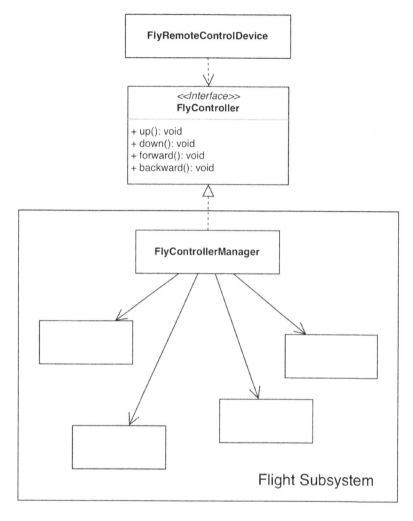

Figure 6.8: Facade of the flight controller subsystem

As you can see, FlyControllerManager, which is a façade, implements the FlyController interface, which has four methods to control the drone, and it delegates calls to other classes inside the flight subsystem. In this way, the client, FlyRemoteControlDevice, doesn't need to know the internal details of the flight subsystem. All it has to do is interact with a simple unified interface, FlyControllerManager. In this design, the client isn't forced to depend on methods that it doesn't need. Therefore, the façade design pattern used in this design doesn't violate the ISP.

The Dependency Inversion Principle (DIP)

The principle focuses on the following two parts:

- **High-level modules should not depend on low-level modules. Both should depend on abstractions**.
- **Abstractions should not depend on details. Details should depend on abstractions**.

First of all, what is a high-level module and a low-level module? In short, high-level modules contain business rules, and low-level modules contain the implementation details.

According to the first part of this principle, high-level modules should only be concerned with high-level abstraction. This high-level abstraction defines what the components are, what the interactions between these components are, and what business rules these components must follow. Low-level modules should also depend on the high-level abstraction. They should not depend on other low-level modules.

According to the second part of this principle, the high-level abstraction should not depend on implementation details, which change frequently. The impact on the high-level abstraction from changes to the implementation details should be minimized so that the abstraction can stay stable. Also, when details depend on high-level abstraction, they are decoupled from each other. Hence, changes are managed inside.

Now, let's look at an example of a data export application. In this application, the `Exporter` class contains high-level abstraction. It uses the `JdbcRepository` class to query records from the database and then uses the `CsvGenerator` class to save the records into a file of the `.csv` format. After that, it will call the `zip()` method of the `ZipCompressor` class to compress the file.

In the design shown in the following diagram, the `Exporter` class depends directly on the `JdbcRepository` class, the `CsvGenerator` class, and the `ZipCompressor` class:

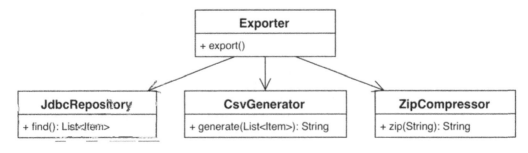

Figure 6.9: Rigid data export application

And here is what the `Exporter` class looks like:

```
public class Exporter {
  public Exporter(JdbcRepository repository,
      CsvGenerator genenerator, ZipCompressor compressor) {
    // ...
  }

  public void export() {
    List<Item> items = repository.find();
    if (items.isEmpty()) {
      // Business rules to handle empty result
      return;
    }
    String csvFilePath = genenerator.generate(items);
    String compressed = compressor.zip(csvFilePath);
    // Business logics to handle the compressed file
    }
  }
}
```

As you can see, the dependencies are injected through the constructor of the `Exporter` class. The `export()` method contains the high-level abstraction of this data export application's main logic. There is no implementation detail of how to retrieve records from the database, how to generate the `.csv` file, or how to compress the file. Those are irrelevant here! The only thing this `Exporter` class cares about is the high-level abstraction of this data exporting logic.

The problem with this design is that the `Exporter` class depends directly on the concrete classes, and changes to these dependencies will have an impact on the `Exporter` class, making it unstable. This is a violation of the DIP. This not only causes the high-level abstraction not closed to change but also makes this `Exporter` class unable to be extended. For example, it cannot be extended to support exporting data out from MongoDB, and it cannot be extended to support exporting data in XML format. All of these changes require the `export()` method to be modified.

As the DIP suggest, high-level modules should depend on abstraction. Let's refactor the data export application to use the design, as shown in the following diagram:

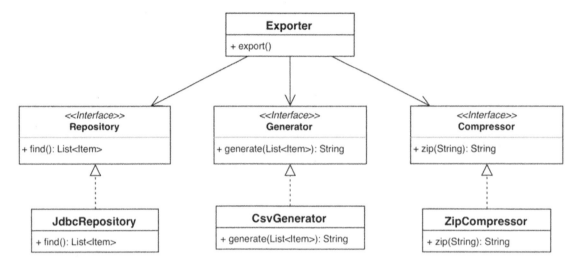

Figure 6.10: Dependency inversion applied to the data export application

As you can see, the `Exporter` class now depends on the `Repository` interface, the `Generator` interface, and the `Compressor` interface. These interfaces are implemented by their corresponding concrete classes. To extend this application to support MongoDB, you just need to add a new implementation of the `Repository` interface, for example, `MongoRepository`, so that the `Exporter` class doesn't have to be modified.

In practice, we can put the `Exporter` class and the three interfaces in the same package and add subpackages for the implementation details, as shown in the following code:

```
app.dataexport.Exporter
app.dataexport.Compressor
app.dataexport.Generator
app.dataexport.Repository
app.dataexport.compressor.ZipCompressor
app.dataexport.generator.CsvGenerator
app.dataexport.repository.JdbcRepository
```

There are other package design options. We will talk about the principles of package design in detail when we implement the TaskAgile application.

TaskAgile code design

For a TaskAgile application, the code design will be at three levels—the architecture level, abstraction level, and implementation level. We will only talk about the architecture level design here. When we start the implementation, we will work on the abstraction level design. Most of the implementation level design will be carried out during the implementation phase. We will practice test-driven development, write acceptance tests, and keep refactoring the code to keep it clean, simple, and expressive.

Now, let's look at the architecture level design. We will introduce two designs—layered architecture and hexagonal architecture. Each design has its pros and cons. Let's go through them one by one.

Layered architecture

The layered architecture pattern is a common technique that's used to break complicated systems into separate layers, where each layer focuses on its own concern. The usual separation is to use layers, that is, the presentation layer, business layer, and data access layer. A higher-layer depends on a lower-layer, while a lower-layer isn't aware of the existence of the high-layer that depends on it. In a strictly layered architecture, a higher-layer can only depend on a direct lower-layer. In a relaxed layered architecture, a higher-layer can depend on any layer underneath it. For example, the presentation layer can only depend on the business layer in a strict layered architecture, while it can depend on the data access layer in a relaxed layered architecture.

Sometimes, the business layer is called the **application layer**, service layer, or domain layer. Or, it might be divided into the application layer and service layer, which creates a four-layered architecture. No matter what the name of this layer is called, it contains the business logic of the application:

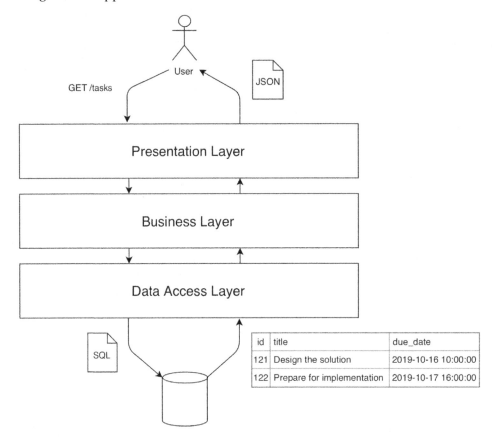

Figure 6.11: Layered architecture

The preceding diagram shows an example of this architecture. The **User** sends a request to get tasks. The **Presentation Layer** receives this request and converts it into an internal call to the API that's provided by the **Business Layer**, which performs a series of business logic and eventually asks the **Data Access Layer** for the data. The **Data Access Layer** generates an **SQL** query and sends it to the database. Once the database returns the result, the Data Access Layer will convert the row-based data into objects which will be sent back all the way to the Presentation Layer, where the result is converted into strings in JSON format and then sent back to the user.

As you can see, the layered architecture is straightforward and easy to understand. And for applications that do not have complex business logic, this architecture works well. It has a tendency to shift the focus from business logic to data manipulation, also known as CRUD. At the bottom of this architecture is the database. For applications that have only a few business rules where most of the requests are about reading data out of the database or saving the data back to the database, this architecture fits well. In these applications, domain models, such as entities, are all POJOs with a bag of getters and setters. They don't contain domain logic. There are often design rules saying that there should be no domain logic in models. Instead, the domain logic should be put into service objects in the business layer. These domain models are usually called **anemic domain models**.

One of the symptoms of this data-centric design is that, as the complexity of the application grows, it is easy to see domain logic leak into other layers. Let's see a simple example of activating a free trial user, as shown in the following code:

```
public class UserController {
  @PostMapping("/users/{userId}/activate")
  public void activate(@PathVariable(value="userId") int userId){
    // get the user and calculate free trial end date
    user.setActive(true);
    user.setInFreeTrial(true)
    user.setFreeTrialEndDate(trialEndDate);
    user.setLastModifiedDate(now);
    userService.save(user);
    sendFreeTrialStartedEmail(user);
  }
}
```

As you can see, in the `activate()` method, we use the setters to modify the user entity and then ask `userService` to save the changes, followed by sending a free trial started email to the user. A better implementation is to add an `activate()` method in the `UserService` API and move the setters and send email logic into that method, and then change `UserController` to the following:

```
public class UserController {
  @PostMapping("/users/{userId}/activate")
  public void activate(@PathVariable(value="userId") int userId){
    // get the user
    userService.activate(user);
  }
}
```

There are still potential and serious issues with this design. As you can see, the User entity has two separate fields, active and inFreeTrial. When a user starts the free trial, both need to be set as true. Imagine this: one day, another developer, Frank, who isn't familiar with this logic, needs to create a new API to allow mobile app users to register, without reading the functional specification; well, he is probably in an Agile team, so there most likely won't be comprehensive specifications, but just user stories. Anyway, Frank doesn't know that when a newly registered user is activated, the inFreeTrial field needs to be set as true. In this way, a serious bug is introduced. Hopefully, the QA team will catch this bug before release.

It is true that, in the example, using layered architecture isn't the cause of this kind of issue. But the point is that layered architecture tends to keep developers looking at the system from the data perspective instead of the domain model perspective.

Hexagonal architecture

Alistair Cockburn came up with the hexagonal architecture, or ports and adapters. In his blog, he wrote the intent of this architecture, as follows:

> *Allow an application to equally be driven by users, programs, automated test or batch scripts, and to be developed and tested in isolation from its eventual runtime devices and databases.*

The following diagram depicts the hexagonal architecture, from Vaughn Vernon's book, *Implementation Domain-Driven Design*, with a few modifications:

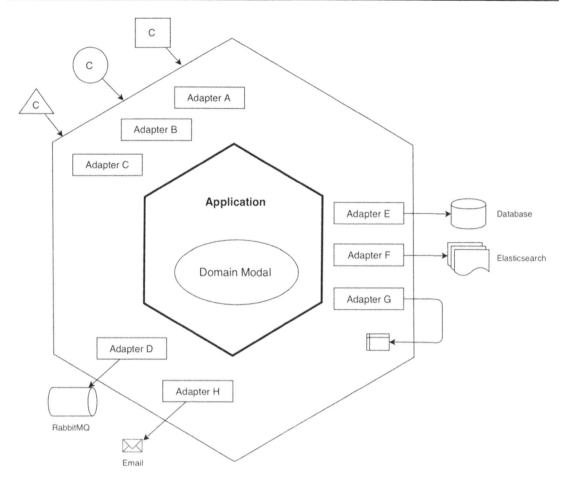

Figure 6.12: Hexagonal architecture

As you can see in the preceding diagram, at the center is the **Application** core. It contains all of the business logic and creates a boundary. And at the heart, it is the **Domain Model**, which contains rich behavior domain models, not anemic ones. Around the **Application** core are the **Adapters** that translate outside events that arrived at different ports into API calls to the **Application** core, such as the **A**, **B**, and **C** adapters in the diagram. Other adapters, such as **Adapter E**, interact with the database, while **Adapter F** interacts with **Elasticsearch**. **Adapter G** saves data in memory. Note that all of the arrows in the diagram are unidirectional to indicate which interactions were triggered from which side. It doesn't mean that the interaction is in one direction.

The hexagonal architecture is a natural fit for **Domain-Driven Design (DDD)**. It isolates the domain logic from the infrastructure, such as the database, search engine, message queue, mail delivery, and the cache system. It can be extended to support different types of clients easily. Just add a new adapter to it.

For TaskAgile, we will use hexagonal architecture and practice DDD. We will discuss this architecture in detail along the way. Meanwhile, if you're interested to learn more about the hexagonal architecture, I recommend that you read Alistair Cockburn's blog on hexagonal architecture and the C2 wiki at `http://wiki.c2.com/?HexagonalArchitecture`.

Summary

In this chapter, you have learned what Agile code design is, the levels of code design, symptoms of bad design, and the levels of code design, as well as how to practice Agile code design.

You also have learned the SOLID design principles and the façade design pattern. After that, you learned about the two types of architecture design: layered architecture and hexagonal architecture.

In the next chapter, you're going to learn how to design the **language** between the frontend and the backend with the RESTful API.

7
RESTful API Design - Building Language Between Frontend and Backend

An API is a contract between the API provider and the API consumers. REST is one of the most popular API styles, mainly because of it being simple to use and easy to understand. The term **REST** stands for **REpresentational State Transfer**, which is an architectural style defined by Roy T. Fielding in his dissertation back in 2000.

Even though REST has been around for 18 years at the time of writing this book, there are still misconceptions of what a RESTful API is. According to Roy T. Fielding, many APIs that call themselves RESTful is not really RESTful. There are even people that think that being RESTful is just *JSON over HTTP*. For years, there have been debates around **HATEOAS** (short for **Hypermedia As The Engine Of Application State**). In this chapter, we will talk about these topics in depth, and so you will learn about the following:

- RESTful API characteristics
- RESTful API design procedure
- RESTful API implementation in Spring MVC
- RESTful API consuming
- RESTful API testing

RESTful API characteristics

Web service APIs that adhere to the REST architectural constraints are called RESTful APIs. Before we talk about the characteristics of RESTful APIs, let's first go through the architectural constraints of this REST architectural style that Roy T. Fielding introduced in his dissertation. This will help us understand what REST is really about.

REST architectural constraints

In his dissertation, Roy T. Fielding listed the following architectural constraints that a RESTful system must conform to.

Client-server

This constraint is about separation of concerns. In the client-server architecture style, user interface concerns are separated from data storage concerns. Web applications fit this style naturally, with the frontend living inside browsers as a client, which then talks to the server through APIs.

Another well-known architectural style is event-based integration architecture, in which components of a system broadcast events over the network and at the same time listen to events that they are interested in.

Stateless

The communication between the client and the server is stateless. Each request from the client to the server contains all of the information about the server that's needed to understand that request. The server should not take advantage of any stored context on its side to fully understand the request.

A common question with this constraint is—should a system that stores session IDs on the server-side for authenticated requests be called RESTful? And should we change it to make such a system RESTful? We will talk about this later in this chapter.

Cache

This constraint is about the performance of a system, in which the response data to a request must be implicitly or explicitly labeled as cacheable or non-cacheable. For a web application, we can use HTTP headers, such as `Cache-Control`, `ETag`, and `Expires` in the response to control the cache.

Uniform interface

This constraint is the central feature that distinguishes the REST architecture style from other styles, such as SOAP. With a uniform interface, the overall system architecture is simplified, and the visibility of interactions is improved. To obtain a uniform interface, there are four interface constraints, including identifications of resources, manipulation of resources through representations, self-descriptive messages, and hypermedia as the engine of application state. We will discuss these constraints in detail later.

Layered system

As we mentioned in `Chapter 6`, *Code Design - Designing for Stability and Extensibility*, layered architecture is also a separation of concerns. In a layered system, an architecture is composed of hierarchical layers by constraining component behavior so that each component cannot *see* beyond the immediate layer that they are interacting with.

Code-on-demand (optional)

This constraint is optional in a REST architecture style. According to Roy T. Fielding, REST allows client functionality to be extended by downloading and executing code in the form of applets or scripts. This simplifies clients by reducing the number of features required to be pre-implemented. In practice, not many RESTful APIs allow code to be downloaded and executed during runtime.

As long as a system adheres to the preceding constraints, it can be known as being RESTful. HTTP isn't mandatory to make a system RESTful, even though most RESTful APIs are built over HTTP, mostly because HTTP, as an open standard, doesn't bind the implementation of the API or the implementation of its clients to a specific technology. Developers who are familiar with HTTP can pick up a RESTful API easily.

RESTful interface constraints

The architectural constraints mentioned previously are high-level. Other types of APIs also share some of these constraints. What distinguishes a RESTful API from others is the uniform interface, mainly the previously mentioned four interface constraints. Let's talk about them in detail one by one.

Identifications of resources

In REST, resources are the key abstraction of information so that a service can make them available to its clients. Essentially, a resource can be anything—a user, a document, an image, or even an operation. Resources must be uniquely identifiable through URIs. For example, the following URI uniquely identifies a task with ID 1:

```
https://api.example.com/v1/tasks/1
```

As you can see, in this URI, we add the version number, v1, in the URI. Some people think it is a bad practice to put version information in the resource URI. They prefer to add it in the HTTP request header. Other people think that using versioning itself is not the right thing to do when building a RESTful API. For example, Roy T. Fielding mentioned the following on Twitter (https://mobile.twitter.com/fielding/status/376835835670167552):

> *The reason to make a real REST API is to get evolvability ... a "v1" is a middle finger to your API customers, indicating RPC/HTTP (not REST).*

So, is versioning really that bad? We will discuss this in detail later.

Manipulation of resources through representations

We mentioned earlier that a resource is an abstraction of information. It has a state, which is described through its representation, which can have different formats, such as XML, HTML, and JSON. Nowadays, JSON is the most popular format of a resource's representation.

In REST, the manipulation of a resource is through sending a representation back to the server using standard HTTP methods. The most common methods are GET, POST, PUT, PATCH, and DELETE. We will discuss them in detail later.

Self-descriptive messages

A self-descriptive message is a message that contains all of the information necessary for the receiver to understand it. Being self-descriptive, requests can be handled separately and the interactions between the client and the server can be stateless. A server that processes a self-descriptive message does not need to remember how it handled previous requests.

Hypermedia as the engine of the application state

This constraint is often known as HATEOAS or **hypermedia constraint**. In Roy T. Fielding's dissertation, there is no detailed explanation of this constraint. The following definition from Wikipedia provides a good definition:

> *Having accessed an initial URI for the REST application—analogous to a human web user accessing the home page of a website—a REST client should then be able to use server-provided links dynamically to discover all the available actions and resources it needs. As access proceeds, the server responds with text that includes hyperlinks to other actions that are currently available. There is no need for the client to be hardcoded with information regarding the structure or dynamics of the REST service.*

This constraint is also called hypertext-driven, and according to Roy T. Fielding, *REST APIs must be hypertext-driven* (`http://roy.gbiv.com/untangled/2008/rest-apis-must-be-hypertext-driven`). Otherwise, an API cannot be RESTful and cannot be called a REST API. This raised lots of debates over whether or not HATEOAS is useful or practical. We will talk about this later in detail.

Those are all of the constraints of REST. As you can see, REST is an architectural style that defines several constraints. It is not a standard of how you should design your API, and it doesn't specify any implementation details. You can use the programming language that you prefer to build RESTful APIs.

Opinionated RESTful API

As mentioned earlier, REST is already 18 years old at the time of writing this book, and there have been lots of discussions and debates about it in the industry. The focus of these debates is HATEOAS. There are advocates and also skeptics. Some people even use a strong word—*Haters*. In this section, we will talk about the two sides of HATEOAS in depth.

Richardson Maturity Model

In 2008, Leonard Richardson developed a model to describe the maturity level of a service in the sense of its REST compliancy after reviewing a hundred different web service designs. There are three factors in his model—URI, HTTP methods, and hypermedia constraints (HATEOAS). The more a service employs these technologies, the more mature it shall be considered:

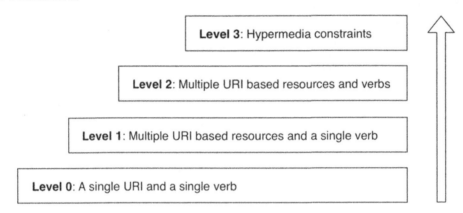

Figure 7.1: Richardson Maturity Model

Level zero

Services in this level have a single URI and a single HTTP verb, typically an HTTP POST method. All of the message exchanges are through that URI using that HTTP method. For example, most **Web Services (WS-*)**-based services use a single URI as the endpoint and transfer SOAP-based payloads using HTTP POST method, even if it is a read action. Another example is XML-RPC-based services.

Level one

Services in this level use a unique URI for each resource but only with a single HTTP verb which, most of the time, is an HTTP POST method. An example of this would be Flickr's web service (https://www.flickr.com/services/api/request.rest.html), which is a popular API. Even though many of these services claim to be RESTful, they are not.

Level two

Services in this level provide numerous URI-addressable resources and support manipulating the exposed resources through different HTTP methods, including GET, POST, PUT, PATCH, and DELETE. A good example of this is Amazon's file hosting service, S3.

Level three

Services in this level provide multiple URI-based resources and operations using different HTTP verbs, and, the most important, hypermedia constraints. According to Roy T. Fielding, a truly RESTful API is one that is driven by hypertext (http://roy.gbiv.com/untangled/2008/rest-apis-must-be-hypertext-driven), which is done to follow the hypermedia constraint. A good example is PayPal's RESTful API (https://developer.paypal.com/docs/api/overview/).

The Richardson Maturity Model provides a good way of thinking about the basic ideas of RESTful APIs. Most RESTful APIs fall into level two, mainly because the gain of being truly RESTful is not worth the overhead of implementing the hypermedia constraint. Or people do not really agree with the benefits brought by HATEOAS. Sometimes, people call level three services **pure RESTful** and level two services **pragmatic RESTful**.

HATEOAS or not?

Regarding the term REST, as is the case with many software terms, there are lots of definitions. Since Roy T. Fielding coined it, his definition should carry more weight than others. However, being RESTful shouldn't be regarded as a religious thing, and being a service at level two doesn't mean that your APIs are inferior to the ones at level three. Whether or not you should implement HATEOAS depends on the nature of your APIs and whether or not it is worth the effort.

What is HATEOAS?

Before we discuss it any further, let's see a popular example of the usage of HATEAOS, which is to buy a cup of coffee via a RESTful API, like the following:

```
POST https://api.examplebucks.org/orders HTTP/1.1
Content-Type: application/json
Content-Length: 33

{"drink": "latte", "quantity": 1}
```

This is a POST request, which has been sent to order a cup of latte. In its response, the server provides information about what the client can do next, as shown in the following code:

```
{
  "id": 12345,
  "drink": "latte",
  "quantity": 1,
  "cost": "5",
  "status": "pending",
  "_links": {
    "self": {
      "href": "https://api.examplebucks.org/orders/12345",
      "type": "GET"
    },
    "payment": {
      "href": "https://api.examplebucks.org/payments/12345",
      "type": "PUT"
    },
    "update": {
      "href": "https://api.examplebucks.org/orders/12345",
      "type": "PUT"
    },
    "cancel": {
      "href": "https://api.examplebucks.org/orders/12345",
      "type": "DELETE"
    }
  }
}
```

As you can see, in the response, the _links property, which is a hypertext that follows the HAL convention, contains operations that the client can take. In this _links object, each key standard for a relationship, and the href property of that relation is the URI of the resource, while the type property is the HTTP method that should be performed on that resource. In this example, the server provides operations, including making a payment, updating the order, and canceling the order. The self relationship is required for referencing the order resource itself.

The following is according to Roy T. Fielding:

> *Hypertext doesn't usually tell you all the operations allowed on any given resource; it tells you which operation to use for each potential transition. The client (user or agent) has to decide what transition to take, not what interface to use.*

So, if a client needs to update an order, it can go through the _links hypertext and find the update operation. And when the client needs to cancel the order, it can find the cancel operation in the hypertext and send a DELETE request to the URI specified in that operation.

Also, with the _links hypertext, API developers can change the URI of a resource without breaking the clients, since the hypertext decouple the clients from the URIs of resources. Clients do not need to hardcode URIs anymore. All they need to understand is the meaning of each operation that was returned in the _links hypertext. This is important when you do not have control of the clients of your APIs. For example, when you are building APIs that are publicly available, such as Twitter's, you won't have the control of most of the clients—and you certainly do not want to break them when you want to fix a typo in a resource URI. According to the HATEOAS advocates, another benefit is that your API becomes more self-descriptive and the clients don't have to look up the documentation that often. They can simply check the hypertext in the API response in order to navigate through your RESTful APIs, making the APIs discoverable.

That's the basic idea of HATEOAS. As mentioned previously, Roy T. Fielding insists that *REST APIs must be hypertext-driven*.

Why you won't need HATEOAS?

In practice, usually, you probably won't need HATEOAS. Here are the reasons:

- First of all, implementing and maintaining HATEOAS requires effort on both the server-side and the client-side. The server-side needs to construct the hypertext based on the state of the resource and the clients need to parse the hypertext and understand the meaning of the hypertext to perform the correct operation. Compared with the API without HATEOAS, what you need to do on the client-side is hard-code the URIs of the resources and decide what operations are available based on the representation of the resource. For example, in our ordering coffee example, you can find out which operations among make a payment, update the order, and cancel the order are available based on the value of the status field of an order. In this way, you avoid the overhead introduced by HATEOAS on the server-side and the parsing of hypertext on the client-side.

- Secondly, the benefit of decoupling the clients with the resources' URIs by adopting HATEOAS isn't bulletproof. The clients still need to know the meanings of the hypertext to find out the operations that can be performed. There is still a coupling between the clients and the hypertext, for example, the `update` operation in the preceding example standards for updating the order. On the client side, `_links.update` is used to find the location of the URI for that operation. It is not `_links.edit` nor `_links.modify`. This `update` operation is a simple example and a generic term. For applications that have unique terms for specific operations, the clients need to bind with those terms. And those terms are also subject to change, similar to URIs. The only difference is that they might be changed less frequently as URIs might have to. But still, it doesn't mean that HATEOAS lets you evolve your API independently without causing any effects on the clients. You still need to put lots of effort in to make sure that the terms you use are extensible. Since most of the time changes to APIs are inevitable, we should come up with an API change strategy to manage these changes. That is why even PayPal's API embraces versioning. Currently, they are in version 3. Even NPR's API, which was used as an example stating that APIs don't require versioning, is now adding version numbers in its API URIs (`https://dev.npr.org/api/`).

- Thirdly, the self-descriptiveness of an API that hypertext provides through the API's response is partial. That is, you still need to check other documents to find all of the information on the operations that are listed in the hypertext. For example, for the `make a payment` and `update a payment` operations, you need to know the representations that you can send to the server, that is, what input parameters those APIs accept, as such information is not revealed in the hypertext. Therefore, for developers of the API clients, they will need to check two places to put together all the pieces of such an API, which is not developer-friendly, making the APIs not easy to use. A more developer-friendly way is to have an API document that provides all of the information developers need to know about the API. An even more pleasant approach is to have a playground so that developers can try it out and see how an API works in action.

- Fourthly, hypertext can be bypassed. Developers can still use the old URI constructing way to identify resources, ignoring the hypertext in the API response. A way to reduce the misuse of APIs is to provide client libraries for different programming languages. For example, Google Drive's API provides client libraries (`https://developers.google.com/drive/api/v3/downloads`), even though it doesn't seem to use hypertext and is still called RESTful. As you can see in the following screenshot, in the representation of the file resource, `capabilities` is used to indicate what the clients can do with this file:

Figure 7.2: The Google Drive API

To sum this up, HATEOAS should be used in places where it can actually help developers of the API clients. For example, the following is a response from the API that can retrieve all of the orders that have been paid. It supports pagination:

```
{
  "items": [{...}],
  "paging": {
    "previous":
      "https://api.examplebucks.org/orders?
      page=1&count=20&status=paid",
        "next":
      "https://api.examplebucks.org/orders?
      page=3&count=20&status=paid",
    "hasMore": true
  }
}
```

As you can see, by adding the URIs of the previous page and the next page, developers of API clients can go through all of the pages easily without constructing the URIs, which is especially useful for remembering all the query parameters that need to be added to the URI.

Opinionated RESTful API characteristics

In this section, we'll talk about the characteristics of opinionated RESTful APIs, which adopt the parts that work great in practice from Roy T. Fielding's REST dissertation.

Resource-centric

The API should be organized around resources. As mentioned earlier, resources are the key abstraction of information so a service makes them available to its clients. The internal structure of a resource should not leak through the APIs. For example, the details of an order might be stored separately in a relational database, so we should not create multiple resources to mirror that internal structure. APIs should focus on business entities and use resources as the abstraction to hide implementation details, making the API implementation evolvable.

Identifiable through URIs

Resources should be identifiable through URIs, which should be based on nouns instead of verbs. The URIs that identify a collection of resources should use plurals. Here are some examples:

- **A collection of orders**: `https://api.examplebucks.org/v1/orders`
- **An order of ID 1234**: `https://api.examplebucks.org/v1/orders/1234`
- **A collection of users**: `https://api.examplebucks.org/v1/users`
- **A user of ID 567**: `https://api.examplebucks.org/v1/users/567`

Defining operations via HTTP methods

The operations that can be performed on resources should be defined via HTTP methods. The following are the common methods that are used in a RESTful API:

- **GET method**: A `GET` method retrieves a representation of the resource at the specified URI. The response of the API contains the details of the requested resource. This method should be implemented as a safe operation, meaning that performing a `GET` operation on resources should not cause any side effects to the state of anything. It can be invoked multiple times and the response of this operation can be cached.

- **POST method**: A POST method creates a new resource at the specified URI. The identifier of the resource is generated by the server. The response of the API contains the details of the new resource. A POST method is an unsafe operation, meaning it has side effects. Multiple POST requests will create different resources on the server-side. A POST request can also be used to perform operations other than creating a new resource, for example, moving a card in the TaskAgile application. We will see how that works when we implement that feature.

- **PUT method**: A PUT method creates a new resource or updates an existing one. The client specifies the URI for the resource and the request body contains a complete representation of the resource. If a resource with the specified URI already exists, it will be replaced. Otherwise, a new resource is created. When creating a new resource, the difference between using PUT and POST is that the resource identifier in the PUT request is specified by the client. If the server doesn't allow the client to choose the resource identifier, PUT should only be used for updating an existing resource, and when no resource exists at the specified URI, a HTTP 404 response should be returned to the client. A PUT method should be implemented in such a way that it can be performed multiple times with the same effects. This means that a PUT method is idempotent.

- **PATCH method**: A PATCH method updates part of an existing resource. The client specifies the URI of the resource, so the request body only contains part of the representation of the resource. The main differences between a PATCH method and a PUT method are that, usually, the request body of a PUT method is a complete representation of the resource, while that of a PATCH method is only a subset of the representation. Another difference is that a PATCH method is not safe nor idempotent.

- **DELETE method**: A DELETE method removes an existing resource at the specified URI. DELETE methods are idempotent, meaning that performing a DELETE method on the same resource multiple times indicates that the resource's state is always the same.

Use of HTTP status codes

A RESTful API should use meaningful status codes that are defined in the HTTP standard to indicate the result of a request. The following are the status codes for different scenarios, which are divided into different types:

- **2xx—Success codes**:
    - `200 OK`: Indicates a successful `GET`, `PUT`, or `PATCH` request. It can also be used for a `POST` request that is not for creating resources, or a `DELETE` request when the response needs to contain the representation of a removed resource.
    - `201 Created`: Indicates a successful `POST` request or a `PUT` request that is for creating a new resource. Usually, a location header is also returned with the URI of the new resource.
    - `204 No Content`: Indicates a successful request that does not contain any response body, such as the `DELETE` request.
- **3xx—Redirections**:
    - `304 Not Modified`: Indicates that a resource hasn't been modified since last requested. Typically, the client will provide a header such as `If-Modified-Since` to provide a time against which to compare.
- **4xx—Client error**:
    - `400 Bad Request`: Indicates that the server cannot or will not process the request due to something that is perceived to be a client error. For example, the request is malformed or failed the validation.
    - `401 Unauthorized`: Indicates a request that doesn't contain authentication credentials or that the authentication failed.
    - `403 Forbidden`: Indicates a request that tries to access a resource that is not allowed for the authenticated user.
    - `404 Not Found`: Indicates a request to a nonexistent resource.
    - `409 Conflict`: Indicates a request that tries to change the state of a resource cannot be processed by the server due to a conflict in the resource's state.
    - `410 Gone`: Indicates that the requested resource is no longer available.

- `429 Too Many Requests`: Indicates that the client has sent too many requests in a given amount of time and that the request has been rejected. The server might include a **Retry-After** header to the response, indicating how long to wait before making a new request.
- **5xx—Server error**:
    - `500 Internal Server Error`: Indicates that the server encountered an unexpected condition and failed to process the request.

Versioning

The most common way to manage changes of an API is to use versioning. Using versioning is basically a way that you can let the developers of the clients of the API know, right from the beginning, that there might be changes in the API that will be backward incompatible as the business model evolves. However, this doesn't mean that you cannot add new APIs to the same version. In fact, you don't have to change the version as long as you do not create backward incompatibility issues in your API. So, versioning is not the cause of backward incompatibilities. On the contrary, it is a way to manage that issue. It is often a lack of consideration during the API design or the changes of the application's business models that introduce backward incompatibilities.

Anyway, once you have a new version, you should announce it to the developers within plenty of time so that they can test and provide feedback before the new version goes live in production. Usually, you will keep the old version running for a period of time so that developers can finish the migration before you retire the old version. It is true that even though you leave plenty of time for the migration, there will still be clients that are stuck with old versions. For example, it is often hard or even impossible for those embedded systems to upgrade to a new version of the API. So, what should you do in that case? From a technical perspective, you can create an autoupgrade mechanism so that the application living in the embedded system can be upgraded as required. Or you can choose to use HATEOAS and provide client libraries to make it easier for those developers to consume your APIs and avoid API misuse. At a certain point, a business decision needs to be made upon which the old version should be shut down.

In reality, there is seldom an API that has pure evolvability plus longevity without breaking clients. Changes are inevitable. Business models can change, the way end users interact with the clients can change, and hence the way of consuming APIs can change. We cannot avoid changes, but we can manage them. And certainly, versioning is not a perfect solution. It is not a silver bullet. But it is an effective way of managing API changes.

There are two ways to manage versions. One is to include the version number in the URI, for example,

`https://api.examplebucks.org/`**`v1`**`/orders` or `https://api.examplebucks.org/orders?version=1`. The other way is put the version number in an HTTP request header, for example, `X-API-Version`. However, this could become a problem when the clients forget to include the version number in the header. You can assume that, without the presence of such a header, the client is requesting the API of the latest version. However, once you upgrade your APIs to a new version, those clients that haven't migrated will break. Preferably, making the version number explicit in the URI is better than being implicit by keeping it in the header.

On the other hand, for a monolithic application where you have the control of both the frontend and the backend, you don't need to use versioning in the API. This is because the API is for internal usage and you can make changes to both the API and the clients at the same time and deploy them together. However, if you're building mobile apps, you might want to treat them separately. This is because, even though you have updated the API version in the mobile app and published it in the app store, end users might be stuck with an old version of the app. Due to the scope of this book, we will not go into the details of mobile apps here.

To sum this up, for public APIs, use versioning, even if your business model is relatively simple at the moment. Remember, things change. For internal APIs, do not use versioning when you have control of the clients.

Stateless

We talked about stateless in the *REST architectural constraints* section. Being stateless makes web services highly scalable. There is no affinity need to retain between the clients and the servers. Any server can process requests from the API clients.

Let's go back to the question of whether or not HTTP sessions should be used in RESTful APIs. If you're creating APIs for internal usage between the frontend and the backend of a monolithic application, HTTP sessions provide a straightforward implementation of the API authentication. You can even archive the scalability using load balancers with the sticky session feature enabled to route the requests of the same session to the same server. Also, you can use Spring Session with Redis to enable clustered sessions to archive high availability so that when the original server that the client interacted with is offline, other servers can pick up the requests from that client transparently. However, it is true that if there is overhead with the clustered sessions, Redis itself could become a single-point-of-failure. For public APIs, you should avoid using HTTP sessions to manage request authentication. Public APIs should be stateless.

For our TaskAgile application, we will use HTTP sessions for the internal APIs that won't be stateless. For future versions of the application, we will create stateless public APIs.

Pagination

When you request for a collection of resources, usually, you don't retrieve all of the resources in a single response because there could be thousands of resources in that collection. Using pagination to return only a subset of the collection is usually more efficient, and it also saves network bandwidth and the processing power on the server-side, since it takes less time to run the database query when pagination is used.

There are two ways to do pagination. The first way is offset-based. The API clients send two parameters in the collection's URI: offset (or `page`) and limit (or `count`), like in the following example, which is used to get the first 20 orders:

```
https://api.examplebucks.org/v1/orders?page=1&count=20
```

The drawback of this approach is that items might either be returned twice or skipped. For example, after the first 20 orders were returned, a new order was created. The collection is sorted by the orders' creation date by default. In this way, when the client requests the second page, the last order shown on the first page will become the first item on the second page. On the other hand, if an order in the first page was deleted after the call, the order that was going to show up as the first item in the second page will be skipped in the request for the second page.

The second way is cursor-based. The API clients will receive a cursor with the result. For example, the following is a response of the getting orders API:

```
{
  "items": [{...}],
  "paging": {
    "previous":
      "https://api.examplebucks.org/v1/orders?count=20&before=101",
    "next":
      "https://api.examplebucks.org/v1/orders?count=20&after=120"
  }
}
```

As you can see, in the URI of `previous` and `next`, the `count` parameter is used for specifying the page size. The value of the `before` parameter is the ID of the first order in the result, while the value of the `after` parameter is the ID of the last order in the result. With cursor-based pagination, no items will be returned twice or skipped. The drawback of this approach is that you cannot jump between pages.

For APIs that support pagination, there should always be a default value for the pagination parameters. For example, when the `page` parameter is not present, by default, the first page will be returned, and when the `count` parameter is not found in the URI, by default, the page will contain 20 items.

Searching and sorting

APIs usually support searching so that a subset of the collection is returned. For example, the following is a request to get only completed orders:

```
https://api.examplebucks.org/v1/orders?status=completed
```

As you can see, we put the `status` field as a query parameter to the URI. This is the preferred way of doing the search for a collection. You don't need to add `/search` to the URI, like in the following code:

```
https://api.examplebucks.org/v1/orders/search?status=completed // Avoid
```

And the following request will return all the completed orders, with the latest completed at the top of the list:

```
https://api.examplebucks.org/v1/orders?status=completed&sort=-completedDate
```

As you can see, we use the `sort` parameter to trigger the sorting. Prepending – is used for specifying a descending sort.

Security

Last but not least is security. First of all, all APIs should use SSL. Requests sent over plain HTTP should fail.

For authentication, there are several approaches. The most basic version is to use basic HTTP so that API clients can use a randomly generated access token as the value of the username field of HTTP basic authentication. Another approach is to support OAuth2 so that end users can grant access to third-party applications to access their data via the APIs. Sometimes, these two approaches won't work or are not ideal. For example, you might require the API clients to pass extra information during authentication. In such a case, you can use **JWT** (short for **JSON Web Tokens**), which is an open standard (**RFC 7519**) that defines a compact and self-contained way for securely transmitting information between the API clients and the server as a JSON object. This doesn't mean to use JWT as a replacement of HTTP session.

The three authentication approaches described previously are for public APIs. For the internal APIs of the TaskAgile application, we will use Spring Security.

Besides authentication, the following are other security considerations:

- Never expose security-related information in URLs, such as usernames, passwords, session tokens, and API keys, since URLs can be captured in web server logs
- Always validate the input parameters of an API and fail the request immediately when there is a validation error

RESTful API design procedure

Now that we've learned what a RESTful API is and the characteristics of a RESTful API, let's talk about how to design a RESTful API; that is, the procedure of API design.

Finding out the requirements

When designing RESTful APIs, you should start by listing what the clients of the APIs need to be able to do. For internal APIs, it is straightforward. You can get these requirements by discussing this with the developers of the frontend to find out the interactions that the frontend needs to have with the backend, which usually involves reviewing user stories and UI design work. For public APIs, you need to talk to the developers of the clients of your APIs, ask them their requirements and what problems they need to solve and find out what is common in their needs.

Identifying resources

Once you have gathered the requirements, you do the domain analysis and identify the resources that need to be exposed. Be careful with the APIs that you make publicly available since, once they are presented, you cannot take them off without breaking clients. Remember, an API is a contract, and once it is offered, you cannot undo it without consequences. In our case, the consequences include breaking clients' apps and losing end users. That's why it often causes trouble when an API is a simple mapping to the internal data storage. You expose too much and create a tight couple between the clients and your internal implementation details. So, expose only what the clients actually need. No more, no less. Always start from simple and gradually evolve your APIs as you learn more about the consumers of your API.

Fleshing out API details

After identifying the resources, you work on the details of each API, that is, what is the input, the validation rules, the output, and status codes. You also need to specify the naming conventions and the data format. Once the details are fleshed out, you shouldn't go straight into the implementation phase. Instead, you should ask the developers of the clients of the API for feedback in order to see what you might have missed, and what further adjustments are required. One thing you should probably avoid is factoring in how the UI of the clients works into the API design consideration. How users interact with the UI of the clients of your API is irrelevant. You want to make the API generic so that it can be used for different types of clients.

Once you have finished the API's detail design, the design phase of the API is over. You then enter the implementation phase, which is what we will talk about in the next section.

RESTful API implementation in Spring MVC

In `Chapter 3`, *Spring 5 - The Right Stack for the Job at Hand*, we mentioned using the `@RestController` annotation to create RESTful APIs in Spring MVC. In this section, we will go through the support that Spring MVC provides for RESTful API implementation.

MVC annotations

Let's have a look in detail about various MVC annotations:

- The `@RestController` annotation is a combination of the `@Controller` annotation and the `@ResponseBody` annotation. As mentioned previously, with the `@ResponseBody` annotation, the return value of the API handlers in controllers will be mapped to the required representation based on the `Content-Type` header in the request.
- The `@RequestMapping` annotation and its convenient aliases, including `@GetMapping`, `@PostMapping`, `@PatchMapping`, `@PutMapping`, and `@DeleteMapping`, can be used to create URIs of resources.
- The `@ResponseEntity` annotation provides the ability to control the HTTP headers and status codes, besides returning the response body.

- The `@RequestParam` annotation provides the ability to specify the URI query parameters of an API.
- The `@PathVariable` annotation provides the ability to extract the variables in the URI, for example, the user ID in the `/users/{userId}` path.
- The `@RequestBody` annotation provides the ability to map the request body into an object. With a `PATCH` request, we can apply this annotation to a parameter of the `Map<String, Object>` type to receive the partial representation of a resource.
- The Spring HATEOAS project provides an easy way to create REST representations that follow HATEOAS constraints, mainly building the links in the representation.

We will use the annotations described in the preceding points during the implementation of the APIs in our TaskAgile application.

Spring HATEOAS

Spring HATEOAS is a library that gives developers the ability to create REST representations that follow the HATEOAS principle in applications using Spring MVC. As the core idea of HATEOAS is to use hypertext to drive a resources' state change, the main function that Spring HATEOAS provides is link creation. It eases the creation of links by providing link builder APIs to create links that point to Spring MVC controller methods. It uses HAL as the hypermedia format of the link. Due to the scope of this book, we won't go into the details of how to use it. If you're interested, you can find tutorials on its official websites: `https://projects.spring.io/spring-hateoas/`.

Spring REST Docs

The Spring REST Docs project helps you document RESTful services. It combines handwritten documentation written with Asciidoctor and autogenerated snippets produced with Spring MVC Test.

This is quite a different approach of other RESTful API documenting tools, such as Swagger, which separate the API documents from the API implementation. Usually, API designers write the API documents during the API design phase and then developers implement the API according to the API designs in the documents. One of the main drawbacks is that you will have to always remember to keep the document up-to-date with the latest implementation. Otherwise, developers of the API clients will see a non-working API, which causes confusion.

Spring REST Docs helps you produce API documentation that is accurate, concise, and well-structured. Every time you run `mvn test`, the document will be updated to the latest implementation. This generation of documents based on unit testing is a brilliant idea. It provides assurance that your API documentation will always be up-to-date and accurate.

However, currently, at the time of writing this book, there are some drawbacks with Spring REST Docs. One of them is that it won't help you that much during the API design phase. You will still need to write API design documents, and there's a good chance that you might have to throw away the API design documents once you can generate the documentation from test cases. If you're working on a big project, this could mean that you will have to throw away or deprecate lots of efforts that you or the team put into the API design documents.

Another drawback is that, currently, there is no support for the API playground. Developers can read the documents but cannot interact with the API, which makes the API harder to use.

Another drawback, which might be a problem for some developers, is that it doesn't support the OpenAPI specification (`https://www.openapis.org`). Hence, developers of API clients cannot generate the client code as they would with Swagger, which supports OpenAPI.

Still, Spring REST Docs is a great project and definitely worth trying. It is under active development at the time of writing this book.

RESTful API consuming

RESTful APIs are usually based on HTTP. To consume a RESTful API, what you actually do is to send out an HTTP request. In this section, we will have a brief introduction of the two scenarios of consuming a RESTful API.

HTTP client

For our TaskAgile application, the frontend is the client of the APIs that the backend provides. We will use Axios (`https://github.com/axios/axios`) as the HTTP client to interact with the APIs. We mentioned this library in `Chapter 3`, *Spring 5 - The Right Stack for the Job at Hand*, and used its `get()` and `post()` methods. Besides these two methods, it also provides the `delete()`, `put()`, and `patch()` methods. Axios also provides an easy way to configure global configurations, as shown in the following code:

```
axios.defaults.baseURL = 'https://api.examplebucks.org/v1';
axios.defaults.headers.common['Authorization'] = AUTH_TOKEN;
axios.defaults.headers.post['Content-Type'] = 'application/json';
```

`baseURL` is used to set the root URL of the APIs, and it is a good place to put the version number. The `Authorization` header is used for API authentication, while the `Content-Type` header is for specifying the data format of the request body.

Server-side consuming

Another scenario of consuming a REST API is that the backend needs to invoke a remote RESTful API. Since RESTful APIs are over HTTP, we can use libraries such as Apache HttpClient to make the call. However, we will have to take care of establishing an HTTP connection, checking the HTTP response, converting a response from a string into required objects, and then closing the connection. There is a lot of boilerplate code. Another option is to use the `RestTemplate` class that Spring provides. This class simplifies communication with HTTP servers by handling HTTP connections, leaving application code to provide URLs (with possible template variables) and extract results. And most importantly, it enforces RESTful principles.

RESTful API testing

There are two ways to test a RESTful API. The first way is to test a RESTful API of a running application that is deployed to a server. In this approach, the test code acts as the client of the API. This is usually called an **integration test** because it tests all of the code that's involved in that the API's execution. Normally, the integration test is executed at a late stage, during **Continuous Delivery (CD)**.

The second way is to isolate the API handler itself, using mocks for its dependencies and writing code to test the logic of the API handler. This is called unit testing and is where we have control of the dependencies and hence can expect the result of the execution to be precisely what we want. This is the approach we will use to test the RESTful API.

Unit testing of the Messages App

In Chapter 2, *Vue.js 2 – It Works in the Way You Expected*, we created a Messages App that has an API to retrieve all of the messages that are received. In this section, we will write unit testing code in that application to test that API.

Before writing any test code, we need to add `spring-boot-starter-test` in the Message App's `pom.xml` file, as shown in the following code. Let's have a look at the `pom.xml` file:

```
<project>
  ...
  <dependencies>
    ...
    <!-- Test -->
    <dependency>
      <groupId>org.springframework.boot</groupId>
      <artifactId>spring-boot-starter-test</artifactId>
      <scope>test</scope>
    </dependency>
  </dependencies>
  ...
</project>
```

For this dependency, we use a test scope so that the related dependencies won't be included in the final package. This starter will add the following libraries to the application:

- **JUnit:** The de facto standard for unit testing in Java applications. The version bundled in Spring Boot 2.0.0.RELEASE is JUnit 4.12.
- **Spring Test and Spring Boot Test:** Utilities and integration test support for Spring Boot applications.
- **AssertJ:** A fluent assertion library for Java.
- **Hamcrest:** A library of matcher objects, which can be combined to create flexible expressions of intent in tests.
- **Mockito:** A Java mocking framework.
- **JSONassert:** An assertion library for writing JSON unit tests in less code.
- **JsonPath:** A Java DSL for reading JSON documents.

The unit testing code for `MessageController#getMessages()` will be put inside a separate class named `MessageControllerTest` that lives in the `/test/java/app/messages/web/` directory. All of the test classes in this book will follow the `<Class>Test` format. Here is what this test class looks like. Let's have a look at the `MessageControllerTest.java` file:

```
...
@RunWith(SpringRunner.class)
@WebMvcTest(MessageController.class)
public class MessageControllerTest {
  @Autowired
  private MockMvc mvc;
  @MockBean
  private MessageService service;
  @Test
  public void getMessages_existingMessages_shouldReturnJsonArray()
  throws Exception {
    Message firstMessage = new Message("First Message");
    List<Message> allMessages = Arrays.asList(firstMessage);
    when(service.getMessages()).thenReturn(allMessages);
    mvc.perform(get("/api/messages").contentType(MediaType.
    APPLICATION_JSON))
    .andExpect(status().isOk())
    .andExpect(jsonPath("$", hasSize(1)))
    .andExpect(jsonPath("$[0].text", is(firstMessage.getText())));
  }
}
```

As you can see, we apply the `@RunWith` and `@WebMvcTest` annotations to set up this test class. The `@RunWith` annotation is a JUnit 4 annotation used to specify the JUnit Runner of this test class. A JUnit Runner is a class that extends JUnit's abstract `Runner` class and is used for running test classes. In our example, the runner will be `SpringRunner`, a class provided by the Spring Test framework. The `@WebMvcTest` annotation is provided by Spring. With its presence, Spring will only autoconfigure the Spring MVC's infrastructure.

Inside the test class, we have two properties: `mvc` of the `MockMvc` class, and `service` of the `MessageService` class, which is annotated by the `@MockBean` annotation. The `MockMvc` class is the main entry point for server-side Spring MVC test support, while the `@MockBean` annotation is used to create a mock of `MessageService`, which is then added to Spring's application context. The mock will also be injected into the service field.

The test method, `getMessages_existingMessages_shouldReturnJsonArray()`, follows the naming convention for unit testing that's suggested by Roy Osherove, which is `[UnitOfWork_StateUnderTest_ExpectedBehavior]`. The `@Test` annotation is from JUnit, which tells JUnit that the `public void` method that it annotated can be run as a test case. Inside this method, first, we create a list called `allMessages` that contains a `Message` object. Then, we use Mockito's `when().thenReturn()` command to set up the details of the service mock. When the `MessageService#getMessage()` method is invoked, the mock will return `allMessages`. In this way, we isolate the `MessageController` class from its dependencies and, at the same time, have full control of those dependencies.

When the pre-condition is ready, we use the `mvc.perform()` method to perform a `GET` request to the API and add assertions to verify the result. Here, we verify that `Content-Type` of the API's response is `application/json`, and that the status code is `200`. We use JsonPath to verify that the resulting JSON has only one item and that the value of the text field is `First Message`.

In VS Code, you can simply click **Run Test** from the class to execute the unit test cases of that class only, as shown in the following screenshot. Or you can execute the `mvn test` command to run all of the unit testing together:

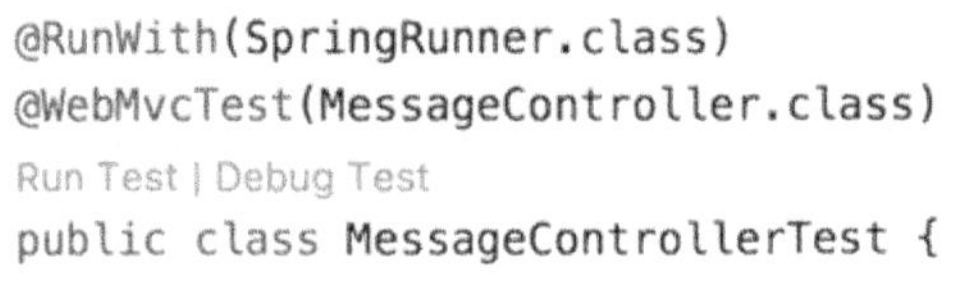

```
@RunWith(SpringRunner.class)
@WebMvcTest(MessageController.class)
Run Test | Debug Test
public class MessageControllerTest {
```

Figure 7.3: Test class in VS Code

Up until this point, we have successfully tested the `MessageController#getMessages()` method. In practice, we will write multiple test cases for a single method to verify the behavior of the method and understand its different conditions. We will talk more about unit testing later in this book.

Summary

In this chapter, you learned what a RESTful API is, the architectural constraints of REST, and the details of the REST uniform interface constraint. You also learned the characteristics of the opinionated RESTful API, that is, the Richardson Maturity Model of the RESTful API. We also talked about how being RESTful isn't a religious thing. Be practical.

You also learned about the design procedure of the RESTful API, the implementation support that Spring MVC provides, as well as the use of an HTTP client to consume a RESTful API. Finally, you tested the Message App's /messages API to see how to perform API unit testing.

In the next chapter, you're going to learn how to set up the scaffold of the frontend and the backend. That's where we will start, as we implement the TaskAgile application.

8
Creating the Application Scaffold - Taking off Like a Rocket

Now, we've entered the implementation phase of this book. It is time to write the code of the TaskAgile application. And, in this chapter, we will focus on setting up the application's scaffold—or you can call it the application skeleton. Because we have the frontend and the backend, we will generate the two parts of the scaffold separately and then put them together. In this chapter, you will learn the following:

- How to set up the development environment
- How to create the backend scaffold with Spring Initializr
- How to create the frontend scaffold with Vue CLI 3
- How to connect the frontend and the backend, putting them together
- How to set up the router in the frontend with `vue-router`

Setting up the development environment

Even though we have created the frontend of the Message App in Chapter 2, *Vue.js 2 - It Works in the Way You Expected*, and the backend in Chapter 3, *Spring 5 - The Right Stack for the Job at Hand*, and mentioned the usage of VS Code, we haven't talked about how to set up the development environment. In this section, we will go through the tools we're going to use to build the TaskAgile application. However, we won't cover the details of a step-by-step installation of those tools. You can use this section as an overview of the development environment requirement.

Our development environment includes mainly the following parts:

- Runtime
- Database
- Code editor/IDE
- Source control system
- Utilities

The runtime for the frontend will be the browser. In our case, it is Chrome. The backend runtime is the **JRE** (short for **Java Runtime Environment**), which is included in the **JDK** (short for **Java Development Kit**). We use JDK 8 (http://www.oracle.com/technetwork/java/javase/overview/index.html).

The database we will use is MySQL 5.7. The code editor we will use is still VS Code. Even though VS Code is not an **IDE** (short for **Integrated Development Environment**), such as IntelliJ IDEA, it can help us with most of our daily coding, debugging through a variety of extensions. In Chapter 3, *Spring 5 - The Right Stack for the Job at Hand*, we have listed those we need for both frontend and backend development. The fascinating part of VS Code is that it is written in TypeScript and open sourced on GitHub (https://github.com/Microsoft/vscode).

The source control system that we will use is Git. And, while we're implementing TaskAgile, we will push the code to vuejs.spring-boot.mysql, a public repository on GitHub (https://github.com/taskagile/vuejs.spring-boot.mysql). In this way, once we finish the implementation, besides a working application, you can also see all of the commits that we make along the way. And we will use GitHub Desktop (https://desktop.github.com) as the GUI client.

The utilities we will use are those for dependency management and building the package. For the frontend, we will use Node.js 8.11.0+. For the backend, we will use Maven 3.2+. And the other tool that we will use is MySQL Workbench 6.3. We have used it in Chapter 5, *Data Modeling - Designing the Foundation of the Application,* for physical data modeling. During the implementation, we mainly use its Visual SQL Editor to check the data records and executing SQL queries.

Before we move on, you will need to have the following installed:

- Node.js 8.11.0 +
- JDK 1.8.0_152 +
- MySQL 5.7 +
- Git 2.15.1 +

Creating the backend scaffold with Spring Initializr

To generate the backend scaffold, instead of creating Maven's pom.xml file manually from scratch, we can use Spring Initializr to generate a Spring Boot application for us. To do that, let's go to https://start.spring.io and switch to the full version by clicking the **Switch to the full version** link, and then fill in form with the following parameters:

- Group: com.taskagile
- Artifact: app
- Name: TaskAgile
- Description: Open source task management tool
- Package Name: com.taskagile
- Dependencies: **Web**, **Thymeleaf**, **JPA**, and **DevTools**

After that, all we need to do is click the **Generate Project** button, as shown in *Figure 8.1*:

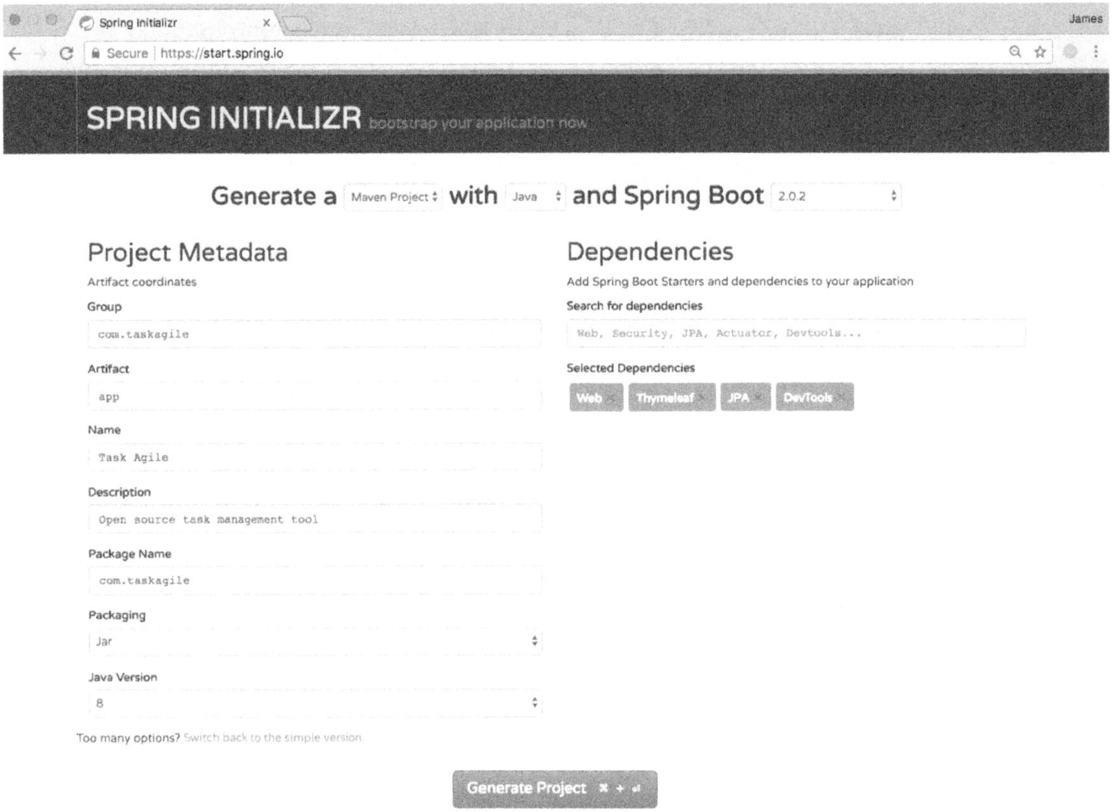

Figure 8.1: Spring Initializr

File structure

Once Spring Initializr finishes the generation of the skeleton of the backend of our
TaskAgile application, we can see the following structure:

```
.
├── .gitignore
├── .mvn
│   └── wrapper
│       ├── maven-wrapper.jar
│       └── maven-wrapper.properties
├── mvnw
├── mvnw.cmd
```

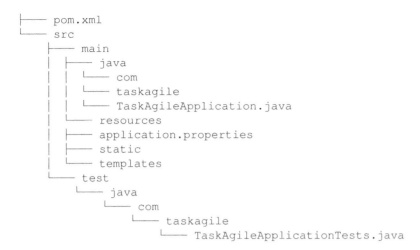

```
├──── pom.xml
└──── src
      ├──── main
      │     ├──── java
      │     │     └──── com
      │     │           └──── taskagile
      │     │                 └──── TaskAgileApplication.java
      │     └──── resources
      │           ├──── application.properties
      │           ├──── static
      │           └──── templates
      └──── test
            └──── java
                  └──── com
                        └──── taskagile
                              └──── TaskAgileApplicationTests.java
```

Let's go through the items in this tree. First of all, the .mvn folder, and the mvnw and mvnw.cmd files, are for Maven Wrapper, which enables you to use a project-specific Maven version, and, when there is no Maven of that version installed or found on the path, it will download it automatically.

The pom.xml file, as we mentioned before, is the configuration file used by Maven, and, with the selected dependencies, Spring Initializer will add the following dependencies in this file:

- spring-boot-starter-data-jpa
- spring-boot-starter-thymeleaf
- spring-boot-starter-web
- spring-boot-devtools
- spring-boot-starter-test

The com.taskagile.TaskAgileApplication.java class is the main entry of the application. And com.taskagile.TaskAgileApplicationTests.java is its unit test.

When Spring Initializr generates a project skeleton, it uses the value of the artifact field as the application's folder name. For TaskAgile, we will rename the application folder to vuejs.spring-boot.mysql.

The application folder's name follows the pattern, `<front-end-technolgoy>.<back-end-technology>.<database-technology>`. This doesn't mean you need to name it the same way in your application. The reason we named it in this way is that, in the future, we will implement TaskAgile using different technologies, such as `react.spring-boot.mysql` or `vuejs.spring-boot.mongodb`.

Before committing the application scaffold, let's add the following, `.editorconfig`, to the root directory.

Let's have a look at the `.editorconfig` file:

```
root = true

[*]
charset = utf-8
indent_style = space
indent_size = 2
end_of_line = lf
insert_final_newline = true
trim_trailing_whitespace = true

[*.md]
trim_trailing_whitespace = false
```

This `.editorconfig` file is used by EditorConfig (`https://editorconfig.org`) to maintain consistent coding styles. You will need to install the VS Code extension, **EditorConfig for VS Code** (`EditorConfig.editorconfig`), to enable this feature.

Committing and pushing

Now, let's initialize our application folder as a Git repository, and make a commit by using the following commands:

```
git init
git add -A
git commit -m "create back-end scaffold"
git remote add origin
https://github.com/taskagile/vuejs.spring-boot.mysql.git
```

If you're writing your own app by following this step-by-step, you will most likely create a repository of your own on GitHub or somewhere else and change the URL in the `git remote add` command to your repository.

After that, we use the following command to push the repository to GitHub:

```
git push -u origin master
```

Now, we have our first commit of the TaskAgile application, as shown in *Figure 8.2*:

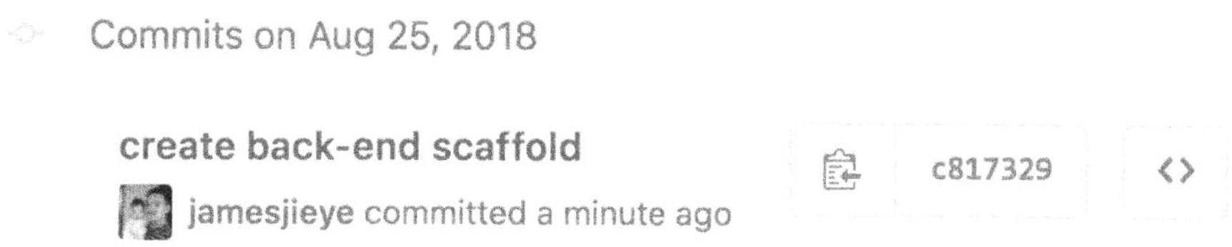

Commits on Aug 25, 2018

create back-end scaffold

jamesjieye committed a minute ago

c817329

Figure 8.2: Creating the backend scaffold commit

As a practice, we will record every commit made to this repository in this book, so that you can use these as references to see the actual code created.

Running the application

We were moving too fast. We haven't tested the code and made sure it works before committing it. This is a bad practice and should be avoided. No matter how eagerly we want to commit the code, we must make sure it compiles and passes tests in the local environment first.

Now, let's run the `mvn install` command to see how it works. Unfortunately, we have a build failure. Our only test, which was generated automatically by Spring Initializr, has failed, as you can see from the following output in the console:

```
. . .
[ERROR] Tests run: 1, Failures: 0, Errors: 1, Skipped: 0, Time elapsed:
2.499 s <<< FAILURE! - in com.taskagile.TaskAgileApplicationTests
[ERROR] contextLoads(com.taskagile.TaskAgileApplicationTests) Time elapsed:
0.007 s <<< ERROR!
. . .
```

And, if you go through the entire error log, you can see the following information provided by Spring Boot:

```
* * * * * * * * * * * * * * * * * * * * * * * * * *
APPLICATION FAILED TO START
* * * * * * * * * * * * * * * * * * * * * * * * * *

Description:
```

```
Failed to configure a DataSource: 'url' attribute is not specified and no
embedded datasource could be configured.
Reason: Failed to determine a suitable driver class
```

It seems like that we forgot to add the database driver and configure the datasource. In Chapter 3, *Spring 5 - The Right Stack for the Job at Hand,* we learned that we need to add the dependency, mysql-connector-java, which contains the MySQL driver class. Let's add the following to pom.xml:

```
<dependency>
    <groupId>mysql</groupId>
    <artifactId>mysql-connector-java</artifactId>
</dependency>
```

And let's also add the following datasource configuration to application.properties:

```
spring.datasource.url=jdbc:mysql://localhost:3306/task_agile?useSSL=false
spring.datasource.username=<username>
spring.datasource.password=<password>
spring.datasource.driver-class-name=com.mysql.jdbc.Driver
```

<username> and <password> are just placeholders. Remember to replace them with your own.

Before we move further, let's initialize the task_agile database using database-setup.sql, which we created in Chapter 5, *Data Modeling - Designing the Foundation of the Application.* Once that is done, let's run another mvn install command to see how things work. There are no more errors. The build has succeeded, as you can see from the output in the console:

```
[INFO] BUILD SUCCESS
```

Even though the build has passed, you might well have spotted something wrong in what we just did. That's right, we put the database's username and password in application.properties, which will be pushed to a public repository that anyone can access. This is a security leak, and it is also problematic when we need to deploy the application to staging and production servers because the MySQL's username and password in those environments will definitely be different, as well as the URL of the database. Furthermore, it will cause issues with team collaboration because it forces everyone to use the same username and password for their local dev environment.

A practical way is to use Spring Profiles to segregate the data source configured so that a different environment has its own settings. And, by default, in a Spring Boot application, the active profile is `dev`. Now, let's change the username and password of the datasource in `application.properties` to placeholders. The reason we do not remove those settings completely is that we want to use `application.properties` as a complete view of our configuration. And we create a different configuration file for each environment to override those settings that will be different in each environment. For now, let's focus on the local dev environment and create `application-dev.properties` with the following properties:

```
spring.datasource.url=jdbc:mysql://localhost:3306/task_agile?useSSL=false
spring.datasource.username=<change to your own username>
spring.datasource.password=<change to your own password>
```

If you run the `mvn install` command again, you can see we still have a successful build. It means the Spring Boot has picked up the settings in `application-dev.properties`. And to keep these settings only visible in the local dev environment, let's add `application-dev.properties` into `.gitignore`.

Now, let's commit the following files and push them to a remote origin, as shown in *Figure 8.3*:

- `.gitignore`
- `pom.xml`
- `application.properties`

The following screenshot shown the preceding commit operation:

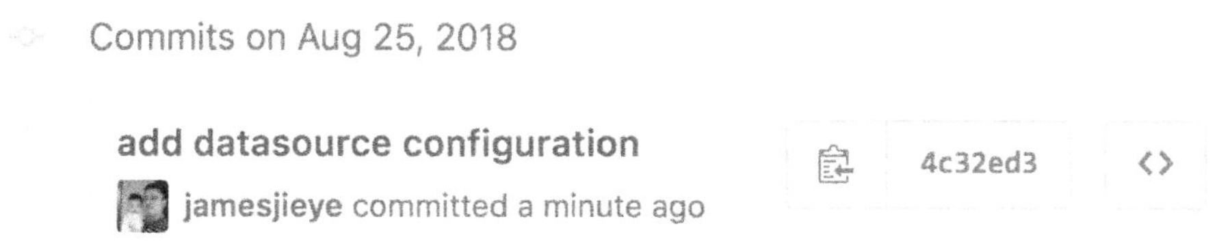

Figure 8.3: Adding the datasource configuration commit

Spring provides a feature called Profile that allows us to set different properties for different environments. And, we can set active profiles to tell Spring which `.properties` should be loaded.

Since we're in the local dev environment, it would be better to make sure we're running in the **dev** profile. As we will mention in `Chapter 14`, *Health Checking, System Monitoring - Getting Ready for Production*, there are many ways to specify the active profile. For a local dev environment, let's use the environment variable to set the active profile.

If you're in a Unix/Linux OS, you can set it by using `export spring_profiles_active=dev` in your bash profile. And if you're in Windows, you will need to add an environment variable.

By now, we have created the backend scaffold of the TaskAgile application. And, as mentioned before, we can use the `mvn spring-boot:run` command to start the Spring Boot application.

Now, let's move on to the next step.

Creating the frontend scaffold

To create the frontend scaffold, we will use Vue.js's command line, `vue-cli`, to generate the code for us. First of all, let's install `vue-cli` with the following commands:

```
npm install -g @vue/cli
```

At the time of writing, the version of `vue-cli` we used here is 3.0.1.

Once `vue-cli` is installed, we can use its `create` command to generate the code. Let's create a Vue application called `front-end` under the root directory of the application by using the following command:

```
vue create front-end
```

And, in the prompt shown in *Figure 8.4*, we choose to manually select the following features: **Babel**, **Router**, **Vuex**, **CSS Pre-processors**, **Linter**, **Unit**, and **E2E**.

We enable the history mode for the router and choose **SCSS/SASS** as the CSS pre-processor. For Linter, we choose the ESLint + **Standard** configuration. And, we choose **Jest** as the unit testing solution and **Nightwatch** as the E2E testing solution. And, we choose **NPM** for package managing:

```
●  ⬚  ▦         ▤ vuejs.spring-boot.mysql — npm • node /usr/local/bin/vue create front-end — 105×12
Vue CLI v3.0.1
? Please pick a preset: Manually select features
? Check the features needed for your project: Babel, Router, Vuex, CSS Pre-processors, Linter, Unit, E2E
[? Use history mode for router? (Requires proper server setup for index fallback in production) Yes        ]
? Pick a CSS pre-processor (PostCSS, Autoprefixer and CSS Modules are supported by default): SCSS/SASS
? Pick a linter / formatter config: Standard
? Pick additional lint features: Lint on save
? Pick a unit testing solution: Jest
? Pick a E2E testing solution: Nightwatch
? Where do you prefer placing config for Babel, PostCSS, ESLint, etc.? In dedicated config files
[? Save this as a preset for future projects? No                                                           ]
? Pick the package manager to use when installing dependencies: NPM
```

Figure 8.4: Vue CLI where manually selecting features

File structure

Once the code generation is finished and all the dependencies are also installed, you can see the following structure in the `front-end` directory:

```
.
├──── .browserslistrc
├──── .eslintrc.js
├──── .gitignore
├──── README.md
├──── babel.config.js
├──── jest.config.js
├──── package-lock.json
├──── package.json
├──── postcss.config.js
├──── public
│      ├──── favicon.ico
│      └──── index.html
├──── src
│      ├──── App.vue
│      ├──── assets
│      │      └──── logo.png
│      ├──── components
│      │      └──── HelloWorld.vue
│      ├──── main.js
│      ├──── router.js
│      ├──── store.js
│      └──── views
│             ├──── About.vue
│             └──── Home.vue
└──── tests
       ├──── e2e
       │      ├──── custom-assertions
```

```
|   |       └── elementCount.js
|   └── specs
|   └── test.js
└── unit
    ├── .eslintrc.js
    └── HelloWorld.spec.js
```

Before we go through each item in this structure, let's switch to the `front-end` directory and run the command, `npm run serve`, to start the Vue application. Behind the scenes, this command calls `vue-cli-service serve` to start a dev server, which is based on `webpack-dev-server`, to serve our Vue application with **Hot-Module-Replacement (HMR)** working out of the box. *Figure 8.5* is how our generated Vue application looks. It is a placeholder page that we will change later:

Welcome to Your Vue.js App

Essential Links

Core Docs   Forum   Community Chat   Twitter
Docs for This Template

Ecosystem

vue-router   vuex   vue-loader   awesome-vue

Figure 8.5: Vue initial page

Now, let's go through the items in the structure one by one. `.browserslistrc` is used by libraries such as Babel and `postcss-preset-env` to define the target browser. `.eslintrc.js` is the configuration file of ESLint. `babel.config.js` is the configuration file of Babel. `jest.config.js` is the configuration file of Jest. And the `package-lock.json` file is automatically generated by npm for describing the exact `node_modules` tree that was generated so that subsequent installs are able to generate identical trees. The `postcss.config.js` file is used to autoload configuration for PostCSS (`https://postcss.org`).

The `public` directory contains the `favicon.ico` file and the `index.html` file, which is the template file of the final generated `index.html` file served by `webpack-dev-server`, as shown in *Figure 8.6*. Let's take a closer look to see the difference. The following is the content of the `index.html` template file:

```
<!DOCTYPE html>
<html lang="en">
  <head>
    <meta charset="utf-8">
    <meta http-equiv="X-UA-Compatible" content="IE=edge">
    <meta name="viewport" content="width=device-width,initial-
    scale=1.0">
    <link rel="icon" href="<%= BASE_URL %>favicon.ico">
    <title>front-end</title>
  </head>
  <body>
    <noscript>
      <strong>We're sorry but front-end doesn't work properly without
      JavaScript enabled. Please enable it to continue.</strong>
    </noscript>
    <div id="app"></div>
    <!-- built files will be auto injected -->
  </body>
</html>
```

Figure 8.6 shows the source code of `index.html` that is served by `webpack-dev-server`:

```
1  <!DOCTYPE html>
2  <html>
3    <head>
4      <meta charset="utf-8">
5      <meta name="viewport" content="width=device-width,initial-scale=1.0">
6      <title>task-agile</title>
7    </head>
8    <body>
9      <div id="app"></div>
10     <!-- built files will be auto injected -->
11     <script type="text/javascript" src="/app.js"></script></body>
12 </html>
13
```

Figure 8.6: Source of Vue initial page

As you can see, in line 7, `<%= BASE_URL %>` is replaced with the / value. And, line 9 and line 16 are auto-injected by webpack. The `app.js` file is generated by webpack on the fly.

Let's change `<title>` in the `index.html` template to `<title>TaskAgile</title>`. And, without refreshing the page, the page title has been updated automatically.

The `src` directory is where we will put the source code of our Vue application. Inside the `src` directory, the `assets` directory is where we put assets that will be processed by webpack. The `components` directory is where we put our shareable components. `App.vue` is the main Vue component of our application that is bootstrapped in `main.js`, which is the application's entry file. And the `router.js` file contains the configuration of `vue-router`, which we will discuss later in this chapter. The `store.js` file is for bootstrapping Vuex, which we will introduce in Chapter 11, *State Management and i18n - Building a Home Page*. The `views` directory is where we put the pages.

The `test` directory contains two types of test code: end-to-end tests and unit tests, which are kept in the `e2e` subfolder and `unit` subfolder respectively. And there are test examples included in the generated code. We can try with the commands, `npm run test:unit` and `npm run test:e2e`, to see the execution.

Let's make the following change to `scripts` and to `package.json` by adding the `test` command so that we can use one single command, `npm test`, to run both the unit test and the E2E test:

```
{
  ...
  "scripts": {
  ...
  "test:unit": "vue-cli-service test:unit",
  "test:e2e": "vue-cli-service test:e2e",
  "test": "npm run test:unit && npm run test:e2e"
  },
  ...
}
```

Cleaning up and reorganizing

As you can see, the auto-generated Vue application contains code examples, which we don't need. Let's clean them up before committing to the repository.

Let's start from `App.vue` by removing the `<img>` tag and the `#app` CSS inside `<style>`, making the file look like this:

```
<template>
  <div id="app">
    <router-view/>
  </div>
</template>

<script>
export default {
  name: 'App'
}
</script>

<style>
</style>
```

In the future, we will add global styles inside the `<style>` tag of `App.vue`.

Now, let's delete `components/HelloWorld.vue`, `views/About.vue`, and `views/Home.vue`. Once these files are deleted, and if you have the frontend running, the webpack will complain about this deletion. And, you can see an error message: `Failed to compile with 2 errors`, in the console. It is because `Home.vue` and `About.vue` are referenced in `router.js`. And webpack monitors the `src` directory. Any change to the `.js` files, `.vue` files, or assets inside of this directory will trigger a compilation of the application. Let's fix this by removing the reference and change `router.js` to the following:

```
import Vue from 'vue'
import Router from 'vue-router'

Vue.use(Router)

export default new Router({
  mode: 'history',
  base: process.env.BASE_URL,
  routes: []
})
```

Now, the compilation finished and webpack automatically updated the page, which is blank now. That's a good base for us to implement TaskAgile. We will talk about more about `router.js` later.

Now, remember the lesson that we learned when we created the backend scaffold—**no commit before all of the tests pass locally**.

Let's run the test on the frontend with the command, `npm test`. Undoubtedly, it failed. Both the unit test in `HelloWorld.spec.js` and the e2e test in `test.js` are expecting contents of `HelloWorld.vue`, which we have deleted. To fix this, one option is to delete these test files, which will work. The other option is to create a Vue component and change the tests accordingly.

Let's take the second option. And, since we're practicing TDD in the book, we won't write the Vue component first. We will create test files and then write the actual component. Before we start practicing TDD, let's describe a little bit about the Vue component that we will create.

As we know, our TaskAgile application is an SPA. So, when we say a page in TaskAgile, we mean a logical page, for example, the login page, the register page, and so on. And we will create a Vue component for each page and put them into the `front-end/src/views` folder. These components will be named in such a way as `LoginPage.vue` and `RegisterPage.vue`. Inside the original `front-end/src/components` folder, we will put components that will be shared between pages, for instances, buttons, and modal windows.

For now, we will write a simple `front-end/src/views/LoginPage.vue` as a placeholder. In this Vue component, we will simply put a heading inside a `<div>` wrapper, which looks like this: `<div><h1>TaskAgile</h1></div>`. Now, we know how the page will look. Let's change the tests.

We will need to rename the unit test file, `HelloWord.spec.js`, to `LoginPage.spec.js` and change it to be like the following:

```
1.  import Vue from 'vue'
2.  import LoginPage from '@/views/LoginPage'
3.
4.  describe('LoginPage.vue', () => {
5.    it('should render correct contents', () => {
6.      const Constructor = Vue.extend(LoginPage)
7.      const vm = new Constructor().$mount()
8.      expect(vm.$el.querySelector('h1').textContent)
9.        .toEqual('TaskAgile')
10.   })
11. })
```

As you can see, line 1 is an import of Vue itself. And line 2 is importing the
LoginPage.vue that we are testing against. Line 4 is using Jest's describe(name, fn)
API to create a test suite that groups related tests together. In our case, we only have one
test right now, that is, the one listed from line 5 to line 10. The it(name, fn, timeout)
function is an alias of Jest's API, test(name, fn, timeout). The first argument is the test
name. The second argument is a function that contains the expectations to test. The third
argument is a timeout in milliseconds, which is optional. And, when not provided, the
default timeout is five seconds. In line 6, we create a LoginPage subclass of the Vue. And
in line 7, we create a Vue instance of LoginPage and then mount it programmatically.
Once the $mount() method is invoked, you can think of this Vue instance as though it has
been rendered on the page. In line 8, we use Jest's API, expect().toEqual(), to assert
that the text content of <h1> tag on the page is of the 'TaskAgile' value. vm.$el is the
root DOM element that the Vue instance, vm, manages. In our case, it is the <div> wrapper,
which is an instance of JavaScript built-in class, Element. The .querySelector('h1')
method is used to find the <h1> element.

Now, let's work on the end-to-end test by starting with renaming the test file from test.js
to login.e2e.js, and changing the tests to be like the following:

```
1. module.exports = {
2.   'login test': function (browser) {
3.     browser
4.       .url(process.env.VUE_DEV_SERVER_URL + 'login')
5.       .waitForElementVisible('#app', 5000)
6.       .assert.containsText('h1', 'TaskAgile')
7.       .end()
8.   }
9. }
```

As you can see in line 1, it is a definition of Node.js module. And we write the Nightwatch
tests inside that module. A Nightwatch test can contain multiple steps and, in our case, we
have only one step, which is named 'login test'. Each step is actually a method of the
module, which accepts a parameter, browser, which is provided by Nightwatch for
controlling the browser. In line 4, we call the .url() method to open the login page that is
served from the development server, which is started by @vue/cli-service. In line 5, the
waitForElementVisible() method is to assert that the #app element will be visible in
five seconds. In line 6, we use Nightwatch's assert API to check the <h1> element contains
the text 'TaskAgile', which is the same assertion we used in LoginPage.spec.js. The
.end() method in line 7 is used to close the test and for the Selenium session to be
properly closed.

This Nightwatch test is quite straightforward, but also brittle. For example, if we change the HTML from `<h1>` to `<h2>` or something else. The test will break, even though we still have the `'TaskAgile'` text on the page. A better way to write E2E tests is to use **Page Objects**, which is a popular pattern of writing end-to-end tests. And, it is the approach we will use in this book. For now, let's we will leave our first E2E test as it is now.

Now, if you run the `npm test` command, without any doubt, it fails. It's time to write the actual code. Let's create the `front-end/src/views/LoginPage.vue` file, which looks like the following:

```
1. <template>
2.   <div>
3.     <h1>TaskAgile</h1>
4.   </div>
5. </template>
6.
7. <script>
8. export default {
9.   name: 'LoginPage'
10.}
11.</script>
```

As you can see, it is quite simple and has only a `<h1>` tag. But it is good enough to pass our unit test. Now, if we run `npm test` again, we can see the unit test has passed, but not the E2E test because we haven't provided a route for `LoginPage.vue` yet.

Let's make changes to `front-end/src/router.js` as the following, so that the `LoginPage.vue` can be rendered:

```
...
import LoginPage from '@/views/LoginPage'
...
export default new Router({
  ...
  routes: [{
    path: '/login',
    name: 'LoginPage',
    component: LoginPage
  }]
})
```

As you can see, we put the login page at the `path '/login'` root. We will talk in detail about how the router works later in this chapter. For now, let's run `npm test` to see how things work. When you see output similar to the following, it means both the unit test and E2E tests have passed:

```
...
Test Suites: 1 passed, 1 total
...
Running: login test
...
OK. 2 assertions passed. (4.746s)
```

Now, let's commit the changes and push it to origin, as shown in *Figure 8.7*:

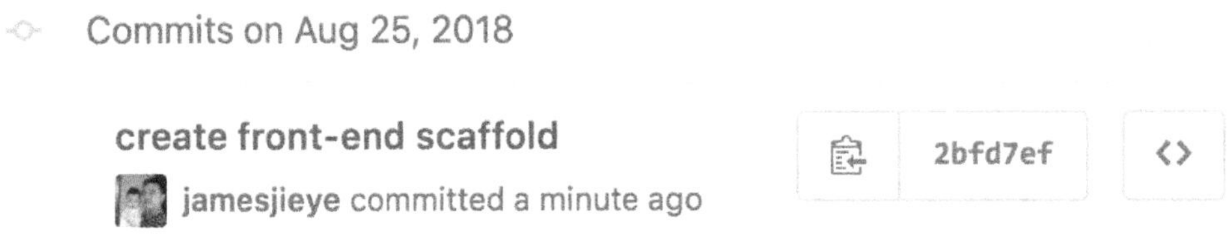

Figure 8.7: Creating the frontend scaffold commit

Didn't we miss something?

Even though we haven't change any backend code, shouldn't we run a test on the backend to make sure everything works? As a matter of fact, it is always recommended to run all of the tests before committing the code, because it is the only way to make sure there are no breaks in the application, which is especially important before leaving the office late in the night after a long day of coding. People make mistakes, but automated tests won't.

There is one issue in our case. Right now, every time we need to run all of the tests, including those of the backend and those of the frontend, we have to do it separately, which is not ideal. A preferred way is to use a single command to run all of the tests of both the backend and the frontend.

And, as you might have noticed, our E2E test isn't really from the frontend to the backend. Currently, the frontend and the backend are isolated, even though they are under the same folder. Let's get them connected.

Putting two ends together

There are two parts that we need to connect between the frontend and the backend. The first part is the build process. Currently, we need to use `mvn` and `npm` to build the two parts separately. Once they are connected, we will only need to execute a single command to build the entire application.

The second part is to bridge the communication between the frontend and the backend. As mentioned, during development, the frontend will be served by `webpack-dev-server` under a different port than the one of the backend. Currently, both ends use the same port, `8080`. We will need to change the port of the frontend to `3000` so that we can have both ends up and running at the same time. When our application is served from `http://localhost:3000`, the requests that the frontend pages send to the backend at `http://localhost:8080`, by default, will be blocked by the browser because they are cross-origin. The frontend won't be able to access the response of those requests unless we bridge the communication. We can achieve this by changing the backend to add HTTP header, `Access-Control-Allow-Origin`, in the HTTP response to allow the frontend to access the response. This will work, but is not ideal in our case, because once we package the whole application, there won't be any cross-origin requests. Instead, we will use another way, which is to add an HTTP proxy on the frontend side to pass the requests to the backend. In this way, all requests will be from the same origin as far as the browser can tell.

 For our TaskAgile application, we put the frontend and the backend in the same package and deploy them together as a whole. This is not the only way to deploy our application. Another common approach is to deploy the frontend and backend separately on different servers. In that case, we should add the `Access-Control-Allow-Origin` header to the HTTP response to bridge the communication.

Building with a single command

Let's start this connection by combining the `build` command. Since we put the frontend inside the backend as a subfolder, we will use Maven to control `npm`. Another important reason of doing this is that Maven has built-in support of various phases of the entire build life cycle that we can leverage. We can use Maven plugins to combine the frontend build steps into Maven's build life cycle. The build life cycle that is shown in *Figure 8.8* here is the one we will implement:

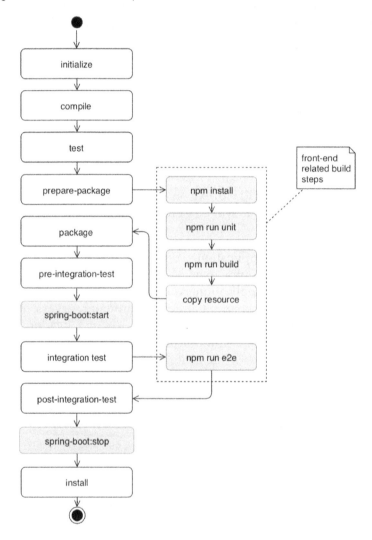

Figure 8.8: Building the life cycle

For simplicity, the life cycle diagram doesn't include all of the default phases that Maven supports. You can find out more about it here: `https://maven.apache.org/guides/introduction/introduction-to-the-lifecycle.html`.

As you can see from the diagram, the build process starts with the initialization, compilation, and test of the backend. And then we include the build steps of the frontend in the **prepare-package** phase. Once the frontend is built, we copy the assets from the `front-end/dist` folder to the `src/main/resources` folder so that in the **package** phase, those assets will be added into the final JAR package. Once that is done, we start the Spring Boot application in Maven's **pre-integration-test** phase and then execute the end-to-end tests that we create in the frontend. When all of the tests pass, we stop the Spring Boot application. And then, Maven installs the JAR package to the repository.

Since we only attach the build steps of the frontend into Maven's packaging phases, when we run `mvn test`, only the backend tests will be executed, which is desired. To run the frontend tests, we will use the `npm` commands. In this way, we won't have coupling between the tests execution of the two ends.

Now, let's see how to implement this unified build process.

We will use **Exec Maven Plugin** (`https://www.mojohaus.org/exec-maven-plugin/index.html`) to execute those `npm` commands and use **Maven Resources Plugin** (`https://maven.apache.org/plugins/maven-resources-plugin`) to copy the frontend resources, and use **Spring Boot Maven Plugin**, which is already included in the generated scaffold, to start and stop the application. All of the required changes are made to the `<plugins>` section of the `<build>` section in `pom.xml`.

First of all, let's add the **Exec Maven Plugin** to the `<plugins>` section, as follows:

```
<plugin>
  <groupId>org.codehaus.mojo</groupId>
  <artifactId>exec-maven-plugin</artifactId>
  <version>1.6.0</version>
  <executions></executions>
  <configuration>
    <workingDirectory>${basedir}/front-end</workingDirectory>
  </configuration>
</plugin>
```

The `<executions>` section is where we will add details of those `npm` commands. And `<workingDirectory>` is to tell `exec-maven-plugin` that the `npm` commands will be executed inside the `front-end/` folder.

The following is `<execution>` that tells `exec-maven-plugin` to execute the `npm install` command:

```
<execution>
  <id>font-end install</id>
  <goals>
    <goal>exec</goal>
  </goals>
  <phase>prepare-package</phase>
  <configuration>
    <executable>npm</executable>
    <arguments>
      <argument>install</argument>
    </arguments>
  </configuration>
</execution>
```

In this `<execution>`, `<id>` is where you name `<execution>` uniquely among the entire build process. The `exec` goal is to tell `exec-maven-plugin` that `npm`, which is specified in the `<executable>` tag, is an external program. And `<phase>` is to tell Maven this plugin's execution should be performed during the `prepare-package` phase. The `<arguments>` section is for specifying the arguments that the executable requires.

The following section is for executing the `npm run` unit during the `prepare-package` phase:

```
<execution>
  <id>font-end unit test</id>
  <goals>
    <goal>exec</goal>
  </goals>
  <phase>prepare-package</phase>
  <configuration>
    <executable>npm</executable>
    <arguments>
      <argument>run</argument>
      <argument>test:unit</argument>
    </arguments>
  </configuration>
</execution>
```

As you can see, since we need to pass two arguments, `run` and `test:unit`, to `npm`, we list them in the `<arguments>` part accordingly. And, since Maven 3.0.3, the `<execution>` of different plugins will be executed in the order that they are listed in `pom.xml`.

The following `<execution>` section is for `exec-maven-plugin` to execute the `npm run build` command during the `prepare-package` phase:

```
<execution>
  <id>font-end build package</id>
  <goals>
    <goal>exec</goal>
  </goals>
  <phase>prepare-package</phase>
  <configuration>
    <executable>npm</executable>
    <arguments>
      <argument>run</argument>
      <argument>build</argument>
    </arguments>
  </configuration>
</execution>
```

The following is `<execution>` for `exec-maven-plugin` to invoke the `npm run test:e2e` command using the `integration-test` phase:

```
<execution>
  <id>front-end e2e test</id>
  <goals>
    <goal>exec</goal>
  </goals>
  <phase>integration-test</phase>
  <configuration>
    <executable>npm</executable>
    <arguments>
      <argument>run</argument>
      <argument>test:e2e</argument>
    </arguments>
  </configuration>
</execution>
```

Now, we have attached all the `npm` commands to the build process. Let's add the Maven Resources Plugin to copy the build result of the frontend to the `src/main/resources` directory.

Here is how the `maven-resources-plugin` section looks overall:

```
<plugin>
  <artifactId>maven-resources-plugin</artifactId>
  <version>3.1.0</version>
  <executions></executions>
</plugin>
```

Because Spring Boot put the HTML template files in the `src/main/resources/templates` folder and static assets in the `src/main/resources/static` folder, we will need to copy `front-end/dist/index.html` and `front-end/dist/static` separately, in two `<execution>` instances.

The following `<execution>` will copy `index.html` to the `src/main/resources/templates` folder during the `prepare-package` phase:

```xml
<execution>
  <id>copy front-end template</id>
  <goals>
    <goal>copy-resources</goal>
  </goals>
  <phase>prepare-package</phase>
  <configuration>
   <outputDirectory>${basedir}/src/main/resources/templates</outputDirectory>
    <resources>
      <resource>
        <directory>front-end/dist</directory>
        <includes><include>index.html</include></includes>
      </resource>
    </resources>
  </configuration>
</execution>
```

The following is `<execution>` that will copy the entire `static` folder into the `src/main/resources/static` folder:

```xml
<execution>
  <id>copy front-end static assets</id>
  <goals>
    <goal>copy-resources</goal>
  </goals>
  <phase>prepare-package</phase>
  <configuration>
    <outputDirectory>${basedir}/src/main/resources/static</outputDirectory>
    <resources>
      <resource>
        <directory>front-end/dist</directory>
        <excludes><exclude>index.html</exclude></excludes>
      </resource>
    </resources>
  </configuration>
</execution>
```

As you can see, the only difference this <execution> has with the previous one is that we use <excludes> to skip index.html during the copying.

Since we specify these two copy <execution> instances to be executed in the prepare-package phase, it is easy to assume that Maven will package the frontend assets into the JAR package. In fact, Maven will do that, but it will only do it the second time you run the mvn install command. Let me explain this. In Maven's default build life cycle, between the initialize phase and the compile phase, there are another four phases, including the following:

- **generate-sources**
- **process-sources**
- **generate-resources**
- **process-resources**

It is in the **process-resources** phase that Maven will copy and process the resources into the destination directory, which is the target/ directory, ready for packaging, as shown in *Figure 8.9*. And the packaging in the package phase happens in the target/ directory:

src/main/resources   target/classes

Figure 8.9: Copying resources to the target directory

As you can see, after we copy the frontend assets to src/main/resources in the prepare-package phase, Maven won't touch src/main/resources anymore. It is only the next time when you execute mvn install that those frontend assets will be picked up by Maven for packaging but, at that moment, they are already stalled since they are not the fresh version that is generated in the later prepare-package phase.

To fix this, let's add another two copy <execution> instances to copy frontend assets to the target/classes directory. The only differences are that they will have a different execution ID and different values for outputDirectory, as you can see here:

```
<execution>
  <id>copy front-end template to target</id>
  ...
  <configuration>
    <outputDirectory>${basedir}/target/classes/templates</outputDirectory>
    ...
  </configuration>
```

```
      </execution>
      <execution>
        <id>copy front-end assets to target</id>
        ...
        <configuration>
          <outputDirectory>${basedir}/target/classes/static</outputDirectory>
          ...
        </configuration>
      </execution>
    </execution>
```

Now, let's get the last part done, which is to start and stop Spring Boot. It is quite straightforward with `spring-boot-maven-plugin`. The following is the change we make to the plugin:

```
<plugin>
  <groupId>org.springframework.boot</groupId>
  <artifactId>spring-boot-maven-plugin</artifactId>
  <executions>
    <execution>
      <id>pre integration test</id>
      <goals>
        <goal>start</goal>
      </goals>
    </execution>
    <execution>
      <id>post integration test</id>
      <goals>
        <goal>stop</goal>
      </goals>
    </execution>
  </executions>
</plugin>
```

As you can see, we simply add two `<execution>` sections which only contain the `start` and `stop` goals. The Spring Boot Maven plugin will tell Maven that the `start` goal is for the `pre integration test` phase and the `stop` goal is for the `post integration test` phase.

Now, if you run the `mvn install` command, you should be able to see the following simplified log information in the output:

```
[INFO] --- maven-compiler-plugin:3.7.0:compile (default-compile) @ app ---
[INFO] --- maven-surefire-plugin:2.21.0:test (default-test) @ app ---
[INFO] --- exec-maven-plugin:1.6.0:exec (font-end install) @ app ---
[INFO] --- exec-maven-plugin:1.6.0:exec (font-end unit test) @ app ---
[INFO] --- exec-maven-plugin:1.6.0:exec (font-end build package) @ app ---
[INFO] --- maven-resources-plugin:3.1.0:copy-resources (copy front-end
```

```
template) @ app ---
[INFO] --- maven-resources-plugin:3.1.0:copy-resources (copy front-end
assets) @ app ---
[INFO] --- maven-resources-plugin:3.1.0:copy-resources (copy front-end
template to target) @ app ---
[INFO] --- maven-resources-plugin:3.1.0:copy-resources (copy front-end
assets to target) @ app ---
[INFO] --- maven-jar-plugin:3.0.2:jar (default-jar) @ app ---
[INFO] --- spring-boot-maven-plugin:2.0.2.RELEASE:start (pre integration
test) @ app ---
[INFO] --- exec-maven-plugin:1.6.0:exec (front-end e2e test) @ app ---
[INFO] --- spring-boot-maven-plugin:2.0.2.RELEASE:stop (post integration
test) @ app ---
[INFO] --- maven-install-plugin:2.5.2:install (default-install) @ app ---
```

As you can see, our build processes of the backend and the frontend are now unified under a single command, `mvn install`. Every time before we commit the code, we should run this command.

Beside a default life cycle, Maven has a clean life cycle, which allows users to use a plugin such as the Maven Clean Plugin (`maven-clean-plugin`) to remove resources that might affect the build, such as those generated resources in previous installs before starting the default life cycle. And, you might also have noticed that those frontend assets that we will copy into the `src/main/resources` folder should be cleaned up. Let's add this plugin underneath `maven-resources-plugin`, as follows:

```xml
<plugin>
  <artifactId>maven-clean-plugin</artifactId>
  <version>3.1.0</version>
  <configuration>
    <filesets>
      <fileset>
        <directory>${basedir}/src/main/resources/static/static</directory>
      </fileset>
      <fileset>
        <directory>${basedir}/src/main/resources/templates</directory>
        <includes>
          <include>index.html</include>
        </includes>
      </fileset>
    </filesets>
  </configuration>
</plugin>
```

As you can see, we don't need to specify the phase and the goal for this plugin. We just tell it what we need to remove. And, in order to trigger this plugin, we need to use the `mvn clean` or `mvn clean install` commands. And, it is preferred to use `mvn clean install` to run the build because it makes sure the installation is not affected by previous builds.

One last thing before we commit our code: let's change the port that `webpack-dev-server` uses from `8080` to `3000`. To do that, we need to create the `front-end/vue.config.js` file, as follows:

```
module.exports = {
  devServer: {
    port: 3000
  }
}
```

`@vue/cli-service` will pick up this configuration and use it to start up `webpack-dev-server`. With this change, our frontend will run under port `3000` while the backend runs under port `8080`.

Now, here is the commit to improve the build process:

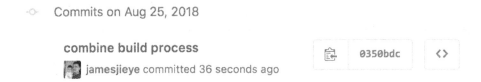

Figure 8.10: Combining the build process commits

Bridging the communication

As we mentioned, we will need to set up an HTTP proxy on the frontend side to solve the cross-origin request restriction. `webpack-dev-server` supports HTTP Proxy through the `http-proxy-middleware` library (`https://github.com/chimurai/http-proxy-middleware`). To bridge the requests, all we need to do is to change `devServer.proxy` in `front-end/vue.config.js`. Before we make the change, we need to come up with a proxy strategy. That is, the requests we will need to use the proxy and how to match those requests.

In general, there are two types of requests in a web application: the page requests and the API requests. The response of a page request is used for rendering a page, while the response of an API request is consumed by JavaScript to fulfill an operation. For example, when you open a login page, the request is a page request. And, when you click the **Login** button to send the credentials for the backend for authentication, that request is an API request. And, during development, since `webpack-dev-server` will serve the pages for the frontend, we won't need to proxy page requests. The API requests are those that we need to bridge because it is our backend that will handle those API requests.

Therefore, we need a way to separate the page requests and API requests. One common approach is to use a specific pattern in the URIs of the API requests. In our case, we will make all of the API requests paths start with `/api/`. In this way, we can use `http-proxy-middleware` context-matching ability to identify these API requests.

Here is the change we make to the `front-end/vue.config.js` file:

```
module.exports = {
  devServer: {
    ...
    proxy: {
      '/api/*': {
        target: 'http://localhost:8080'
      }
    },
    ...
  }
}
```

With this configuration, all the API requests will be bridged to the backend. `http-proxy-middleware` also supports other ways of matching URIs, which you can find in the guide on its repository on GitHub.

How can we verify if this works or not? A very simple way is to type a URI that doesn't exist, such as `http://localhost:3000/api/hello`, and the response should be a *Whitelabel Error Page* that is served by Spring Boot. You will need to start both the backend and the frontend to test this.

Now, let's make the commit and push to origin:

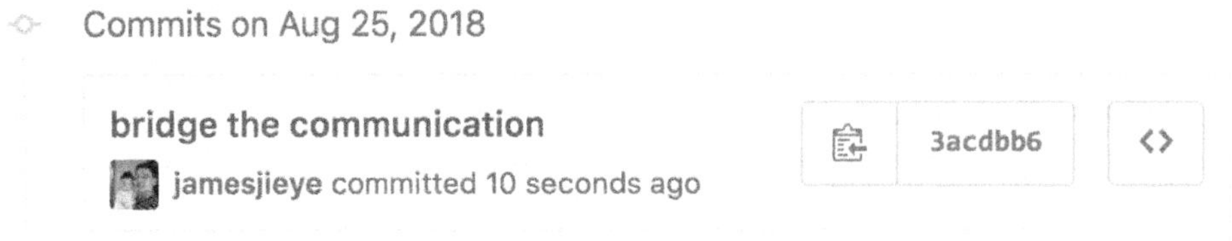

◇ Commits on Aug 25, 2018

bridge the communication

🗃️   3acdbb6   <>

jamesjieye committed 10 seconds ago

Figure 8.11: Bridging the communication commit

Introducing vue-router

For a single-page application, when a user switches from one page (logic page) to another, the application will need to update the URL in the address bar accordingly so that when the user refreshes the page or copies the URL and shares it with others to open, the application will always render the same page. In Vue applications, we can achieve this by using `vue-router` (https://router.vuejs.org/guide), which is already included in the frontend scaffold that we generated.

In this section, we will only cover the features of `vue-router` that we need at the moment. For those features that we don't talk about here, we will introduce them later in this book.

As you probably have noticed, in `App.vue` there is `<router-view>` inside the `#app` div. `vue-router` will render the component that matches the router configuration in `front-end/src/router`, which is used by the root Vue component in `front-end/src/main.js`. When we open a page and there is no match component found on that path, nothing will be rendered.

And when we generate the frontend code using `@vue/cli`, we choose **Yes** to *Use history mode for router?*. With this selection, the `mode` property of the router is set as `"history"`, which enables the router to use HTML5's `history.pushState` API to route the requests, so that we can visit the login page at `http://localhost:3000/login` instead of `http://localhost:3000/#/login`.

Spring MVC request mapping

There is still one issue with the routing, which is on the backend this time. After we do a full installation via mvn install, and then start the application either using mvn spring-boot:run or java -jar target/app-0.0.1-SNAPSHOT.jar, we will see a blank page at http://localhost:8080 and 404 at http://localhost:8080/login.

The reason the root page is blank is because without matched request mapping at the root path, Spring Boot will automatically serve index.html that we copied into the src/main/resources/templates folder. You can open Chrome DevTools to check the requests in the **Network** tab. You will see the .js files and .css files are loaded. The blank page shows up because vue-router doesn't find any match Vue component to render.

The reason the login URL is 404 is that there is no request mapping added in Spring MVC. As far as Spring MVC is concerned, this URL doesn't exist, even though you can access it from webpack-dev-server. So, we can fix this by adding a handler in Spring MVC Controller to map to /login. And, besides the URL of the login page, we will have URLs for other pages (again, those are logical pages). And we will also need to map those URLs accordingly.

The good thing is that Spring MVC's request mapping supports multiple values. We can specify multiple paths for the same handler. Let's create a controller called com.taskagile.web.pages.MainController, which looks like the following:

```
@Controller
public class MainController {

  @GetMapping(value = {"/", "/login"})
  public String entry() {
    return "index";
  }
}
```

For now, we just keep only these two paths, and we will add more values to @GetMapping as needed in the future.

If we run a full build with the `mvn clean install` command and start the application as a whole, we should be able to access the login page now. And, since all tests have passed, let's commit the code and push to origin. The following is the commit of the changes in this section:

Figure 8.12: Adding the backend request mapping commit

Fixes at the end

Starting from this chapter, we will add a small section at the end of each chapter that is about fixing issues that we didn't take care of in the middle of each chapter. All of the TaskAgile code is written in parallel with every other chapter, and bugs and issues are inevitable. This section gives us an opportunity to fix things and start our next chapter from a better code base, and, for the sake of brevity, we will only explain what the issues are and how to fix them, but leave the details out. You can always go to the repository on GitHub (`https://github.com/taskagile/vuejs.spring-boot.mysql`) to check the commit history to see the details. All these types of commits will start with the prefix, *fix* such as the one mentioned here:

- **Fix—Adding the missing README.md commit**: It is always a good practice to add necessary documentation to a project. We forgot to add the `README.md` commit at the application's root directory. Let's add it with some basic descriptions. We will flesh it out later:

Commits on Aug 25, 2018

fix: add missing README.md
jamesjieye committed 11 seconds ago

a5b351c

<>

Figure 8.13: Fix—Adding the missing README.md commit

Summary

In this chapter, you have learned how to use Spring Initializr to generate the backend scaffold and use `@vue/cli` to generate the frontend scaffold. You have also learned how to combine the build process of the two ends and bridge the communication between these two parts.

At the end of the chapter, we also fixed an issue with the missing `README.md` commit. And now, we're ready to move on to the next chapter and to build the `User` module of TaskAgile.

Forms and Validation - Starting with the Register Page

9

Forms are the basic elements of a web application, and data validation is the most basic security mechanism in a web application. User input must always be validated before being processed. We will start the implementation of **TaskAgile** from the register page. In this chapter, we will focus on building the registration form and validating inputs on both the frontend and the backend. Along the way, we will practice TDD while we're building the register page and keep recording the code commits so that you can check the details of each step easily.

In this chapter, you will learn the following:

- How to build a UI with Bootstrap 4
- How to build forms with Vue.js
- How to validate on the frontend with Vuelidate
- How to validate on the backend with Bean Validation
- How to implement registration in the domain model
- How to do full set unit testing

We have a lot to accomplish in this chapter. Let's get started.

Building a UI with Bootstrap 4

Bootstrap (http://getbootstrap.com) is popular and very useful. It changes the way of building UIs for web applications. As you will see when we implement the UI, Bootstrap can boost our productivity by providing features that cover most parts of UI development. It is highly customizable, allowing us to create different themes. In this section, we will learn how to import Bootstrap into a Vue application and use it to build the register page. We will also change webpack's configuration to keep the styles of Bootstrap in a separate .css file.

Install and use Bootstrap

First of all, let's install Bootstrap and its dependencies into our frontend directory by running the following command:

```
npm install jquery popper.js bootstrap --save
```

Once it is installed, we will need to import Bootstrap's compiled CSS into our application. There are many ways to import Bootstrap using webpack. The approach we will use here is to create a new entry in webpack to group all of the third-party styles into a single .css file. The following is the change to frontend/vue.config.js:

```
module.exports = {
  ...
  configureWebpack: {
    entry: {
      app: './src/main.js',
      style: [
        'bootstrap/dist/css/bootstrap.min.css'
      ]
    }
  }
}
```

As you can see, we list the bootstrap.min.css file in the new entry, style. We will add styles of other third-party libraries here when needed. Now, if you execute npm run serve and open the login page at http://localhost:3000/login, you can see the font and size of the text TaskAgile has been changed to the style defined by Bootstrap's default theme.

Implement the UI of the register page

Now, we have Bootstrap ready. Let's use it to create the register page, which looks like the UI design shown in the following figure:

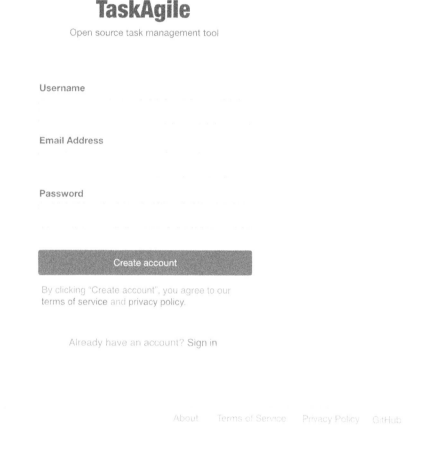

Figure 9.1: UI of the register page

As you can see, on this page, we have a logo, a tagline, three fields, and one submit button. There are also some text, links, and a simple page footer. The main part of this page, the registration form, is positioned in the middle of the screen. Before we write any code, let's see how we're going to structure the layout of this page.

First of all, we will wrap everything on the page inside a container. In Bootstrap, containers are the most basic layout element and are required when we need to use Bootstrap's default grid system, which is flexbox-based and mobile friendly. A grid system, basically, is one that uses rows to divide a page vertically and, inside each row, it uses a *twelve-column system* to divide that row horizontally. In our UI, the logo, the tagline, and the registration form are aligned in the center of the page. Therefore, we will put them in the same wrapper, which will be a `<div>` tag. We will put the page footer inside a `<footer>` tag. This is a high-level overview of the layout. Let's dive deeper.

Create layout diagram

In order to have a better understanding of the layout and the elements of the page, let's draw a layout diagram to break down the structure. In this diagram, we do not need to include every element that will appear on the page. We only need those that will be good enough for us to verify our plan of how to structure the UI. We will give each element in the diagram a name, which will be their class names that we will use in the code. This practice in drawing a layout diagram can be seen as a kind of rehearsal for code writing. It is helpful for those developers who are not familiar with frontend development. Sometimes, experienced frontend engineers will also find it useful when building a complex UI. Once you have completed the diagram, you will be able to write your code more confidently and more quickly.

Figure 9.2 is the layout diagram of the register page:

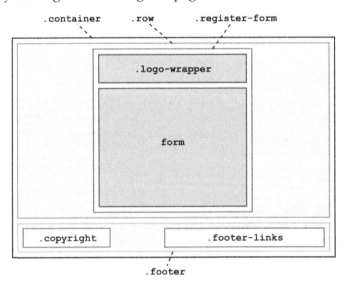

Figure 9.2: The layout of the register page

As you can see, in this diagram we only include high-level structure elements, except .copyright at the bottom. Everything is wrapped inside .container. We put the main body of the page inside .row and keep the footer separately inside .footer. .register-form is for grouping the logo, the tagline, and the form together. It also helps to hold a fixed width and be positioned in the center horizontally. Now, this looks good enough, so let's write the code.

TDD of the register page

The code we will write first is the unit test code. Practicing TDD can be hard if you haven't done it before. If you fight against it, it can be even harder, annoying, and a waste of time. However, with a simple mindset change and several rounds of practicing, you might see it as an extremely valuable technique, especially for Agile projects. We won't go into the details of the benefits of practicing TDD here because we're practicing it in this book and, hopefully, by the end of the journey, you can see the benefits yourselves. For now, just think of all of those unit test methods as mini QA robots that will help us check the health of the application every time we run the mvn clean install command.

We will create the register page in the frontend/src/views/RegisterPage.vue file and the unit test code in the frontend/test/unit/RegisterPage.spec.js file. In this unit test, at this stage, we only need to verify the presence of registration form elements, including the logo, the tagline, three fields, and the submit button. The following is what RegisterPage.spec.js looks like:

```
import Vue from 'vue'
import RegisterPage from '@/views/RegisterPage'

describe('RegisterPage.vue', () => {
  it('should render correct contents', () => {
    const Constructor = Vue.extend(RegisterPage)
    const vm = new Constructor().$mount()
    expect(vm.$el.querySelector('.logo').getAttribute('src'))
      .toEqual('/static/images/logo.png')
    expect(vm.$el.querySelector('.tagline').textContent)
      .toEqual('Open source task management tool')
    expect(vm.$el.querySelector('#username').value).toEqual('')
    expect(vm.$el.querySelector('#emailAddress').value).toEqual('')
    expect(vm.$el.querySelector('#password').value).toEqual('')
    expect(vm.$el.querySelector('form
    button[type="submit"]').textContent)
      .toEqual('Create account')
  })
})
```

As you can see, similar to how to write the test in `LoginPage.spec.js`, we create a Vue subclass with `RegisterPage.vue` and mount it, and then verify the presence of the elements using the `querySelector()` API. This works fine for a simple test, like the one we have one. Later in this chapter, we will use the APIs offered by `vue-test-utils` to create more sophisticated tests.

Implement the UI

Now, if you run the `npm test` command, you can see we have a failed test. Let's write `RegisterPage.vue` to make the test pass.

The following code is the `<template>` section of `RegisterPage.vue`. Some details are excluded here for the sake of brevity:

```
<template>
  <div class="container">
    <div class="row justify-content-center">
      <div class="register-form">
        <div class="logo-wrapper">...</div>
        <form>
          <div class="form-group"></div>
          <div class="form-group"></div>
          <div class="form-group"></div>
          <button type="submit" class="btn btn-primary btn-block">
          </button>
          ...
        </form>
      </div>
    </div>
    <footer class="footer">
      <span class="copyright">...</span>
      <ul class="footer-links list-inline float-right">...</ul>
    </footer>
  </div>
</template>
```

As you can see, in order to keep the content inside the `.row` element in the center, we use the `.justify-content-center` class, which is another utility class of Bootstrap. Inside `<form>`, we add the `.form-group` class to the wrapper of each field. In this way, Bootstrap will organize the padding and margin of these fields nicely for us. In the footer, we use span with the `.copyright` class. `<span>` fits here very well because the copyright information is just text displayed inline, which is the default style of `<span>` tags. We use `<ul>` for the footer links because they are essentially a list of unordered items that are displayed horizontally. Bootstrap's `.list-inline` works perfectly for this scenario. With the help of `.float-right` class, we can pull the list to the right side easily.

The following is the custom style that we need to add to the `<style>` section of `RegisterPage.vue`. The following listing only include those structure-related styles, reformatted into one line for each class:

```
<style lang="scss" scoped>
.container {max-width: 900px;}
.register-form {margin-top: 50px; max-width: 320px;}
.logo-wrapper {margin-bottom: 40px;}
.footer {width: 100%; line-height: 40px; margin-top: 50px; }
</style>
```

As you can see, we set the maximum width of the container to 900 pixels and `.register-form` to 320 pixels. We use margins in these structure classes to keep elements apart from each other. Now, let's run `npm test` and, as you will see, we have a green result. The last thing that we need to do is to add `RegisterPage.vue` to router at the `/register` path. The details of this step won't be covered in this book. You can find them in the code commit record, along with other details of the register page that we have skipped.

By now, we have covered most of creating the UI of the register page. As you can see, we utilized a lot of Bootstrap's built-in classes, which improved our productivity. Let's run the `mvn clean install` command to make sure there are no code breaks introduced accidentally before we commit the code. As you can see, we have a successful build. *Figure 9.3* is the commit record:

Figure 9.3: Implementing the UI of the register page commit

Build registration forms with Vue.js

When we created the UI of the register page, we didn't add any behavior. In this section, we will add the ability to get the values of the fields in the form, the ability to handle the click action on the **Create account** button, and the ability to send registration data to the backend.

Here are the details of what we need to do. First of all, we will create a `form` object with these three properties: `username`, `emailAddress`, and `password`, in the `data` property of the Vue instance. The initial values of these properties will be empty strings. We will bind them to the form's input fields. After that, we will create a `submitForm()` method to handle the submit event of the form. Inside the `submitForm()` method, we will call the `register()` method of the Registration Service that will be written in the `frontend/src/services/registration/index.js` file. Inside that service, we will use `axios` to send the registration details to the backend.

Write test code for the form

It's TDD time. Let's write more tests into `RegisterPage.spec.js`. The tests we need to create include the following:

- Test the initial values of the data model
- Test the binding between the form input fields and the data model
- Test the existence of the event handler of the form

Including the previous test, which is used to verify the form's rendering, we will have four tests in this specification. It's time to do some refactoring to the test specification itself. As mentioned earlier, we will also use `vue-test-utils`, the official unit testing utility library for Vue.js. Let's use the following command to install the library before we start the refactoring:

```
npm install @vue/test-utils --save-dev
```

Once that is done, let's refactor `RegisterPage.spec.js` to the following:

```
1.  import { mount } from '@vue/test-utils'
2.  import RegisterPage from '@/views/RegisterPage'
3.
4.  describe('RegisterPage.vue', () => {
5.    let wrapper
6.    let fieldUsername
7.    let fieldEmailAddress
```

```
8.    let fieldPassword
9.    let buttonSubmit
10.
11.   beforeEach(() => {
12.     wrapper = mount(RegisterPage)
13.     fieldUsername = wrapper.find('#username')
14.     fieldEmailAddress = wrapper.find('#emailAddress')
15.     fieldPassword = wrapper.find('#password')
16.     buttonSubmit = wrapper.find('form button[type="submit"]')
17.   })
18.
19.   it('should render registration form', () => {
20.     expect(wrapper.find('.logo').attributes().src)
21.       .toEqual('/static/images/logo.png')
22.     expect(wrapper.find('.tagline').text())
23.       .toEqual('Open source task management tool')
24.     expect(fieldUsername.element.value).toEqual('')
25.     expect(fieldEmailAddress.element.value).toEqual('')
26.     expect(fieldPassword.element.value).toEqual('')
27.     expect(buttonSubmit.text()).toEqual('Create account')
28.   })
29.})
```

As you can see, in line 1, we import the `mount` function from `vue-test-utils`. This `mount` function will create a `Wrapper` object that contains the mounted and rendered `RegisterPage.vue` component, as you will see in line 12. From line 5 to line 9, we create variables that we need to initialize and use in the tests. From line 11 to line 17, we add `beforeEach()` to initialize the variables before each test in `RegisterPage.spec.js`. In this way, we can be sure that these variables will not be affected by the other tests in this specification file. `wrapper.find()` is the API of `vue-test-utils` for finding HTML elements that match the selector. The result of this API is also a `Wrapper` object, which can be used to retrieve what we need from the HTML element that it wraps. Between line 20 to line 27, we replace the old `vm.$el.querySelector` with the APIs of the `Wrapper` object. We can use `wrapper.element` to access the root `HTMLElement` of this wrapper, and we can use `wrapper.text()` to return the text content of a wrapper and use `wrapper.attributes()` to get the attributes of the DOM node.

Now, let's run the test again using the `npm run test:unit` command to make sure we still have a green result after refactoring. As you should see, everything looks good. Let's start to add the other three new tests.

The first one is to test the initial values of the data model, which look like the following:

```
it('should contain data model with initial values', () => {
  expect(wrapper.vm.form.username).toEqual('')
  expect(wrapper.vm.form.emailAddress).toEqual('')
  expect(wrapper.vm.form.password).toEqual('')
})
```

As you can see, we access the Vue instance through `wrapper.vm`, and from there we can access all of the methods and properties of the wrapped vm. As you can see, we access the `username`, `emailAddress`, and `password` properties through `wrapper.vm.form` to verify that they are all initialized with an empty string.

The next test is to verify the data model binding with the form's inputs. Here is how the test looks:

```
it('should have form inputs bound with data model', () => {
  const username = 'sunny'
  const emailAddress = 'sunny@local'
  const password = 'VueJsRocks!'

  wrapper.vm.form.username = username
  wrapper.vm.form.emailAddress = emailAddress
  wrapper.vm.form.password = password
  expect(fieldUsername.element.value).toEqual(username)
  expect(fieldEmailAddress.element.value).toEqual(emailAddress)
  expect(fieldPassword.element.value).toEqual(password)
})
```

As you can see, at the beginning of the test, we assign new values to those three fields in the data model. With the bindings, those fields should get updated respectively. We can verify that by checking the values of these input fields to see whether they match those we assign to the data model.

The last test that we need to add is to check the existence of the submit handler. The test looks like this:

```
it('should have form submit event handler `submitForm`', () => {
  const stub = jest.fn()
  wrapper.setMethods({submitForm: stub})
  buttonSubmit.trigger('submit')
  expect(stub).toBeCalled()
})
```

As you can see, we create `stub` using Jest and then replace the original submit handler, `submitForm`, with this stub by using the wrapper's `setMethods()` API. Then, we use `buttonSubmit` to trigger the submit event and then verify that `stub` has been called.

Now, our tests are ready. Let's implement the features that have been tested in `RegisterPage.vue` to make the tests pass.

Implement the form bindings

First of all, let's add the three fields to the data model, as follows:

```
export default {
  name: 'RegisterPage',
  data: function () {
    return {
      form: {
        username: '',
        emailAddress: '',
        password: ''
      }
    }
  }
}
```

With this change, the first test that we just added should be able to pass now. Let's run the `npm run test:unit` command to verify that. In the result, you should see something like the following:

```
Tests:       2 failed, 3 passed, 5 total
```

We have made some progress here. Now, let's bind the data model to the inputs in the form and also add the `submitForm()` method to handle the form submit event. The following is the change to `RegisterPage.vue`:

```
<template>
  ...
  <form @submit.prevent="submitForm">
    <div class="form-group">
      <input type="text" class="form-control"
        id="username" v-model="form.username">
    </div>
    <div class="form-group">
      <input type="email" class="form-control"
        id="emailAddress" v-model="form.emailAddress">
    </div>
```

```
          <div class="form-group">
            <input type="password" class="form-control"
              id="password" v-model="form.password">
          </div>
        </form>
        ...
    </template>
    <script>
    export default {
      ...
      methods: {
        submitForm () {
        }
      }
    }
    </script>
```

In the previous listing, we have excluded unnecessary details of the form for the sake of brevity. As you can see, we use the `@submit.prevent` directive to bind the submit event to the `submitForm()` method. Currently, the handler's implementation is left blank. We use `v-model` directives to bind the input fields with the data model. With all of these changes, all four tests in `RegisterPage.spec.js` should be able to pass. Now, let's run the unit tests, and you should see that all of the tests have passed.

Handle form submit

At this moment, our registration form is ready to receive input and handle the submit. We can move forward to implement the logic of sending data the backend, which starts from the `submitForm()` method. Inside this method, we could use the HTTP client, `axios`, directly to do the heavy lifting, as we already introduced in Chapter 3, *Spring 5 - The Right Stack for the Job at Hand*. This time, we will use it differently. We will create a service called `registrationService` in the `frontend/src/services/registration/index.js` file to wrap the details of how to send HTTP requests using `axios`. The benefit of doing this is that we hide the implementation of the communication with the server from `RegisterPage.vue` so that, once we need to change something related to sending HTTP requests that `RegisterPage.vue` doesn't need to be aware of, we can isolate those changes inside `registrationService`, preventing them from ripping out of the service.

Inside the `submitForm()` method, we will call the `registrationService.register()` method with the `vm.form` object. Once the registration succeeds, we will redirect the user to the **Login** page. When it fails, we will display an error message above the form in the UI.

Now, we're clear on what need to implement. Let's think about what we need to test. There are mainly two parts: the `submitForm()` method and the `registrationService.register()` method. Let's start with the first one.

Test the submitForm() method

There are two scenarios we need to cover in the test. One is a successful registration and the other is a failed registration. Our application behaves differently in these two scenarios. It is better that we use a separate test for each scenario.

In the test for the `submitForm()` method, we will isolate the method itself from its dependency, `registrationService`, by creating a mock of the service. In this way, we can define the behavior of the dependency and make sure it won't affect the test result. Using Jest, we will need to put the mocks in a folder named __mocks__ inside the same directory as the dependency. And the following are the paths of `registrationService` and its mock:

```
frontend/src/services/registration/index.js
frontend/src/services/registration/__mocks__/index.js
```

Here is how the mock looks:

```
export default {
  register (detail) {
    return new Promise((resolve, reject) => {
      detail.emailAddress === 'sunny@local'
        ? resolve({result: 'success'})
        : reject(new Error('User already exist'))
    })
  }
}
```

As you can see, the mock has exactly the same API as `registrationService`. The `register()` method is promise-based and its implementation is quite simple. When the email address is `sunny@local`, we will have a success registration; otherwise, we will have a failed registration with the error message **User already exists.**

Now, let's change the `RegisterPage.spec.js` to test specification the following:

```
import { mount, createLocalVue } from '@vue/test-utils'
import VueRouter from 'vue-router'

// Adding Vue Router to the test so that
// we can access vm.$router
```

```
const localVue = createLocalVue()
localVue.use(VueRouter)
const router = new VueRouter()

// Mock dependency registratioService
jest.mock('@/services/registration')

describe('RegisterPage.vue', () => {
  ...
  beforeEach(() => {
    wrapper = mount(RegisterPage, {
      localVue,
      router
    })
    ...
  })

  afterAll(() => {
    jest.restoreAllMocks()
  })
  ...
})
```

As you can see, we import the `createLocalVue` function from `vue-test-utils`. As its name suggests, this function creates a local Vue class so that the changes we make to this local `Vue` class won't affect the actual global `Vue` class. We also import `VueRouter`. Inside the `beforeEach()` method, we provide both the local `Vue` instance and the `router` instance to the `mount` function for creating `wrapper`. The reason we need the `router` instance here is that we will use it to check whether redirection to the login page has occurred or not.

We use `jest.mock('@/services/registration')` to prepare the mock of `registrationService` that we created earlier. We restore `registrationService` by calling `jest.restoreAllMocks()` inside `afterAll()`, which will be invoked once all of the tests in this file have finished their execution.

Now, let's implement the test that is used to verify a successful registration. The test method looks like the following:

```
it('should register when it is a new user', () => {
  const stub = jest.fn()
  wrapper.vm.$router.push = stub
  wrapper.vm.form.username = 'sunny'
  wrapper.vm.form.emailAddress = 'sunny@local'
  wrapper.vm.form.password = 'Jest!'
  wrapper.vm.submitForm()
```

```
    wrapper.vm.$nextTick(() => {
      expect(stub).toHaveBeenCalledWith({name: 'LoginPage'})
    })
  })
})
```

As you can see, we stub the `push()` method of `vm.$router` so that we can check whether the redirect happened or not. After providing values to the data model, we call the `wrapper.vm.submitForm()` method to trigger the form submit. Since the `registrationService.register()` method is promise-based, we need to wrap the expect assertion inside `vm.$nextTick()`, otherwise the assertion would always fail.

The following is the test to verify a failed registration:

```
it('should fail it is not a new user', () => {
  // In the mock, only sunny@local is new user
  wrapper.vm.form.emailAddress = 'ted@local'
  expect(wrapper.find('.failed').isVisible()).toBe(false)
  wrapper.vm.submitForm()
  wrapper.vm.$nextTick(null, () => {
    expect(wrapper.find('.failed').isVisible()).toBe(true)
  })
})
```

As mentioned, when a registration fails, we will display an error message. So, in this test, at the beginning, we verify that the error message is not visible before the `submitForm()` method is invoked. Inside `vm.$nextTick()`, we verify that the error message is visible.

By now, we have finished the tests of the `submitForm()` method. Let's implement the `submitForm()` method itself now.

Implement the submitForm() method

As mentioned earlier, the implementation of the `submitForm()` method depends on `registrationService`, which is not our focus right now; we will simply create a blank implementation of the service. The following is how `frontend/src/services/registration/index.js` looks:

```
export default {
  register (detail) {
    return new Promise((resolve, reject) => {
      resolve()
    })
  }
}
```

As you can see, it is just a placeholder, which is already good enough for us to implement the `submitForm()` method and get those tests to pass.

The following is the change we make to `RegisterPage.vue`:

```
<template>
  ...
  <form @submit.prevent="submit">
    <div v-show="errorMessage" class="alert alert-danger failed">{{
    errorMessage }}</div>
    ...
  </form>
  ...
</template>

<script>
import registrationService from '@/services/registration'

export default {
  name: 'RegisterPage',
  data: function () {
    return {
      ...
      errorMessage: ''
    }
  },
  methods: {
    submitForm () {
      // TODO: Validate the data
      registrationService.register(this.form).then(() => {
        this.$router.push({name: 'LoginPage'})
      }).catch((error) => {
        this.errorMessage = 'Failed to register user. Reason: ' +
          (error.message ? error.message : 'Unknown') + '.'
      })
    }
  }
}
</script>
```

As you can see, inside the `<form>` tag, we add a `<div>` tag to display the error message, which will be highlighted with Bootstrap's `.alert-danger` class. The visibility of the error message is controlled by `vm.errorMessage`, which we defined in the data model.

Inside the `submitForm()` method, for now, we pass the registration details, `vm.form`, to `registrationService`. When the registration succeeds, we will redirect the user. When it fails, we will show the error message. That's all we need to write to make the tests pass. After running the `npm run test:unit` command, you should see all of the tests have passed.

 Normally, when we do TDD, there will be several rounds of trying and fixing to make the tests pass. We skip those steps in this book and show you the final result, and we are going to do the same for the rest of the tests in this book. If you're interested in learning how to practice TDD step by step, Kent Beck's book, *Test-Driven Development by Example*, is highly recommended.

Let's move on to the next part of implementing our registration process in the frontend, which is implementing the `registrationService.register()` method.

Communicate with the backend

In TaskAgile, all communication between the frontend and the backend will be handled by services that we put inside the `frontend/src/services` directory. All the methods of these services will be promise-based, as you have seen in the blank implementation of `registrationService` we created earlier.

Test the register() method

Before writing the test code, let's talk about the behavior of the `registrationService.register()` method so that we can decide what to test. Essentially, this method will send an HTTP `POST` request to the backend and then hand the result back to its caller. The dependency of this method is `axios`, which needs to be mocked so that we can isolate the `register()` method and test its logic without being affected by the dependency.

Let's install `axios` and `moxios`, which mocks `axios` requests, with the following commands:

```
npm install axios --save
npm install moxios --save-dev
```

Once it is done, let's create `frontend/test/unit/services.registration.spec.js`, which looks like the following:

```
1.   import moxios from 'moxios'
2.   import registrationService from '@/services/registration'
3.
4.   describe('services/registration', () => {
5.     beforeEach(() => {
6.       moxios.install()
7.     })
8.
9.     afterEach(() => {
10.     moxios.uninstall()
11.   })
12.
13.   it('should pass the response to caller when request succeeded',
     ()=>{
14.     expect.assertions(2)
15.     moxios.wait(() => {
16.       let request = moxios.requests.mostRecent()
17.       expect(request).toBeTruthy()
18.       request.respondWith({
19.         status: 200,
20.         response: {result: 'success'}
21.       })
22.     })
23.     return registrationService.register().then(data => {
24.       expect(data.result).toEqual('success')
25.     })
26.   })
27.})
```

As you can see, in line 1 to line 2, we import `moxios` and `registrationService`. From line 4 to line 11, we call `moxios.install()` to create the mock for each test and use `moxios.uninstall()` to destroy it afterward.

In the test method, we verify that the service will return the server's response to its caller. In line 14, we use Jest's API, `expect.assertions()`, to make sure the exact number of assertions should be made, which is useful when the method that we're testing against returns a promise.

From line 15 to line 22, the moxios.wait() method is to wait for the request to be made before proceeding. Its implementation is based on setTimeout(). When the waiting is over, as you can see in line 16, we get the most recent request and verify its existence by using the Jest's toBeTruthy() API. This is to ensure that an axios request has actually been issued. After that, we specify the response of the request using the respondWith() moxios method. In this way, we can be sure that the register() method will get a success response.

In line 23, we invoke the register() method and then do a verification to make sure the value of the result property returned by the register() method is success. Since we're using promises here, we need to return a promise as the result of the test method itself so that Jest can wait for it to resolve. When the promise is rejected, the test will automatically fail.

The Promise.prototype.then(onFulfilled[, onRejected]) method also returns a promise. And that's why you can chain other then() methods or catch() methods after it.

Now, let's create a test for the scenario in which the HTTP request fails. Here is how it looks:

```
it('should propagate the error to caller when request failed', () => {
  expect.assertions(2)
  moxios.wait(() => {
    let request = moxios.requests.mostRecent()
    expect(request).toBeTruthy()
    request.reject({
      status: 400,
      response: {message: 'Bad request'}
    })
  })
  return registrationService.register().catch(error => {
    expect(error.response.message).toEqual('Bad request')
  })
})
```

As you can see, this test is very similar to the previous one, except that instead of using respondWith(), we use the request.reject() moxios API to send a failed response, and we chain the register() method with a catch(onRejected) method. Inside of this onRejected handler, we make an assertion of the error response to make sure the error propagates to the caller.

Implement the register() method

Now, let's implement the `register()` method itself, starting with configuring `axios` as follows.

Let's have a look at the `frontend/src/main.js` file:

```
import router from './router'
import axios from 'axios'

// Bootstrap axios
axios.defaults.baseURL = '/api'
axios.defaults.headers.common.Accept = 'application/json'
axios.interceptors.response.use(
  response => response,
  (error) => {
    return Promise.reject(error)
  }
)
```

As you can see, in the `main.js` file, we configure `baseURL` so that we don't have to add `/api` for every request. We make it clear that we only accept responses in JSON format, and we also add an interceptor to the response to propagate errors.

Now, let's change the `register()` method of `registrationService` to the following:

```
import axios from 'axios'

export default {
  register (detail) {
    return new Promise((resolve, reject) => {
      axios.post('/registrations', detail).then(({data}) => {
        resolve(data)
      }).catch((error) => {
        reject(error)
      })
    })
  }
}
```

As you can see, we send a HTTP POST request to the backend with the registration details as the request body. When the request succeeds, we return the response to the caller. When it fails, we reject the error.

Now if we run the `npm run test:unit` command, we should see all tests pass.

By now, we have finished what we planned for this section. If you start the frontend with the `npm run serve` command and go to the register page, then click the **Create account** button, you will see an error similar to the one shown in *Figure 9.4*. If you check the log printed in the Terminal, you can see that there is a proxy error. This is because we haven't built the API handler for `/api/registrations` yet:

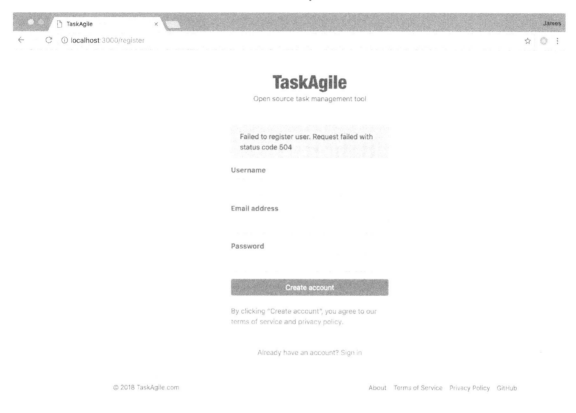

Figure 9.4: The implemented register page

Let's run the `mvn clean install` command before committing the code. As you should see, all tests pass, and the following is the commit history:

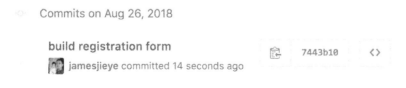

Figure 9.5: Build registration form commit

Validation on the frontend

As mentioned at the beginning of this chapter, we must always validate user input to make sure the data we received is valid. In this section, we will implement validation on the frontend using **Vuelidate** (`https://monterail.github.io/vuelidate`), which is a model-based validation library for Vue.js.

First of all, let's install `Vuelidate` with the following command:

```
npm install vuelidate --save
```

Once it is done, let's write the unit test code for data validation.

Test the data validation

The reason we need to test the data validation is to make sure there is validation in place and user input has been properly validated before being sent to the backend. Let's add the following test to `RegisterPage.spec.js` to verify that, when the value of the email address is invalid, the `registrationService.register()` method won't be invoked:

```
...
import Vuelidate from 'vuelidate'
import registrationService from '@/services/registration'
...
localVue.use(Vuelidate)
...
// Mock dependency registratioService
jest.mock('@/services/registration')

describe('RegisterPage.vue', () => {
  ...
  it('should fail when the email address is invalid', () => {
    const spy = jest.spyOn(registrationService, 'register')
    wrapper.vm.form.emailAddress = 'bad-email-address'
    wrapper.vm.submitForm()
    expect(spy).not.toHaveBeenCalled()
    spy.mockReset()
    spy.mockRestore()
  })
})
```

As you can see, we import `Vuelidate` and then apply it to `localVue`. We also import `registrationService`. Even though importing `registrationService` is placed above `jest.mock('@/services/registration')`, the `jest.mock()` method will still be executed before the import, because Jest will automatically hoist `jest.mock()` calls to the very top of the module, before any imports. In this way, the imported `registrationService` is actually the mock we created earlier, inside the __mock__ folder.

Inside the `test` method, we use `jest.spyOn()` to create a spy of the `register()` method. This spy is also a mock function. As a spy, it has the ability to track calls to the method. As you can see, we use `expect(spy).not.toHaveBeenCalled()` to verify that the `register()` method isn't invoked. At the end of the test, we use `mockReset()` to clear all of the calls stored in the mock and then use `mockRestore()` to restore the original behavior of the `register()` method.

Now, if you run the unit test with the `npm run test:unit` command, you should see that the test failed, which is expected. Let's implement the validation to make the test pass.

Validate form data with Vuelidate

Essentially, Vuelidate is a Vue mixin. We need to apply it to Vue first. To do that, we make changes to the `frontend/src/main.js` file, as follows:

```
import Vuelidate from 'vuelidate'
...
Vue.use(Vuelidate)
```

And the following are the changes we make to `RegisterPage.vue`:

```
<script>
import { required, email, minLength, maxLength, alphaNum } from
'vuelidate/lib/validators'
...
export default {
  ...
  validations: {
    form: {
      username: {
        required,
        minLength: minLength(2),
        maxLength: maxLength(50),
        alphaNum
      },
```

```
          emailAddress: {
            required,
            email,
            maxLength: maxLength(100)
          },
          password: {
            required,
            minLength: minLength(6),
            maxLength: maxLength(30)
          }
        }
      },
    methods: {
      submitForm () {
        this.$v.$touch()
        if (this.$v.$invalid) {
          return
        }
        ...
      }
    }
  }
</script>
```

As you can see, we import several of Vuelidate's built-in validators and then add the `validations` options object, which has the same structure as our data model. In each field of this `validations` object, we specify the rules that each field needs. Once that is done, in the `submitForm()` method, we access the API of Vuelidate through the `$v` object that Vuelidate created and added to the Vue instance. This `$v` object holds the current state of validation. We call its `$v.$touch()` method to trigger the data validation. Then, we verify the result by checking the `$v.$invalid` property. If the validation fails, its value is `true` and we simply abort the registration process.

Now, let's run the test to see how things work. You should see that the result says all of the tests have passed. However, there are lots of warnings from Vue.js, saying the following:

```
Expected mock function to have been called with:
  [{"name": "LoginPage"}]
But it was not called.
```

With a closer look at the warning message, we can see that this warning originates from the following test method:

```
it('should register when it is a new user', () => {
  const stub = jest.fn()
  wrapper.vm.$router.push = stub
```

```
    wrapper.vm.form.username = 'sunny'
    wrapper.vm.form.emailAddress = 'sunny@local'
    wrapper.vm.form.password = 'Jest!'
    wrapper.vm.submitForm()
    wrapper.vm.$nextTick(() => {
      expect(stub).toHaveBeenCalledWith({name: 'LoginPage'})
    })
  })
```

Based on the warning message, `vm.$router.push` was not called. In fact, this should not be taken as a warning because, in this test method, we verify that the user will be redirected to the login page after a success registration. When the method isn't called, the test should fail. Why did Jest still let that test pass? There must be something seriously wrong. We need to dig deep to find out what happened during the test.

Let's think about this. Before we implemented the data validation, this test passed. So, it must have something to do with the validation rules we just added. With a closer look at the data we used in the test, we can see that the email address is invalid, and also the password is shorter than 6 characters. It looks like our test data that is supposed to make the test pass actually caused a validation issue. But still, why did Vue.js throw that warning? Shouldn't Jest be the one to take care of the tests?

Let's walk through the test and the code flow to see what happened. Starting from the test method, we used invalid data, and after the `submitForm()` method was invoked, Vuelidate performed data validation inside of the `submitForm()` method. The validation failed, and the call was returned immediately to the test method. Therefore, the `register()` method didn't get invoked. That means no asynchronous execution occurred and the verification inside `$nextTick()` didn't get evaluated by Jest before the test finished. That's why Jest let the test pass. Later on, no matter whether there is an asynchronous execution or not inside the `submitForm()` method, the next tick will start eventually. That's when the verification inside `$nextTick()` got evaluated and failed. Since Jest has already finished the execution of the test method, the only thing it can do is throw the verification failure as an error. And this error was detected by Vue.js, because the verification happened inside the `$nextTick()` method of Vue.js. Since we didn't provide an error handler to `$nextTick()`, Vue.js didn't know what to do with this error, and it threw that warning at us, basically saying: *Hey, this is an error that you have ignored. Do something about it.*

By now, it all makes sense. This is clearly a defect in the test method. To fix this, first of all let's fix all the test data used in this specification as well the registration service's mock data. Then, we can chain a `catch()` method to `$nextTick()` using promise-chain. Or, we can use `async/await` for asynchronous calls, like the following:

```
it('should fail it is not a new user', async () => {
  // In the mock, only sunny@taskagile.com is new user
  wrapper.vm.form.username = 'ted'
  wrapper.vm.form.emailAddress = 'ted@taskagile.com'
  wrapper.vm.form.password = 'JestRocks!'
  ...
  await wrapper.vm.$nextTick()
  expect(wrapper.find('.failed').isVisible()).toBe(true)
})
```

To use `async/await`, we need to add `async` before the function that contains the asynchronous invocation and then put the await before the invocation that is asynchronous. In this way, JavaScript will wait until that promise settles and returns its result.

Improve the tests

As a matter of fact, the invalid data that we use isn't the primary issue in the test. The actual problem is that the verifications/assertions we add in the test are not evaluated by Jest in time. And hence the tests that we think have passed based on the result from Jest might actually have failed without us noticing. These tests become malfunctioning mini QA robots and will affect the health of our application. As you might have noticed, this kind of issue only happens when there is an asynchronous execution involved.

Another issue in our test is that we jumped to verify the redirection to the login page, which is one of the two possible final results of the `submitForm()` method, by skipping the verification of whether or not the `registrationService.register()` method has been invoked. To write a stronger test, instead of rushing to check the final result, we should verify the behavior of the dependencies of the `submitForm()` method accordingly, so that we can be sure the implementation of the `submitMethod()` method is correct. The implementation of our `submitForm()` method is relatively straightforward. Imagine there was a very complex implementation and there is a chance that the redirection might still happen without the `register()` method being invoked. In our old test method, the mini QA robot would still naively think that the registration had succeeded, leaving a major bug in the application when shipped to production.

Now, we've found the issues in our test. Let's fix them by making the following changes to `RegisterPage.spec.js`:

```
...
describe('RegisterPage.vue', () => {
  ...
  let registerSpy

  beforeEach(() => {
    ...
    // Create spy for registration service
    registerSpy = jest.spyOn(registrationService, 'register')
  })

  afterEach(() => {
    registerSpy.mockReset()
    registerSpy.mockRestore()
  })
  ...
})
```

As you can see, we move `registerSpy` to the test suite level so that all of the tests in this specification can use it. We use `beforeEach()` and `afterEach()` to instantiate it and reset it for each test method. In this way, we can add expectations to the following two tests:

```
it('should register when it is a new user', async () => {
  expect.assertions(2)
  ...
  wrapper.vm.submitForm()
  expect(registerSpy).toBeCalled()
  await wrapper.vm.$nextTick()
  expect(stub).toHaveBeenCalledWith({name: 'LoginPage'})
})

it('should fail it is not a new user', async () => {
  expect.assertions(3)
  expect(wrapper.find('.failed').isVisible()).toBe(false)
  ...
  wrapper.vm.submitForm()
  expect(registerSpy).toBeCalled()
  await wrapper.vm.$nextTick()
  expect(wrapper.find('.failed').isVisible()).toBe(true)
})
```

With this refactoring and improvement, our test is much stronger, since it verifies the behavior of the `register()` method.

And beside the test, *it should fail when the email address is invalid*, let's also add the following two tests to make sure invalid data won't pass the validation:

- It should fail when the username is invalid
- It should fail when the password is invalid

Now, let's run the unit test with `npm run test:unit` to see how things work. You should see a result like the following:

```
Test Suites: 3 passed, 3 total
Tests:       12 passed, 12 total
```

There is one last data validation related change we need to make to the register page, which is to show the validation error of each field in the UI. We won't go into the details of that. If you're interested, check the committed code on GitHub for details.

By now, we've finished the frontend of the register page. Let's run the `mvn clean install` command. As you shall see, all tests have passed, and the following is the commit record:

add validation on front-end

jamesjieye committed a minute ago

Figure 9.6: Add validation on frontend commit

Validation on the backend

Requests received at the backend can be sent over from the UI or be sent by tools such as cURL and Postman. When requests do not originate from the UI, the validations that we added on the frontend can be bypassed completely. Therefore, we must also perform validations of the data on the backend before processing them.

As mentioned in Chapter 5, *Data Modeling - Designing the Foundation of the Application*, we use the Hexagonal Architecture style in the **TaskAgile** application. So, when an HTTP request arrives at the sever end, an adapter will handle it. In our application, the adapter is a handler inside a **Controller**. That's where we will perform the validation. The other thing is that we should leave business logic out of this validation. We should only check whether the data is valid or not based on rules that do not involve any business logic. For example, we might want to reverse a list of usernames in our application, and we will need to check whether the value of the username in the request is allowed or not before we create that user. This verification has a business rule involved and shouldn't be carried out in the adapter. Instead, it should be the responsibility of the services in the **Application Core**. The following figure shows the data validation flow of the backend that we are building in this section:

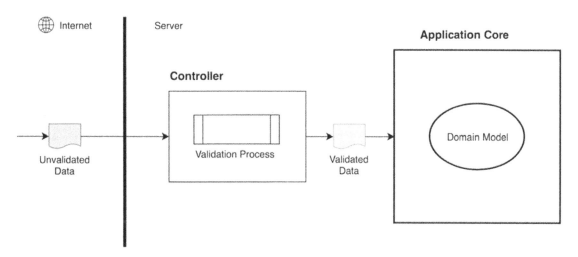

Figure 9.7: Data validation flow

As you can see, we need to make sure that the data we pass to the **Application Core** is always valid.

Creating RegistrationPayload

We will create the com.taskagile.web.apis.RegistrationApiController class in the backend to handle the /api/registrations request. We will create the com.taskagile.web.payload.RegistrationPayload class to map the fields sent in the request body. Spring MVC will instantiate this RegistrationPayload class for us and populate it with the data inside the request body.

Create RegistrationPayloadTests

First of all, let's
create the `com.taskagile.web.payload.RegistrationPayloadTests` unit test class.
In this test class, we will create an instance of `javax.validation.Validator` to perform
data validation. We will still follow the
`[UnitOfWork_StateUnderTest_ExpectedBehavior]` convention for naming the test
methods. Here is how the `RegistrationPayloadTests` looks:

```
...
public class RegistrationPayloadTests {

  private Validator validator;

  @Before
  public void setup () {
    ValidatorFactory factory =
    Validation.buildDefaultValidatorFactory();
    validator = factory.getValidator();
  }

  @Test
  public void validate_blankPayload_shouldFail() {
    RegistrationPayload payload = new RegistrationPayload();
    Set<ConstraintViolation<RegistrationPayload>> violations =
    validator.validate(payload);
    assertEquals(3, violations.size());
  }
}
```

As you can see, we create an instance of `javax.validation.Validator` in the `setup()`
method, which is annotated with the `@Before` annotation so that it will be executed before
running each test method. It is like `beforeEach()` in Jest. The first test method we have
here is quite simple. It tests a blank registration form, and we're expecting to see three
constraint violations.

Create RegistrationPayload

Now, let's move on to create the `RegistrationPayload` class itself. Here is how it looks:

```
...
public class RegistrationPayload {

  @Size(min = 2, max = 50, message = "Username must be between 2 and 50
characters")
```

```
@NotNull
private String username;

@Email(message = "Email address should be valid")
@Size(max = 100, message = "Email address must not be more than 100
characters")
@NotNull
private String emailAddress;

@Size(min = 6, max = 30, message = "Password must be between 6 and 30
characters")
@NotNull
private String password;

// getters and setters
}
```

As you can see, this `RegistrationPayload` class has three fields and the constraints we apply to them match those we added on the frontend. One difference is that the `@Size` annotation considers a `null` value to be valid. That's why we have to put the `@NotNull` annotation for each field too.

We will also need to add the following test methods in `RegistrationPayloadTests` to cover every constraint applied on each field:

- `validate_payloadWithInvalidEmail_shouldFail()`
- `validate_payloadWithEmailAddressLongerThan100_shouldFail()`
- `validate_payloadWithUsernameShorterThan2_shouldFail()`
- `validate_payloadWithUsernameLongerThan50_shouldFail()`
- `validate_payloadWithPasswordShorterThan6_shouldFail()`
- `validate_payloadWithPasswordLongerThan30_shouldFail()`

We will not go through each test method here. If you're interested in the implementation of these methods, you can find them in the commit history on GitHub.

Create RegistrationApiController

Now, let's create the API handler to accept the registration request. The following diagram, *Figure 9.8*, shows the relationship between `RegistrationApiController` and its dependencies:

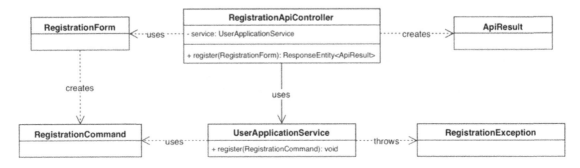

Figure 9.8: The RegistrationApiController class diagram

As you can see, the `RegistrationApiController` class has a field named `service` of the `UserService` type, which provides an API, `register(RegistrationCommand)`, for registering users. This service API returns nothing when it succeeds and throws `RegistrationException` when it fails. In the controller, the `register(RegistrationPayload)` method is the one that we will need to create. The input of this method is an instance of `RegistrationPayload` that Spring MVC will create from the request body and validate its data automatically before passing it over. The return value of this method is an instance of `ResponseEntity` that Spring MVC will use to generate the HTTP response.

Now, let's start the implementation with a unit test.

Create RegistrationApiControllerTests

In `Chapter 7`, *RESTful API Design - Building Language Between Frontend and Backend*, we created the unit test class, `MessageControllerTest`. In this section, we will use the same approach to create the `RegistrationApiControllerTests` class. To test the `register(RegistrationPayload)` method, we will need to provide the input via Spring's `MockMvc`, and mock its dependency, `UserService`. In this way, we can verify the behavior of this API handler.

Now we're clear what need to do, let's add the following test methods that will cover four different scenarios:

- `register_blankPayload_shouldFailAndReturn400()`
- `register_existedUsername_shouldFailAndReturn400()`
- `register_existedEmailAddress_shouldFailAndReturn400()`
- `register_validPayload_shouldSucceedAndReturn201()`

The following is how `RegistrationApiControllerTests` looks with the first test method:

```
...
@RunWith(SpringRunner.class)
@WebMvcTest(RegistrationApiController.class)
public class RegistrationApiControllerTests {

  @Autowired
  private MockMvc mvc;

  @Test
  public void register_blankPayload_shouldFailAndReturn400() throws
Exception {
    mvc.perform(post("/api/registrations"))
      .andExpect(status().is(400));
  }
}
```

As you can see, in this test, we perform a HTTP POST request with an empty request body and expect the API handler to return a response with the HTTP status 400, meaning a bad request.

The second test method, `register_existedUsername_shouldFailAndReturn400()`, looks like the following:

```
...
@MockBean
private UserService serviceMock;
...
@Test
public void register_existedUsername_shouldFailAndReturn400() throws
Exception {
  RegistrationPayload payload = new RegistrationPayload();
  payload.setUsername("exist");
  payload.setEmailAddress("test@taskagile.com");
  payload.setPassword("MyPassword!");
```

```
    doThrow(UsernameExistsException.class)
      .when(serviceMock)
      .register(payload.toCommand());

  mvc.perform(
    post("/api/registrations")
      .contentType(MediaType.APPLICATION_JSON)
      .content(JsonUtils.toJson(payload)))
    .andExpect(status().is(400))
    .andExpect(jsonPath("$.message").value("Username already exists"));
}
```

As you can see, we add the `UserService` dependency here as a mocked bean. Inside the test method, we specify the behavior of `serviceMock`, which throws `RegistrationExcpetion` when the `register(RegistrationCommand)` method is invoked. The `doThrow()` and the `when()` methods are the APIs of Mockito. Once the input and the mock are ready, we call the `/api/registrations` API with registration data passed in as request parameters. And then, we expect the result to be a HTTP `400` failure.

The third test method is similar to the second one. The only different is that inside this test, the exception thrown is `EmailAddressExistException`.

The fourth test method is also similar to the second one. The difference is that, we define the behavior of `serviceMock` differently, as shown in the following code. This is because the return value of the service's method is `void` and no exception will be thrown when the registration succeeds:

```
    doNothing().when(serviceMock).register(form.toCommand());
```

As the name of this Mockito API, `doNothing()`, suggests, nothing will happen after the `register()` method completes, which is the desired behavior.

For the sake of brevity, many details of the `RegistrationApiControllerTests` class have been left out. You can check them in the commit history on GitHub.

Implement RegistrationApiController and its dependencies

Now, let's move on to implement `RegistrationApiControler` and its dependencies. The full name of the controller is `com.taskagile.web.apis.RegistrationApiController`, and it looks like the following:

```
...
@Controller
public class RegistrationApiController {

  private UserService service;

  public RegistrationApiController(UserService service) {
    this.service = service;
  }

  @PostMapping("/api/registrations")
  public ResponseEntity<ApiResult> register(
      @Valid @RequestBody RegistrationPayload payload) {
    try {
      service.register(payload.toCommand());
      return Result.created();
    } catch (RegistrationException e) {
    String errorMessage = "Registration failed";
      if (e instanceof UsernameExistsException) {
      errorMessage = "Username already exists";
      } else if (e instanceof EmailAddressExistsException) {
      errorMessage = "Email address already exists";
      }
      return Result.failure(errorMessage);
    }
  }
}
```

As you can see, we apply the `@Valid` annotation to `RegistrationPayload`. With the presence of this annotation, Spring MVC will perform data validation on `RegistrationPayload` to make sure its data is valid before passing it to the `register()` method. Inside the handler, we call the service API with an instance of the `RegistrationCommand` class that is converted from the `RegistrationPayload` instance. If everything works fine, we call `Result.created()` to return a response with HTTP status `201`. Otherwise, we catch `RegistrationException` and return a `400` response with an message.

The following is how `RegistrationCommand` looks. It is read-only. Once it is created, you cannot change its state because it only provides getters, not setters:

```
public class RegistrationCommand {
   private String username;
   private String emailAddress;
   private String password;

   public RegistrationCommand(String username, String emailAddress, String
password) {
      this.username = username;
      this.emailAddress = emailAddress;
      this.password = password;
   }

   // getters

   @Override
   public boolean equals(Object o) {
      ...
   }

   @Override
   public int hashCode() {
      ....
   }
}
```

As you can see, it also has the `equals()` and `hashCode()` methods. This is because, when Mockito compares the equality of two `RegistrationCommand` instances in the test, it will use these two methods to do the comparison. Otherwise, it will use the memory addresses of the objects to do the comparison of the equality, which will be different and the test will fail.

Here is how the `com.taskagile.domain.application.UserService` interface looks:

```
public interface UserService {
   void register(RegistrationCommand command) throws RegistrationException;
}
```

We put this **Application Service** inside
the `com.taskagile.domain.model.user` package. We won't use the layered architecture packaging style, which typically looks like the following:

- `com.taskagile.web`
- `com.taskagile.service`

- `com.taskagile.domain`
- `com.taskagile.dao`

Even though this structure works great for CRUD applications due to its simplicity, the biggest issue with this approach is that it divides classes of the same domain into different packages. When you look at the structure of the application, you have no idea what it provides.

In **TaskAgile**, we go with a different approach. That is, we put all of the classes of a domain in the same package and all domain knowledge will live inside that package. The following is the structure of our User domain:

- `com.taskagile.domain.application.UserService`
- `com.taskagile.domain.application.commands`
- `com.taskagile.domain.application.commands.RegistrationCommand`
- `com.taskagile.domain.model.user.User`
- `com.taskagile.domain.model.user.UserRepository`
- `com.taskagile.domain.model.user.events.UserRegisteredEvent`
- `com.taskagile.domain.model.user.RegistrationManagement`
- `com.taskagile.domain.model.user.AuthenticationManagement`

As you can see, the `com.taskagile.domain.aplication` package contains the Application Services that Controllers depend on. The `com.taskagile.domain.model.user` package contains the Domain Models, Repository interfaces, and Domain Events, as well as the Domain Services, `RegistrationManagement` and `AuthenticationManagement`. We will talk more about these in detail later in this chapter.

Back to making our test pass; we still need to get these dependencies/changes done:

- Convert a `RegistrationPayload` instance into a `RegistrationCommand` instance
- Create a `com.taskagile.domain.model.user.RegistrationException` exception, as well as `UsernameExistsException` and `EmailAddressExistsException`
- Add a blank implementation of `com.taskagile.domain.application.UserService`
- Add `com.taskagile.web.results.ApiResult` and `com.taskagile.web.results.Result`

Since most of these implementations and changes are quite straightforward, we will not list them in this book. You can find the details in the commit history shown in *Figure 9.10*.

Now, let's run the tests in `RegistrationApiControllerTests` from VS Code by clicking the **Run Test** link, as shown in *Figure 9.9*, and you will see all tests pass:

```
21    @RunWith(SpringRunner.class)
22    @WebMvcTest(RegistrationApiController.class)
      Run Test | Debug Test | ✅
23    public class RegistrationApiControllerTests {
```

Figure 9.9: Run RegistrationApiControllerTests

After running the `mvn clean install` command, you should see that we have a successful installation before committing the changes. *Figure 9.10* shows the commit history:

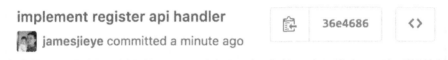

Figure 9.10: Implement register API handler commit

Implement registration in domain model

`UserService` that `RegistrationApiController` depends on is very thin because its responsibility only includes the following:

- Coordinating tasks on the models
- Guarding the domain model with security constraints
- Controlling transactions

Most importantly, its responsibility should not involve any business logic. Business logic should only live in the domain models. *Figure 9.11* shows the relationship between `UserService` and its dependencies:

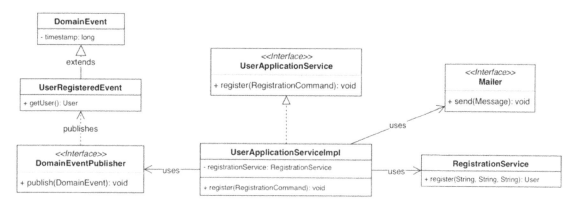

Figure 9.11: UserService class diagram

As you can see, the implementation of `UserService`, which is `UserServiceImpl`, relies on `RegistrationService`, which is a Domain Service to handle the actual registration. It also relies on `MailManager` to send email and `DomainEventPublisher` to publish the `UserRegisteredEvent` domain event.

Implement the UserService application service

As mentioned, Application Services should be kept thin. They can hold references to their dependencies, such as Repositories, Domain Services, and Infrastructure Services, to help it fulfill its role.

Create UserServiceImplTests

First things first: Let's create the unit test class `UserServiceImplTests`. To test `UserServiceImpl`, we will need to mock its dependencies—`RegistrationManagement`, `MailManager`, and `DomainEventPublisher`. There will be at least the following test methods to cover the different scenarios:

- `register_nullCommand_shouldFail()`
- `register_existingUsername_shouldFail()`

- register_existingEmailAddress_shouldFail()
- register_validCommand_shouldSucceed()

The following is how the first test method looks:

```
...
public class UserServiceImplTests {
   private RegistrationManagement registrationManagementMock;
   private DomainEventPublisher eventPublisherMock;
   private MailManager mailManagerMock;
   private UserServiceImpl instance;

   @Before
   public void setUp() {
      registrationManagementMock = mock(RegistrationManagement.class);
      eventPublisherMock = mock(DomainEventPublisher.class);
      mailManagerMock = mock(MailManager.class);
      instance = new UserServiceImpl(registrationServiceMock,
      eventPublisherMock, mailerMock);
   }

   @Test(expected = IllegalArgumentException.class)
   public void register_nullCommand_shouldFail() throws
   RegistrationException {
      instance.register(null);
   }
}
```

As you can see, we use the setUp() method to create the mocks and instantiate UserServiceImpl. In our first test method, register_nullCommand_shouldFail(), we pass a null value to the register() method to let it fail explicitly. We use @Test(expected = IllegalArgumentException.class) to tell JUnit that we're expecting this method to throw an IllegalArgumentException error. If this exception isn't thrown, then this test should be considered failed.

Since the rest of the test methods are similar to those in RegistrationApiControllerTests, we won't list them here. Check the commit history on GitHub for details.

Create MailManager

For now, we will just create the `MailManager` interface and an empty implementation, `DefaultMailManager`. We will finish the implementation later in the next chapter. The following is how the `MailManager` interface looks:

```
public interface MailManager {
   void send(String emailAddress, String subject, String template,
MessageVariable... variables);
}
```

As you can see, the API is quite simple. It requires the recipient's email address, the mail subject, the template of the mail message, and the variables that are used inside that template.

Build domain events

We build domain events based on Spring's `ApplicationEvent`. This allows us to publish and listen to domain events easily. Here is how the `DomainEvent` class looks:

```
...
public abstract class DomainEvent extends ApplicationEvent {
  public DomainEvent(Object source) {
    super(source);
  }
  public long occurredAt() {
    // Return the underlying implementation's timestamp
    return getTimestamp();
  }
}
```

As you can see, it extends from `ApplicationEvent` and provides its own API, the `occurredAt()` method, so that we don't rely too much on `ApplicationEvent` to get the time the event occurred.

The following is how the `DomainEventPublisher` interface looks:

```
public interface DomainEventPublisher {
  void publish(DomainEvent event);
}
```

As you can see, it has only one API, the `publish()` method. Its Spring-based implementation looks like the following:

```
@Component
public class DefaultDomainEventPublisher implements DomainEventPublisher {
  @Autowired
  private ApplicationEventPublisher actualPublisher;

  @Override
  public void publish(DomainEvent event) {
    actualPublisher.publishEvent(event);
  }
}
```

As you can see, we inject the actual publisher, the `ApplicationEventPublisher` instance here, and then delegate the publishing to it. With this implementation, we can publish and listen to domain events inside the same JVM. In the future, we can create implementations based on AMQP or the Redis Pub/Sub, to provide distributed domain event processing. For now, this Spring-based implementation is good enough.

`DomainEvent`, `DomainEventPublisher`, and `DefaultDomainEventPublisher` all live in the `com.taskagile.domain.common.event` package. They can be shared between multiple models.

Even though inside the `User` module we don't need to handle `UserRegisteredEvent`, let's create a handler to see how to receive this domain event.

The following is the `UserRegisteredEventHandler` inside the `com.taskagile.domain.model.user` package:

```
...
@Component
public class UserRegisteredEventHandler {
    ...
  @EventListener(UserRegisteredEvent.class)
  public void handleEvent(UserRegisteredEvent event) {
    log.debug("Handling `{}` registration event",
    event.getUser().getEmailAddress());
    // This is only a demonstration of the domain event listener
  }
}
```

As you can see, an event handler is a standard component that has a method annotated with the `@EventListener` annotation, which is only interested in `UserRegisteredEvent`. The method body itself simply writes debug information into the log. In order to see this log, you will need to add the following logging level in `src/main/resources/application.properties`:

```
logging.level.com.taskagile=DEBUG
```

With this setting, all of the debug information of the application itself will show up in the output.

Implement the UserServiceImpl class

Now, we have the tests ready. Let's implement the `UserServiceImpl` class itself. Here is how it looks:

```
...
@Service
@Transactional
public class UserServiceImpl implements UserService {

  private RegistrationManagement registrationManagement;
  private DomainEventPublisher domainEventPublisher;
  private MailManager mailManager;

  public UserServiceImpl(RegistrationManagement registrationManagement,
                         DomainEventPublisher domainEventPublisher,
                         MailManager mailManager) {
    this.registrationManagement = registrationManagement;
    this.domainEventPublisher = domainEventPublisher;
    this.mailManager = mailManager;
  }

  @Override
  public void register(RegistrationCommand command) throws
  RegistrationException {
    Assert.notNull(command, "Parameter `command` must not be null");
    User newUser = registrationManagement.register(
      command.getUsername(),
      command.getEmailAddress(),
      command.getPassword());

    sendWelcomeMessage(newUser);
    domainEventPublisher.publish(new UserRegisteredEvent(newUser));
  }
```

```
    private void sendWelcomeMessage(User user) {
      mailManager.send(
        user.getEmailAddress(),
        "Welcome to TaskAgile",
        "welcome.ftl",
        MessageVariable.from("user", user)
      );
    }
  }
```

As you can see, we apply the `@Service` annotation and the `@Transactional` annotation to this class. The name of the `@Service` annotation was originally defined in Eric Evans's book, *Domain-Driven Design*. It means that the class with this annotation applied only offers operations for its client. The `UserServiceImpl` class is stateless. It doesn't hold any internal state. In a DDD application, services are partitioned into three types—Application Services, Domain Services, and Infrastructure Services.

Let's talk a little bit more about these services.

First of all, for Application Services, the following applies:

- They only coordinate tasks on the model
- They do not house any business logic
- They are sometimes designed to shield clients from accessing the domain model
- They control transactions, in our case by using the `@Transactional` annotation

One example is our `UserServiceImpl` class. As you can see, it doesn't care about how to register a user. It replies on the Domain Service, `RegistrationManagement`, to take care of that. In Spring, the `@Service` annotation is usually applied to Application Services.

For Domain Services, the following applies:

- They encapsulate business logic that doesn't naturally fit within a domain object and are not typical CRUD operations, which would belong to a repository

One example is our `RegistrationManagement` class, which we will discuss shortly.

For Infrastructure Services, the following applies:

- They typically talk to the external resources, for example, mail servers, databases, messaging queues, cache servers, or third-party RESTful APIs
- They are not part of the primary problem of the domain model

One example is the implementation of `UserRepository` and the mail service, which we will create in the next chapter, and which `DefaultMailManager` depends on.

Back to the code; in this service, we ask Spring to inject its three dependencies via the constructor. Inside the `register()` method, the first thing we do is to add an assertion to make sure the command parameter can never be `null`. If it is null, an `IllegalArgumentException` will be thrown from the `Assert.notNull()` method. Once the parameter is checked, we call the `register()` method of `RegistrationManagement` to register the user. Here, we do not pass the `RegistrationCommand` instance as the parameter anymore because `RegistrationCommand` is for clients of Application Services, such as `Controller`, to use. Inside the Application Core, we avoid using `RegistrationCommand` so that the internals of the Application Core won't be coupled with the outside.

Once the user has been registered, we send a welcome email and also publish the `UserRegisteredEvent` domain event so that others who are interested in (subscribed to) this event can take action accordingly. We will skip the details of the `sendWelcomeMessage()` method for now. You can check the details of the commit. We will talk about sending emails in a later section of this chapter.

For now, we still cannot make the test pass because we haven't created the `RegistrationManagement` class.

Implement RegistrationManagement

The `RegistrationManagement` domain service is where the business logic of registration lives. The business logic includes the following:

- Existing username/email address cannot register
- Encrypt password
- Save the user to the repository

The following diagram, shows the relationship between `RegistrationManagement` and its dependencies:

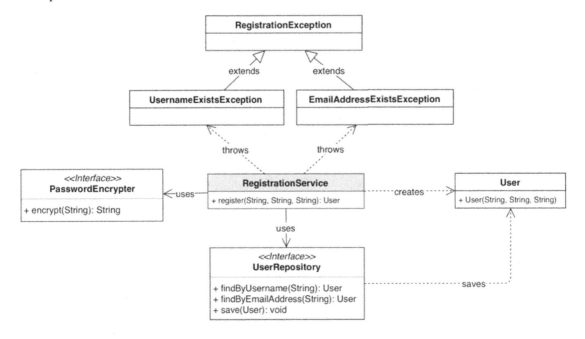

Figure 9.12: RegistrationManagement class diagram

As you can see, `RegistrationManagement` uses `UserRepository` to find a user. It throws `UsernameExistsException` or `EmailAddressExistsException` when there is another user that already exists with the same username or email address. Otherwise, it asks `PasswordEncryptor` to encrypt the password and then asks `UserRepository` to save that user.

Before we create the unit test, let's create the `User` entity first because it is created inside `RegistrationManagement`, and `UserRepository` also depends on it. It looks like the following:

```
...
@Entity
@Table(name = "user")
public class User extends AbstractBaseEntity {
  @Id
  @GeneratedValue(strategy = GenerationType.IDENTITY)
  private Long id;
  @Column(name="username", nullable=false, length=50, unique=true)
  private String username;
```

```
@Column(name="email_address", nullable=false, length=100,
unique=true)
private String emailAddress;

@Column(name="password", nullable=false, length=30)
private String password;

@Column(name="first_name", nullable=false, length=45)
private String firstName;

@Column(name="last_name", nullable=false, length=45)
private String lastName;

@Temporal(TemporalType.TIMESTAMP)
@Column(name = "created_date", nullable=false)
private Date createdDate;

public User() {}

public static User create(String username, String emailAddress,
      String password) {
  User user = new User();
  user.username = username;
  user.emailAddress = emailAddress;
  user.password = password;
  user.firstName = "";
  user.lastName = "";
  user.createdDate = new Date();
  return user;
}
...
}
```

As you can see, this entity's fields map to the columns we created during the data modeling. And for the id field, we use the GenerationType.IDENTITY strategy to tell Hibernate that the value of the id field is generated by the database. For the other fields, we specify the length, nullability, and uniqueness using the @Column annotation. This is required because, when we test repositories, we will use Hibernate's hbm2ddl feature to create the database inside H2, the embedded database that we will use during testing. With these settings in the @Column annotations, the table that is autogenerated will have these constraints as well. In this entity, we also override the equals() and hashCode() method to only compare username and emailAddress of two User objects; as long as those two fields are the same, we consider those two objects to be equal.

Create RegistrationManagementTests

Now, we know what RegistrationManagement does and we have the User entity ready, so let's create the RegistrationManagementTests unit test. We will focus on the following:

- Make sure registering a user with an existing username fails
- Make sure registering a user with an existing email address fails
- Make sure registering a user with valid data succeeds and the password is encrypted
- Make sure all users' email addresses are saved as lowercase in the repository

The following are the test methods we will create to cover the cases listed previously:

- register_existedUsername_shouldFail()
- register_existedEmailAddress_shouldFail()
- register_uppercaseEmailAddress_shouldSucceedAndBecomeLowercase()
- register_newUser_shouldSucceed()

Here is how the first test method in the RegistrationManagementTests class looks:

```
...
public class RegistrationServiceTests {
  ...
  @Test(expected = UsernameExistsException.class)
  public void register_existedUsername_shouldFail() throws
RegistrationException {
    String username = "existUsername";
    String emailAddress = "sunny@taskagile.com";
    String password = "MyPassword!";
    // We just return an empty user object to indicate an existing user
    when(repositoryMock.findByUsername(username)).thenReturn(new User());
    instance.register(username, emailAddress, password);
  }
}
```

The same as UserServiceImplTests, in this test we also need to create mocks and instantiate the RegistrationManagement instance inside the setUp() method.

As you can see, in this test method, we define the behavior of `repositoryMock` to return a user as the result of the `findByUsername()` method. With this setup, we expect `RegistrationManagement` to throw `UsernameExistsException`. If this exception is not thrown, then the implementation of `RegistrationManagement` is incorrect.

The `register_existedEmailAddress_shouldFail()` method is similar to the first method and we will not list it here. The only difference is that we define the mock's behavior for the `findByEmailAddress()` method and expect `EmailAddressExistsException` to be thrown.

Here is how the third method looks:

```
@Test
public void
register_uppercaseEmailAddress_shouldSucceedAndBecomeLowercase()
  throws RegistrationException {
  String username = "sunny";
  String emailAddress = "Sunny@TaskAgile.com";
  String password = "MyPassword!";
  instance.register(username, emailAddress, password);
  User userToSave = User.create(username, emailAddress.toLowerCase(),
password);
  verify(repositoryMock).save(userToSave);
}
```

As you can see, in this test method we call the `register()` method with a mixed-case email address, and we expect the `register()` method to make sure that `repository` saves the user and the email address is in lowercase.

Here is how the last test method looks:

```
@Test
public void register_newUser_shouldSucceed() throws RegistrationException {
  String username = "sunny";
  String emailAddress = "sunny@taskagile.com";
  String password = "MyPassword!";
  String encryptedPassword = "EncryptedPassword";
  User newUser = User.create(username, emailAddress, encryptedPassword);

  // Setup repository mock
  // Return null to indicate no user exists
  when(repositoryMock.findByUsername(username)).thenReturn(null);
  when(repositoryMock.findByEmailAddress(emailAddress)).thenReturn(null);
  doNothing().when(repositoryMock).save(newUser);
  // Setup passwordEncryptor mock
  when(passwordEncryptorMock.encrypt(password))
```

```
        .thenReturn("EncryptedPassword");

    User savedUser = instance.register(username, emailAddress, password);
    InOrder inOrder = inOrder(repositoryMock);
    inOrder.verify(repositoryMock).findByUsername(username);
    inOrder.verify(repositoryMock).findByEmailAddress(emailAddress);
    inOrder.verify(repositoryMock).save(newUser);
    verify(passwordEncryptorMock).encrypt(password);
    assertEquals("Saved user's password should be encrypted",
        encryptedPassword, savedUser.getPassword());
}
```

As you can see, at the beginning of this test method, we prepare all of the test data. Then, we define the behavior of the mocks. As a matter of fact, we don't have to define the behavior of `repositoryMock` here, because by default the behavior of its `findByUsername()` method, the `findByEmailAddress()` method is returned `null`, and its `save()` method does nothing. We add those behavior definitions here to make that explicit, which will make our test stronger. The `encrypt()` method of `passwordEncryptorMock` will return the encrypted password we specified.

In this test, we use Mockito's `InOrder` API to verify that the invocations of the methods of `repositoryMock` occurred in a specific order. Then, we verify that the `encrypt()` method of `passwordEncryptor` has been invoked, and the password stored in the saved user is the encrypted version, not the plain text version.

Implement the RegistrationManagement class

With all of the test methods we created in the preceding section, you probably already have an idea of how `RegistrationManagement` will look, and here it is:

```
...
@Component
public class RegistrationService {

  private UserRepository repository;
  private PasswordEncryptor passwordEncryptor;

  public RegistrationManagement(UserRepository repository,
PasswordEncryptor passwordEncryptor) {
    this.repository = repository;
    this.passwordEncryptor = passwordEncryptor;
  }

  public User register(String username, String emailAddress, String
password) throws RegistrationException {
```

```
      User existingUser = repository.findByUsername(username);
      if (existingUser != null) {
        throw new UsernameExistsException();
      }

      existingUser =
        repository.findByEmailAddress(emailAddress.toLowerCase());
      if (existingUser != null) {
        throw new EmailAddressExistsException();
      }

      String encryptedPassword = passwordEncryptor.encrypt(password);
      User newUser = User.create(
        username, emailAddress.toLowerCase(), encryptedPassword);
      repository.save(newUser);
      return newUser;
    }
  }
```

As you can see, this domain service is quite straightforward. Some might doubt the existence of this `RegistrationManagement` class and argue that this is over-design because this registration logic can be put inside the `register()` method of `UserServiceImpl` so that the effort of creating `RegistrationManagement` can be saved. Others might even prefer to move this registration logic inside `RegistrationController` so that the code can be much simpler. If we look at these two alternatives from a simplicity perspective, there is no doubt that they are both simpler. However, if we look at this from the extensibility and maintainability point of view, the use of `RegistrationManagement` is better because it encapsulates the necessary business rules so that its clients, who invoke its `register()` method, don't need to care about those rules. And, in the future, when we need to add more rules to the registration process, we just need to modify `RegistrationManagement`.

Some might prefer to declare `RegistrationManagement` as an interface and then use `RegistrationManagementImpl`, for example, to implement the actual logic. For Application Services, which set up the boundary between the Application Core and its clients, using an interface is preferred because we don't want `Controller` to directly reference the actual implementation, which gives us a narrow space to evolve the implementation. For Domain Services such as `RegistrationManagement`, there is no need to declare a boundary inside the Application Core. The only time it would make sense to use an interface for Domain Services is when you need to apply the Strategy design pattern, in which case there will be multiple implementations of the same interface and the choice of implementation depends on the strategy that is needed.

Implement RegistrationManagement dependencies

We will introduce the dependencies of RegistrationManagement briefly here. At this stage, our focus is to get the RegistrationManagementTests pass. In the tests, we use mocks to define the behavior of the dependencies. So, we will only need to create a blank implementation of the dependencies, leaving the actual implementation for later sections in this chapter.

Here is the blank implementation of the PasswordEncryptor interface:

```
@Component
public class PasswordEncryptorDelegator implements PasswordEncryptor {
  @Override
  public String encrypt(String rawPassword) {
    // TODO implement this
    return rawPassword;
  }
}
```

As you can see, we name it PasswordEncryptorDelegator, indicating that the actual password encryption logic is delegated to others, in our case, Spring Security's PasswordEncoder, which we will talk about later.

And here is the blank implementation of the MailManager interface:

```
@Component
public class DefaultMailManager implements MailManager {

  @Override
  public void send(String emailAddress, String subject, String template,
MessageVariable... variables) {
    // TODO implement this
  }
}
```

This mail manager is responsible for creating mail messages from the template and the variables, and then calling the mail service API to send the message out.

Here is how the UserRepository interface looks:

```
...
public interface UserRepository {
  User findByUsername(String username);
  User findByEmailAddress(String emailAddress);
  void save(User user);
}
```

As you can see, this interface is clean and easy to understand. We will talk about its implementation shortly.

Now, if you run `RegistrationManagementTests` from VS Code, you should see all of the tests pass.

By now, we have finished the implementation of registration inside the domain model. It's time to save the user in the database.

Implement UserRepository

As mentioned earlier, we will use Hibernate to save data into a MySQL database. The JPA implementation of the Spring Data JPA is based on Hibernate.

The special part of the Spring Data JPA is that it significantly reduces the effort to write the repository by only requiring the developers to write repository interfaces, and it will generate the implementation automatically for us, which sounds perfect and very productive.

To use this autogeneration of the implementation feature that Spring Data JPA provides, we will need to change the `UserRepository` interface to the following:

```
@Repository
public interface UserRepository extends JpaRepository<User, Long> {
  User findByUsername(String username);
  User findByEmailAddress(String emailAddress);
}
```

As you can see, we will need to apply the `@Repository` annotation to the interface and make it extend from Spring's `JpaRepository` or `CurdRepository`. We don't need the `save()` method in the original interface anymore because `JpaRepository` already has one. Besides the `save()` method, we also inherit a bunch of other methods, for example, `saveAll()`, `getOne()`, and `findAll()`.

If we need to find users who registered yesterday, we can declare an API in the `UserRepository` interface like the following:

```
List<User> findByCreatedDateBetween(Date, Date);
```

Or, we can create the following method to find users by last name and sort by first name in descending order:

```
List<User> findByLastNameOrderByFirstNameDesc(String lastName);
```

The Spring Data JPA also supports pagination out of the box, for example, the following methods can find users by last name and return the paginated result:

```
List<User> findByLastName(String lastName, Pageable pageable);
```

The Spring Data JPA provides a list of query keywords that you can put into the method names. Other than that, you can apply the @Query annotation to a method to create a custom query, like the following:

```
@Query("select u from User u where u.emailAddress = ?1")
User findByEmailAddress(String emailAddress);
```

Or, use a native query, like the following:

```
@Query(value = "SELECT * FROM USERS WHERE EMAIL_ADDRESS = ?1", nativeQuery
= true)
User findByEmailAddress(String emailAddress);
```

If this still cannot meet your requirements, you can create a custom repository interface with a custom implementation.

But, is this really a good approach? The answer to this question depends on how you want the Repository interfaces to look like. If you're comfortable with narrowing your method naming options to those keywords, using @Query to specify the query in the interface, or creating another Repository interface for custom queries, the autogeneration of the implementation can be quite productive. And you don't need to worry about doing a unit test of Repository interfaces, because Spring Data JPA provides a nice solution for that.

On the other hand, if you want your Repository interfaces to be clean and implementation neutral so that you can keep the freedom of switching to other implementations from Hibernate, such as MyBatis or Spring JDBC, you probably don't want to use Spring Data JPA the way described previously.

In **TaskAgile**, we want to keep the Repository interfaces clean and keep infrastructure related implementation out of our domain model. So, here is what we will do:

- Keep the UserRespository interface as it is
- Create a HibernateUserRepository implementation in the com.taskagile.infrastructure.repository package
- Let the Spring Data JPA create the DataSource instance and the EntityManager instance for us, as well as setting up the connection pool; from there, we will implement those methods ourselves

Let's get started.

Create HibernateUserRepositoryTests

In `HibernateUserRepositoryTests`, we will create the following test methods to cover different scenarios:

- `save_nullUsernameUser_shouldFail()`
- `save_nullEmailAddressUser_shouldFail()`
- `save_nullPasswordUser_shouldFail()`
- `save_validUser_shouldSuccess()`
- `save_usernameAlreadyExist_shouldFail()`
- `save_emailAddressAlreadyExist_shouldFail()`
- `findByEmailAddress_notExist_shouldReturnEmptyResult()`
- `findByEmailAddress_exist_shouldReturnResult()`
- `findByUsername_notExist_shouldReturnEmptyResult()`
- `findByUsername_exist_shouldReturnResult()`

First of all, let's add a H2 dependency into Maven's `pom.xml` as follows, so that when Spring Boot starts the tests, it knows that we need H2 instead of MySQL:

```xml
<dependency>
  <groupId>com.h2database</groupId>
  <artifactId>h2</artifactId>
  <scope>test</scope>
</dependency>
```

Since the data source configuration that H2 requires is different from the one that MySQL uses in `src/main/resources/application.properties`, let's create `application.properties` in the `src/test/resources/` directory with the following settings for H2:

```
spring.datasource.url=jdbc:h2:mem:taskagile;DB_CLOSE_DELAY=-1;DB_CLOSE_ON_EXIT=FALSE
spring.datasource.username=sa
spring.datasource.password=sa
spring.datasource.driver-class-name=org.h2.Driver

spring.jpa.open-in-view=false
spring.jpa.hibernate.ddl-auto=create-drop
spring.jpa.database-platform=org.hibernate.dialect.H2Dialect
```

As you can see, we use the H2 database by specifying `url` and `driver-class-name` of the data source, and let Hibernate autogenerate and drop the database by specifying `ddl-auto` to `create-drop`. We also turn off Hibernate's **Open Session In View** feature, and then we let JPA know the database platform we're using through the class name of Hibernate's `H2Dialect`.

Since we've added the `spring.jpa.*` settings in `src/`**test**`/resources/application.properties`, let's also add the following settings into `src/`**main**`/resources.application.properties` to make it clear that we need these settings for the environments other than test:

```
spring.jpa.open-in-view=false
spring.jpa.hibernate.ddl-auto=none
spring.jpa.database-platform=org.hibernate.dialect.MySQL5InnoDBDialect
```

It is only when Spring is run in the `test` profile that it will read the settings in the `src/`**test**`/resources/application.properties` file. By default, when you start the Sprint Boot application, it runs in the `dev` profile. We will need to change the active profile so that Spring can know we're doing testing. We can apply the `@ActiveProfiles` annotation to tests, such as the following `TaskAgileApplicationTests`, which is initially generated by Spring Initializr:

```
...
@RunWith(SpringRunner.class)
@SpringBootTest
@ActiveProfiles("test")
public class TaskAgileApplicationTests {
  @Test
  public void contextLoads() {
  }
}
```

As you can see, we use the `@SpringBootTest` annotation here so that Spring Boot will look for a main class, in our case, the `TaskAgileApplication` class, which is annotated with `@SpringBootApplication`, and then start a Spring application context with all of the Spring beans defined in the application loaded into the context. Without specifying the profile by using the `@ActiveProfiles` annotation, when we run the `mvn clean install` command, or `mvn test`, Spring will read `src/main/resources/application.properties` for the `dev` profile and won't be able to initialize the H2 database.

Another property file that we need to add is
`src/test/resources/hibernate.properties`, which looks like the following:

```
hibernate.hbm2ddl.auto=create-drop
hibernate.dialect=org.hibernate.dialect.H2Dialect
hibernate.show_sql=true
hibernate.format_sql=true
```

During the test, Hibernate will pick up the settings from this file.

Now, let's get back to `HibernateUserRepositoryTests`. The following is the first test
method:

```
...
@RunWith(SpringRunner.class)
@ActiveProfiles("test")
@DataJpaTest
public class HibernateUserRepositoryTests {

  @TestConfiguration
  public static class UserRepositoryTestContextConfiguration {
    @Bean
    public UserRepository userRepository(EntityManager entityManager) {
      return new HibernateUserRepository(entityManager);
    }
  }

  @Autowired
  private UserRepository repository;

  @Test(expected = PersistenceException.class)
  public void save_nullUsernameUser_shouldFail() {
User inavlidUser = User.create(
  null, "sunny@taskagile.com", "MyPassword!");
    repository.save(inavlidUser);
  }
}
```

As you can see, we apply the `@ActiveProfiles` annotation to it as well as the
`@DataJpaTest` annotation. Unlike the `@SpringBootTest` annotation, the `@DataJpaTest`
annotation is only for testing JPA components. With its presence, by default, tests will use
an embedded in-memory database, in our case, the H2 database. We create an inner
configuration class to create an instance of `HibernateUserRepository` so that it can be
auto-wired into the test class.

In fact, if we used `UserRepository` the Spring Data JPA way, we wouldn't need to instantiate `UserRepository` like this using a test configuration, because Spring will generate the repository implementation and instantiate it for us automatically with the presence of the `@DataJpaTest` annotation.

In this test, we don't need to create any mocks. All of the database interactions will be performed against the in-memory database.

In the `save_nullUsernameUser_shouldFail()` method, we try to save a user without `username`, and it should fail because, in the `User` entity, we put `nullable=false` in the `@Column` annotation that applied to the `username` field.

We will not go through the rest of the test methods here because the only major difference that this `HibernateUserRepositoryeTests` has with all the previous tests we created is how the embedded database is initialized. You can find the details of this test class in the commit history on GitHub.

Implement HibernateUserRepository

As mentioned, Spring Data JPA will instantiate `EntityManager` for us. `EntityManager` is an interface of JPA. And, in our application, Hibernate is the underlying implementation. Hibernate offers a more powerful API than JPA. For example, the `org.hibernate.query.Query` interface supports `Generics` while the `javax.persistence.Query` interface does not. In this book, we will use Hibernate's API in our repository implementation most of the time.

To make things easier, let's first create an abstract base class, `HibernateSupport`, to retrieve an instance of `org.hibernate.Session` from `EntityManager`. Here is how it looks:

```
...
abstract class HibernateSupport {

  EntityManager entityManager;

  HibernateSupport(EntityManager entityManager) {
    this.entityManager = entityManager;
  }

  Session getSession() {
    return entityManager.unwrap(Session.class);
  }
}
```

As you can see, we ask Spring to inject the `EntityManager` instance here and then inside the `getSession()` method, which returns an instance of `org.hibernate.Session`, we use the `unwrap()` method of `EntityManager` to get an instance of the Hibernate `session`.

And the following is how `HibernateUserRepository` looks:

```
...
@Repository
public class HibernateUserRepository extends HibernateSupport
    implements UserRepository {

  public HibernateUserRepository(EntityManager entityManager) {
    super(entityManager);
  }

  @Override
  public User findByUsername(String username) {
Query<User> query = getSession().createQuery(
  "from User where username = :username", User.class);
    query.setParameter("username", username);
    return query.uniqueResult();
  }

  @Override
  public User findByEmailAddress(String emailAddress) {
Query<User> query = getSession().createQuery(
  "from User where emailAddress = :emailAddress", User.class);
    query.setParameter("emailAddress", emailAddress);
    return query.uniqueResult();
  }

  @Override
  public void save(User user) {
    entityManager.persist(user);
    entityManager.flush();
  }
}
```

As you can see, besides the `save()` method where we use the `EntityManager` API directly, for the other two `find*` methods, we use Hibernate's API. It is true that there is boilerplate code in here. The trade-off is that we keep the infrastructure implementation details out of our domain model.

Now, let's run the `mvn clean install` command to make sure everything works before committing the code. As you should see, it is a successful build. The following is the commit record on GitHub:

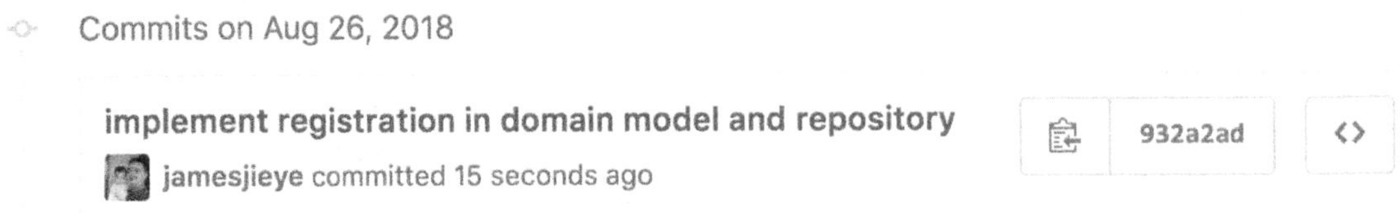

Commits on Aug 26, 2018

implement registration in domain model and repository

jamesjieye committed 15 seconds ago

932a2ad   <>

Figure 9.13: Implement registration in domain model and repository commit

Fixes at the end

Here are the fixes in this chapter:

- **Fix—adding/registering to request mapping**: If you run the `mvn spring-boot:run` command after a clean install and then open the page at `https://localhost:8080/register`, you will see a `404` error page. This is because we haven't added `/register` to `@GetMapping` inside `MainController`. Let's fix it now. Once it is fixed, try to perform a registration from the register page. After registration, you should see the debug information that `UserRegisteredEventHandler` created.

  Not adding `/register` to the mapping reveals a defect in our end-to-end testing. The end-to-end test is supposed to capture this kind of issue during building. Unfortunately, it didn't. We will improve our end-to-end testing in the next chapter. The following is the commit record:

Commits on Aug 26, 2018

fix: add /register to request mapping

jamesjieye committed 12 seconds ago

ee034f4   <>

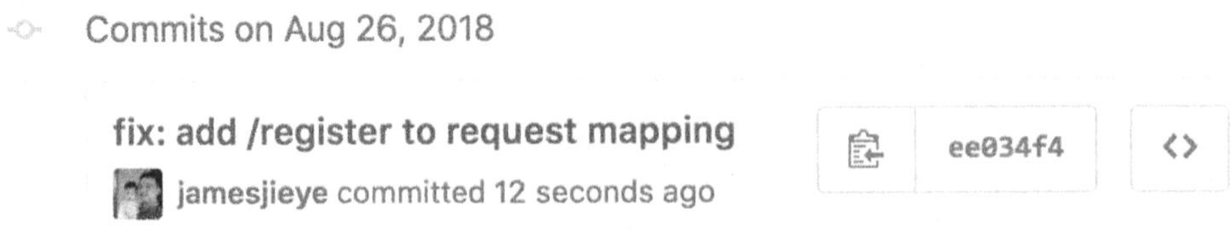

Figure 9.14: Fix—add/register to request mapping commit

- **Fix—invalid return value of** `encrypt()` **method**: In our implementation of `PasswordEncryptor`, `PasswordEncryptorDelegator`, the `encrypt()` method returns a `null` value, which causes the registration failure. Let's change it to return the raw password for now, so that we can have successful registration. We will use Spring Security's `PasswordEncoder` in the next chapter to encrypt the password.

    The following is the commit record:

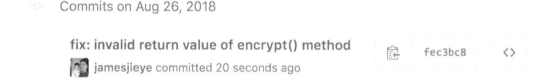

Figure 9.15: Fix—the invalid return value of encrypt method commit

Summary

In this chapter, we've covered the whole set of full-stack development, starting from the UI creation of the register page to the logic and data validation of registration, and then we moved to the backend implementation. We have also demonstrated TDD practices, and we've looked into how to write stronger unit tests.

Due to the scope of this book, not every detail of the implementation of the register page has been covered. You can use the commit record on GitHub to see how the application was created step by step.

In the next chapter, we will introduce Spring Security and implement the login page. We will also refactor our end-to-end testing to make it actually useful.

10
Spring Security - Making Our Application Secure

Security is one of the fundamental requirements of a web application such as TaskAgile. We want to authenticate requests and authorize access to various resources, and we will want to prevent potential attacks that can be performed against our application. Spring Security, originally named Acegi Security, is the most popular security solution adopted in the Spring world. In this chapter, we will introduce the basics of web application security and various authentication processes, including **Single Sign-On** (**SSO**) and OAuth 2.0. We will also introduce Spring Security and explore its features, and then take a deep dive into its architecture to understand how it works. We will also implement the login page of the user module along the way.

In a nutshell, the following is what you will learn in this chapter:

- How to secure a web application
- How Spring Security works
- How to set up Spring Security
- Authenticating requests with Spring Security
- Sending emails using JavaMail
- Performing end-to-end integration tests
- Adding a Java unit test coverage report

How to secure a web application

Security is a very broad topic and it covers many aspects. Due to the scope of this book, we will mainly focus on the security that a web application needs to take care of, which includes authentication, authorization, and preventing attacks such as **Cross-Site Scripting** (**XSS**) and SQL/NoSQL injection. Topics such as how to secure a server or how to prevent a **distributed denial-of-service** (**DDoS**) attack will not be covered here.

So, how do we secure a web application? It really comes down to three aspects:

- Authenticating users
- Authorizing users
- Preventing attacks

Let's take TaskAgile as an example. We want only those users that we have authenticated to access the application. So, people will need to log in to the application before using it, except the register and the login page, which are accessible publicly. We also want to limit the resources that authenticated users can access to only those that they have been authorized for. For example, they should not be able to edit others' personal information or view the cards of boards that they haven't joined yet. We will also want to prevent attacks from malicious users. Let's get into these three aspects in detail.

Authenticating users

To authenticate users, the application needs to be able to identify a user to verify they are who they claim to be. A common authentication process starts with a user who provides either an email address or a username together with a password on the login form, and the application will find the user's record by looking in the database using the email address or the username and then doing a comparison of the password that is stored in the database with the one that the user provides. If the user record does not exist or the passwords do not match, then the authentication fails. Otherwise, the application will consider the user as authenticated and recognize the user in the following requests, usually by storing the user's information in the HTTP session. The following figure is a high-level overview of the authentication process:

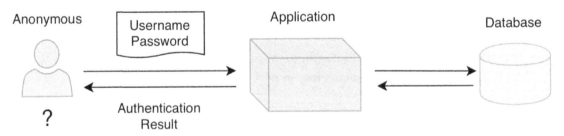

Figure 10.1: Authenticating user

There are many variants of the authentication process. For example, instead of looking up users in a **Database**, the **Application** can talk to a server **Lightweight Directory Access Protocol (LDAP)** such as **Active Directory**, check an XML file that contains user data, or even use the user data stored in memory.

Single Sign-On

Another variant of the authentication process is Single Sign-On (SSO), which uses protocols such as **Security Assertion Markup Language (SAML)** or **Central Authentication Service (CAS)**. When using SSO, the application will redirect users to the identity server, reply on the identity server to perform the authentication, and notify the application about the result. When using SAML, the application, which is known as a **Service Provider (SP)**, will receive an SAML assertion from the identity server, which is known as the **identity provider (IdP)**, after the authentication. The SAML assertion contains information on the user that the application can trust. It usually includes the user's basic information, such as name, email address and user ID on the IdP side. When using CAS, upon a successful authentication on the CAS server side, the application will receive a service ticket once the user is redirected back to the application. With this service ticket, the application will make a request to the CAS server to validate the service ticket to make sure the received service ticket is valid and can be trust. As you can see, in the Single Sign-On process, the application won't have any knowledge of the user's credentials.

OAuth 2.0

The OAuth 2.0 protocol is a very popular way to authenticate a user, even though the protocol was initially designed to be used as a way to authorize third-party services to access the user's data. In a nutshell, the OAuth 2.0 protocol involves four parties:

- **Resource owner**: A person who owns the data in the resource server. For instance, I'm the owner of my data on Twitter.
- **Resource server**: The server that stores the data the client wants to access. For example, the Twitter API server is a resource server.
- **Authorization server**: The server that will perform the authorization of the data access requested from the clients. Usually, the resource server and the authorization server are the same one.
- **Client**: The application that wants to access your data.

In a case where we use OAuth 2.0 for authentication, for example, with GitHub, our application is the client and the user who tries to access our application is the resource owner. GitHub is the resource server and the authorization server. The following figure shows the authentication flow when logging in to our application with GitHub through OAuth 2.0:

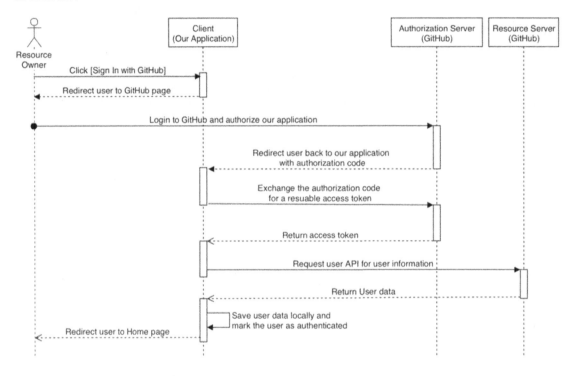

Figure 10.2: OAuth 2.0 authentication flow

As you can see, the authentication process starts with the user clicking the **Sign In with GitHub** button on our application. Our application will redirect the user to the authorization page on GitHub, requesting permission to access the user's data on GitHub. If the user hasn't logged in on the GitHub side, GitHub will show a login form requiring the user to pass the authentication check on GitHub first. After that, the user will be able to grant data access to our application. The user will then be redirected back to our application with an authorization code that our application can use to get an access token from GitHub. Once the access token is retrieved, our application can use it to access the user's data on GitHub, such as the user's name, email address, and profile photo.

In the previous sequence diagram, many details are left out for the sake of brevity. For example, the user, as a **resource owner**, does not interact with our application or GitHub directly. It is through a user agent, most of the time a browser. And it is in the browser that the redirect happens.

In summary, authenticating a user is about verifying the user is really who claimed to be, either through a data source the application manages or through a third party.

Authorizing users

Once authenticated, a user will be able to access the application. However, it doesn't mean the user can do anything at will. The access will be limited to only those resources that the user has been authorized for. For example, a user can edit his/her own personal information and is forbidden to modify another user's. The following figure shows a user trying to access payment information inside an **admin** module and getting an **Access Denied** error, or forbidden error, usually sent back to the client side with the HTTP status `403`:

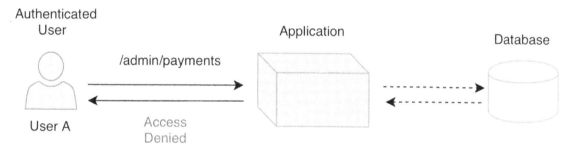

Figure 10.3: Deny unauthorized access

There are two types of authorization. One is role-based authorization, for example, as long as the user has the admin role, he/she will be able to access the **/admin/payments** resource. This is a coarse-grained authorization since it only has the ability to control access at the resource type level, even though you can add a privilege, such as `READ`, `WRITE`, or `DELETE`. Another type of authorization is through an **access control list** (**ACL**), which is a list of permissions attached to a piece of data, as well as a list of users who have been granted access to that piece of data. In this way, users can have fine-grained authorization. For example, with ACL, you can specify that an admin can only view the payment of **User A**, but can manage the refund to User B. In general, role-based authorization is easier to maintain and manage, while ACL-based requires extra effort in maintaining the list and extra steps to determine if a user has the authorization to access a resource or not.

Sometimes, the authorization you want to perform isn't simply either a completely role-based approach or ACL-based approach. For example, as mentioned earlier, in TaskAgile, we only allow users to access cards of the boards that they have joined. So, if you are not a member of that board, you shouldn't be able to view it. Board member seems to be a role. However, it isn't really a role since you will have to join a board to be a board member. The membership is related to a specific board. On the other hand, it feels like a little bit of ACL. However, we won't define an access control list because we have already stored the membership information in `board_member`. (If you do not remember this, you might want to check the data modeling in `Chapter 5`, *Data Modeling - Designing the Foundation of the Application*). Therefore, in TaskAgile, we will create a custom authorization mechanism based on Spring's EL, which we will talk about later in this chapter.

Preventing attacks

The internet is not a safe place. It is extremely dangerous to assume that no one will attack your application, or that putting a firewall in front of the server is enough to stop attackers. According to the **Open Web Application Security Project** (**OWASP**), the following are the top 10 security of web applications:

- Injection
- Broken authentication
- Sensitive data exposure
- **XML External Entities (XXE)**
- Broken access control
- Security misconfiguration
- Cross-Site Scripting (XSS)
- Insecure deserialization
- Using components with known vulnerabilities
- Insufficient logging and monitoring

Clearly, firewalls cannot help with these vulnerabilities. The application itself needs to address these security risks. Due to the scope of this book, we won't go into the details of each item in the list. You can find details about these security issues here: `https://www.owasp.org/images/7/72/OWASP_Top_10-2017_%28en%29.pdf.pdf`.

Introducing Spring Security

In a nutshell, Spring Security uses filters to perform authentication and request-level authorization and uses AOP to fulfill method-level authorization. The following figure shows the components that a request will go through in a web application that is guarded by Spring Security:

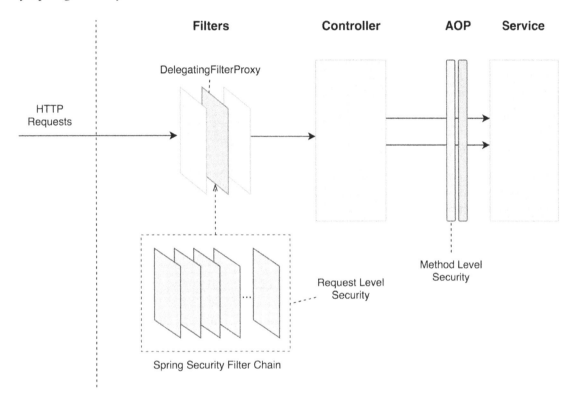

Figure 10.4: Spring Security in an application

As you can see, when a request arrives at the server, it will go through a **Spring Security Filter Chain**, which is delegated through
`org.springframework.web.filter.DelegatingFilterProxy`. This filter chain is usually created as a Spring bean named `springSecurityFilterChain`, which contains a list of filter beans created by Spring Security. Through these filters, Spring performs a series of actions to decide how a request should be handled. Once a request passes all the filters, it arrives at the **Controller** that is registered, through request mapping, to handle the request. Most of the time, controllers will call APIs of services to either execute a command or query for some information. Before the control flows into the **Service**, Spring Security can perform method-level authorization via **AOP**. That's a very high-level introduction to Spring Security for you to understand where Spring Security fits in an application. Now, let's go through some core concepts in Spring Security.

Spring Security core concepts

Before we move forward and talk about Spring Security in depth, let's introduce the core concepts in Spring Security. Understanding these concepts will help us have a better understanding of how it works.

In Spring Security, the core components are `Authentication`, `GrantedAuthority`, `SecurityContext`, and `SecurityContextHolder`.

An `Authentication` object represents the token for an `authentication` request or for an authenticated principal, once the request has been processed by `AuthenticationManager`. An authentication request is usually a login request the frontend sends to the server. In Spring Security, this request's end point is the login processing URL. By default, it is at the `/login` path using the `HTTP POST` method. In an authentication request, the `Authentication` object will usually contain the **username** and the **password** that will be used for authentication. The term principal comes from the `java.security.Principal` interface that `Authentication` extends. In Java, `Principal` represents an individual, a corporation, or a login ID. In Spring Security, an authenticated principal is the currently logged in user's information, which, as mentioned earlier, is usually saved into an HTTP session.

GrantedAuthority is an authority granted to a user. Usually, it is a role name, for example, ROLE_ADMIN or ROLE_SUPERVISOR. You can retrieve the granted authorities of a user through the getAuthorities() method in Authentication. When a logged in user's information, which is an instance of Authentication, is saved to an HTTP session, it is encapsulated inside an instance of SecurityContext. Spring Security has SecurityContextPersistenceFilter responsible for managing the SecurityContext for each request. In the execution of each request, you can retrieve SecurityContext by SecurityContextHolder through the SecurityContextHolder.getContext() method. Internally, SecurityContextHolder keeps SecurityContext in a ThreadLocal variable. In this way, SecurityContext is bound to the current thread that executes the request. When Spring Security performs authorization, it will retrieve SecurityContext from SecurityContextHolder. In Spring Security, at the core, it really comes down to these four concepts. Most of the other components in Spring Security are about either updating SecurityContext or using it to perform authorization.

Spring Security deep dive

Filters are the perfect place to perform various actions on the requests that the application receives, such as auditing and security checking. Spring Security is built on filters. To gain a better understanding of how Spring Security works internally, we're going to look at the following types of requests and see how they are processed by Spring Security filters, as well as the Spring Security components that participate in these requests:

- An unauthenticated request accessing a public resource
- An unauthenticated request accessing a protected resource
- An authentication request
- An authenticated request accessing a protected resource
- An authenticated request accessing an unauthorized resource

What is a better way to understand how Spring Security works than seeing it in action? Before we talk about these requests, let's set up Spring Security in our TaskAgile application.

Setting up Spring Security

To install Spring Security, let's add the following dependency to `pom.xml`:

```xml
<dependency>
  <groupId>org.springframework.boot</groupId>
  <artifactId>spring-boot-starter-security</artifactId>
</dependency>
...
<dependency>
  <groupId>org.springframework.security</groupId>
  <artifactId>spring-security-test</artifactId>
  <scope>test</scope>
</dependency>
```

We add `spring-security-test` so that we can use it in the unit test to make sure the endpoints of our application have permission configured correctly. In order to see what Spring Security does, let's turn on the **debug-level** logging by adding the following configuration to `src/main/resources/application.properties`:

```
logging.level.org.springframework.security=DEBUG
```

Now, let's add Spring Security configuration. To do that, we will extend Spring Security's `WebSecurityConfigurerAdapter` class and apply the `@EnableWebSecurity` annotation to our customization class. Here is how `com.taskagile.config.SecurityConfiguration` looks:

```java
...
@EnableWebSecurity
public class SecurityConfiguration extends WebSecurityConfigurerAdapter {

  private static final String[] PUBLIC = new String[]{
    "/error", "/login", "/logout", "/register", "/api/registrations"};

  @Override
  protected void configure(HttpSecurity http) throws Exception {
    http
      .authorizeRequests()
        .antMatchers(PUBLIC).permitAll()
        .anyRequest().authenticated()
        .and()
      .formLogin()
        .loginPage("/login")
        .and()
      .logout()
        .logoutUrl("/logout")
        .logoutSuccessUrl("/login?logged-out")
```

```
        .and()
      .csrf().disable();
  }

  @Override
  public void configure(WebSecurity web) {
     web.ignoring().antMatchers("/static/**", "/js/**", "/css/**",
"/images/**", "/favicon.ico");
  }
}
```

As you can see, `SecurityConfiguration` overrides two `configure()` methods from `WebSecurityConfigurerAdapter`. In the first `configure(HttpSecurity)` method, we call the `authorizeRequests()` method to let Spring Security know that we're restricting access based on HTTP requests. The return result of this method is an instance of `ExpressionInterceptUrlRegistry`, which allows us to use `antMatchers()` to specify the paths of requests that we want Spring Security to process. In our case, we want all of the paths defined in `PUBLIC` to be allowed by anyone. Then, we say any other requests can be accessed by an authenticated user. After that, we use the `and()` method to restore the chain back to the `http` object. The `formLogin()` method tells Spring Security that our application uses form-based authentication and the `loginPage()` method specifies the path of our login page. The `logout()` method is for defining the logout behavior. In fact, we don't have to define this method here because, with `WebSecurityConfigurerAdapter`, by default, Spring Security provides the support of logging a user out at path `/logout` and redirect the user afterwards to path `/login?success`. In our configuration, we choose to use path `/login?logged-out`. At the end of this chain, we tell Spring Security to disable the **Cross-Site Request Forgery (CSRF)** feature. Now, we have this configuration in place. The configuration will be automatically picked up by Spring Boot when we run the application. You can start the application with the `mvn spring-boot:run` command and try to access `http://localhost:8080`, and you will be redirected to the `http://localhost:8080/login` page. Our settings are working now.

However, in our `RegistrationApiControllerTests` test, things are a little different. With the `@WebMvcTest` annotation, in this test, only `RegistrationApiController` and Spring Security will be instantiated. But our `SecurityConfiguration` won't be picked up in the test. We need to use the `@ContextConfiguration` annotation to apply our customization, like this:

```
@RunWith(SpringRunner.class)
@ContextConfiguration(classes = {SecurityConfiguration.class})
@WebMvcTest(RegistrationApiController.class)
@ActiveProfiles("test")
public class RegistrationApiControllerTests {
```

Let's run the test method, `register_blankForm_shouldFail()`. It failed again, and the test result says `Response status expected:<400>` but was :`<404>`. After checking the test output, we do not see a log about the mapping of the `/api/registrants` endpoint to the handler that `RequestMappingHandlerAdapter` printed out anymore. This doesn't make sense. Looks like we need to do more troubleshooting. Since this happens right after we apply the `@ContextConfiguration` annotation, it must have something to do with that. After checking its JavaDoc, we can find the following description:

- `@ContextConfiguration` defines class-level metadata that is used to determine how to load and configure `ApplicationContext` for integration tests.
- `@ContextConfiguration` can be used to declare the annotated classes. The term annotated class can refer to any of the following:
  - A class annotated with `@Configuration`
  - A component (a class annotated with `@Component`, `@Service`, `@Repository`, and so on)

It looks like, after applying the `@ContextConfiguration` annotation, `RegistrationApiController.class` that we add to `@WebMvcTest` doesn't work anymore. To fix this issue, we will need to change the annotations as the following:

```
@ContextConfiguration(classes = {SecurityConfiguration.class,
RegistrationApiController.class})
@WebMvcTest
```

Now, let's run the test and you can see it passed. Running the `mvn clean install` command will also produce a successful build. Let's commit this and the following is the commit record:

 Commits on Aug 26, 2018

add spring security

jamesjieye committed 15 seconds ago

Figure 10.5: Add Spring Security commit

Spring Security filter chain

Now, let's start the application with the `mvn spring-boot:run` command. Once the application starts, you can see the following information in the output:

```
Mapping filter: 'springSecurityFilterChain' to: [/*]
```

Because it is mapped to a wildcard (`/*`), the Spring Security filter chain will handle all of the requests the application receives.

Another log that you will see in the output is the following:

```
o.s.s.web.DefaultSecurityFilterChain    : Creating filter chain:
org.springframework.security.web.util.matcher.AnyRequestMatcher@1,
[org.springframework.security.web.context.request.async.WebAsyncManagerInte
grationFilter@3c2b5b0a,
org.springframework.security.web.context.SecurityContextPersistenceFilter@2
40d2b4d,
org.springframework.security.web.header.HeaderWriterFilter@711e7156,
org.springframework.security.web.authentication.logout.LogoutFilter@d7be699
,
org.springframework.security.web.authentication.UsernamePasswordAuthenticat
ionFilter@77b0917e,
org.springframework.security.web.savedrequest.RequestCacheAwareFilter@2f67b
8d8,
org.springframework.security.web.servletapi.SecurityContextHolderAwareReque
stFilter@369a4ddd,
org.springframework.security.web.authentication.AnonymousAuthenticationFilt
er@5f6eca45,
org.springframework.security.web.session.SessionManagementFilter@98d744b,
```

```
org.springframework.security.web.access.ExceptionTranslationFilter@7fc7231d
,
org.springframework.security.web.access.intercept.FilterSecurityInterceptor
@5604e1a5]
```

As you can see, with our configuration of `HttpSecurity`, Spring Security created these filters for us. Let's take a look at these filters in a different view. The following figure shows a request comes in from the left side and gets processed by each of these filters in order, and the interaction some of these filters have with `SecurityContext`:

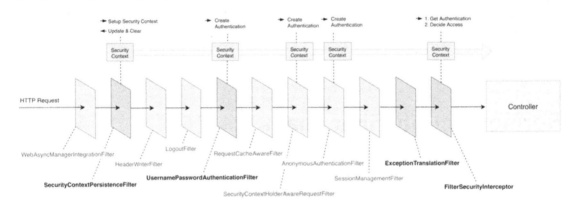

Figure 10.6: Spring Security filters

Among these filters, the most important ones are `SecurityContextPersistenceFilter`, `UsernamePasswordAuthenticationFilter`, `ExceptionTranslationFilter`, and `FilterSecurityInterceptor`. Based on the version of Spring Security you're using, the filters created in this filter chain might be different from the ones we listed. However, these four filters have a very similar responsibility and will still be present in order to make it work. Now, let's go through these Spring Security filters one by one to see what they do:

- `WebAsyncManagerIntegrationFilter`: This filter provides integration between `SecurityContext` and Spring Web's `WebAsyncManager`, which is the central class for managing asynchronous request processing.

- `SecurityContextPersistenceFilter`: The next filter that the request reaches is `SecurityContextPersistenceFilter`, which is one of the filters that must be present in the chain in order to have Spring Security function normally. As you can see in the diagram, when the request comes in, this filter will set up `SecurityContext` by loading it from `SecurityContextRepository`, which is by default implemented based on `HttpSession`. Once `SecurityContext` is loaded, the filter will put it inside `SecurityContextHolder` so that, after this filter, it can be accessed through `SecurityContextHolder.getContext()`. On the other hand, when the request goes out through this filter, `SecurityContext` will be updated back to `SecurityContextRepository` so that any changes to `SecurityContext` will be persisted between requests. The filter will also clear `SecurityContextHolder` to avoid leaking security context to other requests that might not be from the same user.

- `HeaderWriterFilter`: This filter adds headers to the response of the current request. It is useful to add certain headers, which enable browser protection, for example, **X-Frame-Options**, **X-XSS-Protection**, and **X-Content-Type-Options**.

- `LogoutFilter`: As its name states, this filter will log out a user who has been authenticated. By default, the logout processing URL is `/logout`. So, it will only execute the logout procedure when a request is sent to that path. The logout processing URL is configurable through `HttpSecurity`, which is the one we use in our `SecurityConfiguration`.

- `UsernamePasswordAuthenticationFilter`: The `UsernamePasswordAuthenticationFilter` is where the authentication starts. This filter holds a reference to an instance of `ProviderManager`, which is an implementation of the `AuthenticationManager` interface. `ProviderManager` holds a list of `AuthenticationProvider`, which are used to perform the actual authentication. The most commonly used authentication provider is `DaoAuthenticationProvider`, which uses `UserDetailsService` to load `UserDetails` of the same username from the database. Then `DaoAuthenticationProvider` checks if the provided password in the request matches the one in `UserDetails`. If it matches, the authentication passes; otherwise, it fails. When the authentication succeeds, `UsernamePasswordAuthenticationFilter` will update `SecurityContext`, and the user will be regarded as authenticated. `AuthenticationSuccessHandler` will take control of the request. By default, a redirection to the default success URL will occur. When the authentication fails, `SecurityContextHolder` will be cleared and `AuthenticationFailureHandler` will take control of the request. By default, the user will be redirected to the `/login?failed` page. `UsernamePasswordAuthenticationFilter` won't trigger the authentication process for any request. It will only do it for a request that is sent to the `/login` path using the HTTP `POST` method.

- `RequestCacheAwareFilter`: This filter restores the previous cached request, which is usually saved by `ExceptionTranslationFilter` when a request fails. For example, when an authenticated request is sent to access a protected resource, Spring Security will block that request and send the user to the login page. After a successful authentication, the user will be redirected back to the protected resource. Spring Security knows where the user should go after authentication by checking the cached request.

- `SecurityContextHolderAwareRequestFilter`: This filter is responsible for the request with a wrapper that implements servlet API security methods, such as the following:

  - `HttpServletRequest.authenticate(HttpServletResponse)`
  - `HttpServletRequest.login(String, String)`
  - `HttpServletRequest.logout()`

We will not use these APIs in TaskAgile.

- `AnonymousAuthenticationFilter`: What this filter does is update `SecurityContext` with `AnonymousAuthenticationToken` when it finds that no `Authentication` is present in `SecurityContext`. It doesn't really perform authentication for anonymous users. It is more like putting a placeholder authentication in `SecurityContext` to make it clear that the request is sent from an anonymous user.

- `SessionManagementFilter`: This filter is responsible for activating session-fixation protection and controlling the concurrent sessions, which requires `ConcurrentSessionFilter` to be in the chain. To turn on concurrent session management, we can use the following setting provided by `HttpSecurity`. By default, there is no limitation:

  ```
  http.sessionManagement().maximumSessions(n);
  ```

- `ExceptionTranslationFilter`: This is the second to last filter in the chain. As its name states, this filter is responsible for translating Spring Security exceptions. When there is `AuthenticationException` caught, the filter will launch the authentication endpoint. If there is `AccessDeniedException` caught and the user is anonymous, the filter will also launch the authentication endpoint; when the user is not anonymous, `AccessDeniedHandler` will by default send an HTTP `403` response.

- `FilterSecurityInterceptor`: The last filter in the chain is `FilterSecurityInterceptor`, which has a reference to `AccessDecisionManager`. The filter retrieves `SecurityContext` and then delegates to `AccessDecisionManager` to decide whether the request is allowed or not, and raise exceptions when the request is denied. If the request is allowed, it will reach the corresponding `Controller`. The decision that `AccessDecisionManager` makes is based on votes. The decision made here is at the request level. It means that Spring Security checks the path of the request against the configuration on `HttpSecurity` and sees if the granted authorities found inside `SecurityContext` are sufficient to permit access.

 There are many other built-in filters that can be added to the chain by turning on the corresponding features. We're not going to go through every one of them here. If you are interested, you can check Spring Security's reference documentation for details.

Spring Security in action

As mentioned earlier, a better way to understand how Spring Security works is to see it in action. In this section, we will try to access the register page, /register, and the home page, /. Since we haven't implemented the login page, the requests we send will be unauthenticated. So, we will be able to review the following two requests at the moment:

- An unauthenticated request accessing a public resource
- An unauthenticated request accessing a protected resource

Unauthenticated request on public resource

Let's review the first type of request, which is an unauthenticated request accessing a public resource. In our TaskAgile app the register page is publicly available. Let's open the browser at http://localhost:8080/register. Once the page finishes loading, you can see the debug log information in the Spring Security output.

Let's go to the part that was logged by o.s.security.web.FilterChainProxy, which looks like the following:

```
/register at position 1 of 11 in additional filter chain; firing Filter:
'WebAsyncManagerIntegrationFilter'
/register at position 2 of 11 in additional filter chain; firing Filter:
'SecurityContextPersistenceFilter'
```

As you can see, the /register request was processed by WebAsyncManagerIntegrationFilter and SecurityContextPersistenceFilter. Then, it is a log printed by w.c.HttpSessionSecurityContextRepository. The full path of this class is org.springframework.security.web.context.HttpSessionSecurityContextRepository. The log it printed out is the following:

```
No HttpSession currently exists
No SecurityContext was available from the HttpSession: null. A new one will
be created.
```

As you might remember in *Figure 10.6*, it is when a request is processed
by SecurityContextPersistenceFilter that SecurityContext is set up. This log is
saying that SecurityContextPersistenceFilter tried to load
SecurityContext from HttpSession, which did not exist. Therefore, a
new SecurityContext would be created.

Then, FilterChainProxy printed out that the request was through
HeaderWriterFilter and LogoutFilter:

```
/register at position 3 of 11 in additional filter chain; firing Filter:
'HeaderWriterFilter'
/register at position 4 of 11 in additional filter chain; firing Filter:
'LogoutFilter'
```

When the request was processed by LogoutFilter, the filter tried to check if the request
matches the logout processing URL. Since it does not, the filter let the request pass. Then,
FilterChainProxy printed out that the request
reached UsernamePasswordAuthenticationFilter:

```
/register at position 5 of 11 in additional filter chain; firing Filter:
'UsernamePasswordAuthenticationFilter'
```

Still, because the path of the request does not match the login processing URL, the filter let
this request pass quietly. The request passes RequestCacheAwareFilter and
SecurityContextHolderAwareRequestFilter quietly, as shown in the following log:

```
/register at position 6 of 11 in additional filter chain; firing Filter:
'RequestCacheAwareFilter'
/register at position 7 of 11 in additional filter chain; firing Filter:
'SecurityContextHolderAwareRequestFilter'
```

After that, the request arrives at AnonymousAuthenticationFilter. Something interesting happened here, as you can see from the following log:

```
/register at position 8 of 11 in additional filter chain; firing Filter:
'AnonymousAuthenticationFilter'
Populated SecurityContextHolder with anonymous token:
'org.springframework.security.authentication.AnonymousAuthenticationToken@d
6fc3bc2: Principal: anonymousUser; Credentials: [PROTECTED]; Authenticated:
true; Details:
org.springframework.security.web.authentication.WebAuthenticationDetails@b3
64: RemoteIpAddress: 0:0:0:0:0:0:0:1; SessionId: null; Granted Authorities:
ROLE_ANONYMOUS'
```

Since the request wasn't authenticated by UsernamePasswordAuthenticationFilter, AnonymousAuthenticationFilter created AnonymousAutnenticationToken in SecurityContextHolder so that when the authentication is retrieved through SecurityContextHolder.getContext().getAuthentication(), the result won't be null. And as you can see, the authority granted to this authentication is ROLE_ANONYMOUS. FilterChainProxy later points out that the request arrived at SessionManagementFilter:

```
/register at position 9 of 11 in additional filter chain; firing Filter:
'SessionManagementFilter'
```

Because this is an anonymous request, SessionManagementFilter pointed out that the requested session ID is invalid. After that, the request reached ExceptionTranslationFilter. The way this filter works is that it will let the request pass first and it will catch any Spring Security exception that is thrown afterwards. So, when our request went in, nothing happened:

```
/register at position 10 of 11 in additional filter chain; firing Filter:
'ExceptionTranslationFilter'
```

The last filter that the request arrived is FilterSecurityInterceptor. As mentioned earlier, this is where the decision of whether a request can proceed or not is made:

```
/register at position 11 of 11 in additional filter chain; firing Filter:
'FilterSecurityInterceptor'
```

As you can see from the following log, this filter went through the paths that we have in `SecurityConfiguration` one by one to find the authorization settings:

```
AntPathRequestMatcher: Checking match of request : '/register'; against
'/error'
AntPathRequestMatcher: Checking match of request : '/register'; against
'/login'
AntPathRequestMatcher: Checking match of request : '/register'; against
'/logout'
AntPathRequestMatcher: Checking match of request : '/register'; against
'/register'
FilterSecurityInterceptor: Secure object: FilterInvocation: URL: /register;
Attributes: [permitAll]
...
AffirmativeBased: Voter:
org.springframework.security.web.access.expression.WebExpressionVoter@4d127
1da, returned: 1
FilterSecurityInterceptor: Authorization successful
...
FilterChainProxy: /register reached end of additional filter chain;
proceeding with original chain
```

Once a matched configuration is found, it asked `DecisionManager`, which is `AffirmativeBased`, to decide if the request is allowed or not. As you can see, `WebExpressionVoter` gave it a positive vote. The authorization then succeeded. After the request passed the Spring Security filter chain, it proceeded with the original chain.

On its way out, the request still went through the filters it passed on its way in. This time, not all filters were interested in processing it. As you can see from the following log information, `ExceptionTranslationFilter` did nothing because no exception was thrown and `SecurityContextPersistenceFilter` cleared `SecurityContextHolder`:

```
...
ExceptionTranslationFilter : Chain processed normally
SecurityContextPersistenceFilter : SecurityContextHolder now cleared, as
request processing completed
```

In *Figure 10.6*, we only include the direction of a request on its way in and the order of the filters a request will go through. As you can see from the log output, on its way out, the order of the filters that will process the request is reversed.

Unauthenticated request on protected resource

Now, let's see how Spring Security will work when we try to access a protected resource, in our case, the home page at /.

After you open http://localhost:8080 and the page finishes loading, you can see that you have actually landed on the login page at /login. Let's check the debug log information to see what Spring Security did exactly. As you can see from the log, everything Spring Security did this time is the same as the last time when we tried to access a public resource, except what happened at the last filter, FilterSecurityInterceptor. The following is the log printed out when the request was processed by this filter:

```
AffirmativeBased : Voter:
org.springframework.security.web.access.expression.WebExpressionVoter@93d13
c0, returned: -1
ExceptionTranslationFilter : Access is denied (user is anonymous);
redirecting to authentication entry point
org.springframework.security.access.AccessDeniedException: Access is denied
  at
org.springframework.security.access.vote.AffirmativeBased.decide(Affirmativ
eBased.java:84)
...
```

As you can see, DecisionManager has denied access based on the voter's result. It threw AccessDeniedException, which is caught by ExceptionTranslationFilter. Since it is an anonymous user, redirection to the login page occurred.

Spring Security authentication in depth

By now, you should have a good understanding of how Spring Security works. In this section, we're going to dig deeper into how the components in Spring Security work when it authenticates a request. We will mainly focus on the following two filters:

- SecurityContextPersistenceFilter
- UsernamePasswordAuthenticationFilter

SecurityContextPersistenceFilter

As you already know, this filter is responsible for `SecurityContext` persistence between requests. Let's see how it works internally by checking the class diagram shown in the following figure:

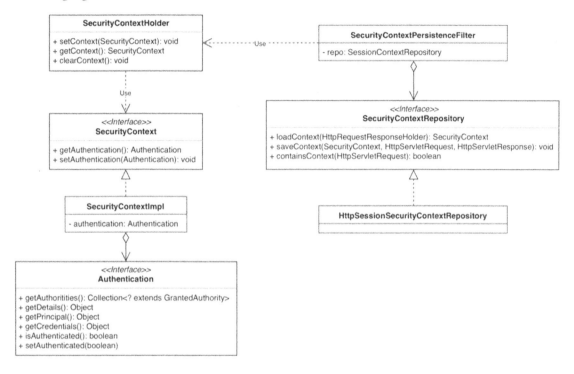

Figure 10.7: SecurityContextPersistenceFilter and its dependencies

As you can see, the filter holds a reference to an instance of `HttpSessionSecurityContextRepository`, which implements the `SecurityContextRepository` interface. The filter also uses `SecurityContextHolder` to set up `SecurityContext` as well as clear it out. The `SecurityContext` implementation, `SecurityContextImpl`, holds an instance of `Authentication`.

In an unauthenticated request, `SecurityContextRepository` contains no
`SecurityContext` object for that request. `SecurityContext` that this filter puts into
`SecurityContextHolder` is an empty one, as `authentication` inside
that `SecurityContext` object is null, as shown in the following figure:

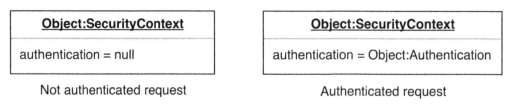

Figure 10.8: SecurityContext object

It is only after a successful authentication that `authentication` inside the
`SecurityContext` will be updated to an `Authentication` object that contains the
information of the user who just logged in. This filter will save `SecurityContext` into
`HttpSession`. In the following requests, `SecurityContextPersistenceFilter` will
load `SecurityContext` from the repository and put it into `SecurityContextHolder`.

UsernamePasswordAuthenticationFilter

Now, let's take a look at `UsernamePasswordAuthenticationFilter` and its
dependencies, as shown in the following figure:

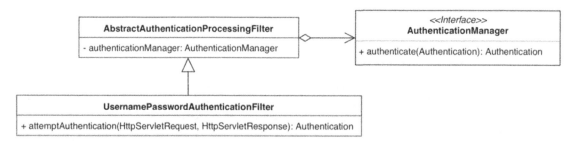

Figure 10.9: UsernamePasswordAuthenticationFilter and its dependencies

As you can see, `UsernamePasswordAuthenticationFilter` extends from
`AbstractAuthenticationProcessingFilter`, which holds a reference to an instance of
`AuthenticationManager`. `AuthenticationManager` is an interface, which has only
method: `authenticate()`. This method takes an unauthenticated `Authentication`
instance as its input and returns an authenticated `Authentication` instance.

The following figure shows the relationship between
`AuthenticationManager`, `AuthenticationProvider`, `UserDetails`,
and `UserDetailsService`:

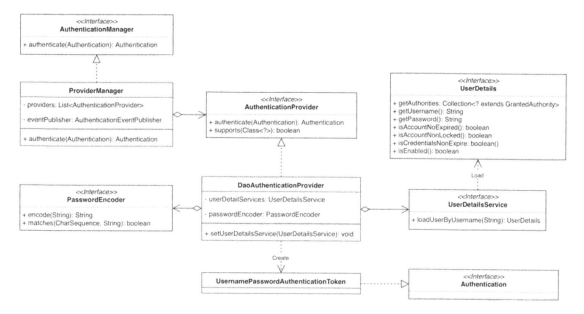

Figure 10.10: AuthenticationManager and its dependencies

As you can see, `ProviderManager`, the implementation of `AuthenticationManager`,
holds a list of `AuthenticationProvider` that it can use to perform the authentication.
`DaoAuthenticationProvider` is one of the implementations of the
`AuthenticationProvider` interface. The followings are the built-in
`AuthenticationProvider`:

- `CasAuthenticationProvider`
- `DaoAuthenticationProvider`
- `LdapAuthenticationProvider`
- `OAuth2LoginAuthenticationProvider`
- `OpenIDAuthenticationProvider`
- `RememberMeAuthenticationProvider`
- `AnonymousAuthenticationProvider`

Through these `AuthenticationProvider`, Spring Security is very flexible with the way to authenticate requests. For now, let's focus on `DaoAuthenticationProvider`, which is the one being commonly used.

As you can see, `DaoAuthenticationProvider` holds an instance of `PasswordEncoder` and an instance of `UserDetailsService`. In the process of authentication, the provider will ask `UserDetailsService` to load an instance of `UserDetails` and, when `UserDetails` exists, it will use `PasswordEncoder` to check the password passed inside the `Authentication` instance matches one of the `UserDetails` instances. When the passwords match, the request will be considered as authenticated and the provider will create an instance of `UsernamePasswordAuthenticationToken`, which is an implementation of `Authentication` interface.
This `UsernamePasswordAuthenticationToken` instance is the one to be returned to `UsernamePasswordAuthenticationFilter` and updated to `SecurityContextHolder`.

In an authentication request, when it arrives at this filter, the `Authentication` object lives inside `SecurityContext` and looks similar to the one on the left in the following diagram. After successful authentication, the `Authentication` object looks like the one on the right. In `SecurityContextPersistenceFilter`, this authenticated `Authentication` object will be saved into `HttpSession`:

Object:Authentication	**Object:Authentication**
principal = "user@taskagile.com" credentials = "MyPassword!" authorities = [ ] authenticated = false	principal = Object:UserDetails credentials = - authorities = ["ROLE_USER"] authenticated = true
Before authentication	After a successful authentication

Figure 10.11: Authentication object

As you can see, before the authentication, the value of the `principal` and the `credentials` properties of the `Authentication` instance is the email address or username and the password that sent in the login request. `authorities` is empty and `authenticated` is `false`. After a successful authentication, the value of `principal` in the `Authentication` object is changed to an instance of `UserDetails` and `credentials` is cleared out to protect the password. In our example, this user's granted authority is `ROLE_USER`.

Spring Security authorization in depth

Now, let's take a look at how Spring Security works internally when it authorizes requests. As mentioned earlier, in `FilterSecurityInterceptor`, Spring Security will perform the authorization at the request level. And with AOP, Spring Security can also perform method-level authorization and secure domain objects.

FilterSecurityInterceptor

First of all, let's take a closer look at `FilterSecurityInterceptor`. The following figure shows the relationship between `FilterSecurityInterceptor` and its dependencies:

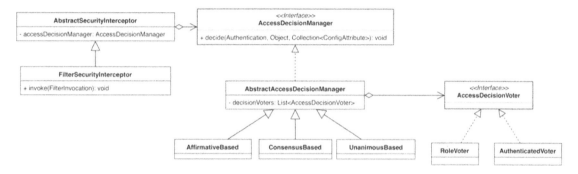

Figure 10.12: FilterSecurityInterceptor and its dependencies

As you can see, `FilterSecurityInterceptor` extends `AbstractSecurityInterceptor`, which holds a reference to an instance of `AccessDecisionManager`. There are three implementations of `AccessDecisionManager`: `AffirmativeBased`, `ConsensusBased`, and `UnanimousBased`. These decision managers holds a list of `AccessDecisionVoter` and there are two implementations of `AccessDecisionVoter`: `RoleVoter` and `AuthenticatedVoter`. The `RoleVoter` implementation checks whether the granted authorities of the `Authentication` instance contain the role required to access the request. If the role is granted, then `RoleVoter` gives an affirmative vote, otherwise, it gives a negative vote. `AuthenticatedVoter` simply checks whether the authentication inside `SecurityContext` is authenticated or not and gives an affirmative vote or a negative vote respectively.

So, `AccessDecisionManager` make the decision based on the votes from the voters they have. `AffirmativeBased` will grant access if any `AccessDecisionVoter` returns an affirmative response, and `ConsensusBased` will grant access when the affirmative votes are greater than the negative votes. `UnanimousBased` requires no negative votes to grant access. When access is granted, nothing will help and the request will move forward to `Controller`. Otherwise, `AccessDeniedException` will be thrown, and the flow of the control will go back to `ExceptionTranslationFilter`.

Method security

As mentioned earlier, Spring Security performs method-level security through AOP, and there are two ways to secure methods. One is to use the `@Secured` annotation or the **JSR-250** `@RoleAllowed` annotation to specify the authority/role required to invoke that method. The other way is to use Spring's expression language through the `@PreAuthorize` and `@PostAuthorize` annotations.

The following is the way to enable method security with the use of the `@Secured` annotation:

```
@EnableGlobalMethodSecurity(securedEnabled = true)
public class MethodSecurityConfig {
  // ...
}
```

The following is the way to enable method security with the use of the `@RoleAllowed` annotation:

```
@EnableGlobalMethodSecurity(jsr250Enabled = true)
public class MethodSecurityConfig {
  // ...
}
```

As you can see, both configurations are applied with the `@EnableGlobalMethodSecurity` annotation.

The following is how to use the `@Secured` annotation:

```
public interface PaymentService {
  @Secured("ROLE_PAYMENT_ADMIN")
  List<Payment> getPayments(Long userId);
}
```

The following code shows how to use the @RoleAllowed annotation:

```
public interface PaymentService {
  @RoleAllowed("ROLE_PAYMENT_ADMIN")
  List<Payment> getPayments(Long userId);
}
```

As you can see, both annotations are used in the same way and work in the same way. An instance of the MethodSecurityInterceptor interface will intercept the method invocation and the access decision will be delegated to AccessDecisionManager. The decision will be made based on the user's roles that is the granted authorities of the Authentication instance in SecurityContext.

As mentioned earlier, role-based authorization is coarse-grained and has its limits, and that's solved by Spring Expression Language-based method security. Instead of being limited to only checking the granted authorities, we can use Spring Expression Language to access the parameters the method takes or the returned result of the method. With the availability of that information, we can make much more complex authorization logic, such as granting access to the invocation on a method that returns all of the cards of a board only when the invocation is from a board member.

The following configuration will enable expression-based method security:

```
@EnableGlobalMethodSecurity(prePostEnabled = true)
public class MethodSecurityConfig {
  // ...
}
```

We can use the @PreAuthorize annotation and the @PostAuthorize annotation to secure methods. As its name suggests, the @PreAuthorize annotation will trigger authorization before the method invocation and the @PostAuthorize annotation will do that after the method has been invoked.

The following is a usage example of the @PreAuthorize annotation:

```
public interface BoardService {
  @PreAuthorize("isBoardMember()")
  List<Card> getCards(long boardId);
}
```

The authorization will be handled by an instance of the SecurityExpressionHandler interface. We will not dig too much into the method security at the moment, because in the next chapter we will implement a handler of the @PreAuthorize annotation to guard our methods in application services. You will see how it works in action.

Building the login page

Now, we've finished the introduction to Spring Security. It's time to implement the login page of the user module. In this section, we will cover the frontend implementation and the backend implementation of the login page, as well as the unit tests of these two parts. However, since most of the implementation of the login page, including the frontend and the backend, is similar to the implementation of the register page, we will only focus on the part that only the login page has, which is to authenticate requests with Spring Security. You can always find the details that are not covered in this book on GitHub by using the commit record.

Implementing the login page UI

Let's implement the UI of the page. The following shows what he login page looks like:

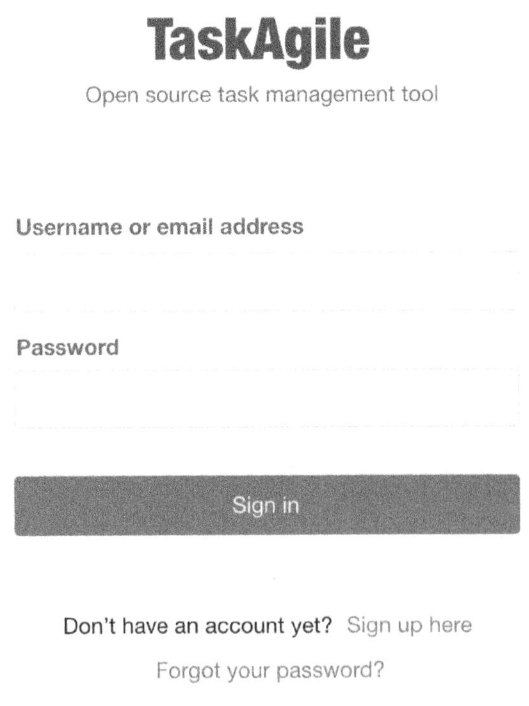

TaskAgile

Open source task management tool

Username or email address

Password

Sign in

Don't have an account yet? Sign up here

Forgot your password?

Figure 10.13: The UI of the login page

As you can see, we support signing in by using either a username or email address. On the login page, there is a link to the register page, as well as another to the forgot password page, which we will implement in a future version of TaskAgile.

The following are the steps to implement the UI of the login page, which is similar to the steps for implementing the register page:

- Write a unit test: `services.authentication.spec.js`
- Create `services/authentication/index.js`
- Write a unit test: `LoginPage.spec.js`
- Create `LoginPage.vue` to make the test pass

In `services.authentication.spec.js`, we will create the following tests:

- It should call the `/authentications` API
- It should pass the response to the caller when the request succeeded
- It should propagate the error to the caller when the request failed

The first test is to make sure the authentication service will call the correct API. The other two are the same as we have in the specification of the registration service, which are used to make sure the authentication service passes results and propagates errors to its caller.

The tests we will create in `LoginPage.spec.js` include the following:

- It should render the login form
- It should contain the data model with initial values
- It should have form inputs bound with the data model
- It should have a form submit event handler, `submitForm`
- It should succeed when credentials are valid
- It should fail when credentials are invalid
- It should have validation to prevent invalid data submission

We will also need to create a mock of the authentication service and a blank home page that users will be redirected to after logging in. We will also need to refactor `RegisterPage.vue` to extract the logo part and the footer as standalone components so that they can be shared with the login page.

Since all of the items mentioned before are similar to what we built for the register page, we will just skip the details here. You can check the commit record to find out more. The following is the commit record:

Figure 10.14: Implementing login page frontend commit

Implementing PasswordEncryptorDelegate

As mentioned, our implementation of `PasswordEncryptor` will delegate the actual encryption to Spring Security's `PasswordEncoder` implementation. Here is how `PasswordEncryptorDelegate` looks:

```
...
@Component
public class PasswordEncryptorDelegate implements PasswordEncryptor {

  private PasswordEncoder passwordEncoder;

  public PasswordEncryptorDelegator(PasswordEncoder passwordEncoder) {
    this.passwordEncoder = passwordEncoder;
  }

  @Override
  public String encrypt(String rawPassword) {
    return encoder.encode(rawPassword);
  }
}
```

As you can see, this is quite straightforward. Spring Security offers multiple implementations of `PasswordEncoder`, and we will use `BCryptPasswordEncoder` here. Let's instantiate `BCryptPasswordEncoder` as the following in `SecurityConfiguration` so that Spring can inject it into `PasswordEncryptorDelegate`:

```
@Bean
public PasswordEncoder passwordEncoder() {
 return new BCryptPasswordEncoder();
}
```

`BCryptPasswordEncoder` uses the `BCrypt` strong hashing function and it is considered to be more secure than algorithms such as **SHA-256**. Now, we can try to register new users. As you should see, in the database the password is encrypted now. As usual, let's commit the change after a successful build with the `mvn clean install` command. Here is the commit record:

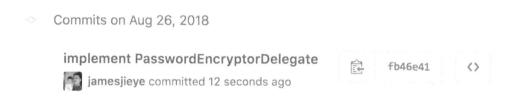

Figure 10.15:Implementing PasswordEncryptorDelegate commit

Implementing authentication in the backend

As you can see in the commit record in *Figure 10.15*, the authentication service in the frontend sends a `HTTP POST` request to `/api/authentications`. This is different from the standard way of using Spring Security for authentication. As mentioned earlier, by default, Spring Security will process the login request at the `/login` path using HTTP `POST` method and we expect the content type of the request to be `application/x-www-form-urlencoded`. After successful authentication, by default, Spring Security will redirect the user to a target page. Usually, it is the home page. The redirection will be done using the `sendRedirect()` method of an instance of `HttpServletResponse`. When the authentication fails, it redirects the user to an error page. This default behavior of Spring Security won't work with our frontend login process. In the frontend, we send a login request using Ajax with content type `application/json` and expect a JSON response.

We will need to customize the authentication part in Spring Security in order to make the backend work with the frontend. Here is what we will do:

- Add `AuthenticationFilter` to replace Spring Security's built-in `UsernamePasswordAuthenticationFilter` so that we can retrieve the username and the password from a JSON format request body
- Implement the `UserDetailsService` interface to provide the ability to load a user by either username or email address
- Implement the `UserDetails` interface to control what will be saved in an authenticated `Authentication` that will be saved in `HttpSession` between requests

- Add `AuthenticationSuccessHandler` to send the authentication success result in JSON
- Add `AuthenticationFailureHandler` to send the authentication failure result in JSON
- Add `LogoutSuccessHandler` to send the logout success result in JSON

This time we will skip introducing unit tests. You can find the details in the commit record. We will focus on the implementation of `AuthenticationFilter`, `UserDetailsService`, and `UserDetails`.

Implementing AuthenticationFilter

Spring Security is very flexible and highly customizable. We can replace the built-in implementation with our own implementation easily. We sometimes do not need to write everything from scratch because Spring Security does a very good job at abstraction. For our `AuthenticationFilter` implementation, we can extend from `AbstractAuthenticationProcessingFilter`, which is also the base class that the built-in `UsernamePasswordAuthenticationFilter` extends.

Since `AuthenticationFilter` deals with API requests, we will put it inside the `com.taskagile.web.apis.authenticate` package. Here is how `AuthenticationFilter` looks:

```
...
public class AuthenticationFilter extends
AbstractAuthenticationProcessingFilter {
  ...
  public AuthenticationFilter() {
    super(new AntPathRequestMatcher("/api/authentications", "POST"));
  }

  @Override
  public Authentication attemptAuthentication(HttpServletRequest
    request, HttpServletResponse response)
    throws AuthenticationException, IOException {

    log.debug("Processing login request");

    String requestBody = IOUtils.toString(request.getReader());
    LoginRequest loginRequest = JsonUtils.toObject(requestBody,
    LoginRequest.class);
    if (loginRequest == null || loginRequest.isInvalid()) {
      throw new InsufficientAuthenticationException("Invalid
```

```
      authentication request");
    }

    UsernamePasswordAuthenticationToken token =
      new UsernamePasswordAuthenticationToken(loginRequest.username,
      loginRequest.password);
    return this.getAuthenticationManager().authenticate(token);
  }
  ...
}
```

As you can see, in the constructor, we specify that this filter will process the requests with the `/api/registrations` path in the `HTTP POST` method. In the `attemptAuthentication()` method, all we do is read the request body from `request.getReader()` into a string, which we expect to be in JSON format. `IOUtils` is a utility class from the Apache Commons IO project. Then, we use `JsonUtils` to convert the JSON string into an instance of `LoginRequest`. `JsonUtils` is a utility class that we create to handle JSON string conversion. `LoginRequest` is a simple inner class of the filter and is only used for parsing the JSON string.

After converting, we throw `AuthenticationException` when `loginRequest` is not valid, either because the request body is not in JSON format or is missing required fields. The exception thrown here will eventually be handled by `AuthenticationFailureHandler` we need to implement. When `loginRequest` is valid, we will create `UsernamePasswordAuthenticationToken`, which, as mentioned earlier, is an `Authentication` object, similar to the one shown on the left in *Figure 10.11*. We then invoke `AuthenticationManager` to take care of the actual authentication.

Implementing UserDetailsService

We will implement `UserDetailsService` inside the existing `UserApplicationServiceImpl` and let's change the `UserApplicationService` interface to extend `UserDetailsService`, as shown here:

```
public interface UserApplicationService extends UserDetailsService {
  ...
}
```

Here is the change to `UserApplicationServiceImpl`:

```
...
public class UserApplicationServiceImpl implements UserApplicationService {
  ...
  @Autowired
```

```
    private UserRepository userRepository;

    @Override
    public UserDetails loadUserByUsername(String username) throws
UsernameNotFoundException {
        if (StringUtils.isEmpty(username)) {
            throw new UsernameNotFoundException("No user found");
        }

        User user;
        if (username.contains("@")) {
            user = userRepository.findByEmailAddress(username);
        } else {
            user = userRepository.findByUsername(username);
        }
        if (user == null) {
            throw new UsernameNotFoundException("No user found by `" +
            username + "`");
        }
        return new SimpleUser(user);
    }
    ...
}
```

As you can see, we add a reference to `UserRepository` here. Inside the `loadUserByUsername()` method, we make sure `username` is not empty; otherwise, we simply throw the exception with no need to go further. The way of finding the user depends on whether the `username` property contains an @ or not. When no user is found, we throw an exception. Otherwise, we return an instance of `SimpleUser`, which implements the `UserDetails` interface.

Implementing UserDetails

As mentioned earlier, the `UserDetails` object will be saved in the `Authentication` object, which will be saved into `HttpSession`. So, it is important that we keep less data inside of `UserDetails`. The following is `SimpleUser`, which implements `UserDetails`:

```
    ...
    public class SimpleUser implements UserDetails, Serializable {
        ...
        private long userId;
        private String username;
        private String password;

        public SimpleUser(User user) {
```

```
    this.userId = user.getId();
    this.username = user.getUsername();
    this.password = user.getPassword();
  }

  // Getters of the three properties
  ...
  public Collection<? extends GrantedAuthority> getAuthorities() {
    return Collections.singleton(new
    SimpleGrantedAuthority("ROLE_USER"));
  }
  public boolean isAccountNonExpired() { return true; }
  public boolean isAccountNonLocked() { return true; }
  public boolean isCredentialsNonExpired() { return true; }
  public boolean isEnabled() { return true; }
  ...
}
```

As you can see, this `SimpleUser` is read-only after being created from a `User` object. `username` is kept here so that we can use it to find out who the authenticated user is.

Updating SecurityConfiguration

Now, let's update `SecurityConfiguration` to make Spring Security aware of the new filter and handlers:

```
...
public class SecurityConfiguration extends WebSecurityConfigurerAdapter {
  ...
  @Override
  protected void configure(HttpSecurity http) throws Exception {
    http
      .authorizeRequests()
        .antMatchers(PUBLIC).permitAll()
        .anyRequest().authenticated()
      .and()
        .addFilterAt(authenticationFilter(),
        UsernamePasswordAuthenticationFilter.class)
        .formLogin().loginPage("/login")
      .and()
        .logout().logoutUrl("/logout")
        .logoutSuccessHandler(logoutSuccessHandler())
      .and()
        .csrf().disable();
  }
  ...
```

```java
@Bean
public AuthenticationFilter authenticationFilter() throws Exception {
  AuthenticationFilter authenticationFilter = new
  AuthenticationFilter();
authenticationFilter.setAuthenticationSuccessHandler(authenticationSuccessH
andler());
authenticationFilter.setAuthenticationFailureHandler(authenticationFailureH
andler());
authenticationFilter.setAuthenticationManager(authenticationManagerBean());
  return authenticationFilter;
}

@Bean
public AuthenticationSuccessHandler authenticationSuccessHandler() {
  return new SimpleAuthenticationSuccessHandler();
}

@Bean
public AuthenticationFailureHandler authenticationFailureHandler() {
  return new SimpleAuthenticationFailureHandler();
}

@Bean
public LogoutSuccessHandler logoutSuccessHandler() {
  return new SimpleLogoutSuccessHandler();
}
}
```

As you can see, we use the `http.addFilterAt()` method to replace
`UsernamePasswordAuthenticationFilter` with `AuthenticationFilter`, which is
initialized in the `authenticationFilter()` method. We also change
`LogoutSuccessHandler` to our implementation, `SimpleLogoutSuccessHanlder`. You
can find the details of this handler along with the other two handlers in the commit record.
Inside `authenticationFilter()`, we create a new `AuthenticationFilter` and provide
the handlers, as well as `AuthenticationManager`, which is gained through the
`authenticationManagerBean()` method that `WebSecurityConfigurerAdapter`
provides.

That's it. We've implemented authentication using Spring Security with some customization. As usual, let's make sure there is a successful build before committing the code. The following is the commit record:

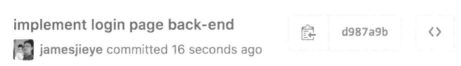

Figure 10.16: Implementing login page backend commit

Sending emails using JavaMail

Now, let's implement the sending email feature using JavaMail. We will also use **FreeMarker** as the template engine to create the body of the email message.

First of all, let's add the following dependencies to `pom.xml`:

```
<dependency>
  <groupId>org.springframework.boot</groupId>
  <artifactId>spring-boot-starter-mail</artifactId>
</dependency>
...
<dependency>
  <groupId>org.freemarker</groupId>
  <artifactId>freemarker</artifactId>
</dependency>
```

The `spring-boot-starter-mail` starter provides interfaces, such as `JavaMailSender`, to make the implementation of sending email relatively easy, as you will see in this section. With the presence of the FreeMaker library, Spring Boot will automatically create an instance of `freemarker.template.Configuration`. By default, the template loader path is `classpath:/templates/`, which has been used to store **Thymeleaf** view templates. It is better that we separate the view templates from the mail templates by putting them in different folders. Let's change the loader path of FreeMarker by adding the following property to `application.properties`:

```
spring.freemarker.template-loader-path=classpath:/mail-templates/
```

To send emails out, JavaMail needs to connect to a **Simple Mail Transfer Protocol (SMTP)** server. In our local **development** environment, we have several options. We can send emails through Gmail's SMTP server or Amazon's SES Service. However, this requires the recipient's email address to be valid. In fact, in our local dev environment, we usually do not need to actually receive the email but only to verify that our application does send out the correct message. For that, what we actually need is an SMTP server that we can use to check the email message the application sends out. The `DebuggingServer` implementation of Python's standard library, `smtpd`, provides exactly that. It will discard the messages received and print them out to the Terminal. After installing Python, you can start a debugging SMTP server using the following command:

```
python -m smtpd -n -c DebuggingServer localhost:1025
```

As you can see, in this command, the SMTP server's host is `localhost` and it listens to port `1025`. We will use this SMTP server for our local dev environment in this book. Now, let's add the following configuration to `application.properties` so that JavaMail can connect to this SMTP server:

```
spring.mail.host=localhost
spring.mail.port=1025
spring.mail.properties.mail.smtp.auth=false
```

MailManager and its dependencies

Now, let's take a look at `MailManager` and its dependencies. `DefaultMailManager`, the implementation of `MailManager`, will need to create the message body based on the template and then use the mail service API to send the message. The following figure shows the relationship between `MailManager` and its dependencies:

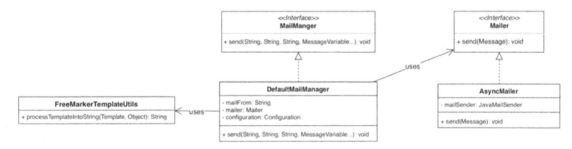

Figure 10.17: MailManager and its dependencies

As you can see, `DefaultMailManager` uses `FreeMarkerTemplateUtils` to create a message body from the template and uses `Mailer`, the mail service API, to send the message. The implementation of the `Mailer` interface is `AsyncMailer`, which will use Spring's `JavaMailSender` to send out a message.

Testing DefaultMailManager

Before we implement `DefaultMailManager`, let's create the unit test, `com.taskagile.domain.common.mail.DefaultMailManagerTests`:

```
@RunWith(SpringRunner.class)
@ActiveProfiles("test")
public class DefaultMailManagerTests {

  @TestConfiguration
  static class DefaultMessageCreatorConfiguration {
    @Bean
    public FreeMarkerConfigurationFactoryBean
    getFreemarkerConfiguration() {
      FreeMarkerConfigurationFactoryBean factoryBean = new
      FreeMarkerConfigurationFactoryBean();
      factoryBean.setTemplateLoaderPath("/mail-templates/");
      return factoryBean;
    }
  }

  @Autowired
  private Configuration configuration;
  private Mailer mailerMock;
  private DefaultMailManager instance;

  @Before
  public void setUp() {
    mailerMock = mock(Mailer.class);
    instance = new DefaultMailManager("noreply@taskagile.com",
    mailerMock, configuration);
  }
  ...
}
```

As you can see, this test class requires a `DefaultMailManager` instance and a mocked version of the `Mailer` instance, which will be used to verify the message. We also create an instance of `freemarker.template.Configuration`, which is required to generate the body of the email from the template. We create an instance of `FreeMarkerConfigurationFactoryBean` inside the test configuration so that a `Configuration` instance will be auto-wired into the test.

In this test class, we have the following test methods:

- `send_nullEmailAddress_shouldFail()`
- `send_emptyEmailAddress_shouldFail()`
- `send_nullSubject_shouldFail()`
- `send_emptySubject_shouldFail()`
- `send_nullTemplateName_shouldFail()`
- `send_emptyTemplateName_shouldFail()`
- `send_validParameters_shouldSucceed()`

The first six methods are making sure the `send()` method will complain about bad parameters by throwing `IllegalArgumentException`.

The last one is to verify successful message sending. The test method looks like this:

```
@Test
public void send_validParameters_shouldSucceed() {
  String to = "user@example.com";
  String subject = "Test subject";
  String templateName = "test.ftl";

  instance.send(to, subject, templateName, MessageVariable.from("name",
"test"));
  ArgumentCaptor<Message> messageArgumentCaptor =
ArgumentCaptor.forClass(Message.class);
  verify(mailerMock).send(messageArgumentCaptor.capture());

  Message messageSent = messageArgumentCaptor.getValue();
  assertEquals(to, messageSent.getTo());
  assertEquals(subject, messageSent.getSubject());
  assertEquals("noreply@taskagile.com", messageSent.getFrom());
  assertEquals("Hello, test\n", messageSent.getBody());
}
```

As you can see, after invoking the `send()` method of `DefaultMailManager`, we use `ArgumentCaptor` to capture the message that passes to `Mailer`; we use the `send()` method, and then make assertions of its values. We won't go into the details too much here. You can check the commit record to find out the other parts that have been skipped.

Implementing DefaultMailManager

The implementation of `DefaultMailManager` is quite straightforward. As mentioned earlier, it uses **FreeMarker** to create a message body from the template and uses the `Mailer` API to send the message. Here is how its `send()` method looks:

```
@Component
public class DefaultMailManager implements MailManager {

  private String mailFrom;
  private Mailer mailer;
  private Configuration configuration;

  public DefaultMailManager(@Value("${app.mail-from}") String mailFrom,
                            Mailer mailer,
                            Configuration configuration) {
    this.mailFrom = mailFrom;
    this.mailer = mailer;
    this.configuration = configuration;
  }

  @Override
  public void send(String emailAddress, String subject, String
    template, MessageVariable... variables) {
    Assert.hasText(emailAddress, "Parameter `emailAddress` must not be
    blank");
    Assert.hasText(subject, "Parameter `subject` must not be blank");
    Assert.hasText(template, "Parameter `template` must not be blank");

    String messageBody = createMessageBody(template, variables);
    Message message = new SimpleMessage(emailAddress, subject,
    messageBody, mailFrom);
    mailer.send(message);
  }
  ...
}
```

As you can see, through the constructor, its dependencies are injected. Inside the `test()` method, it calls its `createMessageBody()` method to create the message body and then instantiates an instance of `Message` and sends it via the `mailer.send()` method.

Here is how the `createMessageBody()` method looks:

```
private String createMessageBody(String templateName, MessageVariable...
variables) {
  try {
    Template template = configuration.getTemplate(templateName);
    Map<String, Object> model = new HashMap<>();
    if (variables != null) {
      for (MessageVariable variable : variables) {
        model.put(variable.getKey(), variable.getValue());
      }
    }
    return FreeMarkerTemplateUtils.processTemplateIntoString(template,
    model);
  } catch (Exception e) {
    log.error("Failed to create message body from template `" +
    templateName + "`", e);
    return null;
  }
}
```

As you can see, inside this method, we use the instance of `freemarker.template.Configuration` to get a `Template` instance and then use `FreeMarkerTemplateUtils` to convert the template into a string.

Implementing AsyncMailer

`AsyncMailer`, as its name suggests, sends a message asynchronously. And, as shown in the UML diagram in *Figure 10.17*, it relies on `JavaMailSender` to actually send messages. Its implementation looks like the following:

```
@Component
public class AsyncMailer implements Mailer {
  ...
  @Async
  @Override
  public void send(Message message) {
    Assert.notNull(message, "Parameter `message` must not be null");

    try {
      SimpleMailMessage mailMessage = new SimpleMailMessage();
```

```
    if (StringUtils.isNotBlank(message.getFrom())) {
      mailMessage.setFrom(message.getFrom());
    }
    if (StringUtils.isNotBlank(message.getSubject())) {
      mailMessage.setSubject(message.getSubject());
    }
    if (StringUtils.isNotEmpty(message.getBody())) {
      mailMessage.setText(message.getBody());
    }
    if (message.getTo() != null) {
      mailMessage.setTo(message.getTo());
    }

    mailSender.send(mailMessage);
  } catch (MailException e) {
    log.error("Failed to send mail message", e);
  }
  }
  }
}
```

As you can see, we use the `@Async` annotation to tell Spring that this
`send(Message)` method should be invoked asynchronously. Inside the method, we create
an instance of `org.springframework.mail.SimpleMailMessage` and then pass it to
Spring's `JavaMailSender`. Underneath, `JavaMailSender` depends on the JavaMail APIs
to send out messages.

Application properties

In `DefaultMailManager`, we use `@Value("${app.mail-from}")` to assign the value of
the `app.mail-from` property that we add in `application.properties`. The following
figure shows that the `app.mail-from` property is added to the top of
`application.properties`:

```
application.properties ✕
1    app.mail-from=noreply@taskagile.com
2
```

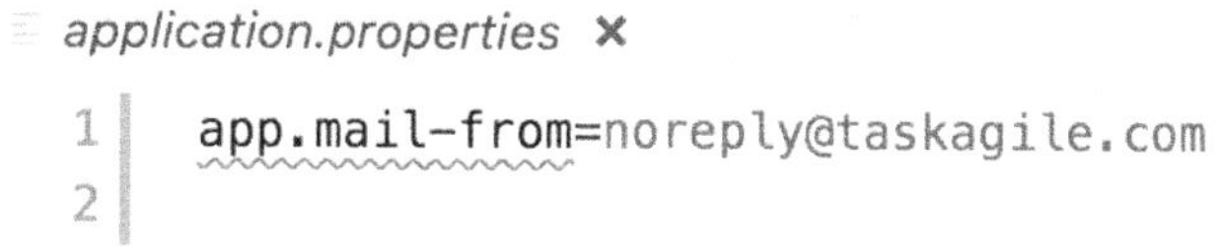

Figure 10.18: Wavy line under unrecognized property

You can see that there is a wavy line under `app.mail-from`. That is because there is no metadata available for this property, and VS Code is complaining about this and lists it in the **Problems** tab. Even though the application will still function normally, leaving it like this will create a tendency to ignore the problems that VS Code finds and lists in the **Problems** tab, which is not a good practice. To fix this, we need to use the `spring-boot-configuration-processor` library provided by Spring Boot.

We will need to create a configuration class to specify the properties of our app, and after a successful installation of the application with the `mvn clean install` command, the library will generate metadata in `target/META-INF/spring-configuration-metadata.json`, which will be used by VS Code to analyze the properties inside of `application.properties`.

Let's create the `com.taskagile.config.ApplicationProperties` configuration class as follows:

```
@Configuration
@ConfigurationProperties(prefix="app")
@Validated
public class ApplicationProperties {
  /**
   * Default `from` value of emails sent out by the system
   */
  @Email
 @NotBlank
  private String mailFrom;

  // getter and setter
}
```

As you can see, we use the `@ConfigurationProperties` annotation here to let Spring Boot know that this configuration defines the properties that have the prefix app. With the `@Validated`, `@Email`, and `@NotBlank` annotations, Spring Boot will perform validation for the properties during the starting phase of the application. For example, if the value of the `app.mail-from` property is not a valid email address, the application will fail to start because of the validation error. This is the actual benefit of defining this `ApplicationProperties` class. It helps us to validate the value of our custom properties. The JavaDoc we add to the `mailFrom` field will show up as a tooltip in VS Code, as the following figure:

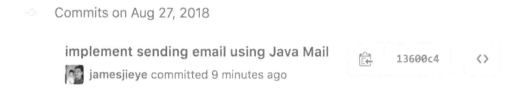

```
  1   app.mail-from=noreply@taskagile.com
  2
        app.mail-from
  3                                               :3306/task_agile?useSSL=false
        java.lang.String
  4
  5     Default from value of emails sent out by the system
  6   spring.datasource.driver-class-name=com.mysql.jdbc.Driver
```

Figure 10.19: Tooltip in application.properties

As usually, let's commit the code after a successful build with `mvn clean install`. Here is the commit record:

Commits on Aug 27, 2018

implement sending email using Java Mail

jamesjieye committed 9 minutes ago

13600c4

<>

Figure 10.20: Implementing sending emails using JavaMail commit

Performing end-to-end integration tests

Now, we've finished both the register and login feature of the User module. It's time to work on the end-to-end test now. Before we continue, let's review our current end-to-end test. By now, we only have a very basic `login.e2e.js`, which only tests against `http://localhost:3000` and does not use Page Objects. In this section, we will make the following improvements to our end-to-end test:

- Correct the port so that tests can be run against `http://localhost:8080` during a Maven build
- Use Page Objects in tests
- Automatically generate a user's test data, which can be shared across tests
- Execute multiple tests in a specific order

Let's go through these one by one.

Correcting the port

In order to run the test against the URL through port 8080, we will need to ask @vue/cli-service to not start the dev server by providing a --url parameter to the command, like the following:

```
"scripts": {
  ...
  "test:e2e": "vue-cli-service test:e2e",
  "test:integration": "vue-cli-service test:e2e --url
http://localhost:8080/",
  ...
},
```

Then, let's change the execution of the integration test in pom.xml to the following:

```
<execution>
  <id>frontend e2e test</id>
  ...
  <configuration>
    <executable>npm</executable>
    <arguments>
      <argument>run</argument>
      <argument>test:integration</argument>
    </arguments>
  </configuration>
</execution>
```

In this way, with the npm test command, we will still run tests against http://localhost:3000 and, with the mvn clean install command, we run tests against http://localhost:8080.

After that, we need to add frontend/nightwatch.config.js to specify launch_url, as follows:

```
module.exports = {
  test_settings: {
    default: {
      launch_url: (process.env.LAUNCH_URL ||
process.env.VUE_DEV_SERVER_URL)
    }
  }
}
```

The launch URL passed in the `test:integration` script will be set to `process.env.LAUNCH_URL`. In this way, **Nightwatch** will pick up the correct URL when we run `npm run test:e2e` and `npm run test:integration`. One last change is `login.e2e.js`. With the setting in `nightwatch.config.js`, we will need to get the launch URL via `browser.launchUrl`:

```
'login test': function (browser) {
  browser
    .url(browser.launchUrl + 'login')
    ...
}
```

Now, if you run `mvn clean install`, you can see the integration is performed against `http://localhost:8080`.

Using Page Objects

To use Page Objects, we will need to create a separate **JS** file for each page. We need to specify the folder that contains these page files in the configuration file. The following is the change we make to `nightwatch.conf.js`:

```
module.exports = {
  ...
  page_objects_path: 'tests/e2e/page-objects',
  ...
}
```

The following is the Page Object for the login page, `tests/e2e/page-objects/LoginPage.js`:

```
module.exports = {
  url: function () {
    return this.api.launchUrl + '/login'
  },
  elements: {
    app: '#app',
    logoImage: 'img.logo',
    usernameInput: '#username',
    passwordInput: '#password',
    submitButton: 'button[type=submit]',
    formError: '.failed'
  },
  commands: [{
    login: function (username, password) {
      this
```

```
        .setValue('@usernameInput', username)
        .setValue('@passwordInput', password)
        .click('@submitButton')
    }
  }]
}
```

As you can see, this Page Object has three parts: `url`, `elements`, and `commands`. `url` is used to specify the page's URL. The `elements` object is a definition of the named page elements with CSS selectors. The `commands` array contains the behavior this page supports. In our case, it is login. To use a Page Object, we will call `browser.page.<PageObjectFileName>()`, as follows:

```
module.exports = {
  'login page renders elements': function (browser) {
    const loginPage = browser.page.LoginPage()
    loginPage
      .navigate()
      .waitForElementVisible('@app', 500)
      .assert.visible('@usernameInput')
      .assert.visible('@passwordInput')
      .assert.visible('@submitButton')
      .assert.hidden('@formError')

    browser.end()
  },
  ...
}
```

As you can see, once the `loginPage` constant is ready, we call its `navigate()` method to go to the login page and then do assertions. Once that is done, we call `browser.end()`. This test only verifies that the page is rendered correctly. The following shows how to make a login request:

```
'login with email address': function (browser) {
  const loginPage = browser.page.LoginPage()
  const homePage = browser.page.HomePage()
  loginPage
    .navigate()
    .login(data.emailAddress, data.password)

  browser.pause(500)

  homePage
    .navigate()
    .expect.element('@pageTitle').text.to.contain('Home Page')
```

```
    browser.end()
  }
```

As you can see, after navigating to the login page, we simply call the `login()` command defined in the Page Object. Once that is done, we wait for half a second and then navigate to the home page and check the page title on that page to verify the login has succeeded. Due to the scope, we won't list all the details here. You can find them in the commit record.

Autogenerating user test data

We cannot rely on fixed data in our test because previously registered users cannot register. We need to autogenerate the user's test data, mainly username, email address, first name, and last name. We can use a fixed password. The generated data must be accessible by other tests as well.

The perfect place to do that is in the end-to-end test file for the register page. We can add the logic of auto-generating to the `before()` method and save the data into `frontend/tests/e2e/data/user.js`. In the tests for the register page, we will use the generated user data to test the registration. In other tests, like the tests on the login page, we can import `data/user.js` and use the generated data to log in.

Testing in specific order

Nightwatch runs test files in alphabetical order. The first one in the `frontend/tests/e2e/specs` directory will be executed first. We can change the filename of the tests to list them in the order that is required, as follows:

```
specs/
  0.register.e2e.js
  1.login.e2e.js
```

In this way, registration will always happen first and then login. In future, we can add other test files after `1.login.e2e.js`, such as `2.home.e2e.js`. In this way, we will start the whole end-to-end test by registering a new user, and then logging in with that user to the application, followed by other operations that we will build later. As you can see, we have skipped a lot of details of the end-to-end test because of the scope of this book. In future chapters, we will only mention the commit record of the end-to-end test and will not discuss them unless it is necessary.

As usual, let's run the `mvn clean install` command and then commit the code once the build is successful. Here is the commit record:

Commits on Aug 27, 2018

implement e2e tests of login and register
jamesjieye committed 13 seconds ago
70d9be6
<>

Figure 10.21: Implement end-to-end tests for login and register commit

Fixes at the end

The following are the fixes for this chapter. You can find the commit history on GitHub for each fix as follows:

- **Fix—rename router**: The name of the router is better if it excludes page and is lowercase. In this way, it is cleaner:

Commits on Aug 27, 2018

fix: rename router
jamesjieye committed 10 seconds ago
5d7795f
<>

Figure 10.22: Fix—renaming router commit

- **Fix—add the missing test of** `services.registration.spec.js`: The test of the registration service doesn't include verification for calling `/api/registrations`, which could fail to verify the behavior of the registration service because the `register()` method might even skip sending the request to the backend:

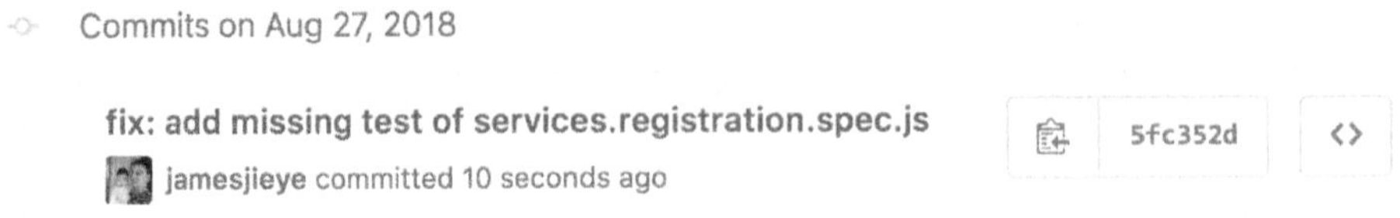

Commits on Aug 27, 2018

fix: add missing test of services.registration.spec.js
jamesjieye committed 10 seconds ago
5fc352d
<>

Figure 10.23: Fix—add the missing test of services.registration.spec.js commit

- **Fix—error handling on frontend**: Different errors returned from the backend sometimes need to show the same message to users. It is better to have an error parser, otherwise known as an error translator, in the service to parse the error before forwarding it to the caller:

Commits on Aug 27, 2018

fix: error handling on front-end

 jamesjieye committed 13 seconds ago

Figure 10.24: Fix—error handling on frontend commit

- **Fix—Jest warning of duplicate manual mock**: In the frontend, the mock file for the `registration` service and the one for the `authentication` service have the same name, `index.js`, as follows:

```
frontend/src/services/authentication/__mocks__/index.js
frontend/src/services/registration/__mocks__/index.js
```

Jest thinks they are mocks for the same JavaScript file and will ignore one of them. It is better to change `services/authentication/index.js` to `services/authentication.js` and `services/registration/index.js` to `services/registration.js` instead:

Commits on Aug 27, 2018

fix: jest warning of duplicate manual mock

 jamesjieye committed a minute ago

Figure 10.25: Fix—Jest warning of duplicate manual mock commit

Summary

In this chapter, we've learned about Spring Security and how it works internally. We also briefly reviewed how Single Sign-On and OAuth 2.0 work. We've also implemented the login page's frontend and backend, as well as using Spring Security's `PasswordEncoder` to encrypt passwords. We've also implemented a feature for sending email using JavaMail and FreeMarker. We've improved our end-to-end testing by using Page Object and generating test user data, as well as running the test against `http://localhost:8080` during the full build with the `mvn clean install` command.

In the next chapter, we will implement the home page, and we will focus on the use of Vuex, as well as the technique of mocking RESTful APIs to get more freedom for the development of the frontend.

11
State Management and i18n - Building a Home Page

The register page and login page that we built in the previous two chapters mainly handle form submissions, which are relatively simple. In this chapter, we are building the home page of TaskAgile, which contains more functionalities, as you will see. We will introduce Vuex, the official library for state management in Vue applications.

As usual, in this chapter, we will show you how the home page will look and then break down the task of implementing that page into small steps so that you can see how it is created step by step. We will skip the details of the parts that have already been mentioned before. As always, you can find those skipped details in the commit history.

In this chapter, you will learn about the following:

- Introduction of frontend state management with Vuex
- Building a modal window with the Bootstrap modal component
- Different ways to manage one-to-many and many-to-many relationships
- Add i18n support with Vue-i18n
- Logging SQL queries that Hibernate sends to the database for performance tuning

State management with Vuex

Before we introduce Vuex, let's take a look at different methods of state management in different web apps.

In a traditional web application that creates fresh pages when navigating through hyperlinks, there is very little state management required because the state is lost once users navigate to another page. In these applications, pages are generated dynamically on the backend. Most of the state of the application is kept on the server side.

Another type of web application is a **single-page application** (**SPA**). Different from a traditional app, an SPA has no page refreshes and it moves some of the logic from the backend to the frontend. Accordingly, it needs to keep some of the states on the client side. This brings complexity to frontend development. With frameworks such as Backbone.js, patterns similar to MVC are introduced into the frontend. (These patterns are usually referred to as **MV***.) And, usually, the state of the application is kept inside global variables or, if you're using a library like RequireJS, you will define a data model in a JS file and import it into other modules. The code that imports the data model can do anything to it, even replacing it entirely. It is true that you can add some protection to the data model, but you cannot control the data flow, as you will see in the next section when we talk about the drawbacks of traditional state management.

Nowadays, when we create an SPA, such as our TaskAgile application, without using Vuex, we can create a single object and store state in that object and share it across Vue components. For example, we can create `front-end/src/local-data.js` as follows:

```
export default {
  name: 'Unknown'
}
```

And we can then import it into different Vue components, for example, `front-end/src/components/ComponentA.vue`, as follows:

```
<template>
  <div>{{ name }} in Component A</div>
</template>
<script>
Import localData from '../local-data'
export default {
  data: function () {
    return localData
  }
}
</script>
```

Vue component `front-end/src/components/ComponentB.vue`, as follows:

```
<template>
  <div>{{ name }} in Component B</div>
</template>
<script>
Import localData from '../local-data'
export default {
  data: function () {
    return localData
  },
```

```
    mounted: function () {
      this.name = 'Sunny'
    }
  }
</script>
```

As you can see, inside the `<template>` sections of both components, we can reference the `name` property defined in `local-data.js` directly. In `ComponentB`, we can change its value. This change will be updated to `ComponentA` automatically. Vue.js takes care of that, which is quite convenient.

Drawbacks of traditional state management

The three types of state management that we have described are considered the traditional ways of managing state in the frontend. Even though the last type in Vue applications provides reactivity to the data model, they suffer the same drawback, which is the lack of control over the data flow. This wouldn't be an issue for small applications or applications that do not need to share state across components. On the other hand, for large-scale applications, this lack of control of the data flow will introduce data inconsistency issues.

Let's say you have a component, for example, `Messages`, showing a list of messages and another component `UnreadMessageCounter` showing the total count of unread messages. Once a new message has been read, in `Messages` component, its status will be marked as read. The unread counter in `UnreadMessageCounter` component should be updated accordingly. At the same time, the application might receive new messages through a real-time connection. A newly arrived message will be appended to the messages list and the unread counter will be updated as well. When everything works correctly, the count of unread messages in the `Messages` component will match the number of the unread message in the `UnreadMessageCounter` component. In reality, these two numbers sometimes would not match, which causes bugs that seem unlikely to happen yet pop up now and then randomly and are hard to reproduce and fix.

This is actually the chat issue that Facebook had in 2011. Back then, the unread messages counter at the top of the Facebook page sometimes showed there were new messages. But when the chat window was opened, no new messages showed up, which is quite annoying. To solve this issue, Jing Chen, an engineer from Facebook, came up with an application architecture called Flux, which essentially is a pattern that enforces one-way data flow. For large-scale applications, it solves issues caused by poor state management. There are many state management libraries that are inspired by Flux, including, Redux, Vuex and Alt.

If you're interested in finding out more about Flux and how it solves Facebook's chat issue, you can check out this talk on YouTube, *Hacker Way: Rethinking Web App Development at Facebook* (`https://www.youtube.com/watch?v=nYkdrAPrdcw`).

Modern state management

Modern state management begins with Flux, which is not a library or framework. It is more a pattern that is different from the traditional MVC pattern.

In a large-scale application that uses MVC, you can easily end up with something like the following:

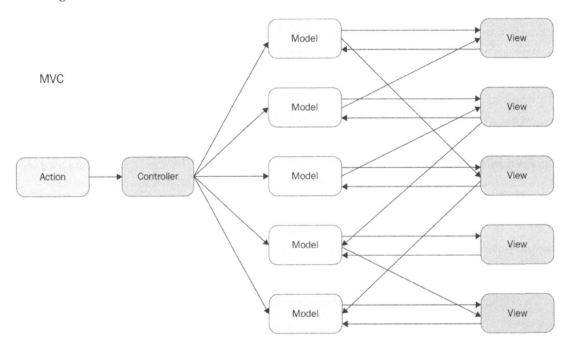

Figure 11.1: Unmanaged data flows (source: https://www.youtube.com/watch?v=nYkdrAPrdcw)

As you can see, the data that flows between **Models** and **Views** is unmanageable. It would be hard to try to figure out the data change flow.

In Flux, data flows in the same direction, as you can see in *Figure 11.2*:

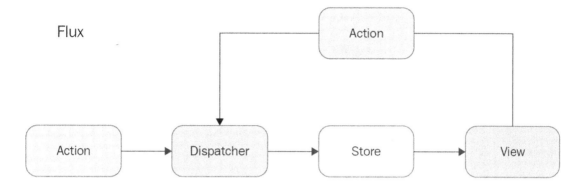

Figure 11.2: Unidirectional data flow in Flux (source: https://www.youtube.com/watch?v=nYkdrAPrdcw)

When users interact with a component on a page, which is called a view, the **View** will propagate an action through a central **Dispatcher** to the **Store** that holds the application's data, and the changes made in the store will be updated to all the associated views accordingly.

As you can see, the data flow is much simpler and easier to follow in Flux than in MVC.

Vuex in a nutshell

Vuex is a state management solution that is tailored specifically for Vue applications. As mentioned, it is inspired by Flux. You can use Vuex as a centralized store for the state, which is shared between components of your application. It has rules to ensure that the state can only be changed in a predictable way.

As you can see in *Figure 11.1*, in Vuex data flows in one direction. Usually, it starts from a Vue component, which dispatches an action that can commit a mutation and only the mutation can make changes to the state, which live inside a store. The store is the center of every Vuex application. Different from `localData` we saw earlier, Vuex stores are reactive. That is, the changes made to the store through a mutation will be synced to the Vue component through the reactivity system of Vue.js:

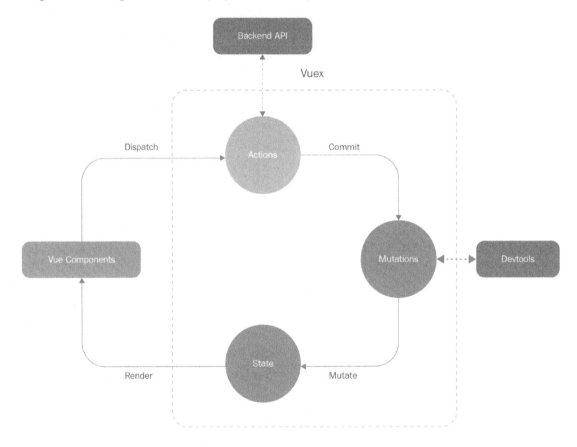

Figure 11.3: Vuex overview (source: https://vuex.vuejs.org)

Besides committing mutations, actions can also communicate with the backend API or make arbitrary asynchronous operations before committing mutations. Through mutations, a Vuex application can integrate with Vue.js DevTools to provide advanced features such as time-travel debugging and state snapshot export/import.

In Vuex, the state is a single object that contains all of our application-level state. It serves as the *single source of truth*. Usually, we will only create one store for each Vue application to hold the state. Putting all of the state of the application in one single object can bloat the store as our application grows. To solve this issue, Vuex provides support for modularity. It allows us to divide our store into modules and each module can contain its own state. We will see how that works later in this chapter.

Besides state, actions, mutations, and modules, Vuex also provides getters. These are useful when we need to compute the derived state based on the store state. For example, if we put all of the messages in the store, we can create a getter to calculate the number of unread messages. You can think of Vuex's getters as computed properties for stores. We will see how that works later in this chapter.

Building home page frontend

Different from the login and the register pages, which are mostly about form and validation, the frontend of the home page is more about how to render items, how to manage app state, and how to support **internationalization (i18n)**.

UI of the home page

First of all, let's take a look at the UI of the home page to see what we are building in this chapter. *Figure 11.4* shows a blank home page. This is how the application will look after a user logs in:

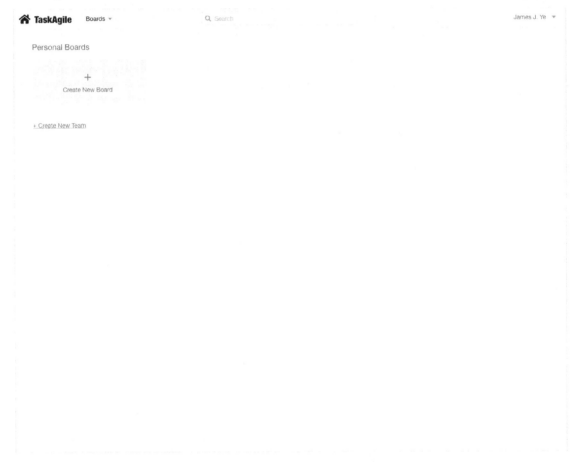

Figure 11.4: Blank home page

At the top of this page is the page header, which includes a logo, a boards menu, a search box, and a profile menu. On the boards menu, all of the boards that the user has access to will be listed. Users can use this menu to navigate among boards easily. The search box at the center of the header is for searching boards and cards globally. The main area of this page is for showing a list of boards that the user has access to, and the boards will be grouped by teams. Those personal boards that do not belong to any team will be listed at the top. For a new user, this home page will be empty at first. The user can click **Create New Board** to create a personal board or click **Create New Team** to set up a team and then create boards under that team, as shown in *Figure 11.5*:

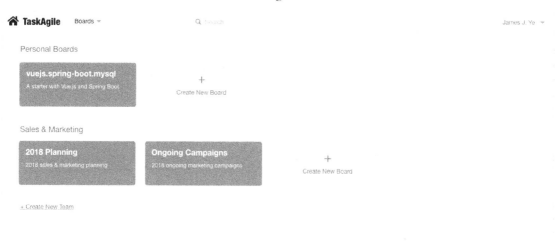

Figure 11.5: Team boards

Home page layout and components

Now, let's think about how to implement the UI of this home page. It is better to start with a layout diagram, the same way we did when creating the register page. *Figure 11.6* shows the layout of the home page:

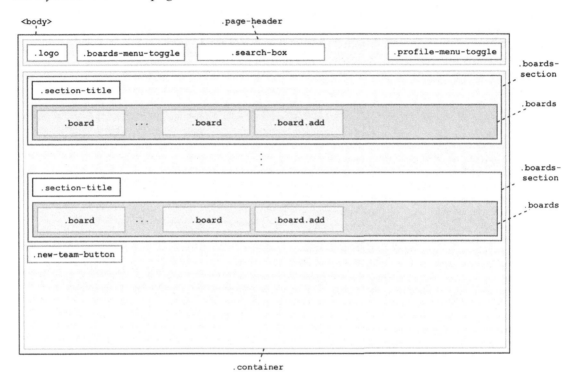

Figure 11.6: The layout of the home page

As you can see, we use an ellipsis between `.board` elements to represent that there could be zero or multiple `.board` elements, similar to the vertical ellipsis between `.boards-section` elements.

For the `.page-header` element, we will need to put it in a Vue component, called `PageHeader.vue`, so that we can share it with other pages. For the `.boards-section` element, we can create a Vue component, for example, `BoardsSection.vue`, and use a list to repeat it. However, this is not what we are going to do, because this element is not used anywhere else besides the home page. There is no real benefit of keeping it in a separate component.

Figure 11.7 shows the how the boards menu and the profile menu look:

Figure 11.7: Boards menu and profile menu

For these pop up windows and the menus, we won't create layout diagrams, because the layout of these elements is relatively easy to figure out.

Data structure and state management

Before writing the frontend code, let's think about the structure of the data that is required on the home page and what data we will need to put into Vuex.

After going through the UI of the home page, we can see that we need the following three pieces of data to initialize the home page:

- Name of logged in user
- Teams the user has joined
- Boards the user has access

There are two ways to get a user's name. The first one is to add it into the login response so that once a user is logged in, we can get the name and keep it in the Vuex store. There is an issue with this approach. Since the Vuex store will be initialized after a page refresh, the user's name will be lost after refreshing. It is true that we can put the name into the browser's local storage so that it can be recovered between page refreshes. However, this would introduce an unnecessary burden, as we will have to manage the local storage. We will also need to clean the user's name after logging out and plug the local storage into the Vuex store. This makes the code more complex than it needs to be.

The second way, which is much simpler and more effective, is to get all three of these pieces of data in one request that will be sent to the server during page initialization. So, from where should we trigger this request? From `HomePage.vue`, `PageHeader.vue` or somewhere else?

Before answering that, let's think about the data structure. What is the data structure that `HomePage.vue` and `PageHeader.vue` require?

For the user's name, this is straightforward. In `PageHeader.vue`, we need something like this:

```
{
  "user": {
    "name": "Sunny Hu"
  }
}
```

For the teams and boards data, we can have the personal boards and the team boards together and then use a computed property to get the personal boards to populate the first `.boards-section` element at the top, as personal boards will always be placed at the top. And we will need another computed property to get the teams and related boards to populate a list of `.boards-section` elements. If we do it this way, we will have duplicated code for extracting different types of boards in `HomePage.vue` and `PageHeader.vue`.

It would be much easier and more straightforward to use a data structure like the following in `HomePage.vue` and `PageHeader.vue`:

```
{
  "personalBoards": [{
    "id": 1,
    "name": "vuejs.spring-boot.mysql",
    "description": "An implementation of TaskAgile application with
    Vue.js, Spring Boot, and MySQL"
  }],
  "teams": [{
    "id": 1,
    "name": "Sales & Marketing",
    "boards": [{
      "id": 2,
      "name": "2018 Planning",
      "description": "2018 sales and marketing plan"
    }, {
      "id": 3,
      "name": "Ongoing Campaigns",
      "description": "2018 ongoing marketing campaigns"
    }]
  }]
}
```

How about the structure of the data that we put into the Vuex store? For the user's name, it will be the same structure as the one mentioned before. For teams and boards, it would be better that we keep team and board data in two separate arrays, as follows:

```
{
  "boards": [{
    "id": 1,
    "name": "vuejs.spring-boot.mysql",
    "description": "An implementation of TaskAgile application with
    Vue.js, Spring Boot, and MySQL",
    "teamId": 0
  }, {
    "id": 2,
    "name": "2018 Planning",
    "description": "2018 sales and marketing plan",
    "teamId": 1
  }, {
    "id": 3,
    "name": "Ongoing Campaigns",
    "description": "2018 ongoing marketing campaigns",
    "teamId": 1
  }],
  "teams": [{
```

```
      "id": 1,
      "name": "Sales & Marketing"
    }]
  }
```

As you can see, the link between `"boards"` and `"teams"` is the `teamId` property. This structure is very similar to how the teams and boards are kept in the database on the server side. We will need to convert this data structure into the one needed by `HomePage.vue` and `PageHeader.vue`. In Vuex, we have a perfect place for this conversion—getters. Vuex allows us to define getters in the store, similar to the computed properties in a Vue instance. The result of a getter is cached based on its dependencies. Once the dependencies have changed, Vuex will re-evaluate the getter and update others that depend on it automatically. We will see how that works later in this chapter.

Backend APIs

Now, we know what data we need and how it looks. Let's think about the backend APIs that are required by the home page frontend to fulfill the following actions:

- Create a personal board
- Create a team
- Create a team board
- Get a user's name, boards, and teams

We will discuss each one in detail.

Creating a personal board API

This will be a `POST` request sent to `/api/boards` with the following payload:

```
{
  "name": "<Board name>",
  "description": "<Board description>"
  "teamId": 0
}
```

We will use the 0 value for the `teamId` parameter to indicate that this is a personal board. A successful response to this request will have the status code 201, and the body will be as follows:

```
{
  "id": 12345,
  "name": "<Board name>",
  "description": "<Board description>"
  "teamId": 0
}
```

Once a board is created, the frontend will redirect the user to the board page, which we will create in the next chapter.

Creating the team API

This will also be a POST request, which is sent to /api/teams with a payload similar to the following:

```
{
  "name": "Sales & Marketing"
}
```

A successful response will also have the status code 201 and the body will be as follows:

```
{
  "id": 123
  "name": "Sales & Marketing"
}
```

Once a team is created, it will show up on the home page with no board under it.

Creating team board API

This API is similar to the one for creating a personal board. The only exception is that the value of the `teamId` parameter will be a valid ID of a team.

A combined API to get the user's name, boards, and teams

As mentioned, we will use one request to get the user's name, the boards, and the teams that the user has access to. There are several benefits to combining the requests:

- Most importantly, it reduces the numbers of the requests required to get all of the data for initializing the home page.
- Second, it saves the effort to combine the results of two different responses. Otherwise, you will need to use a mechanism such as Bluebird's `Promise.all` to wait for both requests to finish before rendering the page.
- As a result, it improves the user experience because, in our case, fewer requests mean faster page rendering.

The GET request will be sent to `/api/me`, and the response body will be as follows:

```
{
  "user": {
    "name": "Sunny Hu"
  },
  "boards": [{
    "id": 1,
    "name": "vuejs.spring-boot.mysql",
    "description": "An implementation of TaskAgile application with
     Vue.js, Spring Boot, and MySQL",
    "teamId": 0
  },
  ...],
  "teams": [{
    "id": 1,
    "name": "Sales & Marketing"
  }]
}
```

As you can see, the data structure of the response is the same as the one we put into the Vuex store.

Implementing home page frontend

Now, let's do a task breakdown to see what we need to do to implement the home page:

- Create a service to interact with backend APIs
- Save the user's name, boards, and teams in a Vuex store

- Add `PageHeader.vue`
- Add `HomePage.vue`
- Add the create board pop up window
- Add the create team pop up window
- Create a blank board page for redirecting users to it after board creation

In this section, we will start writing code for the frontend, and we will skip those parts that we have already covered when building the register page and the login page. We will focus on the following topics:

- How to use Vuex
- How to implement pop up windows with the Bootstrap model

Before we move on, let's create the UI of the home page. Here is the commit record:

Figure 11.8: Adding the home page UI commit

Implementing the services and Vuex store

Before we implement the Vuex store, let's get those services created. We will need to create `teamService` in the `front-end/src/services/teams.js` file, which looks like this:

```
...
export default {
  /**
   * Create a team
   * @param {*} detail the detail of the team
   */
  create (detail) {
    return new Promise((resolve, reject) => {
      axios.post('/teams', detail).then(({data}) => {
        resolve(data)
      }).catch((error) => {
        reject(errorParser.parse(error))
      })
    })
  }
}
```

As you can see, this service only has one method, `create()`, which send the team's detail to `/api/teams` in a `POST` request.

We will also need to create `boardService`, which is very similar to `teamService`, as you can see:

```
...
export default {
  /**
   * Create a new board
   * @param {*} detail the board detail
   */
  create (detail) {
    return new Promise((resolve, reject) => {
      axios.post('/boards', detail).then(({data}) => {
        resolve(data)
      }).catch((error) => {
        reject(errorParser.parse(error))
      })
    })
  }
}
```

The only difference is that the request is sent to `/api/boards`. As for the parameter details, it is up to the Vue instance, in our case `HomePage.vue`, to decide which data will be included, as services do not need to care about it.

The last service we need to create at this stage is `meService`, and here is how it looks:

```
...
export default {
  /**
   * Fetch current user's name, boards, and teams
   */
  getMyData () {
    return new Promise((resolve, reject) => {
      axios.get('/me').then(({data}) => {
        resolve(data)
      }).catch((error) => {
        reject(errorParser.parse(error))
      })
    })
  }
}
```

As you can see, all it does is send a `GET` request to `/api/me`.

Now, let's implement the Vuex store. The default generated `front-end/src/store.js` puts Vuex's `actions`, `mutations`, `getters`, and `state` in a single file. It would be more practical to reorganize it by separating `actions`, `mutations`, and `getters` into separate files or by separating it by modules. For large applications, it is better to split Vuex by modules. Inside each module, we can put `actions`, `mutations`, and `getters` in separate files. For our application, we will go with the first way. Let's delete the `front-end/src/store.js` file and create the `front-end/src/store` folder with the following structure:

```
.
└── store
    ├── actions.js
    ├── getters.js
    ├── index.js
    └── mutations.js
```

Here is how `store/index.js` looks:

```
import Vue from 'vue'
import Vuex from 'vuex'
import * as getters from './getters'
import * as actions from './actions'
import mutations from './mutations'
import createLogger from 'vuex/dist/logger'

Vue.use(Vuex)

const state = {
  user: {
    name: null
  },
  teams: [/* {id, name} */],
  boards: [/* {id, name, description, teamId} */]
}

export default new Vuex.Store({
  state,
  getters,
  actions,
  mutations,
  plugins: process.env.NODE_ENV !== 'production'
    ? [createLogger()]
    : []
})
```

As you can see, we define the data structure of `state` and then create an instance of `Vuex.Store` with `state`, `getters`, `actions`, and `mutations`.

The comments we put inside teams and boards are reminders of what fields the items in these two arrays will have.

By design, only `mutations` can change the state saved in the Vuex store. Here is how our `store/mutations.js` looks:

```
export default {
  updateMyData (state, data) {
    state.user.name = data.user.name
    state.teams = data.teams
    state.boards = data.boards
  },
  addTeam (state, team) {
    state.teams.push(team)
  },
  addBoard (state, board) {
    state.boards.push(board)
  }
}
```

As you can see, we define three `mutation` methods, `updateMyData()`, `addTeam()`, and `addBoard()`. The `updateMyData()` method is for updating the user's name, and all of the teams and boards the user can access with the result of the `/api/me` request. The `addTeam()` method and `addBoard()` method are for adding the newly created team and the newly created boards respectively. The first parameter, `state`, in these methods is provided by Vuex. The second parameter is the payload of the mutation, which is passed through from the actions.

As mentioned earlier, only actions can `commit` mutations. Let's see how our `store/actions.js` looks:

```
import meService from '@/services/me'

export const getMyData = ({ commit }) => {
  meService.getMyData().then(data => {
    commit('updateMyData', data)
  })
}

export const addTeam = ({commit}, team) => {
  commit('addTeam', team)
}
```

```
export const addBoard = ({commit}, board) => {
  commit('addBoard', board)
}
```

As you can see, we define three actions, getMyData, addTeam, and addBoard. We call meService.getMyData(), which is an asynchronous call, inside the getMyData action. Then, we commit the updateMyData mutation with the result of the call. In this way, we save the server's response into the store. Inside addTeam and addBoard actions, we simply commit a mutation with the data passed to the action. The first argument passed to an action method is the context provided by Vuex. It has a commit method. We use argument destructuring here to simplify the method's parameter.

As you might remember, actions are dispatched from Vue components. For now, let's see how to do that from PageHeader.vue to get the current user's data, as shown in the following code snippet:

```
<script>
export default {
  name: 'PageHeader',
  created () {
    this.$store.dispatch('getMyData')
  }
}
</script>
```

We use this.$store.dispatch('getMyData') inside the created() life cycle hook of the Vue instance, and we will see how to dispatch addTeam and addBoard actions later.

Now, let's take a look at store/getters.js, which looks as follows:

```
export const user = state => state.user

export const hasBoards = state => {
  return state.boards.length > 0
}

export const personalBoards = state => {
  return state.boards.filter(board => board.teamId === 0)
}

export const teamBoards = state => {
  const teams = []

  state.teams.forEach(team => {
    teams.push({
      id: team.id,
```

```
      name: team.name,
      boards: state.boards.filter(board => board.teamId === team.id)
    })
  })

  return teams
}
```

As you can see, we define four `getters`—user, `hasBoards`, `personalBoards`, and `teamBoards`. The first three `getters` are straightforward. Inside the last one, `teamBoards`, instead of sending the teams directly from the state, we create a new array and filter `state.boards` to get those that belong to the related team.

Now, let's see how we can use `getters`. To access `getters`, we can use a helper method, `mapGetters`, provided by Vuex to add these `getters` into a Vue component as computed properties. The following is the change we make to `PageHeader.vue`:

```
<script>
...
import { mapGetters } from 'vuex'

export default {
  name: 'PageHeader',
  computed: {
    ...mapGetters([
      'user',
      'hasBoards',
      'personalBoards',
      'teamBoards'
    ])
  },
  created () {
    this.$store.dispatch('getMyData')
  },
  ...
}
</script>
```

As you can see, we use `...mapGetters([])` to map the required `getters` into the computed properties. In this way, in the view, we can access these `getters` directly. For example, use `{{ user.name }}` to get the user's name.

We won't go into the rest of the details of how to render the boards menu, the teams, and the boards on the home page. You can check the commit history for details. Since the backend /api/me API isn't ready yet, we cannot test the implementation of the Vuex store, unless we use mock data. So, in this commit, you will see store/getters.js is actually returning mock data:

Figure 11.9: Implementing Vuex store commit

Implementing popup windows with Bootstrap modal

Now, let's implement the create board and create team pop up windows. Since these two popup windows are similar, we will only go through the details of implementing a create board popup window. We will create it in front-end/src/modals/CreateBoardModal.vue, and all of the popup windows will also be placed inside this modals folder.

Before implementing this component, we need to figure out answers to the following questions first:

- What are the responsibilities of HomePage.vue and CreateBoardModal.vue?
- How does HomePage.vue communicate with CreateBoardModal.vue?

To the first question, since the create board window shows up on the home page, it is naturally the responsibility of HomePage.vue to open the window. So, we will need to import CreateBoardModal.vue into HomePage.vue, bootstrap it, and open it up once the **Create New Board** button is clicked. HomePage.vue should redirect the user to the board page once the board is created. CreateBoardModal.vue is responsible for calling the boardService.create() method to save the board and then dispatch an addBoard action to the Vuex store when the request succeeds or display an error message on the window when the request fails.

For the second question, inside HomePage.Vue, the value of teamId will be passed to CreateBoardModal.vue via its properties. And HomePage.vue will listen to the created event that CreateBoardModal.vue emits.

The following is the change we make to `HomePage.vue`:

```
<template>
  <div>
    ...
    <CreateBoardModal
      :teamId="selectedTeamId"
      @created="onBoardCreated" />
  </div>
</template>

<script>
...
import CreateBoardModal from '@/modals/CreateBoardModal.vue'

export default {
  name: 'HomePage',
  ...
  components: {
    ...
    CreateBoardModal
  },
  methods: {
    ...
    createBoard (team) {
      this.selectedTeamId = team ? team.id : 0
      $('#createBoardModal').modal('show')
    },
    ...
    onBoardCreated (boardId) {
      this.$router.push({name: 'board', params: {boardId: boardId}})
    }
  }
}
</script>
```

As you can see, we import `CreateBoardModal.vue`, add it to the `components` list and then bootstrap it in the view. The `createBoard()` method is simply to open the window. Inside the `onBaordCreated()` method, we redirect the user to the board page.

Here is how `CreateBoardModal.vue` looks. For simplicity, `<template>` and `<style>` are not listed:

```
<script>
...
export default {
  name: 'CreateBoardModal',
```

```
props: ['teamId'],
...
mounted () {
  $('#createBoardModal').on('shown.bs.modal', () => {
    $('#boardNameInput').trigger('focus')
  })
},
methods: {
  saveBoard () {
    this.$v.$touch()
    if (this.$v.$invalid) { return }

    const board = {
      teamId: this.teamId,
      name: this.board.name,
      description: this.board.description
    }

    boardService.create(board).then((createdBoard) => {
      this.$store.dispatch('addBoard', createdBoard)
      this.$emit('created', createdBoard.id)
      this.close()
    }).catch(error => { this.errorMessage = error.message })
  },
  close () { ... },
}
}
</script>
```

As you can see, we define a `teamId` property for this component. We make the
`boardNameInput` field focused once the window is open inside the `mouted()` life cycle
hook. Inside the `saveBoard()` method, we perform data validation using Vuelidate. When
all the fields are valid, we call the `boardService` to save the board. Once the board is
saved, we dispatch the action to put it into the Vuex store and then tell the `HomePage.vue`
that the ID of the new board by emitting the created event. Then, we close the modal
window. Inside the `close()` method, we will need to clean up, such as by resetting the
data model to the initial values. When things go wrong, we will show the error message in
the same way we did in `LoginPage.vue`.

Since `CreateTeamModal.vue` is similar to `CreateBoardModal.vue`, we won't list it here. The following is the commit history of creating these two windows:

Figure 11.10: Implementing create team and create board window commit

Building the home page backend

Now, the frontend is ready. Let's implement the backend, which includes the following subtasks:

- Create API handlers in the `com.taskagile.web.apis` package
- Create application services in the `com.taskagile.domain.application` package
- Create models in the `com.taskagile.domain.model` package
- Create a repository implementation in the `com.taskagile.infrastructure.repository` package

Domain models

With ORM, there is a tendency to use the `@OneToMany` and `@ManyToMany` annotations to build the relationship between entities, and you can go from one entity to another easily. It does provide some convenience and reduces the amount of code.

Here, we are going to go with a different approach; we won't use these annotations to build the relationship. We will use a wrapper ID to build the relationship.

The following is how the `com.taskagile.domain.model.team.Team` model looks like. Some fields and methods are not listed here:

```
@Entity
@Table(name = "team")
public class Team extends AbstractBaseEntity {
  ...
  @Column(name = "userId")
```

```
  private long userId;
  ...
  /**
   * Create new team
   */
  public static Team create(String name, UserId creatorId) {
    Team team = new Team();
    team.name = name;
    team.archived = false;
    team.userId = creatorId.value();
    team.createdDate = new Date();
    return team;
  }

  public TeamId getId() { return new TeamId(id); }
  public UserId getUserId() { return new UserId(userId); }
  ...
}
```

As you can see, we use a simple `userId` to connect to the user who created this team. In the `create()` factory method, we need to pass in an instance of `UserId`, which is simply a wrapper of the long value.

The following is how the `com.taskagile.domain.model.board.Board` model looks like. Some fields and methods are not listed:

```
@Entity
@Table(name = "board")
public class Board extends AbstractBaseEntity {
  ...
  @Column(name = "user_id")
  private long userId;

  @Column(name = "team_id")
  private Long teamId;
  ...
  /**
   * Create new board
   */
  public static Board create(UserId userId, String name, String
  description, TeamId teamId) {
    Board board = new Board();
    board.userId = userId.value();
    board.name = name;
    board.description = description;
    board.teamId = teamId.isValid() ? teamId.value() : null;
    board.archived = false;
    board.createdDate = new Date();
```

```
      return board;
   }

   public BoardId getId() { return new BoardId(id); }

   public UserId getUserId() { return new UserId(userId); }

   public TeamId getTeamId() {
      return teamId == null ? new TeamId(0) : new TeamId(teamId);
   }
   ...
}
```

Because a personal board doesn't belong to any team, we need to define the `teamId` field as a `Long` value. Also, in the `create()` factory method, we pass in wrapped IDs of the user who created the board and the team that this board belongs to. For creating a personal board, the `teamId` parameter will be null. An improvement we can make here is to separate the creation of personal boards and team boards by using methods such as `createPersonalBoard()` and `createTeamBoard()`.

The `com.taskagile.domain.model.board.BoardMember` model appears as follows:

```
@Entity
@Table(name = "board_member")
public class BoardMember extends AbstractBaseEntity {

   @EmbeddedId
   private BoardMemberId id;

   public static BoardMember create(BoardId boardId, UserId userId) {
      BoardMember boardMember = new BoardMember();
      boardMember.id = new BoardMemberId(boardId, userId);
      return boardMember;
   }
   ...

   @Embeddable
   public static class BoardMemberId implements Serializable {

      @Column(name = "board_id")
      private long boardId;

      @Column(name = "user_id")
      private long userId;
      ...
   }
}
```

As you can see, we create `BoardMemberId` with the `@Embeddable` annotation so that we can use the board ID and user ID as the composite id of the `BoardMember` entity.

API handlers

We will put API handlers in separate controllers for different resources. The controllers that we will need to create are the following:

- `com.taskagile.web.apis.MeController` to handle the `/api/me` request
- `com.taskagile.web.apis.BoardController` to handle the `/api/boards` request
- `com.taskagile.web.apis.TeamController` to handle the `/api/teams` request

One difference from `RegistrationApiController` is that we will need to get the information of the logged in user, or, let's call it *the current user*, from Spring Security's `SecurityContext`. There are several ways of retrieving the current user's information:

- We can get it from `HttpServletRequest.getUsePrincipal()`. That will require Spring to inject `HttpServletRequest` into the API handler method.
- We can also get it from `SecurityContextHolder` directly, like this—`SecurityContextHolder.getContext().getAuthentication()`.
- We can create an annotation that is applied with Spring Security's `@AuthenticationPrincipal`, and then we can ask Spring to inject our implementation of `UserDetails` into the API handler method.

We will take the last approach since it makes the code easy to understand and easy to test. The annotation we create is called `@CurrentUser`, which looks like this:

```
@Target({ElementType.PARAMETER, ElementType.TYPE})
@Retention(RetentionPolicy.RUNTIME)
@Documented
@AuthenticationPrincipal
public @interface CurrentUser {
}
```

As you can see, it is a very simple annotation. The key here is to apply the `@AuthenticationPrincipal` annotation to it.

With this annotation, we can get the current user information in `BoardController`, `TeamController`, and `MeController` easily. `BoardController` looks as follows:

```
@Controller
public class BoardApiController {
  ...
  @PostMapping("/api/boards")
  public ResponseEntity<ApiResult> createBoard(
    @RequestBody CreateBoardPayload payload,
    @CurrentUser SimpleUser currentUser) {
    Board board =
    boardService.createBoard(payload.
    toCommand(currentUser.getUserId()));
    return CreateBoardResult.build(board);
  }
}
```

As you can see, in the `createBoard()` API handler method, we apply the `@CurrentUser` annotation to the `currentUser` parameter, and Spring will pass an instance of `SimpleUser` to our method. For this method, we use it to retrieve the current user's ID and create `CreateBoardCommand` from the instance of `CreateBoardPayload`, which is a class for capturing the parameters in the request body. Once the board is created by the service, we use the `CreateBoardResult` class to create `ResponseEntity` to send the new board information back to the frontend.

`TeamController` is similar to `BoardController`, and we will not list its code here. `MeController` looks as follows:

```
@Controller
public class MeApiController {
  ...
  @GetMapping("/api/me")
  public ResponseEntity<ApiResult> getMyData(
  @CurrentUser SimpleUser currentUser) {

    List<Team> teams =
    teamService.findTeamsByUserId(currentUser.getUserId());
    List<Board> boards =
    boardService.findBoardsByMembership(currentUser.getUserId());
    return MyDataResult.build(currentUser, teams, boards);
  }
}
```

As you can see, we call the `teamService.findTeamsByUserId()` method and `boardService.findBoardsByMembership()` method to get all the teams and boards the current user has access to, and then use `MyDataResult` to create `ResponseEntity`.

Application services

In our application core, we will need to create two application services, `TeamService` and `BoardService`, to provide the abilities that `Controller` requires. As mentioned earlier, application services need to be kept as thin as possible; they should try not to involve any business logic because business logic should be kept inside domain models and domain services.

The following is the implementation of `com.taskagile.domain.application.TeamService`:

```
@Service
@Transactional
public class TeamServiceImpl implements TeamService {
  ...
  @Override
  public List<Team> findTeamsByUserId(UserId userId) {
    return teamRepository.findTeamsByUserId(userId);
  }

  @Override
  public Team createTeam(CreateTeamCommand command) {
    Team team = Team.create(command.getName(), command.getUserId());
    teamRepository.save(team);
    domainEventPublisher.publish(new TeamCreatedEvent(this, team));
    return team;
  }
}
```

As you can see, the `findTeamsByUserId()` method is quite straightforward, and the `createTeam()` method takes one parameter, `CreateTeamCommand`. It keeps all of the necessary information the `Team.create()` factory method requires to create a new team, and we only use this command inside the application service. We do not use it in our domain models or domain services because `CreateTeamCommand` is part of the API contract of the application service and it might be changed in the future. We certainly do not want a change to `CreateTeamCommand` to impact our domains. Application services should depend on domains and not the other way around.

The following is the implementation of `com.taskagile.domain.application.BoardService`:

```
@Service
@Transactional
public class BoardServiceImpl implements BoardService {
  ...
```

```
@Override
public List<Board> findBoardsByMembership(UserId userId) {
  return boardRepository.findBoardsByMembership(userId);
}

@Override
public Board createBoard(CreateBoardCommand command) {
 Board board = boardManagement.createBoard(
     command.getUserId(), command.getName(),
     command.getDescription(), command.getTeamId());
  domainEventPublisher.publish(new BoardCreatedEvent(this, board));
  return board;
 }
}
```

As you can see, in the `createBoard()` method of `BoardServiceImpl`, we call the `createBoard()` method of `BoardManagement`, which encapsulates the business logic of creating a board. That's something the application service does not need to know.

The following is how `com.taskagile.domain.model.board.BoardManagement` looks:

```
@Component
public class BoardManagement {
  ...
  public Board createBoard(UserId creatorId, String name, String
  description, TeamId teamId) {
    Board board = Board.create(creatorId, name,
      description, teamId);
    boardRepository.save(board);
    // Add the creator to as a board member
    BoardMember boardMember = BoardMember.create(board.getId(),
    creatorId);
    boardMemberRepository.save(boardMember);
    return board;
  }
}
```

As you can see, in its `createBoard()` method, we use the `Board.create()` factory method to create a board and then save it to a repository. After that, we create an instance of `BoardMember` and save it into its repository as well. As you saw earlier, the `BoardMember` model is quite simple. It only has `boardId` and `userId` properties. In a future version of TaskAgile, we can add properties such as a `joinedDate` field to keep the date and time when a user joined a board and a `permissions` field to indicate what a member can do inside that board, as well as a `memberType` field to differentiate between a guest member who is a client or a partner. Given the limited scope of the first version of TaskAgile, we will only keep `boardId` and `userId` in it.

Repositories and the generic save() method

The last part of the backend implementation of the home page is implementing repositories for each entity. We will need to create the following repositories:

- com.taskagile.domain.model.board.BoardRepository
- com.taskagile.domain.model.board.BoardMemberRepository
- com.taskagile.domain.model.team.TeamRepository

These repositories, as well as UserRepository, all have a save() method to persist entities. The only difference between the save() methods of different repositories is the entity to be saved. It would be better that we create a generic save() method in HibernateSupport to eliminate the code duplication.

The following is the change to HibernateSupport:

```
abstract class HibernateSupport<T> {
  ...
  public void save(T object) {
    entityManager.persist(object);
    entityManager.flush();
  }
}
```

As you can see, we add a generic type, <T>, to the class and use it in the save() method.

The following is the Hibernate implementation of TeamRepository:

```
@Repository
public class HibernateTeamRepository extends HibernateSupport<Team>
implements TeamRepository {
  ...
  @Override
  public List<Team> findTeamsByUserId(UserId userId) {
    String sql =
      " SELECT t.* FROM team t WHERE t.user_id = :userId " +
      " UNION " +
      " ( " +
      " SELECT t.* FROM team t, board b, board_member bm " +
      " WHERE t.id = b.team_id AND bm.board_id = b.id AND bm.user_id =
      :userId " +
      " ) ";
    NativeQuery<Team> query = getSession().createNativeQuery(sql,
    Team.class);
    query.setParameter("userId", userId.value());
    return query.list();
```

```
    }
  }
```

As you can see, it only needs to implement the `findTeamsByUserId()` method and inherit the `save()` method from `HibernateSupport`. Inside this `findTeamsByUserId()` method, we use a `UNION` operation to retrieve the teams that the user created, as well as those teams that the current user has access to because they joined boards. We use Hibernate's `NativeQuery` to execute the query.

The following is the Hibernate implementation of `BoardRepository`:

```
@Repository
public class HibernateBoardRepository extends HibernateSupport<Board>
implements BoardRepository {
  ...
  @Override
  public List<Board> findBoardsByMembership(UserId userId) {
    String sql = "SELECT b.* FROM board b LEFT JOIN board_member bm ON
    b.id = bm.board_id WHERE bm.user_id = :userId";
    NativeQuery<Board> query = getSession().createNativeQuery(sql,
    Board.class);
    query.setParameter("userId", userId.value());
    return query.list();
  }
}
```

As you can see, in the `findBoardsByMembership()` method, we need to do a `LEFT JOIN` operation between the `board` table and the `board_member` table because we didn't use the `@ManyToMany` annotation to build the relationship between the `Board` entity and `User` entity. Instead, we create the `BoardMember` entity to keep the board membership information. As mentioned earlier, with the `BoardMember` entity, we can extend this board membership in a future version.

We skip `BoardMemberRepository` here because it inherits the `save()` method from `HibernateSupport` and does not have any other methods.

The following is the commit record of the backend:

Commits on Aug 30, 2018

implement home page back-end
jamesjieye committed an hour ago

85c019a   <>

Figure 11.11: Implementing the home page backend commit

Adding i18n support with Vue-i18n

Now, let's see how to add support for i18n in a Vue application with Vue-i18n (`https://kazupon.github.io/vue-i18n`).

First of all, we will create a `front-end/src/locale` directory to put our localized message in. This folder looks as follows:

```
.
└── locale
    ├── index.js
    └── messages
        ├── en_US.json
        └── zh_CN.json
```

The following is what `front-end/src/locale/index.js` looks like:

```
import enUSMessages from './messages/en_US.json'
import zhCNMessages from './messages/zh_CN.json'

export const enUS = enUSMessages
export const zhCN = zhCNMessages
```

`en_US.json` and `zh_CN.json` are simply JSON files that contain a localized message. For example, the following is a snippet of `en_US.json`:

```
{
  "logo": {
    "tagLine": "Open source task management tool"
  },
  ...
  "error": {
    "request": {
      ...
      "notAuthorized": "Request not authorized.",
      ...
    }
  }
}
```

Please note that we do not have to use JSON for localized messages. We can just use a JavaScript file. For example, we can change `en_US.json` to `en_US.js` with content like this:

```
export default {
  "logo": { ... },
  ...
  "error": { ... }
}
```

Now we have the localized messages ready, let's create an instance of `VueI18n` in `front-end/src/i18n.js`, which looks as follows:

```
import Vue from 'vue'
import VueI18n from 'vue-i18n'
import { enUS, zhCN } from './locale'

Vue.use(VueI18n)

// Create VueI18n instance with options
export const i18n = new VueI18n({
  locale: 'en_US',
  messages: {
    'en_US': enUS,
    'zh_CN': zhCN
  }
})
```

As you can see, we import the `enUS` and `zhCN` messages from the `./locale` folder and then map them to the `en_US` locale and the `zh_CN` locale. In the `VueI18n` instance, we set the default locale to `en_US` by setting the `locale` property of the `VueI18n` options.

Now, let's make the following changes to `front-end/src/main.js` to bootstrap `VueI18n`:

```
...
import { i18n } from './i18n'
...
new Vue({
  router,
  store,
  i18n,
  render: h => h(App)
}).$mount('#app')
```

As you can see, we import the `VueI18n` instance, `i18n`, and add it to the root Vue instance.

To use localized messages in a Vue component, we can use the $t() instance method that VueI18n creates. For example, in front-end/src/components/Logo.vue, we can use {{ $t("logo.tagLine") }} to get the localized message:

```
<template>
  <div class="logo-wrapper">
    <img class="logo" src="/images/logo.png">
    <div class="tagline">{{ $t("logo.tagLine") }}</div>
  </div>
</template>
```

To use VueI18n in JavaScript files, we can import front-end/src/i18n.js and use the i18n.t() method. For example, the following is the change made to front-end/src/utils/error-parser.js:

```
import { i18n } from '@/i18n'

export default {
    ...
    } else if (status === 401) {
      return new Error(i18n.t('error.request.notAuthorized'))
    }
    ...
  }
}
```

Once all of the labels have been localized, if you run the npm run test:unit command, you will see errors, complaining of _vm.$t is not a function or [vue-i18n] Cannot find VueI18n instance!, and so on. It is because we haven't added VueI18n to these tests.

Let's do that now. In LoginPage.spec.js and RegisterPage.spec.js, we add the VueI18n instance, i18n, into wrapper as follows:

```
...
import { i18n } from '@/i18n'
...
describe('LoginPage.vue', () => {
  ...
  beforeEach(() => {
    wrapper = mount(LoginPage, {
      localVue,
      router,
      i18n
    })
    ...
```

```
  })
    ...
})
```

You can find details about adding i18n support in the commit history:

◇ Commits on Aug 30, 2018

add i18n support

jamesjieye committed 13 minutes ago

877a183 <>

Logging SQL queries and performance tuning

In this section, we will introduce one way to log the SQL queries that `JdbcDriver` sends to the database. We will use P6Spy (`https://github.com/p6spy/p6spy`).

The first change we need to make is to add the following dependencies into `pom.xml`:

```xml
<dependency>
  <groupId>p6spy</groupId>
  <artifactId>p6spy</artifactId>
  <version>${p6spy.version}</version>
</dependency>
```

At the time of writing, the P6Spy version we use is 3.7.0. To customize P6Spy, we can add the `src/main/resources/spy.properties` configuration file. The one that we will use looks as follows:

```
driverlist=com.mysql.jdbc.Driver
logfile=spy.log
dateformat=yyyy-MM-dd HH:mm:ss.SS
logMessageFormat=com.p6spy.engine.spy.appender.CustomLineFormat
customLogMessageFormat=- %(currentTime) | took %(executionTime)ms |
connection %(connectionId) \nEXPLAIN %(sql);\n
filter=true
exclude=select 1 from dual
```

In order to let P6Spy capture the SQL queries, we will need to change the datasource configuration. Let's make changes to `application-dev.properties`, as follows:

```
spring.datasource.url=jdbc:p6spy:mysql://localhost:3306/task_agile?useSSL=false
spring.datasource.username=root
spring.datasource.password=1234
spring.datasource.driver-class-name=com.p6spy.engine.spy.P6SpyDriver
```

As you can see, we need to change the URL's `jdbc:mysql` to `jdbc:p6spy:mysql` and change the driver class name to `com.p6spy.engine.spy.P6SpyDriver`.

With everything ready, once the application starts, you can see SQL queries captured in `spy.log`, which looks as follows:

```
- 2018-08-30 20:55:53.333 | took 1ms | connection 0
EXPLAIN SELECT b.* FROM board b LEFT JOIN board_member bm ON b.id =
bm.board_id WHERE bm.user_id = 34;
```

The `EXPLAIN` keyword is added in the `customLogMessageFormat` custom format of `spy.properties`. In this way, you can copy the SQL to do a MySQL explain of the query and figure out how to tune the performance of the query.

The following is the commit record:

Commits on Aug 30, 2018

add p6spy to log SQL queries
jamesjieye committed 8 minutes ago

948ff96   ⟨⟩

Figure 11.13: Adding P6Spyto log SQL queries commit

Fixes at the end

Let's have a look at the fixes done as follows:

- **Fix—use a wrapped ID instead of a native ID in**
  `BoardMember`: In `com.taskagile.domain.model.board.BoardMember`, `getU serId()` and `getBoardId()` return a native long value. It is better to use wrapped IDs:

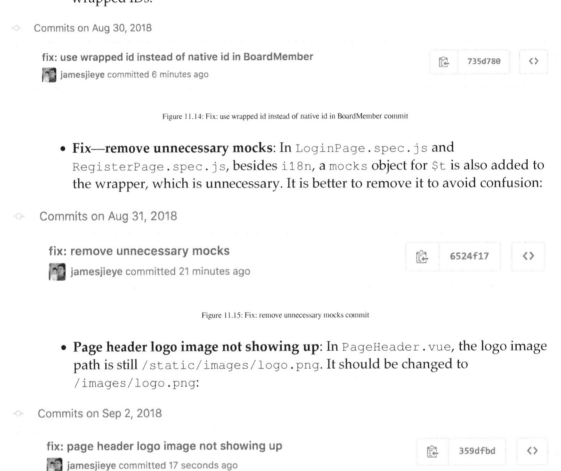

Commits on Aug 30, 2018

fix: use wrapped id instead of native id in BoardMember

jamesjieye committed 6 minutes ago   735d780   <>

Figure 11.14: Fix: use wrapped id instead of native id in BoardMember commit

- **Fix—remove unnecessary mocks**: In `LoginPage.spec.js` and `RegisterPage.spec.js`, besides i18n, a `mocks` object for `$t` is also added to the wrapper, which is unnecessary. It is better to remove it to avoid confusion:

Commits on Aug 31, 2018

fix: remove unnecessary mocks

jamesjieye committed 21 minutes ago   6524f17   <>

Figure 11.15: Fix: remove unnecessary mocks commit

- **Page header logo image not showing up**: In `PageHeader.vue`, the logo image path is still `/static/images/logo.png`. It should be changed to `/images/logo.png`:

Commits on Sep 2, 2018

fix: page header logo image not showing up

jamesjieye committed 17 seconds ago   359dfbd   <>

Figure 11.16: Fix: page header logo image not showing up

Summary

In this chapter, we learned the different ways of state management in the frontend, and we compared data flows in an MVC application and the one Flux uses. Later on, we learned the core concepts of Vuex and how to use them in an application. We also learned how to create pop up windows with the Bootstrap modal component.

We also implemented the home page's frontend and backend. Due to the limited scope, we didn't cover unit testing and end-to-end test for the home page in this chapter. You're encouraged to try that yourself. You can use those in Chapter 9, *Forms and Validation - Starting with the Register Page*, and Chapter 10, *Spring Security - Making Our Application Secure*, as examples.

Besides that, we added i18n support to our frontend, and we introduced the way to log SQL queries with P6Spy.

In the next chapter, we will create the board page and implement real-time updates with WebSocket, as well as global search with Elasticsearch.

12
Flexbox Layout and Real-Time Updates with WebSocket - Creating Boards

The CSS3 Flexbox layout is the new model used to build the layout of a web application. It makes building flexible responsive layout structures easier, without using floats or positioning, and we will use it to build our board page.

Real-time collaboration nowadays has become popular and common in web applications, especially with the standardization of the WebSocket API. In the TaskAgile application, we will implement the real-time update of card changes based on SockJS, which is a cross-browser library that provides a WebSocket-like interface. On the server side, we will use a Spring WebSocket implementation.

In this chapter, you will learn the following:

- Implementing the UI of the board page with Flexbox
- Implementing a drag and drop feature for a card list and cards
- Implementing real-time updates with WebSocket
- Creating an event bus for cross-component communication
- Using JWT for authentication

Building the frontend of the board page

In this section, we will focus on two parts of building the frontend of the board page. The first one is how to make the height of the page the same height as the screen. The second is how to implement the feature of reorganizing the card list and cards by dragging and dropping.

The UI of the board page

Now, let's take a look at the UI of the board page that we're building. *Figure 12.1* is the UI design of the page:

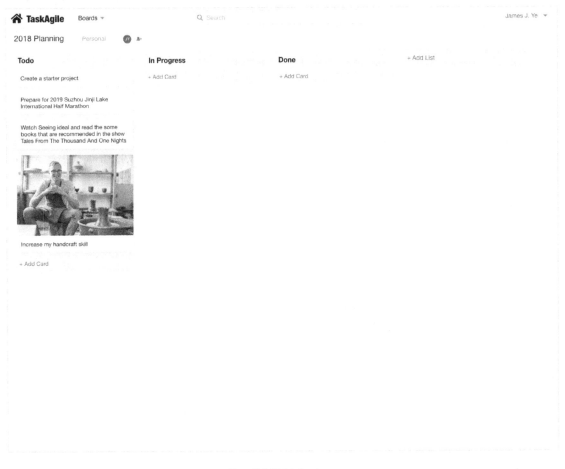

Figure 12.1: UI of the board page

As you can you see, we have the card lists shown as columns on the page. In the **Todo** list, the cards are listed vertically with their titles showing. For cards that have images uploaded, we will show a thumbnail as the card cover, as shown in the fourth card. In this chapter, the cards will only be listed with their titles. We will implement the cover image in the next chapter, once we have uploaded an attachment feature implemented.

Figure 12.2 shows the UI of the board page when the (+ **Add List**) button is clicked; and the Add List form shows up inline. The user can type the list's name and press the *Enter* key or click the (+ **Add List**) button to add a new list. Clicking anywhere outside the form will automatically close the form:

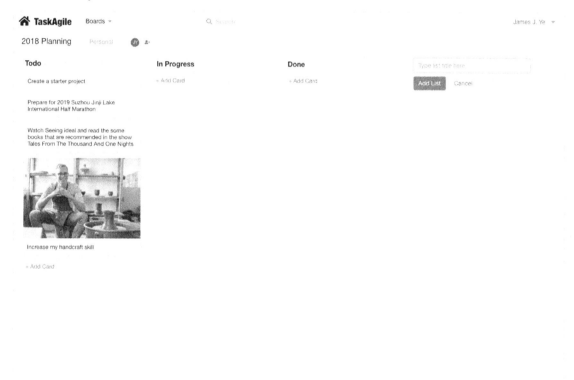

Figure 12.2: UI of the add list field

Figure 12.3 shows the UI when the (**+ Add Card**) button is clicked. As you can see, when the button is clicked, the add card form is shown inline, inside the card list. The user can press the *Enter* key or click the (**Add**) button to submit the form. Also, clicking anywhere outside the form will close the form. We will implement it using the same mechanism as the add list form:

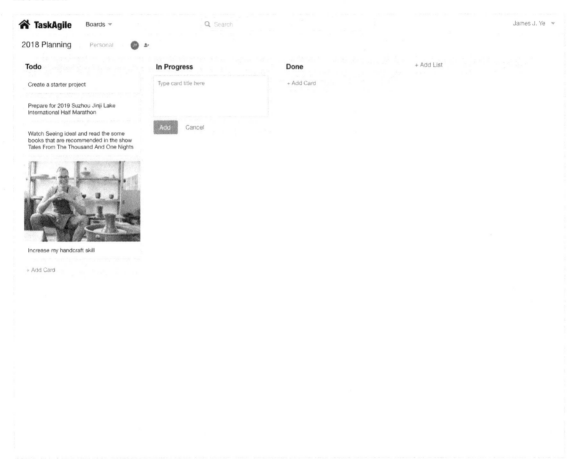

Figure 12.3: UI of the add card field

Users can click on the list header, such as **Waiting, In Progress**, or **Done**, and drag the card list to its left side or right side to change the position of the card list. In the same way, using drag and drop, users can move a card up and down in the same card list or move it to another card list.

Users can add as many card lists to the board as needed. When there are more card lists to show on the screen, the card lists will overflow to the outside of the page and there will be a horizontal scrollbar at the bottom of the page. When a card list contains more cards than can be displayed on the screen, those at the bottom will be hidden and a vertical scrollbar will be shown. *Figure 12.4* shows how the page will look when the card lists overflow horizontally and cards are hidden at the bottom of a card list:

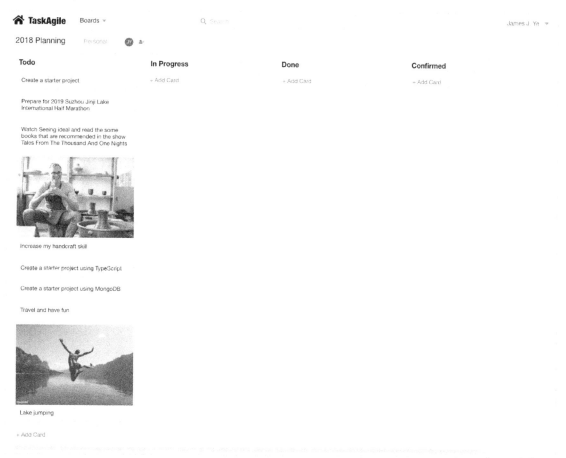

Figure 12.4: UI of the full height card list and overflow card list (source 1: https://www.rawpixel.com/image/53168/artisan-pottery-shop, source 2: https://www.rawpixel.com/image/412056/man-jumping-joy-lake)

The layout of the board page

Now, let's think about how to implement the UI of the board page. Comparing to all the pages we've implemented, the biggest difference this page has is that its height needs to be fixed to the same height as the screen. The height of the card list will not exceed the available area of the page, as you can see in *Figure 12.4*.

One way to archive this is to use JavaScript to calculate the available height of the screen, and then set the height of the card list in JavaScript. This would also require attaching a listener to the browser's resize event so that the height of the card list can be adjusted accordingly. A better way is to use CSS's Flexbox layout to implement it. We will use Flexbox to build the layout of the board page.

Designing the overall layout

The overall layout of the board page is different from all of the other pages in the application. We will put everything inside a .page division, which looks like the following; the height of the <body> tag and #app divisions will be 100%:

```
<body>
  <div id="app">
    <div class="page">
      <div class="page-header"></div>
      <div class="page-body">
        <div class="board-wrapper">
          <div class="board"></div>
        </div>
      </div>
    </div>
  </div>
</body>
```

Inside the `.page` element, we will have a `.page-header` element, which is the same header as the home page, and a `.page-body` element, which contains a `.board-wrapper` element. Inside the `.board-wrapper`, we will put a `.board` element. *Figure 12.5* shows the high-level layout of the board page:

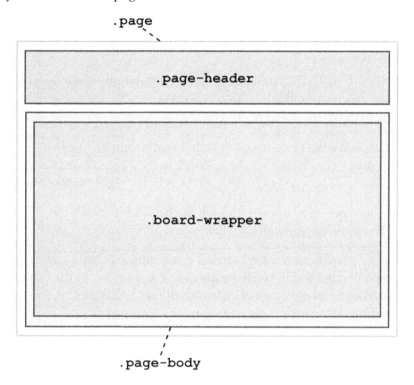

Figure 12.5: Overall layout of the board page

Here is the CSS of the divisions shown previously:

```
.page {
  display: flex;
  flex-direction: column;
}

.page-header {
  flex: none;
}

.page-body {
  flex-grow: 1;
  position: relative;
```

```
}

.board-wrapper {
  position: absolute;
  top: 0;
  right: 0;
  bottom: 0;
  left: 0;
}
```

As you can see, we use the `.page` division as a flex container by assigning `flex` to its `display` property. Since we will align the divisions vertically, we assign the `column` value to the `flex-direction` property.

For `.page-header`, we use `flex: none`, which is equivalent to `flex: 0 0 auto`, which is itself a shorthand of `flex-grow: 0 flex-shrink: 0 flex-basis: auto`. In this way, `.page-header` will be sized according to the width/height of its content.

For `.page-body`, we use `flex-grow: 1` to tell the browser to make the `.page-body` element take up all the vertically available area on the screen.

For `.board-wrapper`, as its name suggested, it is a wrapper of the `.board` division. We make it absolute positioned to fill up all the area of `.page-body`. In this way, the `.board` division, which serves as the flex container for the divisions inside of it, can use 100% of the height to fill up all the area inside `.board-wrapper`.

 If you're not familiar with Flexbox, you can find a detailed introduction to Flexbox on MDN here: `https://developer.mozilla.org/en-US/docs/Learn/CSS/CSS_layout/Flexbox` and CSS trick at: `https://css-tricks.com/snippets/css/a-guide-to-flexbox/`.

Figure 12.6 shows the layout of the parts inside `.board-wrapper`. Inside the `.board` flex container, `.board-header` and `.board-body` have similar CSS properties to `.page-header` and `.page-body`:

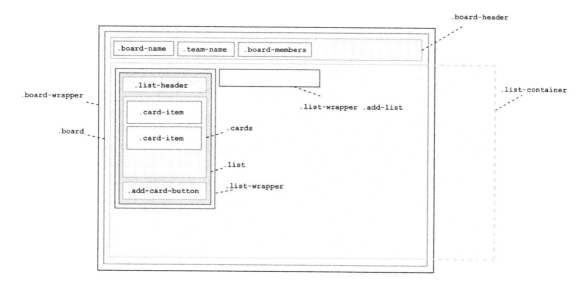

Figure 12.6: Detailed layout of the board page

The following is the CSS of the divisions inside .board-wrapper:

```css
.board {
  display: flex;
  flex-direction: column;
  height: 100%;
}

.board-header {
  flex: none;
  height: auto;
}

.board-body {
  flex-grow: 1;
  position: relative;
}

.list-container {
  position: absolute;
  bottom: 0;
  left: 8px;
  right: 0;
  top: 0;
  overflow-x: auto;
  overflow-y: hidden;
```

```
    }

    .list-wrapper {
      display: inline-block;
      height: 100%;
      vertical-align: top;
    }
```

As you can see, `.board`, `.board-header`, and `.board-body` define the same layout, which can have `.board-body` fill up all of the vertically available area. For `.list-container`, we allow it to be horizontally scrollable by using `overflow-x: auto`. For each card list, we will put it inside `.list-wrapper`, which is positioned side by side horizontally using `display: inline-block`.

Inside `.list-wrapper`, the `.list` is a flex container of its child elements, `.list-header`, `.cards`, and `.add-card-button`. As you can see next, for `.list`, we give it a maximum height of `100%` to make sure it won't exceed the available area. For `.cards`, we allow it to be scrollable vertically so that it can hold as many `.card-items` inside it as needed:

```
    .list {
      display: flex;
      flex-direction: column;
      max-height: 100%;
    }

    .cards {
      min-height: 1px;
      overflow-y: auto;
    }
```

For any other details, you can find them in the commit history on GitHub.

Implementing drag and drop

Dragging and dropping elements on the page has become a common user experience nowadays. There are many libraries to help developers implement this feature with ease. We will use Vue.Draggable (`https://github.com/SortableJS/Vue.Draggable`), which is a Vue component based on the Sortable.js library (`https://github.com/RubaXa/Sortable`).

After installing it via the `npm install vuedraggable --save` command, we will need to import it into `BoardPage.vue`, as follows:

```
    <script>
    import draggable from 'vuedraggable'
```

```
  ...
export default {
  name: 'BoardPage',
  ...
  components: {
    ...
    draggable
  },
  ...
}
</script>
```

To make the card lists support drag and drop, we will need to wrap the `.list-wrapper`
elements as follows:

```
<div class="board-body">
  <draggable v-model="cardLists" class="list-container"
    @end="onCardListDragEnded" :options="{handle: '.list-header',
    ...}">
    <div class="list-wrapper" v-for="cardList in cardLists" v-
    bind:key="cardList.id">
      <div class="list">
        <div class="list-header">{{ cardList.name }}</div>
        ...
      </div>
    </div>
    ...
  </draggable>
</div>
```

As you can see, the `<draggable>` component has a `v-model` attribute that binds
to `cardLists`, which is defined in the `data` properties. In this way, the changes to the card
lists after dragging and dropping will be synced to the `cardLists` data model
automatically. It will emit an `end` event once the drag ends. In our code, we use
the `onCardListDragEnded(event)` handler to listen to that event and save the changes to
the card list positions on the server side. In its `:options` property, we specify that the
dragging can only be triggered by the `.list-header` element. With this `<draggable>`
component, all `.list-wrappers` inside it can be dragged and dropped.

The following is how to make `.card-items` draggable:

```
<div class="list">
  <div class="list-header">{{ cardList.name }}</div>
  <draggable class="cards" v-model="cardList.cards"
    @end="onCardDragEnded" :options="{draggable: '.card-item', group:
    'cards', ghostClass: 'ghost-card', ...}" ...>
```

```
          <div class="card-item" v-for="card in cardList.cards" ...>
            <div class="card-title">{{ card.title }}</div>
          </div>
          <div class="add-card-form-wrapper">
            ...
          </div>
        </draggable>
      ...
    </div>
```

As you can see, we wrap `.card-items` as well as `.add-card-form-wrapper` inside another `<draggable>` component, which is nested inside the `<draggable>` component that makes the card list draggable. We also define an event listener `onCardDragEnded(event)` method to save the card position changes to the server. In the value of the `options` property, we use the `draggable` option to specify that only the elements with the `.card-item` class can be dragged. In this way, the `.add-card-form-wrapper` won't be draggable, which is what we want. We use the option `group` from Sortable.js so that a `.card-item` element can be dragged from one `.cards` element to another `.cards` element. In this way, we can move one card between card lists. The `ghostClass` option is used to define the CSS class of the drop placeholder.

We won't discuss the other details of the implementation of the UI for `BoardPage.vue` in this book. You can find all of the details in the commit record on GitHub.

Building the backend of the board page

Now, let's take a look at what we will need to do to implement the backend of the board page. In a nutshell, we will need to do the following:

- Create the domain models of the card list, the card, and `BoardMember`
- Create the application services
- Create the repository implementations
- Create the API handlers in controllers

APIs for the board page

First of all, let's see the APIs that we will need to implement:

- The API to get a board
- The API to add a board member

- The API to add a card list
- The API to change the positions of card lists
- The API to add a card
- The API to change card positions

Let's take a look at each one of them, as follows:

- **Get board API**: This will be a GET request sent to /api/boards/{boardId}. Through this API, we will return the board information, as well as the board members, card lists, and its cards. If this is a team board, we will also need to return the team information. The following is how the response will look:

```
{
  "team": {
    "name": "Sales & Markerting"
  },
  "board": {
    "name": "Ongoing Campaigns",
    "personal": false,
    "id": 1
  },
  "members": [{
    "userId": 1,
    "shortName": "JY"
  }],
  "cardLists": [{
    "id": 1,
    "name": "Todo",
    "position": 1,
    "cards": [{
      "id": 1,
      "title": "Come up with a marketing strategy",
      "position": 1
    }]
  }]
}
```

- **Add board member API**: This will be a POST request sent to /api/boards/{boardId}/members with the username as the payload:

```
{ "usernameOrEmailAddress": "sunny" }
```

Or, we can use an email address like in the following:

```
{ "usernameOrEmailAddress": "sunny@taskagile.com" }
```

The API response will look like the following:

```
{ "id": 3, "shortName": "SH" }
```

- **Add card list API**: This will be a POST request sent to /api/card-lists with a payload similar to the following:

```
{
  "boardId": 1,
  "name": "Todo",
  "position": 1
}
```

The API response will look like the following:

```
{
  "id": 2,
  "name": "Todo"
}
```

As you can see, in the response, the server will send back the newly created card list.

- **Change card list positions API**: This will be a POST request sent to /api/card-lists/positions with a payload similar to the following:

```
{
  "boardId": 6,
  "cardListPositions": [
    { "cardListId": 1, "position": 1 },
    { "cardListId": 2, "position": 3 },
    { "cardListId": 3, "position": 2 }
  ]
}
```

As you can see, in the request we send the positions of all of the card lists to the server. When the request succeeds, the server will simply return an HTTP status of 200 with no response body.

- **Add card API**: This will be a POST request sent to `/api/cards` with a payload similar to the following:

```
{
  "boardId": 1,
  "cardListId": 1,
  "title": "Come up with a marketing strategy",
  "position": 1
}
```

The API response will look similar to the following when it succeeds:

```
{
  "id": 1,
  "position": 1,
  "title": "Come up with a marketing strategy"
}
```

As you can see, in the response, the server will send back the newly created card.

- **Change card positions API**: This will be a POST request sent to `/api/cards/positions` with a payload similar to the following:

```
{
  "boardId": 6,
  "cardPositions": [
    { "cardListId": "1", "cardId": 2, "position": 1 },
    { "cardListId": "1", "cardId": 3, "position": 2 },
    { "cardListId": "2", "cardId": 1, "position": 1 },
    { "cardListId": "2", "cardId": 4, "position": 2 }
  ]
}
```

When a card is simply moved up and down in the same card list, in the `cardPositions` array, we will only send the positions of all of the cards in that list. When a card is moved from one list to another, we will send the positions of all of the cards in both lists. When the request succeeds, the server will simply return an HTTP status of 200 with no response body.

Changing positions in batch

Among the implementations of the domain models, application services, and repositories, most of them are similar to those we have covered in previous chapters. In this section, we will focus on how to change the positions of card lists and cards.

As you have seen in the APIs used to change card list and card positions, in a single request, there could be multiple position changes. We will implement the changes using the batchUpdate() method of Spring's JdbcTemplate.

Let's take a look at HibernateCardRepository, which looks like the following:

```java
...
@Repository
public class HibernateCardRepository extends HibernateSupport<Card>
implements CardRepository {
  private JdbcTemplate jdbcTemplate;
  HibernateCardRepository(EntityManager entityManager,
      JdbcTemplate jdbcTemplate) {
    super(entityManager);
    this.jdbcTemplate = jdbcTemplate;
  }
  ...
  @Override
  public void changePositions(final List<CardPosition> cardPositions) {
    String sql = "update card set card_list_id=?, `position`=? where
    id=?";

    jdbcTemplate.batchUpdate(sql, new BatchPreparedStatementSetter() {
      @Override
      public void setValues(PreparedStatement ps, int i)
          throws SQLException {
        CardPosition cardPosition = cardPositions.get(i);
        ps.setLong(1, cardPosition.getCardListId().value());
        ps.setInt(2, cardPosition.getPosition());
        ps.setLong(3, cardPosition.getCardId().value());
      }
      @Override
      public int getBatchSize() {
        return cardPositions.size();
      }
    });
  }
}
```

As you can see, besides EntityManager, we ask Spring to inject an instance of JdbcTemplate through the constructor. Inside the changePositions() method, we create an implementation of BatchPreparedStatementSetter to set the values for each SQL query, by using an instance of java.sql.PreparedStatement, and provide the size of the batch through the getBatchSize() method. In this way, we can update the positions of multiple cards in a single update SQL statement.

The implementation of changing card list positions is similar to the implementation of changing card positions. We won't list it here. Here is the commit record for implementing the board page:

Figure 12.7: Implementing the board page commit

Implementing real-time updates with WebSocket

There are two parts we need to build to implement real-time communication—one is the client side and the other is the server side. As mentioned earlier, we will use SockJS (http:/ /sockjs.org) to implement the client side and Spring's WebSocket implementation on the server side.

Introduction to SockJS

Under the hood, the SockJS client will try to use the native WebSocket that the browser provides. If it is not available, it will fall back to other transport protocols, such as XHR-Streaming and XHR-Polling. Its API is very simple to use. The following is an example of establishing a WebSocket connection with a local server at the /rt path:

```
let socket = new SockJS('http://localhost:8080/rt')
socket.onopen = function (event) {
  // Connection established
  console.log(socket.readyState)
}

socket.onmessage = function (message) {
  // Message received via WebSocket
}

socket.onclose = function (event) {
  // Connection closed
}
```

```
socket.onerror = function (error) {
  // An error occurred
}
```

As you can see, it has four event handlers:

- The `onopen()` event handler will be invoked when the connection to the server has been established. At this stage, the `readyState` property of the `SockJS` object has been changed from `SockJS.COLLECTING` to `SockJS.OPEN`.
- The `onmessage()` event handler will be invoked when the client receives a message from the server side.
- The `onclose()` event handler will be invoked when the WebSocket connection has been closed.
- The `onerror()` event handler will be invoked when an error occurs.

Besides these event handlers, SockJS provides the `send()` method for the client to send data to the server. The API is quite simple. It looks like this:

```
socket.send(data)
```

The data can be a string, blob, `ArrayBuffer`, or `ArrayBufferView`.

Also, SockJS provides a `close()` method for the client to close the connection from the server, as follows:

```
socket.close()
```

The biggest advantage of SockJS is that its API follows the HTML5 WebSocket API closely. It provides a generic base layer for applications to build their own communication modes. If you are interested in the latest WebSocket API specification, you can find it here: `https://html.spec.whatwg.org/multipage/web-sockets.html`.

Introduction to Spring WebSocket

Spring's WebSocket implementation provides an abstraction layer on top of other WebSocket runtimes, such as Tomcat, Jetty, and Undertow. With Spring's abstraction, creating a WebSocket server is as simple as implementing the `WebSocketHandler` interface. Spring also provides base classes, such as `TextWebSocketHandler` and `BinaryWebSocketHandler`, that we can extend directly.

Besides implementing `WebSocketHandler`, we will also need to provide the configuration so that Spring knows how to bootstrap our WebSocket server. We can do this by implementing the `WebSocketConfigurer` interface. Here is an example of how a simple WebSocket configuration looks:

```
@Configuration
@EnableWebSocket
public class WebSocketConfig implements WebSocketConfigurer {

  @Override
  public void registerWebSocketHandlers(WebSocketHandlerRegistry registry)
{
    registry.addHandler(realTimeHandler(), "/ws");
  }

  @Bean
  public WebSocketHandler realTimeHandler() {
    return new RealTimeHandler();
  }
}
```

As you can see, we apply the `@EnableWebSocket` annotation to the configuration class and in the `registerWebSocketHandlers()` method, we register `realTimeHander` to the `/ws` path. In this way, requests sent to the `/ws` path will be handled by the `RealTimeHandler` class.

The channel-based communication pattern

As mentioned earlier the SockJS' API is generic. It doesn't force any communication pattern. What it does is provide a real-time connection between the clients and the server through WebSocket. This gives us the freedom to build the communication pattern that suits our application.

In our application, when multiple users open the same board, everything that happens on that board needs to be updated to all the other users automatically, without refreshing the page. For example, once a user adds a new card to the **Todo** list, that card should show up immediately in all other users' **Todo** lists. The communication here is a publish/subscribe pattern. The user who added the new card triggers the publishing of the new card added message on the server side. The server publishes this message to all the clients that have subscribed to this message. This message shouldn't be published to any other clients.

Besides the *new card added* message, we could have many other messages, for example, *new card list added card position changed*. If we require the clients to subscribe to each of these messages individually, there will be a lot of boilerplate code. In our application, this is unnecessary because everybody who has access to a board should be able to receive messages from that board.

So, instead of requiring the clients to subscribe to individual messages, we can create a message channel and send various messages to that channel. Clients that have subscribed to that channel will receive those messages. It is up to the clients to decide what to do with each message. A channel is simply a string that starts with /. We can name the channel whatever we want, as long as it is unique and makes sense to our application. For example, we can create a board channel called /board/1. 1 is the ID of the board.

With the board channel, everyone who opens a board will send a message to the server to subscribe to that board channel. After the user leaves the board, the client side will send another message to unsubscribe from that board channel.

Frontend implementation of the real-time client

In our implementation, we will create a RealTimeClient class to wrap a SockJS object to provide channel-based communication. We will bind the instance of this client to Vue.prototype.$rt so that all of the Vue components can access the real-time client via the instance's $rt property. The following is an overview of the RealTimeClient class.

Let's have a look at the frontend/src/real-time-client.js file:

```
import Vue from 'vue'
import SockJS from 'sockjs-client'

class RealTimeClient {
  constructor () {
    ...
  }
  init (serverUrl, token) {
    ...
  }
  logout () {
    ...
  }
  connect () {
    ...
  }
  subscribe (channel, handler) {
    ...
```

```
    }
    unsubscribe (channel, handler) {
      ...
    }
  }

  export default new RealTimeClient()
```

As you can see, besides the constructor, it provides the `init()`, `logout()`, `connect()`, `subscribe()`, and `unsubscribe()` APIs. The instance of `RealTimeClient` is the default export of `real-time-client.js`. In this way, there will only be one `RealTimeClient` instance in the application.

Inside the constructor, the properties of `RealTimeClient` are initialized, as shown here:

```
  constructor () {
    this.serverUrl = null
    this.token = null
    this.socket = null
    this.authenticated = false
    this.loggedOut = false
    this.$bus = new Vue()
    this.subscribeQueue = {
      /* channel: [handler1, handler2] */
    }
    this.unsubscribeQueue = {
      /* channel: [handler1, handler2] */
    }
  }
```

`serverUrl` is the URL of the WebSocket server and it is set to `null` by default. `token` is the real-time token that the client uses to perform authentication on the server side. It is a JWT token string. We will talk about JWTs in detail in the next section. The `socket` property is an instance of `SockJS`, which will be created inside the `connect()` method. The `authenticated` property is used to mark whether or not the client has been authenticated on the server side. The `loggedOut` property is used to indicate whether or not the user has logged out and the real-time client has been closed because of them logging out.

The `$bus` property is an instance of `Vue`. It serves as the internal event bus of the real-time client. `subscribeQueue` and `unsubscribeQueue` hold the subscribing and unsubscribing actions, respectively, before the real-time client has established a connection with the server. Once the connection is established, the real-time client will perform all of the subscribing and unsubscribing actions in the queue, and empty the queue. We will see how this can make using the real-time client a little bit easier.

The init() method is where we initialize the connection. It looks like the following:

```
init (serverUrl, token) {
  if (this.authenticated) {
    console.warn('[RealTimeClient] WS connection already authenticated.')
    return
  }
  console.log('[RealTimeClient] Initializing')
  this.serverUrl = serverUrl
  this.token = token
  this.connect()
}
```

As you can see, we put a guard at the beginning of the method to make sure that the connection won't be initialized again once the real-time client has been authenticated, that is, the connection has been established. At the end of this method, we call the connect() method to perform the actual connection initialization.

The logout() method, which looks like the following, is used to clear the state of the real-time client by resetting its properties to the initial values and then closing the socket:

```
logout () {
  console.log('[RealTimeClient] Logging out')
  this.subscribeQueue = {}
  this.unsubscribeQueue = {}
  this.authenticated = false
  this.loggedOut = true
  this.socket && this.socket.close()
}
```

The connect() method is where the connection between the real-time client and the server is established. It looks like the following:

```
connect () {
  console.log('[RealTimeClient] Connecting to ' + this.serverUrl)
  this.socket = new SockJS(this.serverUrl + '?token=' + this.token)
  this.socket.onopen = () => {
    this.authenticated = true
    this._onConnected()
  }
  this.socket.onmessage = (event) => {
    this._onMessageReceived(event)
  }
  this.socket.onerror = (error) => {
    this._onSocketError(error)
  }
  this.socket.onclose = (event) => {
```

```
    this._onClosed(event)
  }
}
```

As you can see, we establish the connection by creating an instance of `SockJS` with `serverUrl` and `token` as a query parameters. Then, we assign event handlers to the socket instance. We will not go into the details of every event handler here. You can find the implementation in the commit history.

The `subscribe()` method is the API that the clients of the real-time client will use to subscribe to the channel that they are interested in. It looks like the following:

```
subscribe (channel, handler) {
  if (!this._isConnected()) {
    this._addToSubscribeQueue(channel, handler)
    return
  }
  const message = {
    action: 'subscribe',
    channel
  }
  this._send(message)
  this.$bus.$on(this._channelEvent(channel), handler)
  console.log('[RealTimeClient] Subscribed to channel ' + channel)
}
```

As you can see, at the beginning of the method, we check whether the real-time client is connected to the server. If it isn't, we will add the `'subscribe'` action to the queue for processing once the connection is established or restored. Then, we call the internal `_send()` method to send the subscribe message to the server so that the server will add this client to the subscribers of the channel, and then we bind the `channel` message handler to the internal event bus so that, when there is a message from the server received, we will notify all of the handlers of this channel by using the internal event bus `$emit()` method. In this way, we can subscribe to a channel inside `BoardPage.vue`, as follows:

```
this.$rt.subscribe('/board/' + this.board.id, this.onRealTimeUpdated)
```

The `unsubscribe()` method is the opposite of the `subscribe()` method, as you can see here:

```
unsubscribe (channel, handler) {
  // Already logged out, no need to unsubscribe
  if (this.loggedOut) {
    return
  }
```

```
  if (!this._isConnected()) {
    this._addToUnsubscribeQueue(channel, handler)
    return
  }
  const message = {
    action: 'unsubscribe',
    channel
  }
  this._send(message)
  this.$bus.$off(this._channelEvent(channel), handler)
  console.log('[RealTimeClient] Unsubscribed from channel ' + channel)
}
```

As you can see, at the beginning of the method, we check whether the real-time client has already logged out or not. If it has already logged out, we don't need to perform an unsubscribe action anymore because, on the server side, once a real-time client is logged out, all of the subscribe actions will be cleared. When the real-time client isn't logged out, we will check whether it is connected. For an offline real-time client, the unsubscribe actions will be added to the queue for later processing. To unsubscribe from a channel, the real-time client will also send a message to the server with the action's value as `'unsubscribe'`. After that, we will remove the handler from the internal event bus.

As you can see, the implementation of the real-time client is quite straightforward. One thing that we haven't mentioned here is where we will invoke the init() method of the real-time client. Since there will be only one real-time client instance in the application, the perfect place to initialize the connection is inside the created() life cycle hook of App.vue.

Another question is—when should we do the initialization? As you can see, the init() method requires two parameters—serverUrl and token. We will pass these two values to the client from the server. A good place to put these two values is the response of the getMyData API (/api/me). Once the response is received, we will use the global event bus that we created in frontend/src/event-bus.js to notify App.vue.

The following is the change we made to App.vue:

```
<script>
export default {
  name: 'App',
  created () {
    this.$bus.$on('myDataFetched', myData => {
      // Initializing the real time connection
      this.$rt.init(myData.settings.realTimeServerUrl,
      myData.user.token)
    })
```

```
      }
   }
   </script>
```

As you can see, inside the `created()` hook of `App.vue`, we listen to the `myDataFetched` event and use the two values to initialize the real-time connection.

For other details of the frontend implementation of the real-time client, you can find them in the commit history.

Authenticating a real-time client with JWT

Spring's WebSocket implementation provides a `WebSocketSession` interface that allows you to access the authenticated user's information from the `WebSocketSession.getPrincipal()` method. When the user is not authenticated, the result of this method will be `null`. We can use this to determine whether the user has been authenticated or not, which is very convenient.

However, when we need to separate the real-time-related feature into a standalone application, we cannot use the `WebSocketSession.getPrincipla()` method to retrieve the authenticated user's information unless we set up a clustered session using Spring Session. But that's not the only way. We can also use JWT to perform the authentication.

In this section, we will introduce how to generate a JWT real-time token to perform authentication on a WebSocket connection in our application.

As mentioned earlier, the real-time token will be sent to the client in the response of the `/api/me` API. It is where we will generate the token with the user ID as the JWT subject. We will use the `jjwt` library (`https://github.com/jwtk/jjwt`) to generate and verify the token.

We will create `TokenManager` to isolate the logic for generating the JWT from the rest of the application. Here is how `com.taskagile.domain.common.security.TokenManager` looks:

```
@Component
public class TokenManager {
  private Key secretKey;
  public TokenManager(
      @Value("${app.token-secret-key}") String secretKey) {
    this.secretKey =
      Keys.hmacShaKeyFor(Decoders.BASE64.decode(secretKey));
  }
```

```
public String jwt(UserId userId) {
  return Jwts.builder()
    .setSubject(String.valueOf(userId.value()))
    .signWith(secretKey).compact();
}
public UserId verifyJwt(String jws) {
  String userIdValue = Jwts.parser().setSigningKey(secretKey)
    .parseClaimsJws(jws).getBody().getSubject();
  return new UserId(Long.valueOf(userIdValue));
}
}
```

As you can see, we will inject a secret key that will be added to `application.properties` into `TokenManager`. There are two methods in this class, `jwt()`, which is used to generate a JWT string based on `UserId` and the `verifyJwt()` method, which is used to verify the token we receive from the client.

Here is the change to `MeApiController`:

```
@Controller
public class MeApiController {
  ...
  private TokenManager tokenManager;
  public MeApiController(...TokenManager tokenManager) {
    ...
    this.tokenManager = tokenManager;
  }

  @GetMapping("/api/me")
  public ResponseEntity<ApiResult> getMyData(@CurrentUser SimpleUser
  currentUser) {
    ...
    String realTimeToken = tokenManager.jwt(user.getId());
    return MyDataResult.build(user, teams, boards, realTimeServerUrl,
    realTimeToken);
  }
}
```

As you can see, we inject the instance of `TokenManager` and use it to generate a JWT string as a real-time token.

Once the real-time client initializes the connection with the token, our implementation of WebSocketHandler will receive the request in its afterConnectionEstablished() method. That's where we will perform the authentication by verifying the real-time token.

Our implementation of WebSocketHandler is a request dispatcher, called WebSocketRequestDispatcher. It has the following responsibilities:

- Authenticating the request once the connection is established
- Dispatching requests to channel handlers, which we will discuss in detail in the next section
- Cleaning up the session once a connection is closed

For now, we will only implement the first one. Here is how WebSocketRequestDispatcher looks:

```
@Component
public class WebSocketRequestDispatcher extends TextWebSocketHandler {
  private TokenManager tokenManager;
  public WebSocketRequestDispatcher(TokenManager tokenManager,
      ChannelHandlerResolver channelHandlerResolver) {
    this.tokenManager = tokenManager;
  }

  @Override
  public void afterConnectionEstablished(WebSocketSession
  webSocketSession) {
    log.debug("WebSocket connection established");
    RealTimeSession session = new RealTimeSession(webSocketSession);
    String token = session.getToken();

    try {
      UserId userId = tokenManager.verifyJwt(token);
      session.addAttribute("userId", userId);
      session.reply("authenticated");
    } catch (JwtException exception) {
      log.debug("Invalid JWT token value: {}", token);
      session.fail("authentication failed");
    }
  }
}
```

As you can see, we inject the instance of `TokenManager` into the request dispatcher, and use it to verify the token received inside the `afterConnectionEstablished()` method. `RealTimeSession` is a wrapper over `WebSocketSession` to provide some convenient methods.

With the implementation of `WebSocketRequestDispatcher`, our real-time client can be authenticated. Let's commit the code, and here is the commit record:

Figure 12.8: Implementing the real-time client commit

Server implementation of channel handlers

Now, let's start the rest of the implementation of our real-time communication on the server side. As introduced earlier, we build the communication using a channel-based pattern, but the default API that `WebSocketHandler` provides doesn't have the concept of the channel. It defines a generic interface. We will need to extend it.

As mentioned earlier, our implementation of this interface is `WebSocketRequestDispatcher`. It is inspired by Spring MVC's `DispatcherServlet`. Inside the `handleTextMessage()` method of `WebSocketRequestDispatcher`, we will ask `ChannelHandlerResolver` to find the channel handler that is registered to handle the message sent to the specified channel. Once the channel handler is located, we will use corresponding `ChannelHandlerInvoker` to invoke the channel handler's action method that is bound to process the message. When the channel handler or the action method isn't found, the server will send an error message to the client. Otherwise, the action method of the channel handler will take over the processing of the message.

The following is a diagram to show `WebSocketRequestDispatcher` and its dependencies:

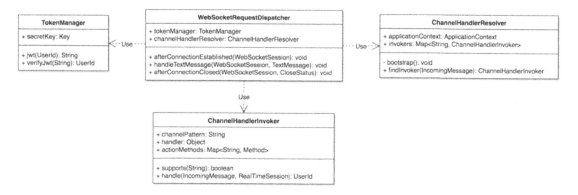

Figure 12.9: WebSocketRequestDispatcher and its dependencies

We will not dig into the details of these classes. You can find them in the commit record. Instead, let's take a look at the handler of
the `com.taskagile.web.socket.handlers.BoardChannelHandler` board channel, which looks like the following:

```java
@ChannelHandler("/board/*")
public class BoardChannelHandler {

  @Action("subscribe")
  public void subscribe(RealTimeSession session, @ChannelValue String
  channel) {
    log.debug("RealTimeSession[{}] Subscribe to channel `{}`",
    session.id(), channel);
    SubscriptionHub.subscribe(session, channel);
  }

  @Action("unsubscribe")
  public void unsubscribe(RealTimeSession session, @ChannelValue String
  channel) {
    log.debug("RealTimeSession[{}] Unsubscribe from channel `{}`",
    session.id(), channel);
    SubscriptionHub.unsubscribe(session, channel);
  }
}
```

As you can see, this `BoardChannelHandler` is a simple Java class. You don't need to extend any base class or implement any interface. All you need to do is to apply the `@ChannelHandler` annotation at the class level and apply the `@Action` annotation to the methods that will process the request.

The two parameters passed in the `subscribe()` action method and the `unsubscribe()` action method are passed by `ChannelHandlerInvoker`. This is inspired by the way that Spring MVC passes parameters to controllers' methods. If you do not need the invoker to pass the `RealTimeSession` instance or the channel, you simply do not add it as a parameter of the action method.

As you might remember, in the `subscribe()` method of `RealTimeClient`, the message we send to the server has two parameters, action, and channel:

```
subscribe (channel, handler) {
  ...
  const message = {
    action: 'subscribe',
    channel
  }
  this._send(message)
  ...
}
```

The `channel` parameter will match the one we specify in `@ChannelHandler("/board/*")`. The `action` parameter will match the value we specify in `@Action("subscribe")`. You can create actions other than `subscribe` and `unsubscribe` in the `channel` handler.

Due to the scope of this book, we will only implement the real-time update of adding a new card. In a future version of TaskAgile, we will add the rest of the real-time updates. You can find the details of how to perform the real-time update of adding a new card in the frontend in the following commit record:

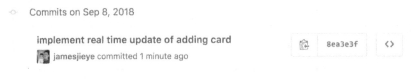

Figure 12.10: Implementing real-time update of adding card commit

Fixes at the end

Let's have a look at the following fixes:

- **Fix—switch board from menu does not work**: The implementation
  of `BoardPage.vue` doesn't work when we switch boards from the **Boards** menu
  in the header. The cause of the issue is that we only load the board when we
  enter the router. After that, switching boards using the Board menu doesn't really
  trigger the router entering, instead, it triggers an update to the router. The fix is
  to move the logic for loading the board data into a standalone method and
  invoke it from both the `beforeRouteEnter()` navigation guard and the
  `beforeRouteUpdate()` navigation guard:

Figure 12.11: Fix switch board from menu not work commit

- **Fix—add missing mapping of the board page**:

Figure 12.12: Fix add missing mapping of board page commit

Summary

In this chapter, we implemented the board page. We used CSS3 Flexbox to design the layout so that the height of the board can be stretched to fill up the screen without using JavaScript hacks. We also implemented real-time communication based on SockJS and Spring's WebSocket API.

We introduced the way to perform batch updates to the database by using Spring's `JdbcTemplate`, as well as the way to authenticate requests using JSON Web Tokens, based on the `jjwt` library.

In the next chapter, we will see how to implement the card window.

File Processing and Scalability - Playing with Cards

13

In this chapter, we will focus on implementing the card modal window. As with Trello's card, in TaskAgile, each card will have a unique URL that allows us to open it directly. Users will be able to change the card title, edit the description, upload attachments, and add comments to a card.

In this chapter, we will learn how to do the following:

- Add Markdown format support to the card description
- Handle file uploads on the client side and the server side
- Create thumbnails with GraphicMagick
- Scale file storage with AWS S3
- Track activities asynchronously with AMQP

Building the frontend of the card modal

In this section, we will focus on implementing the frontend of the card modal window. Instead of opening cards in a standalone page, opening a card in a modal window is very convenient for browsing cards. When you open a card to check its details, you stay on the same board page with everything else unchanged. This will help you focus, avoiding distractions caused by jumping between pages.

The UI of the card modal window

Now, let's take a look at the UI of the card modal window. *Figure 13.1* shows its UI design:

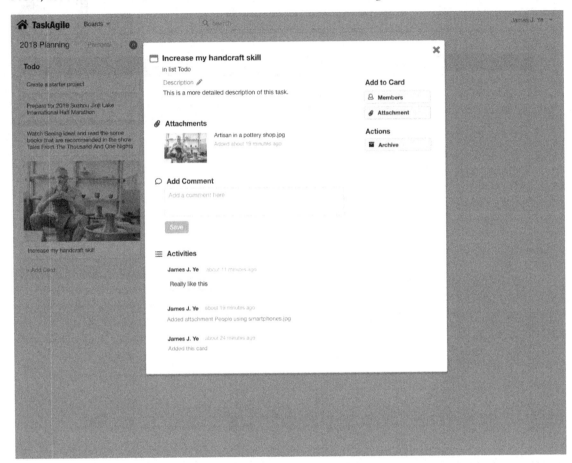

Figure 13.1: UI of the card modal window

As you can see, the card opened in a modal window with a dark transparent mask behind it. The title of the card is showing at the top of the modal window. You will also be able to check the title to enable the edit mode, which we will talk about later. Under the title is the description of the card. You can click the edit icon to open the edit description form, and when there are attachments added to the card, they will show up as a list under the description. When the attachment is an image, the thumbnail of the image will show up in the preview section. Otherwise, the file type will show up in the preview section.

For every card, you will be able to add comments, and they will show up in the **Activities** list. In the **Activities** list, other activities will show up too, including adding a card, changing the title, changing the description, and adding attachments.

On the right-hand side of the modal window are the control buttons. You can click the **Members** button to assign a member to the card. You can click the **Attachment** button to upload files. You can click the **Archive** button to archive the card. In this version of TaskAgile, we will only implement the adding attachments feature.

The layout of the card modal window

We're building the card modal window based on Bootstrap's modal plugin, and the layout of the card modal is simple, as you can see from the layout diagram here:

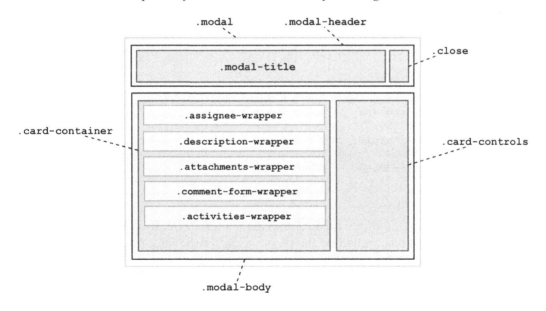

Figure 13.2: The layout of the card modal window

The card title will be placed inside the .modal-title element, and inside .modal-body, we will use Flexbox to put the .card-container element and the .card-controls element side by side, with the width of .card-controls fixed, and .card-container takes all the remaining space using flex-grow. For the details of the UI layout, you can check the commit history on GitHub.

Router for board URL and card URL

We will give each card a unique URL so that users can use that URL to open the card directly, and a card URL will not contain any board information so that when a card is moved between boards, the card URL will always be able to open that card correctly. We will implement the moving of cards between boards feature in a future version.

The card URL will use this format: https://taskagile.com/card/{cardId}/{card-title}. For example, the URL of the *Increase my handcraft skill* card, whose ID is 4, will be this: https://taskagile.com/card/4/increase-my-handcraft-skill.

So, how are we going to use the card URL to open a card and also have the board fully loaded behind the mask? The answer is by using vue-router. We can add the card route to router.js, as shown in the following:

```
...
export default new Router({
  ...
  routes: [...
  {
    path: '/board/:boardId',
    name: 'board',
    component: BoardPage
  }, {
    path: '/card/:cardId/:cardTitle',
    name: 'card',
    component: BoardPage
  }]
})
```

As you can see, component of the card route is also BoardPage. In this way, requests that go to the card URL will be handled by the BoardPage component. This is the first step to the route board URL and card URL. We will need to refactor BoardPage to make both routes work.

Previously, we relied on the following navigation guards of `vue-router` to trigger the loading of the board as well as unsubscribing from the real-time update channel:

```
beforeRouteEnter (to, from, next) {
  next(vm => {
    vm.loadBoard()
  })
},
beforeRouteUpdate (to, from, next) {
  next()
  this.unsubscribeFromRealTimeUpdate()
  this.loadBoard()
},
beforeRouteLeave (to, from, next) {
  next()
  this.unsubscribeFromRealTimeUpdate()
}
```

Right now, because we map two paths, one for the board URL and the other for the card URL, to the `BoardPage` component, the `vue-router` library would not invoke the `beforeRouteUpdate` guard when we open the page with a board URL and then open a card, close it, and then switch to another card, or when we open the page using a card URL and then switch to another board using the **Boards** menu at the top. According to the documentation of `vue-router` (`https://router.vuejs.org/guide/advanced/navigation-guards.html#per-route-guard`), the `beforeRouteUpdate` guard will be invoked when we switch from `/board/1` to `/board/2`, but not when we switch from `/board/1` to `/card/1/card-title1`.

Therefore, we cannot rely on the navigation guards to detect the changes to the route when we stay on the `BoardPage` page. We will need to watch the `this.$route` object to detect the route change, as in the following:

```
<script>
...
export default {
  name: 'BoardPage',
  ...
  watch: {
    '$route' (to, from) {
      // Switch from one board to another
      if (to.name === from.name && to.name === 'board') {
        this.unsubscribeFromRealTimeUpdate(from.params.boardId)
        this.loadBoard(to.params.boardId)
      }
      // Open a card
      if (to.name === 'card' && from.name === 'board') {
```

```
                this.loadCard(to.params.cardId).then(() => {
                  this.openCardWindow()
                })
            }
            // Close a card
            if (to.name === 'board' && from.name === 'card') {
              this.closeCardWindow()
              this.openedCard = {}
            }
        }
      },
      ...
  }
</script>
```

As you can see, we use `to.name` and `from.name` to detect three scenarios: switching between boards, opening a card, and closing a card. With this watcher, we do not need the navigation guards, `beforeRouteEnter` and `beforeRouteUpdate`. We will still need the `beforeRouteLeave` guard to detect the exit from the board page, which is not detected by the `$route` watcher.

Inside the `mounted()` hook of the `BoardPage` component instance, we will need to trigger the data loading of the board page when users open a board URL or a card URL directly or refresh the page. The refactored `mounted()` method looks like the following:

```
mounted () {
  console.log('[BoardPage] Mouted')
  this.loadInitial()
  this.$el.addEventListener('click', this.dismissActiveForms)
  // Closing card window will change back to board URL
  $('#cardModal').on('hide.bs.modal', () => {
    this.$router.push({name: 'board', params: {boardId: this.board.id}})
  })
}
```

As you can see, we add two logics into this method. We call the `loadInitial()` method to load the data from the server when `BoardPage` is mounted, and we also bind to the close event of the card modal window to change the URL back to the board URL.

The following shows the `loadInitial()` method, as well as the `loadCard()` and `loadBoard()` methods:

```
methods: {
  loadInitial () {
    // The board page can be opened through a card URL.
    if (this.$route.params.cardId) {
```

```
        console.log('[BoardPage] Opened with card URL')
        this.loadCard(this.$route.params.cardId).then(card => {
          return this.loadBoard(card.boardId)
        }).then(() => {
          this.openCardWindow()
        })
      } else {
        console.log('[BoardPage] Opened with board URL')
        this.loadBoard(this.$route.params.boardId)
      }
    },
    ...
  }
```

Inside the `loadInitial()` method, we check to see if it is a card URL or a board URL. When it is a card URL, we will call the `loadCard()` method first which returns a promise, and once the card is retrieved from the server, we use it to load the board. Once the board is loaded, we call the `openCardWindow()` method to show the card modal window. On the other hand, when it is a board URL, we load the board as we used to do, and in order to chain the actions, both the `loadCard()` method and `loadBoard()` method return a promise.

Now, let's take a look at the `loadCard()` method, which looks like the following:

```
methods: {
  ...
  loadCard (cardId) {
    return new Promise(resolve => {
      console.log('[BoardPage] Loading card ' + cardId)
      cardService.getCard(cardId).then(card => {
        this.openedCard = card
        resolve(card)
      }).catch(error => {
        notify.error(error.message)
      })
    })
  },
  ...
}
```

As you can see, all this method does is call the `getCard()` method of `cardService` to retrieve the card information and assign it to the `openedCard` property of the component. This `openedCard` property is used to pass the card information to the `CardModal.vue` component that we will create.

Implement auto-resize of card title editing

Inside the `CardModal.vue` component, we will display the card title in a `textarea` element, which will be in edit mode once you click on the title. *Figure 13.3* shows how the edit mode looks:

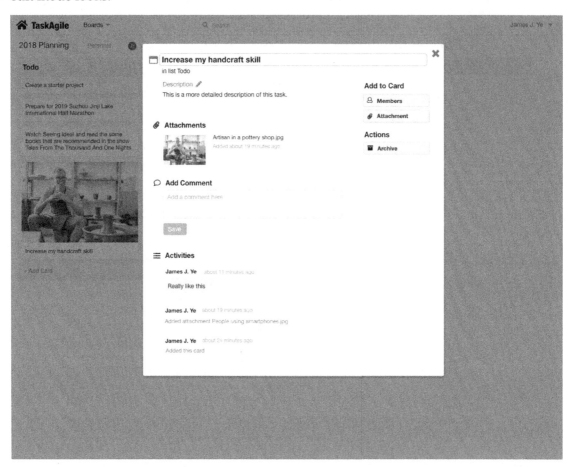

Figure 13.3: Card title edit mode

The `textarea` of the card title needs to auto-resize so that when a user types more characters it will grow, and when the user deletes characters it will decrease its height to make it always fit the card title, and once a user presses the *Enter* key, we will save the card title to the server.

To do the auto-resize, we will use `autosize` (`https://github.com/jackmoore/autosize`), which is small, standalone, and easy to use.

The following shows how to auto-resize, as implemented in `frontend/src/modals/CardModal.vue`:

```
<template>
  <div class="modal" id="cardModal">
    <textarea id="cardTitle" class="auto-size" v-model="title"
      @keydown.enter.prevent="changeCardTitle"></textarea>
  </div>
</template>

<script>
import autosize from 'autosize'
...
export default {
  name: 'CardModal',
    ...
  mounted () {
    setTimeout(() => {
      autosize($('.auto-size'))
    }, 0)

    $('#cardModal').on('show.bs.modal', () => {
      setTimeout(() => {
        autosize.update($('.auto-size'))
      }, 0)
      ...
    })
  },
    ...
}
</script>
```

As you can see, we add class `auto-size` to the `textarea`. In the `mounted()` method, we initialize the auto-resize ability of all the `.auto-size` elements by calling the `autosize()` method inside a `setTimeout()` callback. When the card modal window is opened, we call the `autosize.update()` method to resize the `textarea` to the required height.

Implementing support of the Markdown format

Markdown format is popular. It is simple, easy to read, and widely supported. That's why we choose it as the format of the card description.

We will convert the card description written in Markdown format to HTML on the fly so that we do not need to store converted HTML in the database. To implement this feature, we will use the library, Showdown (`https://github.com/showdownjs/showdown`).

The following is how to use Showdown to support the Markdown format:

```
<template>
  <div class="modal" id="cardModal">
    ...
    <div class="description" v-show="description &&
    !editingDescription"
      v-html="descriptionHtml"></div>
    ...
  </div>
</template>

<script>
...
import showdown from 'showdown'

showdown.setOption('strikethrough', true)
showdown.setOption('tables', true)
const markdownConverter = new showdown.Converter()

export default {
  name: 'CardModal',
  ...
  computed: {
    descriptionHtml () {
      if (!this.description) {
        return ''
      }
      return markdownConverter.makeHtml(this.description)
    },
    ...
  },
  ...
}
</script>
```

As you can see, we create a `showdown` converter instance which can be reused, and we use `v-html` to bind the `.description` element to the converted HTML code, which is a computed property, called `descriptionHtml`. Inside the property, we call the `makeHtml()` method of the markdown converter instance. That's it. We now support Markdown format in our card description.

Implementing file uploads

In the card modal window, once a user clicks the **Attachment** button, the native file manager window will show up. Once the user selects a file, the frontend will send that file to the server and receive the saved file's information.

There are two parts to implementing this file upload feature. One is that we need to build a consistent UI of the **Attachment** button. By default, the UI of the element `<input type="file" />` looks different in Chrome, Firefox, Safari, and IE, which is the only HTML element that will trigger the opening of the native file manager window. The second one is to send the file. Within `<form>`, we can add the file input to send the selected file when the form is submitted. However, in our card modal window, we need to send the file immediately after it is selected. Users won't need to click another button to do that.

To implement this file upload feature, we will use the library, jQuery File Upload (`https://github.com/blueimp/jQuery-File-Upload`), and we will create a standalone component, called `Uploader.vue`, to isolate the library from the other parts of the application.

The following is how the `<template>` part of `Uploader.vue` looks:

```
<template>
  <div class="fileinput-button">
    <font-awesome-icon :icon="icon" class="icon" v-if="icon"/> {{ label }}
    <input :id="id" type="file" name="file" multiple>
  </div>
</template>
```

As you can see, we wrap the file input inside a `.fileinput-button` element with an icon and the label. The `multiple` attribute indicates that users will be able to select multiple files in the native file manager window.

jQuery File Upload will make this file input invisible by applying the following style to it:

```
.fileinput-button input {
  position: absolute;
  top: 0;
  right: 0;
```

```
        margin: 0;
        opacity: 0;
        font-size: 200px !important;
        direction: ltr;
        cursor: pointer;
    }
```

In this way, the user will only see the button's icon and label, but will still be able to click the button to open the native file browser.

The following is the `<script>` part of `Uploader.vue`:

```
<script>
...
export default {
    name: 'Uploader',
    props: ['id', 'url', 'icon', 'label'],
    watch: {
        url () {
            if (!this.url) {
                return
            }

            $('#' + this.id).fileupload({
                url: this.url,
                dataType: 'json',
                add: (e, data) => {
                    this.$emit('uploading', data.files[0])
                    data.submit()
                },
                fail: (e, data) => {
                    this.$emit('failed',
                    data._response.jqXHR.responseJSON.message)
                },
                done: (e, data) => {
                    this.$emit('uploaded', data.result)
                },
                progress: (e, data) => {
                    let progress = parseInt(data.loaded / data.total * 100, 10)
                    this.$emit('progress', progress)
                }
            })
        }
    }
}
</script>
```

This `Uploader` component has four properties, `id`, which is used to specify the ID attribute of the file input, `url`, which is used to specify the server's endpoint that will receive the uploaded file, `icon`, which is used to display an icon in the button, as well as `label`, which is used to specify the label of the **Upload** button.

We add a watcher to the `url` property. Its value is different for each card. For upload card attachment, the value of the `url` property will be in this format: `/api/cards/{cardId}/attachments`. As you can see in the `url` watcher method, we initiate the jQuery File Upload plugin for the file input. The `add`, `fail`, `done`, and `progress` methods are the event listeners that will be invoked when a file is added to the upload queue, when an upload has failed, when an upload is done, and when an upload is in progress, respectively, and once an event listener is invoked, we will publish a corresponding event to the client of the `Uploader` component, which is the `CardModal` in this case.

The following is how the `Uploader` component looks in `CardModal.vue`:

```
<template>
  <div class="modal" id="cardModal">
    ...
    <uploader
      id="cardAttachment"
      :url="attachmentUploadUrl"
      icon="paperclip"
      label="Attachment"
      @uploading="onUploadingAttachment"
      @progress="onUploadingProgressUpdated"
      @failed="onAttachmentUploadFailed"
      @uploaded="onAttachmentUploaded"/>
    ...
  </div>
</template>
```

For the `id` property, we use a static ID, and the `url` property is bound to the `attachmentUploadUrl`, which is a computed property. We also listen to the four events that `Uploader` emits, as in the following:

```
<script>
...
export default {
  name: 'CardModal',
  ...
  data () {
    return {
      ...
```

```
              uploadingCount: 0
         ...
    }
  },
  computed: {
    ...
    attachmentUploadUrl () {
      return this.card.id ? '/api/cards/' + this.card.id + '/attachments' :
''
    }
  },
  ...
  methods: {
    ...
    onUploadingAttachment () {
      this.uploadingCount++
    },
    onUploadingProgressUpdated (progress) {
      console.log('Uploading progress: ' + progress + '%')
    },
    onAttachmentUploadFailed (error) {
      this.uploadingCount--
      notify.error(error)
    },
    onAttachmentUploaded (attachment) {
      this.uploadingCount--
      this.attachments.push(attachment)
      ...
    },
    ...
  }
}
</script>
```

As you can see, we use a counter, `uploadingCount`, to track if there is any file being uploaded. Inside the `onUploadingAttachment` method, we increase it every time the uploading event is triggered, and we decrease it accordingly inside the `onAttachmentUploadFailed` method and the `onAttachmentUploaded` method, and once a file is uploaded successfully, we will add it into the attachments array so that it will be shown in the attachments list.

For other parts of the `CardModal.vue`, such as adding comments, and listing activities, you can find the details in the commit record.

Building the backend of the card modal

Now, let's focus on implementing the backend of the card modal window, and start with the API handlers.

APIs for the card modal

The following are the APIs that we will need to create for the card modal window:

- The API to get a card
- The API to change the card title
- The API to change the card description
- The API to add comments to a card
- The API to get the activities from a card
- The API to add attachments to a card
- The API to get attachments from a card

Let's take a look at the individual APIs:

Get card API

This will be a GET request sent to /api/cards/{cardId}. Through this API, we will get the following card information:

```
{
  "id": 4,
  "title": "Increase my handcraft skill",
  "boardId": 1,
  "description": "",
  "cardListId": 1
}
```

Change card title API

This will be a PUT request sent to /api/cards/{cardId}/title with a payload similar to the following:

```
{
  "title": "This is a new card title"
}
```

The response of the API will be simply an HTTP status of 200 when the change succeeds.

Change card description API

This will be a PUT request sent to /api/cards/{cardId}/description with a payload similar to the following:

```
{
    "description": "This is the card's description."
}
```

The response of the API will be simply an HTTP status of 200 when the change succeeds.

Add comment API

This will be a POST request sent to /api/cards/{cardId}/comments with a payload similar to the following:

```
{
    "comment": "This is a test comment."
}
```

The response of the API will be similar to the following when it succeeds:

```
{
    "id": 1,
    "detail": "{\"comment\":\"This is a test comment.\"}",
    "type": "add-comment",
    "userId": 1,
    "cardId": 4,
    "boardId": 1,
    "createdDate": 1538239135000
}
```

Get activities API

This will be a GET request sent to /api/cards/{cardId}/activities.

The response of the API will be similar to the following:

```
{
  "activities": [{
    "id": 3,
    "type": "add-comment",
    "detail": "{\"comment\": \"This is a test comment.\"}",
    "userId": 1,
    "createdDate": 1538239135000
  }]
}
```

Add attachment API

This will be a POST request with the content type *multipart/form-data*, sent to /api/cards/{cardId}/attachments, and the file will be sent in a parameter named file. The response of the API will be similar to the following:

```
{
  "id": 5,
  "fileName": " Artisan in a pottery shop.jpg",
  "fileType": "jpg",
  "fileUrl": "/local-file/attachments/1538189609099.b2e98bbb-0a9d-49ee-
  bff2-2a4a14b38dba.jpg",
  "previewUrl": "/local-file/attachments/1538189609099.b2e98bbb-0a9d-
  49ee-bff2-2a4a14b38dba.thumbnail.jpg",
  "userId": 1,
  "createdDate": 1538189609000
}
```

previewUrl will be used for previewing the attachment when it is an image. When the file is not an image, its value will be an empty string.

Get attachments API

This will be a GET request sent to /api/cards/{cardId}/attachments with a response similar to the following:

```
{
  "attachments": [{
    "id": 5,
    "fileName": " Artisan in a pottery shop.jpg",
    "fileType": "jpg",
    "fileUrl": "/local-file/attachments/1538189609099.b2e98bbb-0a9d-
    49ee-bff2-2a4a14b38dba.jpg",
```

```
      "previewUrl": "/local-file/attachments/1538189609099.b2e98bbb-0a9d-
      49ee-bff2-2a4a14b38dba.thumbnail.jpg",
      "userId": 1,
      "createdDate": 1538189609000
   }]
 }
```

In the next few sections, we will focus on the implementation details of the add attachment API to see how to save an uploaded file on the server or save it to AWS S3, as well as generating a thumbnail when an attachment is an image.

Saving the uploaded file

In this section, we will discuss how to save the uploaded file to the server's local file system, as well as save it to AWS S3.

The main API of file saving is the `FileStorage` interface, which has three methods:

- `saveAsTempFile(String, MultipartFile): TempFile`
- `saveTempFile(TempFile)`
- `saveUploaded(String, MultipartFile): String`

The first method, `saveAsTempFile()`, is used to save the `MultipartFile` instance to the server's `temp` folder, which is specified in `application.properties`. This is useful when we need to create a thumbnail image before saving the file to S3. The second method, `saveTempFile()`, is used to save the temporary file to the final location, and the last method, `saveUploaded()`, is used to save the uploaded `MultipartFile` to the final location.

There are two implementations of `FileStorage`. They are `LocalFileStorage` and `S3FileStorage`. *Figure 13.4* shows the relationships between `FileStorage` and its implementations:

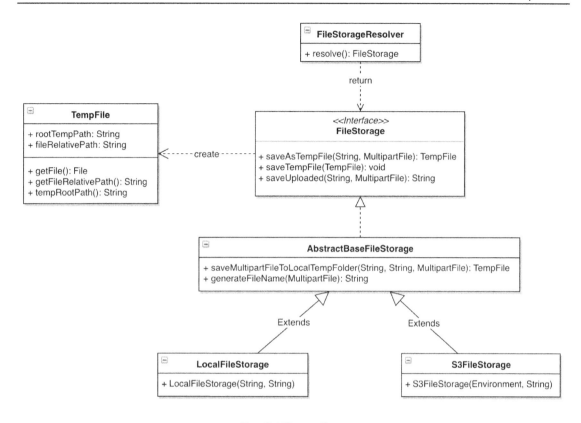

Figure 13.4: File storage diagram

`FileStorageResolver` is responsible for finding what is the active file storage and returning the corresponding `FileStorage` instance. It will look for the `app.file-storage.active` property to decide the active file storage. You can find details of the file saving in the commit history on GitHub.

Generating thumbnails for images

In this section, we will introduce a way to generate thumbnails for images of extension
.jpg, jpeg, and .png. We will create a class called ThumbnailCreator to take care of the
thumbnail creation. *Figure 13.5* shows its relationship with its dependency,
ImageProcessor, which is responsible for the actual image resizing and retrieving the
image's actual size:

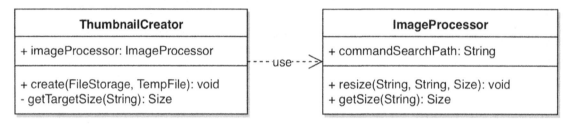

Figure 13.5: ThumbnailCreator diagram

The following is how the create() method of ThumbnailCreator looks:

```
...
@Component
public class ThumbnailCreator {
  ...
  public void create(FileStorage fileStorage, TempFile tempImageFile) {
    Assert.isTrue(tempImageFile.getFile().exists(), "Image file `" +
      tempImageFile.getFile().getAbsolutePath() + "` must exist");

    String ext =
    FilenameUtils.getExtension(tempImageFile.getFile().getName());
    if (!SUPPORTED_EXTENSIONS.contains(ext)) {
      throw new ThumbnailCreationException("Not supported image format
      for creating thumbnail");
    }
    ...
    try {
      ...
      String tempThumbnailFilePath =
       ImageUtils.getThumbnailVersion(tempImageFile.getFile()
      .getAbsolutePath());
      Size resizeTo = getTargetSize(sourceFilePath);
      imageProcessor.resize(sourceFilePath, tempThumbnailFilePath,
      resizeTo);

      fileStorage.saveTempFile(TempFile.create
      (tempImageFile.tempRootPath(), Paths.get
```

```
        (tempThumbnailFilePath)));
        // Delete temp thumbnail file
        Files.delete(Paths.get(tempThumbnailFilePath));
    } catch (Exception e) {
        log.error("Failed to create thumbnail for file `" +
        tempImageFile.getFile().
        getAbsolutePath() + "`", e);
        throw new ThumbnailCreationException("Creating thumbnail failed",
        e);
    }
  }
  ...
}
```

As you can see, in the beginning, we use assertion to make sure the source file, `tempImageFile`, exists on the server. Then we check whether we can support creating a thumbnail of the image by checking its extension, and we create the thumbnail's file path based on the source file by adding the `.thumbnail` part before the extension. For example, the source file path is `/data/temp/image.jpg`, so the thumbnail file path will be `/data/temp/image.thumbnail.jpg`.

We will also need to get the size of the thumbnail that we will create by calling the `getTargetSize()` method, which calls the `getSize()` method of `ImageProcessor` to get the source image file's actual size, and then calculates the thumbnail's size. After that, we invoke the `resize()` method of `ImageProcessor` to create the thumbnail that is saved as a temporary image file. After the thumbnail is saved to the file storage, we delete the thumbnail temporary file.

Now, let's take a look at `ImageProcessor`. Currently, `ImageProcessor` is defined as a class that relies on GraphicMagick (http://www.graphicsmagick.org/) to do all the heavy lifting. We use the library, `im4java`, to bridge the call between Java and the GraphicMagick commands.

Here is how the `resize()` method of `ImageProcessor` looks:

```
  ...
  @Component
  public class ImageProcessor {
    ...
    public void resize(String sourceFilePath, String targetFilePath, Size
    resizeTo) throws Exception {
      Assert.isTrue(resizeTo.getHeight() > 0, "Resize height must be
      greater than 0");
      Assert.isTrue(resizeTo.getWidth() > 0, "Resize width must be
      greater than 0");
```

```
        ConvertCmd cmd = new ConvertCmd(true);
        cmd.setSearchPath(commandSearchPath);
        IMOperation op = new IMOperation();
        op.addImage(sourceFilePath);
        op.quality(70d);
        op.resize(resizeTo.getWidth(), resizeTo.getHeight());
        op.addImage(targetFilePath);
        cmd.run(op);
    }
    ...
}
```

As you can see, all the `resize()` method does is to build a command similar to the following GraphicMagick `convert` command using `im4java` API:

```
gm convert -resize 300x185 -quality 70 source.jpg  source.thumbnail.jpg
```

The reason we need to set the search path of the `ConvertCmd` instance is because on Mac, when GraphicMagick is installed via Homebrew, the GraphicMagick command is in `/usr/local/bin`, rather than `/usr/bin`.

The following is how the `getSize()` method looks:

```
...
@Component
public class ImageProcessor {
  ...
  public Size getSize(String imagePath) throws IOException {
    try {
      ImageCommand cmd = new ImageCommand();
      cmd.setCommand("gm", "identify");
      cmd.setSearchPath(commandSearchPath);

      ArrayListOutputConsumer outputConsumer = new
      ArrayListOutputConsumer();
      cmd.setOutputConsumer(outputConsumer);

      IMOperation op = new IMOperation();
      op.format("%w,%h");
      op.addImage(imagePath);
      cmd.run(op);

      List<String> cmdOutput = outputConsumer.getOutput();
      String result = cmdOutput.get(0);
      Assert.hasText(result, "Result of command `gm identify` must not
      be blank");

      String[] dimensions = result.split(",");
```

```
      return new Size(NumberUtils.toInt(dimensions[0]),
      NumberUtils.toInt(dimensions[1]));
    } catch (Exception e) {
      throw new IOException("Failed to get image's height/width", e);
    }
  }
}
```

As you can see, all the `getSize()` method does is to build a command similar to the following:

gm identify -format '%w,%h' image.jpg

This command uses the GraphicMagicks identify command to retrieve the image's basic information—width and height.

GraphicMagick is a very powerful tool. Due to the limited scope of this book, we're only touching the surface of its power here. You can find more about what GraphicMagick can do on its home page: `http://www.graphicsmagick.org`.

Storing files to S3

To store files to S3, the best way is to use S3 SDK. To use the API of the SDK, we will need to create an S3 client that can be reused between multiple requests.

The following is how we initialize the `S3FileStorage`, our `FileStorage` implementation based on S3:

```
...
@Component("s3FileStorage")
public class S3FileStorage extends AbstractBaseFileStorage {

  private Environment environment;
  private String rootTempPath;
  private AmazonS3 s3;

  public S3FileStorage(Environment environment,
                       @Value("${app.file-storage.temp-folder}") String
    rootTempPath) {
    this.environment = environment;
    this.rootTempPath = rootTempPath;
    if ("s3FileStorage".equals(environment.getProperty("app.file-
    storage.active"))) {
      this.s3 = initS3Client();
    }
```

```
    }
    ...
  }
```

As you can see, in its constructor, we use a guard to initialize the S3 client only when the active file storage is S3.

This is how `initS3Client()` looks:

```
private AmazonS3 initS3Client() {
  String s3Region = environment.getProperty("app.file-storage.s3-
  region");
  Assert.hasText(s3Region, "Property `app.file-storage.s3-region` must
  not be blank");

  if (environment.acceptsProfiles("dev")) {
    log.debug("Initializing dev S3 client with access key and secret
    key");

    String s3AccessKey = environment.getProperty("app.file-storage.s3-
    access-key");
    String s3SecretKey = environment.getProperty("app.file-storage.s3-
    secret-key");

    Assert.hasText(s3AccessKey, "Property `app.file-storage.s3-access-
    key` must not be blank");
    Assert.hasText(s3SecretKey, "Property `app.file-storage.s3-secret-
    key` must not be blank");

    BasicAWSCredentials awsCredentials = new
    BasicAWSCredentials(s3AccessKey, s3SecretKey);
    AWSStaticCredentialsProvider credentialsProvider = new
    AWSStaticCredentialsProvider(awsCredentials);

    AmazonS3ClientBuilder builder = AmazonS3ClientBuilder.standard();
    builder.setRegion(s3Region);
    builder.withCredentials(credentialsProvider);
    return builder.build();
  } else {
    log.debug("Initializing default S3 client using IAM role");
    return AmazonS3ClientBuilder.standard()
      .withCredentials(new InstanceProfileCredentialsProvider(false))
      .withRegion(s3Region)
      .build();
  }
}
```

As you can see, we use `AmazonS3ClientBuilder` to create the client instance. We provide two pieces of information to the builder. One is the region, which is configured in our `application.properties`. The other is the credentials. Since our application will be pushed to Amazon's EC2, we have two options with the credentials. One is to use the access key + secret key to create `BasicAWSCredentials`. The other is to use the IAM role defined in the EC2 instance to provide the credential information, and in our case, when we're in dev environment, which will be on our laptop, we use the access key + secret key. When we're running on the server, we will use the IAM role.

The following is `S3FileStorage` implementation of the `saveAsTempFile()` method:

```
public TempFile saveAsTempFile(String folder, MultipartFile multipartFile)
{
   return saveMultipartFileToLocalTempFolder(rootTempPath, folder,
multipartFile);
}
```

As you can see, we simply call the `saveMultipartFileToLocalTempFolder()` method of `AbstractBaseFileStorage`.

Here is the implementation of the `saveTempFile()` method:

```
public void saveTempFile(TempFile tempFile) {
   Assert.notNull(s3, "S3FileStorage must be initialized properly");

   String fileKey = tempFile.getFileRelativePath();
   String bucketName = environment.getProperty("app.file-storage.s3-
     bucket-name");
   Assert.hasText(bucketName, "Property `app.file-storage.s3-bucket-
     name` must not be blank");

   try {
     log.debug("Saving file `{}` to s3", tempFile.getFile().getName());
     PutObjectRequest putRequest = new PutObjectRequest(bucketName,
     fileKey, tempFile.getFile());
     putRequest.withCannedAcl(CannedAccessControlList.PublicRead);
     s3.putObject(putRequest);
     log.debug("File `{}` saved to s3", tempFile.getFile().getName(),
     fileKey);
   } catch (Exception e) {
     log.error("Failed to save file to s3", e);
     throw new FileStorageException("Failed to save file `" +
     tempFile.getFile().getName() + "` to s3", e);
   }
}
```

In this method, we use the file's relative path as the bucket file key and get the bucket name from `application.properties`, and to upload a file to S3 with the S3 client is quite straightforward, as you can see. We create `PutObjectRequest` and make the file accessible publicly. After that, we call the client's `putObject()` method to save the file to S3.

Here is the implementation of the `saveUploaded()` method:

```
public String saveUploaded(String folder, MultipartFile multipartFile) {
  Assert.notNull(s3, "S3FileStorage must be initialized properly");

  String originalFileName = multipartFile.getOriginalFilename();
  ObjectMetadata metadata = new ObjectMetadata();
  metadata.setContentLength(multipartFile.getSize());
  metadata.setContentType(multipartFile.getContentType());
  metadata.addUserMetadata("Original-File-Name", originalFileName);
  String finalFileName = generateFileName(multipartFile);
  String s3ObjectKey = folder + "/" + finalFileName;

  String bucketName = environment.getProperty("app.file-storage.s3-
  bucket-name");
  Assert.hasText(bucketName, "Property `app.file-storage.s3-bucket-
  name` must not be blank");

  try {
    log.debug("Saving file `{}` to s3", originalFileName);
    PutObjectRequest putRequest = new PutObjectRequest(
      bucketName, s3ObjectKey, multipartFile.getInputStream(),
      metadata);
    putRequest.withCannedAcl(CannedAccessControlList.PublicRead);
    s3.putObject(putRequest);
    log.debug("File `{}` saved to s3 as `{}`", originalFileName,
    s3ObjectKey);
  } catch (Exception e) {
    log.error("Failed to save file to s3", e);
    throw new FileStorageException("Failed to save file `" +
    multipartFile.getOriginalFilename() + "` to s3", e);
  }

  return s3ObjectKey;
}
```

In this method, we save the uploaded file, the `MultipartFile` instance, to S3 directly. It is almost the same as the `saveTempFile()` method; the only difference is that we create an `ObjectMetadata` instance to add custom metadata, `Original-File-Name`, which will show up as a header, `x-amz-meta-original-file-name`, in the response of the request for getting this file.

The following is the commit record of implementing the card frontend and backend:

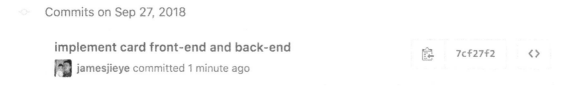

Figure 13.6: Implementing the card frontend and backend commit

Tracking activity asynchronously with AMQP

In this section, we will implement activity tracking using RabbitMQ (`https://www.rabbitmq.com`), which is an AMQP implementation. We will need to refactor the domain event publishing and listening mechanism that we implemented earlier and remove the Spring's application event-related code.

At a high level, the new domain event **Publisher**, `AmqpDomainEventPublisher`, will send domain events to RabbitMQ's **Exchange**, which is a fan-out exchange that binds to one or more queues. Once an **Exchange** receives a message, it will broadcast the message to all the queues it knows, and consumers who listen to those queues will receive the message. *Figure 13.7* shows the message flows using AMQP to implement the domain event publishing and consuming:

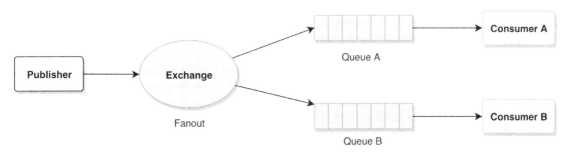

Figure 13.7: AMQP publisher and consumers

The following shows com.taskagile.config.MessageConfiguration, where we configure the exchange, queue, and binding:

```
...
@Configuration
public class MessageConfiguration {

  @Bean
  public FanoutExchange domainEventsExchange() {
    return new FanoutExchange("ta.domain.events", true, false);
  }

  @Bean
  public Queue activityTrackingQueue() {
    return new Queue("ta.activity.tracking", true);
  }

  @Bean
  public Binding bindingActivityTracking(FanoutExchange exchange, Queue
activityTrackingQueue) {
    return BindingBuilder.bind(activityTrackingQueue).to(exchange);
  }
}
```

As you can see, in the domainEventsExchange() method, we create a durable FanoutExchange, named "ta.domain.events", and in the activityTrackingQueue() method, we create a durable queue named "ta.activity.tracking", and in the bindingActivityTracking() method, we bind the activity tracking queue to the exchange.

The following is how AmqpDomainEventPublisher looks:

```
...
@Component
public class AmqpDomainEventPublisher implements DomainEventPublisher {
  ...
  private RabbitTemplate rabbitTemplate;
  private FanoutExchange exchange;

  public AmqpDomainEventPublisher(RabbitTemplate rabbitTemplate,
                                   @Qualifier("domainEventsExchange")
FanoutExchange exchange) {
    this.rabbitTemplate = rabbitTemplate;
    this.exchange = exchange;
  }

  @Override
```

```
    public void publish(DomainEvent event) {
      log.debug("Publishing domain event: " + event);
      try {
        rabbitTemplate.convertAndSend(exchange.getName(), "", event);
      } catch (AmqpException e) {
        log.error("Failed to send domain event to MQ", e);
      }
    }
  }
}
```

In this publisher, we inject a `RabbitTemplate` instance and the `domainEventsExchange` through the constructor, and inside the `publish()` method, we use the `convertAndSend()` method of the `rabbitTemplate` to send the domain event as a RabbitMQ message.

Listening to a queue is quite simple with Spring. The following shows `ActivityTracker`, which listens to the activity tracking queue that we defined in the configuration:

```
@Component
public class ActivityTracker {
  ...
  private ActivityService activityService;
  private DomainEventToActivityConverter
  domainEventToActivityConverter;

  public ActivityTracker(ActivityService activityService,
                         DomainEventToActivityConverter
    domainEventToActivityConverter) {
    this.activityService = activityService;
    this.domainEventToActivityConverter =
    domainEventToActivityConverter;
  }

  @RabbitListener(queues = "#{activityTrackingQueue.name}")
  public void receive(DomainEvent domainEvent) {
    log.debug("Receive domain event: " + domainEvent);

    Activity activity =
    domainEventToActivityConverter.toActivity(domainEvent);
    // Save the activity only when there is an activity
    // result from the domain event
    if (activity != null) {
      activityService.saveActivity(activity);
    }
  }
}
```

As you can see, `ActivityTracker` is a simple Spring bean. The only special part is that the `receive()` method is annotated with the `@RabbitListener` annotation. With this annotation, Spring will convert the received RabbitMQ message to a `DomainEvent` object automatically. `DomainEventToActivityConverter` is a converter that converts the received domain event into a corresponding activity so that `ActivityService` can save it.

The following is the commit history of implementing activity tracking:

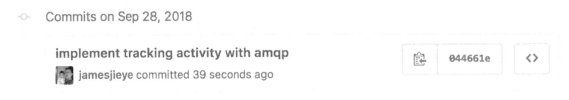

Figure 13.8: Implementing tracking activity with the AQMP commit

Adding card cover images and activity tracking

Now, we can upload an attachment to cards and tracking activities. We can implement the card cover image and the activity detail of the card. However, we will not discuss the details of the implementation here because they are similar to what we have introduced before. The following is the commit history on GitHub:

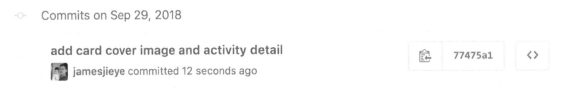

Figure 13.9: Adding the card cover image and activity detail commit

Fixes at the end

There are two types of fixes. Let's discuss them here as follows:

- **Fix—add mapping for card URL**: This is an oversight. Without adding the card URL to `@GetMapping` in `MainController`, refreshing the page will show an HTTP `404` error page. The following is the commit record:

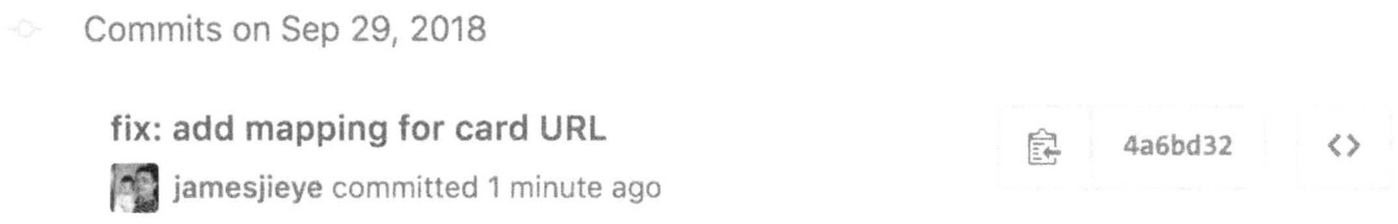

Commits on Sep 29, 2018

fix: add mapping for card URL

4a6bd32 <>

jamesjieye committed 1 minute ago

Figure 13.10: Fix—add mapping for card URL commit

- **Fix—unsubscribe from board channel when opening a card**: The `vue-router` will trigger the `beforeRouteLeave` navigation guard when the URL is switched from the board URL to the card URL. The fix involves simply adding a condition guard to the unsubscribe method. The following is the commit history:

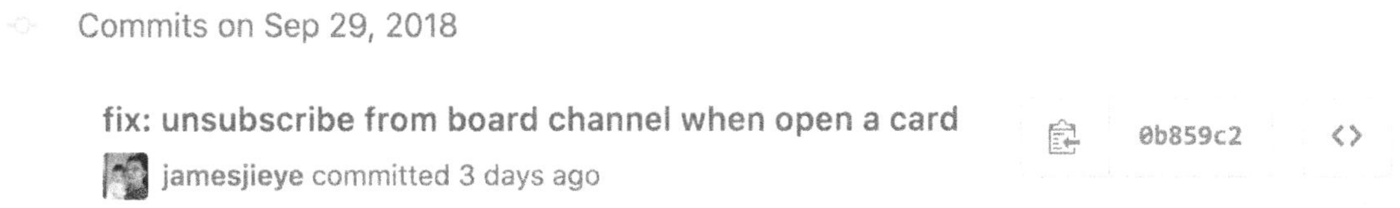

Commits on Sep 29, 2018

fix: unsubscribe from board channel when open a card

0b859c2 <>

jamesjieye committed 3 days ago

Figure 13.11: Fix—unsubscribe from board channel when opening a card commit

Summary

In this chapter, we implemented the router for both the board URL and card URL by using a watcher to `this.$route`. We also implemented the auto-resizing of the card title editing, support of the Markdown format, as well as file uploading in the frontend.

We implemented saving files to both the server and AWS S3, as well as thumbnail generating with GraphicMagick. We refactored the publish and subscribe domain events to use RabbitMQ as the message broker. We also added the final touch to the application of this version by adding card cover images and showing activity details on the card modal window.

In the next chapter, we will see what preparation we will need before pushing a build to production.

14
Health Checking, System Monitoring - Getting Ready for Production

By now, we've finished all the main features of the TaskAgile application. Those that are in the user stories list but haven't been implemented will be done in future versions. It is time to prepare for our production deployment.

In this chapter, we will learn about the following:

- Installing applications as a service
- Spring Profile
- Spring Boot Actuator
- Monitoring with Icinga 2

Installing as a service

We will deploy our application to an AWS EC2 instance, and we will deploy it as a standalone `.jar` file and use an embedded application server, which, by default, is the Tomcat server. It would be better that we simply use a command such as the following to start and stop the application:

```
service taskagile start|stop
```

We can achieve this by installing the application as an `init.d` service. To do that, first of all, we will need to make the `.jar` file fully executable by adding a configuration to `spring-boot-maven-plugin` in the `pom.xml` file:

```
<plugin>
  <groupId>org.springframework.boot</groupId>
  <artifactId>spring-boot-maven-plugin</artifactId>
  <configuration>
    <executable>true</executable>
  </configuration>
  <executions>
    ...
  </executions>
</plugin>
```

Once we deploy the application to the server, we will put it in `/opt/taskagile/app.jar`. To install the application as an `init.d` service, we will need to create a symlink, like the following:

```
$ sudo ln -s /opt/taskagile/app.jar /etc/init.d/taskagile
```

With this symlink, we are able to do the following:

- Start the service as the user who owns the `jar` file
- Track the application's PID with the `/var/run/taskagile/taskagile.pid` file
- Write logs to `/var/log/taskagile.log`

Spring Profile

When we deploy our application to the server, we will need to use a different set of configurations, such as the database's username, password, and URL, and so on. Spring Profiles provides a way to segregate the configuration for different environments.

We have the following environments for this:

- **dev**: The local development environment
- **test**: The unit test environment
- **e2e**: The end-to-end test environment
- **staging**: The staging environment
- **production**: The production environment

With Spring Profile, we can create a profile-specific configuration file, for example, the `application-dev.properties` file that we created for the local development environment, and, we use `application.properties` as the base configuration. Other configurations will override the defaults in the base configuration. For example, in our `application.properties`, we use `<username>` and `<password>` for the database connection:

```
spring.datasource.username=<username>
spring.datasource.password=<password>
```

In `application-dev.properties`, we override these two configurations with the actual username and password in the local development environment. We will do the same for other environments, especially, the staging and the production environment.

Now, let's take a look at each environment profile.

The dev profile

In the local development environment, as we mentioned in Chapter 8, *Creating the Application Scaffold - Taking off Like a Rocket*, we can set the active profile to be `dev` by setting the environment variable, `spring_profiles_active`.

If you want to override the `active` profile, for example, by changing it to be `production`, you can pass a command line argument when you start the application, as shown in the following:

```
java -jar -Dspring.profiles.active=production app.jar
```

Or, when using the `mvn` command, as follows:

```
mvn spring-boot:run -Dspring-boot.run.profiles=production
```

The test profile

For any tests, it is ideal to keep the configuration for them in an isolated environment. The "test" profile is for this purpose. As you have already seen, we use @ActiveProfiles("test") in the unit test code. Instead of looking for src/main/resources/application-test.properties, Spring will look for src/test/resources/application.properties, in which the biggest difference is the datasource configuration. In test "test" profile, we use H2 to speed up the performance. In other environments, we use MySQL.We want to keep H2 only for the tests, and that is why we add the H2 dependency in pom.xml with the test scope.

One interesting thing about the "test" profile is that if you set the active profile to be "test" by using methods other than using the @ActiveProfiles annotation, Spring will look for src/main/resources/application-test.properties. For example, the following are ways to set the active profile to be "test". You will need to have application-test.properties ready if want you do that:

```
// Set active profile through using the @Profile annotation
@Profile("test")
// Set active profile through Environment.setActiveProfiles()
env.setActiveProfiles("test");
// Set active profile through JVM parameter
$ java -jar -Dspring.profiles.active=test app.jar
# Set active profile through environment variable
export spring_profiles_active=test
```

The usage of the "test" profile in places other than the unit tests could be confusing because we need to have two .properties for the same profile. Because of this, we will only use the "test" profile in unit tests with the @ActiveProfiles annotation.

The end-to-end test profile

Even though it has the word *test* in its name, the end-to-end test, or, E2E test for short, is quite different from unit tests. The E2E test has nothing to do with those unit tests code or the @ActiveProfiles annotation. You can think of those E2E tests as mini robots. They can open browsers with the help of tools like Nightwatch, and test the application's features directly from the browser as an actual application user.

In Chapter 8, *Creating the Application Scaffold - Taking off Like a Rocket*, we combined the build steps of the frontend into Maven's build process. In this process, before the E2E test starts, we start the application by running mvn spring-boot:start, and then we execute the E2E test cases. Once that is done, we stop the application. Because we have set the environment variable, spring_profiles_active, to be dev. (see Chapter 8, *Creating the Application Scaffold - Taking off Like a Rocket*), when we run the E2E tests with the mvn clean install command, we're actually using the dev profile. That's why you see those autogenerated users showing up in the user table in the database.

This build process that has the E2E test combined into Maven's build lifecycle seems to be working well. However, it will become an issue when we build the application with Jenkins. We will talk about Jenkins in the next chapter. On the Jenkins server, the environment is not the dev environment. Thus, we cannot use the "dev" profile when we build with Jenkins. We need an isolated and refreshed environment to perform the E2E test before the code is deployed to the production. It is better that we give this environment a profile, such as "e2e".

Let's add src/main/resources/application-e2e.properties, and set the active profile to be "e2e" in spring-boot-maven-plugin, as in the following:

```
<plugin>
  <groupId>org.springframework.boot</groupId>
  <artifactId>spring-boot-maven-plugin</artifactId>
  <executions>
    <execution>
      <id>pre integration test</id>
      <goals>
          <goal>start</goal>
      </goals>
      <configuration>
        <profiles>
          <profile>e2e</profile>
        </profiles>
      </configuration>
    </execution>
    ...
  </executions>
</plugin>
```

The `<profile>` we added to `spring-boot-maven-plugin` is to set the active Spring Profile. It is not the profile that Maven supports. We will talk about Maven's profile in the next chapter.

Here is how `src/main/resources/application-e2e.properties` looks:

```
spring.datasource.url=jdbc:mysql://localhost:3306/task_agile_e2e?useSSL=fal
se
spring.datasource.username=root
spring.datasource.password=1234

spring.jpa.hibernate.ddl-auto=create-drop
```

As you can see, we use a different database, `task_agile_e2e`, for the E2E test, and we ask the JPA to autogenerate the tables and drop them after the testing. All the other settings will come from the base configuration, `application.properties`.

 In the `User.java` entity, we set the length of the password field to be 30 characters, which is not enough to store the encrypted version of the password. We need to fix it by changing it to 128 characters. See the *Fixes at the end* section for more details.

In the next chapter, we will do a refactoring to our build process to make it fit the continuous delivery's life cycle.

The staging and production profile

For staging and production environments, we will add `application-staging.properties` and `application-production.properties` to `src/main/resources` to provide configurations that are suitable for these environments. For example, you might want to, by default, set the log level of the application to be `"debug"` in the staging environment, and set it to be `"info"` in the production environment.

When we deploy our application to these environments, we will put it in /opt/taskagile directory. We will also add /opt/taskagile/config/application-staging.properties in the staging environment and /opt/taskagile/config/application-production.properties in the production environment. The purpose of these two .properties files is to put sensitive configurations outside of the source code. For example, we do not want to put the database username and password of these two environments in the source code. We want to keep them secret. The other reason it is better to keep them it outside the jar file is that you might need to change it. You do not want to do a new build and deployment simply for changing these configurations. For now, all we need to put inside ./config/application-staging.properties and ./config/application-production.properties are the following database settings:

```
spring.datasource.username=app_user
spring.datasource.password=Uqx$UV!TabRfu1vm
```

Spring Boot Actuator

Actuator is the feature that Spring Boot provides for monitoring and managing applications in the production environment. It has features for health checking, auditing, metrics tracking, HTTP tracking, showing environment variables, and dumping threads. In this section, we will explore some of these features and turn on those that we will need for monitoring our application.

First of all, for the use Actuator, we need to add the following dependencies to pom.xml:

```
<dependency>
    <groupId>org.springframework.boot</groupId>
    <artifactId>spring-boot-starter-actuator</artifactId>
</dependency>
```

At the time of writing, with JDK 8 we will also need to include the following dependency to avoid a compilation error:

```
<dependency>
    <groupId>javax.interceptor</groupId>
    <artifactId>javax.interceptor-api</artifactId>
    <version>${javax.interceptor.version}</version>
</dependency>
```

And now, let's add the following settings to `application.properties`:

```
management.server.port=9000
management.endpoint.health.show-details=always
management.endpoints.web.exposure.include=health, info, metrics, env
```

As you can see, we open the Actuator at port `9000` and make it always show health details. The actuator points that we choose to expose are the following:

- `/actuator/health`: Allows us to check the health status of the application. For example, if the application is still up, if the database, mail server, or the RabbitMQ server is up, as well as server disk space usage, and so on.
- `/actuator/info`: Displays the general information about the application.
- `/actuator/metrics`: Shows various sensitive metric information of the application.
- `/actuator/env`: Displays the current environment properties, which is sensitive information.

There are many other built-in endpoints that Actuator supports. You can also create custom endpoints. We will not discuss them here. For our application, these four endpoints are good to go with.

The health endpoint

For the `/actuator/health` endpoint, Spring Boot Actuator provides various built-in autoconfigured health indicators. We can also create a custom health indicator by implementing the `HeathIndicator` interface. It is useful when we need to check our application's health in our own way. Currently, the built-in health indicators are good enough.

The info endpoint

The /actuator/info endpoint, by default, is empty. We will need to add the following settings to application.properties so that we can see the basic information:

```
info.app.name=@name@
info.app.description=@description@
info.app.encoding=@project.build.sourceEncoding@
info.app.java.source=@java.version@
info.app.java.target=@java.version@
```

We can use @..@ placeholders to refer to our Maven properties because we use spring-boot-starter-parent. Beside this basic information, we can add build information into this endpoint by adding the build-info goal to the spring-boot-maven-plugin:

```
<plugin>
  <groupId>org.springframework.boot</groupId>
  <artifactId>spring-boot-maven-plugin</artifactId>
  ...
  <executions>
    <execution>
      <goals>
        <goal>build-info</goal>
      </goals>
    </execution>
    ...
  </executions>
</plugin>
```

We can add the following git-commit-id-plugin to add the Git commit information to the endpoint:

```
<build>
    <plugins>
      <plugin>
        <groupId>pl.project13.maven</groupId>
        <artifactId>git-commit-id-plugin</artifactId>
      </plugin>
      <plugin>
      ...
    </plugins>
</build>
```

With these plugins, we can use the `/actuator/info` endpoint to verify whether the application has the current build and commit to detect situations such as having an old incompatible version of the application running.

The metrics endpoint

This endpoint gathers and publishes information of the OS, JVM, and application-level metrics. By default, the `/actuator/metrics` endpoint will return all the names of the metrics that are supported, for example, if it has a metric such as `"jvm.memory.used"`. We can query the details by using `/actuator/metrics/jvm.memory.used` and get a result similar to the following:

```
{
  "name": "jvm.memory.used",
  "description": "The amount of used memory",
  "baseUnit": "bytes",
  "measurements": [{
    "statistic": "VALUE",
    "value": 2.13495176E8
  }],
  "availableTags": [{
    "tag": "area",
    "values": ["heap", "nonheap"]
  }, {
    "tag": "id",
    "values": ["Compressed Class Space", "PS Survivor Space", "PS Old
    Gen", "Metaspace", "PS Eden Space", "Code Cache"]
  }]
}
```

As you can see, the application has used 213 megabytes of memory.

The environment endpoint

The environment endpoint, `/actuator/env`, provides information about the environment properties, which can be very helpful during troubleshooting issues. As you can see in *Figure 14.1*, this endpoint shows properties from different property sources:

```
{
  - activeProfiles: [
        "dev"
  ],
  - propertySources: [
      - {
          name: "server.ports",
        + properties: {…}
      },
      - {
          name: "servletContextInitParams",
          properties: { }
      },
      - {
          name: "systemProperties",
        + properties: {…}
      },
      - {
          name: "systemEnvironment",
        + properties: {…}
      },
      - {
          name: "applicationConfig: [classpath:/application-dev.properties]",
        + properties: {…}
      },
      - {
          name: "applicationConfig: [classpath:/application.properties]",
        + properties: {…}
      },
      - {
          name: "refresh",
        + properties: {…}
      }
    ]
}
```

Figure 14.1: The environment endpoint

We can use the property's name to ask Actuator to return only the related information. For example, we can use `/actuator/env/app.mail-from` to see the value of the `app.mail-from` property.

Endpoint security

Most of the information exposed through the Actuator's endpoints are sensitive. That's why Spring Boot disables endpoints, besides `/health` and `/info`, by default. There are several ways to protect these endpoints. In this section, we will explore a few of them.

Using a different port and firewall

In our configuration, we separate Actuator's endpoints from our APIs and make it available on port `9000`. On the server, we will make port `9000` only accessible from the internal network by using the firewall. For example, we can create a standalone admin application, which is also a Spring Boot application. In this admin application, it can access the Actuator's endpoints from the server side through the internal network and display the result on a page that only authorized administrators can see.

Because port `9000` is only accessible from the internal network, behind the firewall, we can change the Spring Security configuration, as in the following, to make the endpoints accessible without authentication:

```
public class SecurityConfiguration extends WebSecurityConfigurerAdapter {
  ...
  protected void configure(HttpSecurity http) throws Exception {
    http
      ...
        .antMatchers(PUBLIC).permitAll()
        .requestMatchers(EndpointRequest.toAnyEndpoint()).permitAll()
        .anyRequest().authenticated()
      ...
  }
  ...
}
```

Using the same port and Spring Security

With Spring Security, we can define a role, for example, ACTUATOR_ADMIN, and make the endpoints only accessible to authenticated users who are in this role, as shown in the following:

```
public class SecurityConfiguration extends WebSecurityConfigurerAdapter {
    ...
  protected void configure(HttpSecurity http) throws Exception {
    http
      ...
        .antMatchers(PUBLIC).permitAll()
        .requestMatchers(EndpointRequest.toAnyEndpoint()).
        hasAnyRole("ACTUATOR_ADMIN")
        .anyRequest().authenticated()
      ...
  }
  ...
}
```

In `application.properties`, we will comment out the port setting, as in the following:

```
# management.server.port=9000
```

In this way, we can access the Actuator's endpoints with an authenticated user who has the required role.

Using a custom filter

In case we need to access the Actuator's endpoints from the outside, for example, from another AWS's region, and we want to authenticate the request using JWT, we can exclude these endpoint requests from Spring Security's verification by permitting all these requests, and then create a custom filter to process these requests by verifying the JWT token.

Monitoring with Icinga 2

Once the application is deployed to the production environment, we will need a way to constantly monitor the application's status, for example, by checking those Actuator's endpoints. When there is an outage or the system is in a critical status, for example, if the server is overloaded, we need a way to get notified.

Icinga 2 is a great fit for this purpose. It is an open source monitoring system. It uses monitoring plugins to check various services' statuses and generates performance data for reporting. Each plugin is a standalone command-line tool that performs a specific type of check. There are more than fifty standard plugins available on `https://www.monitoring-plugins.org`. Besides these plugins, you can also create your own check plugin. Icinga 2 also provides REST API and Web UI.

Because of the scope of this book, we will not go into the details of Icinga 2. You can find out more about it on its website, at: `https://www.icinga.com/docs/icinga2/latest`.

The following is the commit record of adding profile properties and turning on Actuator:

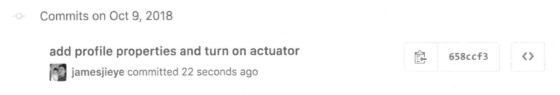

Figure 14.2 Adding profile properties and turning on the actuator commit

Fixes at the end

Let's have a look at a few fixes:

- **Fix—increase password field length**: As mentioned earlier, the password field's length, defined in `User.java`, was too small for an encrypted password. It causes an error when we run the end-to-end testing in the `"e2e"` profile:

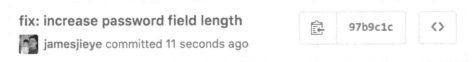

Figure 14.3: Fix—increase password field length

Summary

In this chapter, we learned how to use Spring Profile to separate the configuration for different environments. We also learned how to use Spring Actuator to provide endpoints for health checking and system monitoring. We also introduced Icinga 2, briefly.

In the next chapter, we will talk about continuous delivery, Docker, and how to use Jenkins to deploy the application.

15
Deploying to the Cloud with Jenkins - Ship It Continuously

Finally, it is time to ship our application. There are many ways to get our application deployed to the production environment. We can choose to do it manually, starting from running the `mvn clean install` command, to sending the `.jar` file to servers using tools such as FTP or the `scp` command, then stopping the old version of the application and starting the new version, followed by initiating the E2E test. Or, we can write Python/shell scripts to automate some of the steps. Either way, there are manual steps, which creates room for errors. That's why rolling out an application manually or half-manually is always stressful. Constant focus is required throughout the entire release.

Nowadays, there are various tools that can help us with that. Many of these tools provide deep integration with **Version Control Systems (VCS)**, such as Git, and are free for open source projects. For example, Travis CI will build your application once you push code to GitHub. After the build passes, it will automatically deploy the application to the servers that you specified, then it will inform you of the successful deployment by sending you an email or telling you on Slack. It will also notify you in case the build fails. This whole process is triggered by the push of the code.

In this chapter, we will create a continuous delivery process using Jenkins 2. You will learn the following:

- What continuous delivery is
- How continuous delivery is different from continuous integration and continuous deployment
- How to use Jenkins 2 to build a continuous delivery process

Continuous delivery

In this section, we will talk about continuous delivery and other two related practices—continuous integration and continuous deployment. The following diagram shows the differences between these three practices:

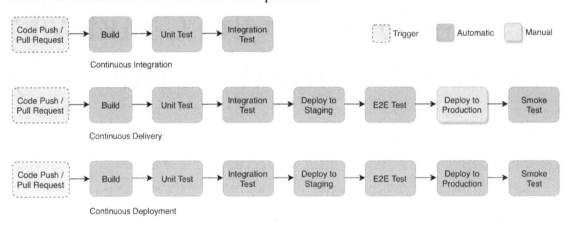

Figure 15.1: Continuous integration, continuous delivery, and continuous deployment

As you can see, the processes of these three practices can be triggered by a **Code Push** or **Pull Request**. For continuous integration, it focuses on building the code and execute those tests, including unit tests as well as integration tests. The integration test we talk about here is on the backend. To do that, we will need to start the Spring Boot application with all the components initialized, including controllers, services, repositories, and all other dependents, and then send API requests to see if the backend functions as expected.

Registration API integration test

We haven't added any integration test to our application yet. Let's create one for the registration API as an example. To keep the integration tests separate from the unit tests, we will put all the integration tests inside the `src/test/java/integration` package, and name these tests with the suffix `IntegrationTests`.

The following is what the
register_existedUsername_shouldFailAndReturn400() test
method in RegistrationApiIntegrationTests looks like:

```
...
@RunWith(SpringRunner.class)
@SpringBootTest(webEnvironment = SpringBootTest.WebEnvironment.MOCK,
                classes = TaskAgileApplication.class)
@ActiveProfiles("test")
@AutoConfigureMockMvc
public class RegistrationApiIntegrationTests {

  @Autowired
  private MockMvc mvcMock;

  @Test
  public void register_existedUsername_shouldFailAndReturn400() throws
  Exception {
    RegistrationPayload payload = payload("exist",
    "test1@taskagile.com");
    mvcMock.perform(
      post("/api/registrations")
        .contentType(MediaType.APPLICATION_JSON)
        .content(JsonUtils.toJson(payload)))
      .andExpect(status().is(201));

    // Try to register again with the same username
    RegistrationPayload payload2 = payload("exist",
    "test2@taskagile.com");
    mvcMock.perform(
      post("/api/registrations")
        .contentType(MediaType.APPLICATION_JSON)
        .content(JsonUtils.toJson(payload2)))
      .andExpect(status().is(400))
      .andExpect(jsonPath("$.message").value("Username already
      exists"));
  }
  ...
}
```

As you can see, this test is also written as a unit test, very similar to the
RegistrationApiControllerTests. The biggest difference is that, in this test, we use
the @SpringBootTest annotation to start the entire application, whereas
in RegistrationApiControllerTests, we used the @WebMvcTest annotation to focus
only on the tests of Spring MVC components. In this test, we do not need to provide
a @MockBean of UserService, because Spring will initialize the actual UserServiceImpl
in the container.

In the register_existedUsername_shouldFailAndReturn400() method, instead of
mocking the behavior of UserService to throw UsernameExistsException, we call the
registration API to create a user first and then call the API with the same username. In this
test, the first user will be saved into the H2 database. The second API call will cause the
throw of UsernameExistException. There is no mocked behavior in the test. That's why
it is an integration test.

The following screenshot shows the commit record of this integration test:

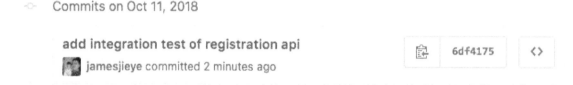

Figure 15.2: Commit record of the integration test

Maturity and cost

As you can see from the previous flowchart, continuous integration only covers the build
and the test steps. It ensures that the code is tested before deploying to servers. Even
though it is considered the least mature practice among the three, we still need to write
enough unit tests and integration tests to keep the test coverage at a high percentage.
Otherwise, it cannot really be called continuous integration.

To achieve continuous delivery, we will need to deploy the code to the staging environment automatically and then execute E2E tests automatically. In our application, we write our E2E tests based on Nightwatch.js. As mentioned before, in those tests, those **mini-robots** will actually open the application inside a browser and then test features the same way a human being would do. It is a test from the frontend all the way to the backend. Sometimes, these tests are called **automation tests**, in contrast with the manual test a QA colleague will do. Using an automatic E2E test is a great improvement for the entire software development process because it releases us from having to do those tedious tasks ourselves so that we can focus on building a better application. However, this benefit comes with a cost that is the effort to write a comprehensive E2E test suite.

Between continuous delivery and continuous deployment, the difference is that, in continuous deployment, the build is automatically shipped to the production environment. This is the most mature process that, on the other hand, requires the best testing culture. Since a change is shipped automatically, our tests need to be able to protect the quality of the release. Broken features or issues must be detected during the test phases. Sometimes, it requires feature flags that we can use to turn new features off by default when they are shipped to production so that we can coordinate with other team members to roll the feature out gradually, as well as keep the damage, if there is any, manageable.

Refactoring E2E tests

In `Chapter 8`, *Creating the Application Scaffold - Taking off Like a Rocket*, we added the build process of the frontend into Maven's build life cycle and added the executing of E2E tests in Maven's `integration-test` phase. However, as shown in the flowchart earlier in this chapter, we will need to execute E2E tests once the application is deployed to the staging environment. In this section, we will refactor our build process. Before we jump into that, let's review different scenarios in which we need to execute E2E tests.

Running E2E tests during the writing

When we write E2E tests, we usually will start the backend and the frontend separately. The backend will keep running while we're writing tests. After we finish a new E2E test, let's say, `0.register.e2e.js`, we will run it with the following command inside the `front-end` directory:

```
node_modules/.bin/vue-cli-service test:e2e \
  -t tests/e2e/specs/0.register.e2e.js
```

Or if your npm version is 5.2.0 or later, use the following code instead:

```
npx vue-cli-service test:e2e \
  -t tests/e2e/specs/0.register.e2e.js
```

Once we finish all the tests, it is a good practice to run all the tests again to make sure there is no accidental break. Use the following command:

```
npm run test:e2e
```

In both of these scenarios, we run our E2E tests in the local environment.

Running E2E tests before pushing the code to VCS

We've been doing this since Chapter 9, *Forms and Validation - Starting with the Register Page*, with the mvn clean install command. Currently, we have only created two E2E test suites, one for the register page and the other for the login page. Both of them are lightweight. That's why our build completes fast. However, in the future, once we create enough tests to cover all the features of the application, it could take more than fifteen minutes or half an hour to finish all the tests. The situation could be worse for large-scale applications. Even for a tiny change, such as a typo, we would have to sit there and wait for all E2E tests to finish before committing the code.

It is better that we make the step of executing the E2E tests optional in the Maven build process. That is, by default, with the mvn clean install command, E2E tests won't be executed. When you want to execute the E2E tests, you can opt-in using a flag. Maven's profile feature is perfect for these kinds of requirements. As you can see in the following diagram, we will extract the steps with a flag into a Maven profile, called local-e2e. We name it local-e2e to make it clear that executing the E2E tests using the Maven command is only used in the local development environment. As you will see in the next section, with Jenkins, we will not use Maven to trigger the E2E tests. The Maven build process is shown here, with optional steps included:

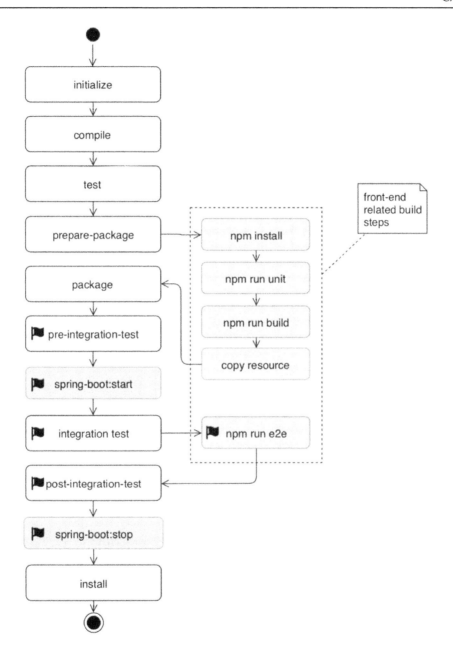

Figure 15.3: The Maven build process with optional steps

Here is the change to `pom.xml`. We extract the `spring-boot:start`, `integration-test`, and `spring-boot:stop` steps into the `local-e2e` profile as follows:

```xml
<profiles>
 <profile>
    <id>local-e2e</id>
    <build>
      <plugins>
        <plugin>
          <groupId>org.springframework.boot</groupId>
          <artifactId>spring-boot-maven-plugin</artifactId>
          <executions>
            . . .
          </executions>
        </plugin>
        <plugin>
          <groupId>org.codehaus.mojo</groupId>
          <artifactId>exec-maven-plugin</artifactId>
          <version>${codehaus.version}</version>
          <executions>
            . . .
          </executions>
          . . .
        </plugin>
      </plugins>
    </build>
  </profile>
</profiles>
```

With this change, when we execute the `mvn clean install` command, no E2E test will be executed. We can add the `-P` argument, followed by the Maven profile's ID, to include the E2E tests, such as the following:

```
mvn clean install -P local-e2e
```

To avoid confusion, we rename the `test:integration` npm script to `test:local-e2e`. We also add another script, `test:staging-e2e`, for executing E2E tests in the staging environment. You can check the commit record shown at the end of this section for details.

Run E2E tests after deploying to staging

The last scene in which we will run the E2E tests is after we deploy the build to the staging environment. Instead of using a Maven command, we will use the `npm run test:staging-e2e` command to start the E2E testing.

Since the staging environment is close to the production environment, when a test fails on staging, it will most likely fail on production too. In practice, we will keep the staging environment up and running, so that when there is a test failure, we can investigate it by going into the servers to find out what went wrong.

One drawback of using the staging environment as the E2E test environment is that we cannot have multiple builds running at the same time, otherwise, they will overwrite each other when they deploy the build to the staging environment. Everybody else has to wait until the current build finishes.

To solve this, instead of deploying a build to the staging environment for E2E testing, we can spin up an isolated refresh E2E test environment and shut down that environment when the E2E testing is done. In case there is a failure during the test, we will keep the environment up for the investigation of the issue and shut it down manually after locating the root cause. With this approach, we would still need the staging environment for other purposes, such as verifying an integration with a third party before rolling it out to the production environment.

Our recommendation is to start by performing the E2E test on the staging environment. When you have so many builds in parallel that using the staging environment for the E2E test is no longer applicable, then switch to isolated E2E test environments.

The following screenshot shows the commit record of the refactoring of the Maven build process:

Commits on Oct 11, 2018

refactor maven build process
jamesjieye committed 30 seconds ago

3881393   <>

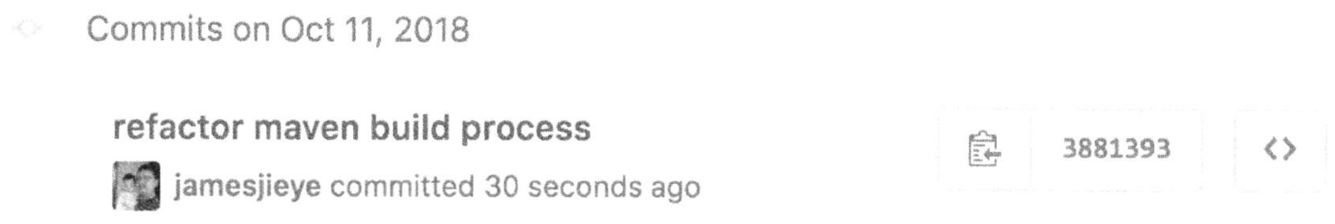

Figure 15.4: Commit record of the Maven build process

Last fix before rolling out

Fix—add test profile and turn off the debug-level log: This is a minor fix to add a test profile to unit tests that run with `SpringRunner`, and turn off the debug-level log in `application.properties`. The commit for this fix was as follows:

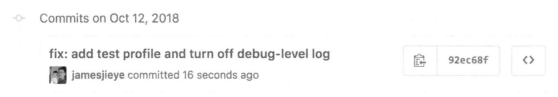

Figure 15.5: Commit record for the fix

Let's ship it

In this section, we will use Jenkins 2 and Docker to build the application and ship it to the cloud. The following diagram shows the continuous delivery process built with Jenkins:

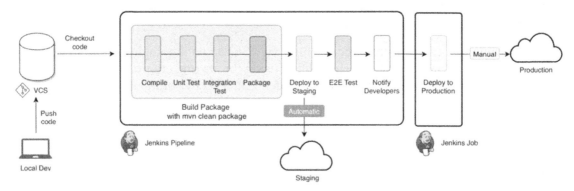

Figure 15.6: The continuous delivery process with Jenkins

As you can see, Jenkins will manage the packaging, deploying, and triggering of the E2E testing, and then notify developers when the build completes. All these steps are streamlined inside the **Jenkins Pipeline** plugin. If you're not familiar with Jenkins Pipeline, you might want to check out Jenkins user handbook at `https://jenkins.io/doc/book/pipeline`. When a build succeeds, we can use another Jenkins job to manually trigger the deployment of the application to the production environment.

When we deploy the application to the staging/production environment, we will need to prepare AWS EC2 instances by installing the dependencies our application requires, for example, OpenJDK, GraphicMagicks, and so on. Once the EC2 instance is ready, we will install our application as a service, which we talked in the last chapter. Then we use the `taskagile` command service to start the application.

All these extra steps we just described might not seem like too much work at the moment. However, imagine that our application grows, and we have more dependencies. Since we will need to make sure the versions of those dependencies in all the environments are exactly the same, the preparation of the server instances could be a tedious and time-consuming task. It can also be easier for us to make mistakes during the preparation.

The following diagram shows an improved version of this process:

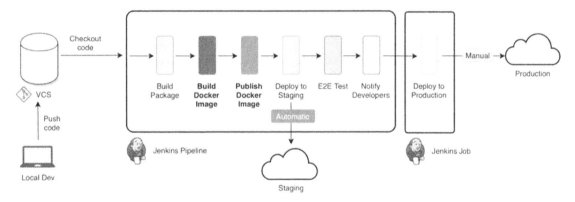

Figure 15.7: An improved continuous delivery process with Jenkins and Docker

As you can see, after building the package with the `mvn clean package` command, we will build a Docker image to wrap all the dependencies our application has inside of it and then ship the Docker image to different environments, in which we only need to execute the `docker run` command to start the Docker container and boot up the application. Much simpler and more efficient.

Let's use this approach to ship our application.

Preparing a Dockerfile

To build a Docker image, we need to create a file called `Dockerfile` to specify the environment inside the Docker container. Our application will be securely isolated inside the container. If you're not familiar with Docker, the official documentation at `https://docs.docker.com` is a great place to start your exploration.

Before we start, we need to make sure that Docker is installed in our local environment so that we can test `Dockerfile` locally. In case you haven't installed it, you can download it from `https://www.docker.com/get-started` and follow the install instructions.

We will create a folder called `docker` in the root folder with the following structure:

```
├── docker
    ├── Dockerfile
    ├── application-docker.properties
    ├── env.list
    └── start.sh
```

Let's go through these files one by one. The following is how the `Dockerfile` should look:

```
1.  From openjdk:8-jre-alpine
2.
3.  RUN apk add graphicsmagick=1.3.30-r0
4.  RUN ln -s /usr/bin/gm /usr/local/bin/gm
5.
6.  ADD app.jar /opt/taskagile/app.jar
7.  ADD application-docker.properties /config/application-
    docker.properties
8.
9.  EXPOSE 8080 9000
10.
11. ENTRYPOINT ["java", "-jar", "/opt/taskagile/app.jar"]
```

Every `Dockerfile` begins with the `From` instruction, which tells Docker to initialize a new build stage and, in our case, use `openjdk:8-jre-alpine` as the base image. This OpenJDK image comes from Docker's public repository. In line 3, with `RUN` instruction, we ask Docker to install the GraphicMagick dependency. In line 4, we create a soft link from `/usr/bin/gm` to `/usr/local/bin/gm`, which is used for creating image thumbnails in our application. In line 6, we add the `docker/app.jar` file to the Docker image. The `docker/app.jar` file will be copied from the `target` folder into the `docker` folder by command defined in `Jenkinsfile`, as you will see in the next section. In line 7, we add the `application-docker.properties` file to the `/config` folder inside the Docker image. After that, we use an `EXPOSE` instruction to inform Docker that the container will listen to the `8080` and `9000` ports at runtime. The `EXPOSE` instruction does not actually publish the port. It is more like a document between the builder of the Docker and the runner of the container, about which ports are intended to be published. In line 11, the `ENTRYPOINT` instruction allows us to run the Docker container as an executable, and the `java -jar /opt/taskagile/app.jar` command will be executed when the container starts.

As you might remember, in the last chapter, when we prepared for the `rolling-out` phase, we mentioned that we will put the `.properties` file in `/opt/taskagile/config/`, so that when we execute the `service taskagile start` command, Spring Boot will pick up the properties defined in that file. When we run with Docker, we no longer need to install the application as a service. We will use the `java -jar` command to start it and, by default, Docker will run this command from the root path inside the container. That's why we put the `application-docker.properties` inside `/config` folder.

`application-docker.properties` is the properties file that we use to provide the ability for Docker to override settings through environment variables. Here is how it looks:

```
spring.datasource.url=jdbc:mysql://${TASK_AGILE_DB_HOST}:3306/${TASK_AGILE_
DB_NAME}?useSSL=false
spring.datasource.username=${TASK_AGILE_DB_USERNAME}
spring.datasource.password=${TASK_AGILE_DB_PASSWORD}

spring.rabbitmq.host=${TASK_AGILE_MQ_HOST}
spring.rabbitmq.port=${TASK_AGILE_MQ_PORT}
spring.rabbitmq.username=${TASK_AGILE_MQ_USERNAME}
spring.rabbitmq.password=${TASK_AGILE_MQ_PASSWORD}

spring.mail.host=${TASK_AGILE_MAIL_HOST}
spring.mail.port=${TASK_AGILE_MAIL_PORT}
```

As you can see, in this properties file, we use environment variables for external resources that the application depends on. These environment variables will be defined in Docker's `env.list` environment file and passed to the container via the `--env-file` argument of the `docker run` command. Here is how it looks:

```
TASK_AGILE_TOKEN_SECRET_KEY=60dKuW2Qpc3YkUoaa9i6qY5cyaGgQM8clfxpDGWS3sY=

TASK_AGILE_DB_HOST=<Your DB host>
TASK_AGILE_DB_NAME=task_agile
TASK_AGILE_DB_USERNAME=<Your DB username>
TASK_AGILE_DB_PASSWORD=<Your DB password>

TASK_AGILE_MQ_HOST=<Your MQ host>
TASK_AGILE_MQ_PORT=5672
TASK_AGILE_MQ_USERNAME=<Your MQ username>
TASK_AGILE_MQ_PASSWORD=<Your MQ password>

TASK_AGILE_MAIL_HOST=<Your Mail host>
TASK_AGILE_MAIL_PORT=25

TASK_AGILE_CDN_URL=<Your CDN URL>
```

In our production environment, `https://taskagile.com`, given the fact that it will be just a demo, we will host everything inside a single EC2 instance, including the database, the messaging queue, and the Docker container of our application. Both the database and the message queue will be installed in the same EC2 instance directly. In reality, a more practical way is either to put them both inside separate containers or use corresponding cloud services, like AWS's RDS and AWS's MQ. Here, we simply put them in the same box to save a few bucks.

If you're using Docker for Mac locally, you can also use the special `host.docker.internal` DNS name as the value of `TASK_AGILE_DB_HOST`, `TASK_AGILE_MQ_HOST`, and `TASK_AGILE_MAIL_HOST`. On Linux, you can use the host's private IP for these hosts. Using `127.0.0.1` or `localhost` won't work.

In practice, the `env.list` file in the `docker` folder is used as a template. We will save the actual `env.list` file in S3 and download it during deployment.

You can use the following command to test Docker in your local environment:

```
$ mvn clean package
$ cp target/app-0.0.1-SNAPSHOT.jar docker/app.jar
$ docker build -t taskagile:latest docker/
$ docker run --rm --name taskagile -e "SPRING_PROFILES_ACTIVE=dev" \
  -p 8080:8080 -p 9000:9000 taskagile
```

> If you experience a *database connection refused* issue when the connection from the inside of the container to the MySQL database in the host, then you might want to create a MySQL user that has been granted to access from addresses other than localhost.

The following is how `start.sh` looks:

```
docker pull taskagile/vuejs.spring-boot.mysql:$1
docker container stop taskagile
docker run --detach --rm --name taskagile --env-file ./env.list \
  -e "SPRING_PROFILES_ACTIVE=staging,docker" \
  -p 8080:8080 -p 9000:9000 \
  taskagile/vuejs.spring-boot.mysql:$1
```

The `start.sh` shell script serves as a bootstrap of the application. First, it pulls the Docker image of a specific tag from Docker's repository. `$1` is a variable used to get the first argument passed to the script. Once the Docker image is pulled, the script stops the current Docker container and then starts a new one. Let's go through the options in this command in detail:

- With the `--detach` option, the container will run in the background.
- With the `--rm` option, Docker will automatically remove the `"taskagile"` container when it exists.
- With the `--name` option, the started new container will be named `"taskagile"`.
- With the `--env-file` option, Docker will read the environment variables from the `env.list` file.
- With the `-e` option, Docker will set the `SPRING_PROFILES_ACTIVE` environment variable with the `staging,docker` value. Make sure to put `"docker"` as the last profile, so that settings in `env.list` can be applied.
- With the `-p` option, Docker will bind port `8080` of the container to port `8080` of the host machine, as well as port `9090`.

The `env.list` and `start.sh` files will be copied over to the server during the deployment, as we will see in the next section.

Preparing a Jenkinsfile

Jenkins Pipeline is used to streamline the build process. With various Jenkins plugins, we can define an automated continuous delivery process. Creating `Jenkinsfile` and committing it to the source code is the current best practice.

The following is how the `Jenkinsfile` looks at a high level:

```
pipeline {
  ...
  environment {...}
  stages {
    stage("Build package") {...}
    stage("Build Docker image") {...}
    stage("Push Docker build image") {...}
    stage("Deploy to staging") {...}
    stage("Run E2E tests") {...}
  }
  post {...}
}
```

Let's go through each stage, one by one. The following is how the `"Build package"` stage looks:

```
stage("Build package") {
  steps {
    echo "Git commit: ${env.GIT_COMMIT}"
    sh "mvn clean package"
  }
}
```

In this stage, we print out the ID of the last commit for reference. Then we invoke the `mvn clean package` command to build the application.

The following is how the `"Build Docker image"` stage looks:

```
stage("Build Docker image") {
  steps {
    sh "cp target/app-0.0.1-SNAPSHOT.jar docker/app.jar"
    sh "docker build -t ${DOCKER_REPO}:${env.GIT_COMMIT} docker/"
  }
}
```

In this stage, we copy the `.jar` package into the `docker` folder. Then we build the Docker image and tag it with the last commit ID. The `${DOCKER_REPO}` variable is an environment variable we defined in environment section. The `${env.GIT_COMIT}` variable is an environment variable created by Jenkins's Git plugin, with the value of the last commit ID. We can also add the prefix `env` to our own variables. Here, we omit it to make it easier to tell if a variable is defined by us or not.

The following is how the `"Push Docker build image"` stage looks:

```
stage("Push Docker build image") {
  steps {
    withDockerRegistry([ credentialsId: DOCKER_CREDENTIAL, url: '' ]) {
      sh "docker push ${DOCKER_REPO}:${env.GIT_COMMIT}"
    }
  }
}
```

In this stage, we publish the Docker image we just built to `https://hub.docker.com`.

The following is how the `"Deploy to staging"` stage looks:

```
stage("Deploy to staging") {
  steps {
    sh "ssh ${JENKINS_AT_STAGING} rm -fr /app/env.list /app/start.sh"
    sh "scp ./docker/env.list ./docker/start.sh
    ${JENKINS_AT_STAGING}:/app"
    sh "ssh ${JENKINS_AT_STAGING} \"cd /app && ./start.sh
    ${env.GIT_COMMIT}\""
  }
}
```

In this stage, we connect to the staging server via SSH to remove the existing `env.list` and `start.sh`, then copy the new version over. Once that is done, we switch to the `/app` directory and execute the `start.sh` bootstrap script with the last commit ID.

The following is how the `"Run E2E test"` stage looks:

```
stage("Run E2E tests") {
  steps {
    sh "cd ${env.WORKSPACE}/frontend && npm run test:staging-e2e"
  }
}
```

In this `stage`, we switch to the `front-end` directory and run the E2E test against the staging environment.

The following is how the "`post`" section looks:

```
post {
  always {
    emailext (
      subject: "[Jenkins] ${env.JOB_NAME} Build #${env.BUILD_NUMBER} -
      ${currentBuild.currentResult}",
      recipientProviders: [[$class: 'DevelopersRecipientProvider'],
      [$class: 'RequesterRecipientProvider']],
      body: "${currentBuild.currentResult}\n\nJob:
        ${env.JOB_NAME}\nBuild: #${env.BUILD_NUMBER}\nGit commit:
        ${env.GIT_COMMIT}\nMore detail at: ${env.BUILD_URL}"
    )
    sh "docker rmi -f ${DOCKER_REPO}:${env.GIT_COMMIT}"
  }
}
```

In this section, we define an `always` condition. The steps defined inside it will be executed, no matter whether the build succeeded or failed. As you can see, we use Jenkins Email Extension Plugin to send an email to the developers, as well as those who requested to be notified. Then, we remove the Docker image we just built.

 Due to the scope of this book, we didn't go in the details of Pipeline syntax here. If you're not familiar with `Jenkinsfile` and Pipeline syntax, you can find more details at `https://jenkins.io/doc/book/pipeline/syntax` and `https://jenkins.io/doc/book/pipeline/jenkinsfile`.

The following is the commit record of adding `Dockerfile` and `Jenkinsfile`:

Commits on Oct 15, 2018

add Dockerfile and Jenkinsfile

 jamesjieye committed 13 seconds ago

Figure 15.8: The commit record for Dockerfile and Jenkinsfile

Server preparation

Before we build the application, we need to prepare a server. Our `taskagile.com` server is an instance of Amazon EC2. Its operating system is Amazon Linux 2 AMI. Its type is `t2.micro`. MySQL, RabbitMQ, and NGINX are installed manually on the same box. The mail server is the pre-installed Postfix. During the launching of the EC2 instance, we will also need to open port `80` and port `443` by adding inbound rules. For more details on how to do that, you can check Amazon AWS's user guide.

Installing MySQL

For anyone who is not familiar with installing MySQL on Amazon Linux, you can use the following steps to install it:

1. Download the MySQL Yum repository as follows:

   ```
   wget
   http://dev.mysql.com/get/mysql57-community-release-el7-8.noarch.rpm
   ```

2. Install the Yum repository file using the following commands:

   ```
   sudo yum localinstall mysql57-community-release-el7-8.noarch.rpm
   ```

   This will add the MySQL Yum repository to our system's repository list and downloads the GnuPG key to check the integrity of the package we will download.

3. Install the MySQL community server as follows:

   ```
   sudo yum install mysql-community-server
   ```

4. Start the MySQL server using this command:

   ```
   sudo service mysqld start
   ```

5. Get the generated root password from the log file as follows:

   ```
   sudo grep 'temporary password' /var/log/mysqld.log
   ```

6. Change the root password, as shown here:

```
mysql -u root -p
mysql> ALTER USER 'root'@'localhost' IDENTIFIED BY
'k7Ayy$KTCcrM%2F3';
```

7. Create a database as follows:

```
CREATE DATABASE task_agile CHARACTER SET utf8mb4 COLLATE
utf8mb4_unicode_ci;
```

8. Create a database user as follows:

```
CREATE USER 'app_user'@'%' IDENTIFIED BY '12$456!';
GRANT ALL PRIVILEGES ON task_agile . * TO 'app_user'@'%';
FLUSH PRIVILEGES;
```

Installing RabbitMQ

RabbitMQ is written in Erlang. We need to install Erlang first. The Erlang version we will install is the customized version that the RabbitMQ team provides at `https://github.com/rabbitmq/erlang-rpm`.

Here are the steps to install the Erlang RPM:

1. Download the RPM package using the following command:

```
wget
https://github.com/rabbitmq/erlang-rpm/releases/download/v21.1/erla
ng-21.1-2.el6.x86_64.rpm
```

2. Install RPM package with `sudo`:

```
sudo rpm -ivh erlang-21.1-2.el6.x86_64.rpm
```

Now, let's install RabbitMQ. We use the RPM package provided by Bintray:

1. Download the RPM package:

```
wget
https://dl.bintray.com/rabbitmq/all/rabbitmq-server/3.7.8/rabbitmq-
server-3.7.8-1.el6.noarch.rpm
```

2. Install the RPM package with the following commands:

```
sudo rpm -ivh rabbitmq-server-3.7.8-1.el6.noarch.rpm
```

3. Set RabbitMQ to autostart when the server reboots, as follows:

```
sudo chkconfig rabbitmq-server on
```

4. Create a user with the username `app_user` and the password `GxweRTK`, as shown here:

```
sudo rabbitmqctl add_user app_user GxweRTK
```

Do not add special characters to a RabbitMQ user's password, such as `G$xweRTK`. If so, the user will be able to log in with the command but will not able to pass authentication from the application. RabbitMQ will, for some reason, truncate the password to remove the special character. Authentication is done with the following syntax: `rabbitmqctl authenticate_user <username> <password>`.

5. Add the user to the `administrator` tag:

```
sudo rabbitmqctl set_user_tags app_user administrator
```

6. Grant permissions to the user as follows:

```
sudo rabbitmqctl set_permissions -p / app_user ".*" ".*" ".*"
```

7. Enable the management plugin (optional):

```
sudo rabbitmq-plugins enable rabbitmq_management
```

You can choose to enable the management plugin so that you can monitor the server from UI. For more information, check RabbitMQ's documentation at http://www.rabbitmq.com/management.html.

8. Restart the server, as shown here:

```
sudo service rabbitmq-server restart
```

We do this because when you enable the management plugin, you will need to restart the server to make it work.

The preparation we use here is only for experimental purposes when you want to get your hands dirty. In practice, you will probably want to use a more automated way of preparing servers, such as Ansible, Puppet, Chef, and so on. Due to the fact that those topics are really out of the scope of this book, we introduce one of the most straightforward ways of setting up a server.

Installing NGINX and the SSL certificate

Installing NGINX on Amazon Linux is straightforward, with only one command:

```
sudo yum install nginx
```

Once NGINX is ready, let's install the SSL certificate with Let's Encrypt (https://letsencrypt.org). Hats off to the Let's Encrypt team! Before installing the SSL certificate, we need to make sure the taskagile.com domain points to the server. We will use Certbot (https://github.com/certbot/certbot) to automate the generated certificate by using the following command:

```
sudo yum install -y certbot python2-certbot-nginx
```

Once Certbot is installed, start the generating process with the following command and follow the instructions to finish the certificate generation:

```
sudo certbot
```

When you see a success message similar to the following, it means the SSL certificate has been installed successfully, and Certbot has updated NGINX's /etc/nginx/nginx.conf configuration file to enable HTTPS automatically:

```
Congratulations! You have successfully enabled https://taskagile.com
```

Now, we need to do a reverse proxy, by asking NGINX to forward requests to our application at port 8080. Open /etc/nginx/nginx.conf, and update the location / subsection of the http section as follows:

```
...
http {
  ...
  server {
    server_name taskagile.com;
    ...
    location / {
      proxy_read_timeout 1000;
      proxy_send_timeout 1000;
```

```
    proxy_pass http://127.0.0.1:8080;
    proxy_buffering on;
    proxy_connect_timeout 15;
    proxy_intercept_errors on;
    proxy_set_header Host $http_host;
    proxy_set_header X-Real-IP $remote_addr;
    proxy_set_header X-Forwarded-For $proxy_add_x_forwarded_for;
  }
  ...
}
}
...
```

And with that, we've completed the preparation of the server.

Building with Jenkins

Now that we have `Dockerfile` and `Jenkinsfile` ready, let's build the application with Jenkins.

In case you do not have a Jenkins server up and running, you can use the following steps to spin up one easily:

1. Download Jenkins from `http://mirrors.jenkins.io/war-stable/latest/jenkins.war`
2. Open up a Terminal in the download directory
3. Run `java -jar jenkins.war --httpPort=9090`
4. Browse to `http://localhost:9090`
5. Follow the instructions to complete the installation

 The preceding steps are copied from the *Guided Tour of Jenkins*, available at `https://jenkins.io/doc/pipeline/tour/getting-started`. The port is changed from `8080` to `9090`.

The following screenshot shows how the Jenkins server looks after a fresh installation:

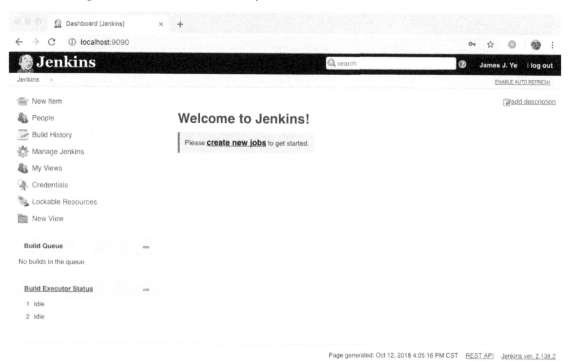

Figure 15.9: A fresh installation of Jenkins

You can click the **New Item** on the left menu, or **create new jobs**, to create a job. On the **New Item** page, type in `TaskAgile - vuejs.spring-boot.mysql` as the name and choose **Pipeline**, as shown in the following screenshot. Click the **OK** button to proceed:

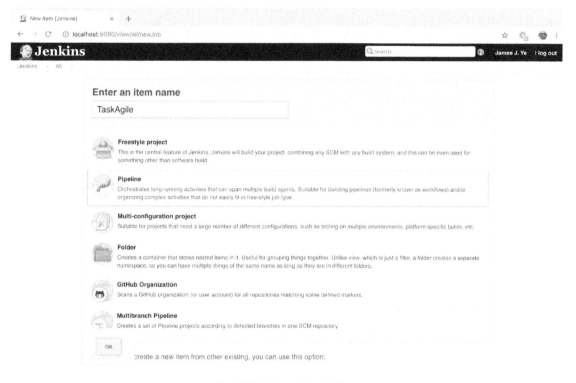

Figure 15.10: Creating new item in Jenkins

Once Jenkins creates the job, you will be redirected to the configuration page. Click the **Pipeline** tab to go to the Pipeline configuration section, as shown in the following screenshot:

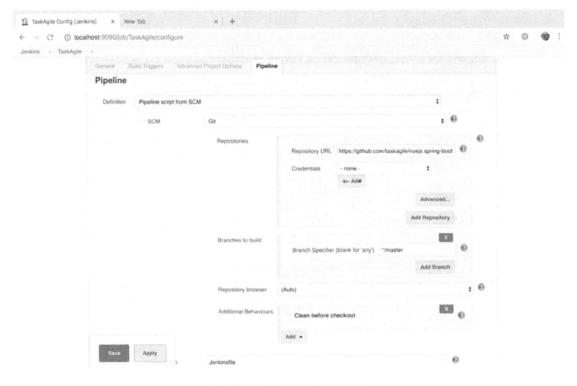

Figure 15.11: Setting up the Pipeline plugin in Jenkins

Use the following configuration for the Pipeline setup:

- **Definition:** `Pipeline script from SCM`
- **SCM:** `Git`
- **Repository URL:** `https://github.com/taskagile/vuejs.spring-boot.mysql`
- **Credentials:** `none`
- **Branch specifier:** `*/master`
- **Additional behaviors:** **Clean before checkout**

Then, click the **Apply** button to apply the settings, and then click the **Save** button. Jenkins will redirect you to the Jenkins jobs' page. Click **Build Now** on the left menu. Once the build has started, you should be able to see the **Stage View** like the following:

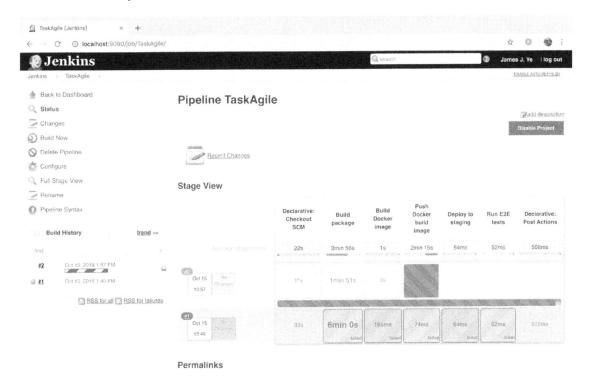

Figure 15.12: The Pipeline Stage View in Jenkins

This is how our TaskAgile application looks in production (`https://taskagile.com`):

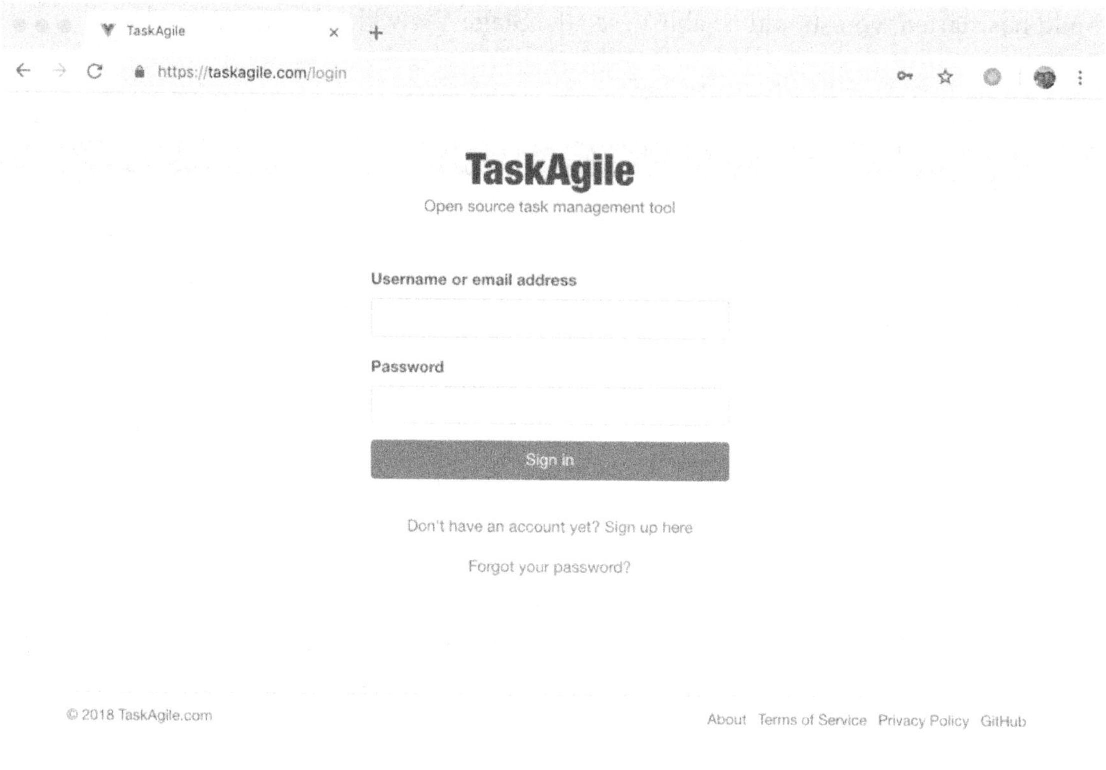

Figure 15.13: The application is launched!

Summary

In this chapter, we've talked about continuous delivery briefly and compared it with continuous integration and continuous deployment. We've also created `RegistrationApiIntegrationTests` to demonstrate one way of doing an integration test in Spring Boot. We also further improved our Maven build process by making executing the E2E test optional. We also created `Dockerfile` for building our Docker image, and `Jenkinsfile` to perform the continuous delivery of our application.

By now, we've built the first version of TaskAgile application using Vue.js, Spring Boot, and the MySQL database. Due to the scope of the book, we do not have enough time to finish all the user stories that we wrote in `Chapter 4`, *TaskAgile - A Trello-like Task Management Tool*. In the future, we will keep improving this open source application and deploying it to `https://taskagile.com`.

Further reading

In case you have any questions, ideas, or issues, please visit the GitHub repository. In particular, the following pages may be of use:

- The Wiki is available here: `https://github.com/taskagile/vuejs.spring-boot.mysql/wiki`
- Report any issues here: `https://github.com/taskagile/vuejs.spring-boot.mysql/issues`

Other Books You May Enjoy

If you enjoyed this book, you may be interested in these other books by Packt:

Full-Stack Web Development with Vue.js and Node
Aneeta Sharma

ISBN: 978-1-78883-114-7

- Build an application with Express.js
- Create schemas using Mongoose
- Develop a single-page application using Vue.js and Express.js
- Create RESTful APIs using Express.js
- Add test cases to improve the reliability of the application
- Learn how to deploy apps on Heroku using GitHub
- Add authorization using passports

Hands-On Full Stack Development with Spring Boot 2.0 and React
Juha Hinkula

ISBN: 978-1-78913-808-5

- Create a RESTful web service with Spring Boot
- Understand how to use React for frontend programming
- Gain knowledge of how to create unit tests using JUnit
- Discover the techniques that go into securing the backend using Spring Security
- Learn how to use Material UI in the user interface to make it more user-friendly
- Create a React app by using the Create React App starter kit made by Facebook

Leave a review - let other readers know what you think

Please share your thoughts on this book with others by leaving a review on the site that you bought it from. If you purchased the book from Amazon, please leave us an honest review on this book's Amazon page. This is vital so that other potential readers can see and use your unbiased opinion to make purchasing decisions, we can understand what our customers think about our products, and our authors can see your feedback on the title that they have worked with Packt to create. It will only take a few minutes of your time, but is valuable to other potential customers, our authors, and Packt. Thank you!

Index

Made in the USA
Coppell, TX
20 April 2020